Daily Guideposts, 1999

Publishers Since 1798

THOMAS NELSON PUBLISHERS
Nashville

Published in Nashville, Tennessee, by Thomas Nelson, Inc.

ACKNOWLEDGMENTS

All Scripture quotations, unless otherwise noted, are from *The King James Version of the Bible.*

Scripture quotations marked (NIV) are from the *Holy Bible, New International Version.* Copyright © 1973, 1978, 1984 International Bible Society. Used by permission of Zondervan Bible Publishers.

Scripture quotations marked (RSV) are from the *Revised Standard Version of the Bible.* Copyright © 1946, 1952, 1971 by the Division of Christian Education of the National Council of Churches of Christ in the U.S.A. and are used by permission.

Scripture quotations marked (NAS) are from the *New American Standard Bible,* © 1960, 1962, 1963, 1968, 1971, 1972, 1973, 1975, 1977 by The Lockman Foundation. Used by permission.

Scripture quotations marked (TLB) are from *The Living Bible,* © 1971. Used by permission of Tyndale House Publishers, Inc., Wheaton, IL 60189. All rights reserved.

"Lessons in Listening" series was written by Elizabeth Sherrill.
"Six for Working, One for Rest" series was written by Isabel Wolseley.
"Through the Valley" series was written by Shari Smyth.
"Trial by Fire" series was written by Carol Knapp.
"Journey of the Soul" series was written by Marilyn Morgan Helleberg.
"A Fork in the Road" series was written by Eric Fellman.
"The Paths to Christmas" series was written by Julia Attaway.

http://www.guideposts.org
Designed by Holly Johnson
Artwork by Viqui Maggio
Indexed by Patricia Woodruff
Jacket photo by H. Abernathy / H. Armstrong Roberts, Inc.
Typeset by Com Com, an R.R. Donnelley & Sons Company
Printed in the United States of America

ISBN 0-7852-7024-8

1–99

TABLE OF CONTENTS

TABLE OF CONTENTS

INTRODUCTION

Many of us can't remember a time when we didn't know the Twenty-third Psalm. Along with the Lord's Prayer, it was one of the first pieces of Scripture we committed to memory. Its images of green pastures and still waters, of plenteous tables and overrunning cups are permanent parts of our imaginations. Its simple but beautiful message of God's care and provision for us, in life and in death, has strengthened us in danger, consoled us in sorrow and given a thankful voice to our hearts' rejoicing.

This year, we are preparing to say farewell to the decade of the nineties, to our incredible but often harrowing twentieth century and to the second millennium of the Christian era. It's natural to want to look back over where we've been and to look ahead to where we're going, and in our reflection on our journey, to seek to see the hand of God leading us forward. What better way to express our thankfulness and strengthen our hope than with words we have lived with all our lives. So our theme for *Daily Guideposts, 1999*—our twenty-third annual edition—comes from that most familiar of psalms: "He Leadeth Me."

We invite you to join us as our fifty-two writers share their stories of the wonderful ways in which God has led them through the joys and sorrows, the dangers and opportunities of life. Sometimes they've recognized God's providential care in a moment of joyful recognition or surprised laughter. Sometimes they've found it only as an unlooked-for peace within a storm of tears. However they've discovered it, it has fortified their faith and confidence in God. And by following their journeys, we'll be able to see more clearly how God is working in our own lives today, and will be better able to look forward with confidence as God leads us into tomorrow.

At the beginning of every month, in "Lessons in Listening," Elizabeth Sherrill shares the experiences that have helped her learn to listen prayerfully for God's guidance. In February, Isabel Wolseley takes a look back at "Six for Working, One for Rest"—the weekly routines of her growing-up years—and shares the spiritual lessons they taught her. During Holy Week, Shari Smyth joins the journey of the disciples of Jesus through the streets of Jerusalem, under the shadow of the Cross and into the joy of Easter, sharing her own struggle to walk "Through the Valley." In June, Carol Knapp takes us to Alaska, into the raging inferno of the Miller's Reach Fire, where she finds a new appreciation for the providence and mercy of God. In August, Marilyn Morgan Helleberg invites us to take a "Journey of the Soul" to find God's guidance in prayer and solitude. In October, Eric Fellman looks for the signs of God's leading in his life as he faces "A Fork in the Road." For Advent, Julia Attaway shares some of "The Paths to Christmas" down which God has led her to a richer appreciation of the birth of Jesus. And throughout the year, Van Varner shares the things God has taught him through his love of ships and the sea. Join him aboard the SS *Rotterdam* for a glimpse of God's glory in a comet's tail!

"Each year's new *Daily Guideposts* is like a family reunion," our readers tell us, and we're happy to welcome back such beloved members as Drue Duke, Arthur Gordon, Marjorie Holmes, Oscar Greene, Ruth Stafford Peale, Fred Bauer, Phyllis Hobe, Daniel Schantz, Carol Kuykendall and Marion Bond West, among many others.

Every family grows by welcoming new members, and this year we welcome five new friends to our feast of faith: Libbie Adams, a housewife from Richlands, North Carolina; Melody Bonnette, a wife, mother and high school teacher from Mandeville, Louisiana; Helen Grace Lescheid, a writer and mother from Sumas, Washington; Allison Sample, a young working woman living in Brooklyn, New York; and Gail Thorell Schilling, a single mother and teacher from Lander, Wyoming.

We've added someone else to our family conversation this year—you. Each month in "The Reader's Room," we'll feature a testimony to the wonderful things God is doing in the lives of *Daily Guideposts* readers from the letters you've sent us. As we walk together through the days ahead, we'll ask you to jot down your own experiences in listening to God's leading so we can hear your voice, too.

And, of course, you're invited to visit the Fellowship Corner, where old friends are waiting to catch you up on what's happened to them in the year just past, and new friends are waiting to get acquainted.

So as this new year begins, let's set off together joyfully, with prayer and praise, wherever God leads us.

—*THE EDITORS*

January

The Lord is my shepherd, I shall not want.
—PSALM 23:1 (RSV)

S	M	T	W	T	F	S
					1	2
3	4	5	6	7	8	9
10	11	12	13	14	15	16
17	18	19	20	21	22	23
24	25	26	27	28	29	30
31						

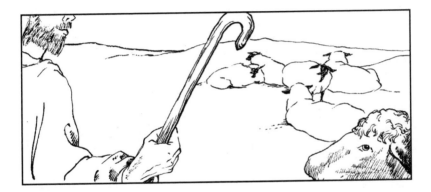

1

God saw every thing that he had made, and, behold, it was very good.... —GENESIS 1:31

When I was in high school, I worked at a neighborhood grocery. It was a valuable experience, because I learned to do many things—deal with the public, order merchandise, figure prices, keep the books, write advertisements, cut meat, run the cash register and, at the end of the year, take inventory. That is, count everything on the shelves, in the storerooms and in the freezers. The store owner explained that without an inventory of goods he wouldn't know his financial status.

"Of course, I could operate like old Jake Thomas, a hardware store owner I once knew," my boss chuckled. "He never made an accounting, and it didn't seem to matter until he decided to sell the business. The prospective buyer was taken aback. 'How do you determine your profit or loss at the end of the year?' he asked. 'All I know,' Jake responded, 'is that I always have more cash in the drawer at night than I did in the morning.'"

Some people, myself included, like to take personal inventory at this time of the year, not so much financial as spiritual. Questions I ask are: Am I using my time more wisely? Am I a better listener—to God and others? Am I more Christlike, more giving, more loving, more understanding? Am I kinder, gentler, more thoughtful of others? Am I more helpful to people (especially strangers) with needs (especially silent ones)?

Some day at the final accounting, I wonder how I'll measure up. Remind me in the New Year, Lord...

> *When my spirit wills, but my flesh won't,*
> *That the things I count, often don't.*

—FRED BAUER

LESSONS IN LISTENING

It's the last year of our century—one that's seen more change than any time in human history. All we know of the millennium about to begin is that changes will come faster still! How can we move forward with confidence when we don't know what's ahead? By claiming the promise God has given: "I will instruct you and teach you the way you should go; I will counsel you with my eye upon you" (Psalm 32:8, RSV).

At the beginning of each month, Elizabeth Sherrill looks at some of the ways we can learn to listen for God's guidance in a fast-changing world. What can we know about the third millennium after Christ? Only that He will be with us every day, every hour, instructing, guiding, pointing the way. —THE EDITORS

2

SATURDAY

GREAT EXPECTATIONS
Hope and quietly wait for the salvation of the Lord.
—LAMENTATIONS 3:26

One day in the early 1950s, when *Guideposts* magazine was new and struggling, I went with others on the very small staff to the home of a well-to-do New Yorker with a list of needs: new typewriter; stapling machine; desks instead of card tables. We'd hoped that Tessie Durlach would get out her checkbook. Instead, she got out pencils and pads of paper. "Let's all be quiet now," she said as she handed them around, "and see what God has in mind for *Guideposts.*"

To my surprise, the others were soon scribbling furiously, their pads filling up with messages from what to me was empty air. Listen though I would, I heard nothing. As people began to read aloud what they'd written—page after page of insights and ideas—it was apparent to me that this was more than just a human planning session.

From that meeting came a long-term vision for *Guideposts*: The sense that God had more in mind than simply publishing a magazine; an understanding of readers' needs and how to meet them; recognition of our own need for daily prayer backup by people outside the staff.

All this and much more the others heard, while I sat deaf and dumb. "Thou hast given me an open ear," the psalmist rejoices (Psalm 40:6). *Does God give ears to some and not to others?* I wondered. *Or is listening something all of us can learn to do?* Ever since that morning in Tessie's apartment, I've devoured books on guidance, talked to the spiritually sensitive and discovered aids for those who, like me, are hard of hearing.

But that morning, already I'd learned the first lesson: Expect more than you ask for! To be guided is to grasp a whole new dimension to daily living. I'd watched us arrive at Tessie's with expectations low— a little equipment for the office. I saw us leave carrying infinitely more—a king's treasure of energy, direction, confidence. We'd asked God for a crumb from His table. He answered: *Sit at My banquet, be My welcome guest. I have much to say to you.*

Father, teach me to listen.   —ELIZABETH SHERRILL

EDITOR'S NOTE: We hope you'll take time out during the year to listen for God's leading in your own life. Use the diary pages at the end of each month to jot down your own "My Faith Journey."

3   *SUNDAY*

In simplicity and godly sincerity, not with fleshly wisdom, but by the grace of God, we have had our conversation in the world.... —II CORINTHIANS 1:12

My husband Lynn and I quietly slipped into a pew at the back of our church just as the Sunday morning service began. For the next several minutes, I mechanically sang the songs, yawned my way through the call to worship and numbly recited the Lord's Prayer.

Then came the children's sermon, and I peered around the people in front of me so I could see the boys and girls who came skipping and running pell-mell down the aisles to the front. They sat on the chancel steps, listening with wide-eyed interest while the minister showed them a wooden replica of Noah's ark and explained how

Noah built the huge boat in the midst of a drought, simply because he trusted God and wanted to obey Him. The children's faces clearly reflected their eager and open response to this story, just the opposite of my own nonchalance this morning.

No wonder Jesus used children to remind grown-ups to come to Him with childlike faith. In fact, He told the disciples that unless they changed and became like children, they would never even enter the kingdom of heaven.

How do I need to change? I wondered. *What is childlike faith, and how do grown-ups like me need to "grow down" in order to experience this kind of faith?*

With these children before me, I saw one obvious answer: I needed to come to church as they came down the aisles: eagerly, with greater openness and expectancy to hear and accept God's truth. So as the children made their way back down the aisles and we entered into a time of silent prayer, this is what I prayed:

Jesus, help me recognize the ways I need to change in order to come to You like a child.   —CAROL KUYKENDALL

4

MONDAY

For the Son of God, Jesus Christ, whom we preached among you...was not Yes and No; but in him it is always Yes.   —II CORINTHIANS 1:19 (RSV)

Last January I went through a terrible three-week depression. Alaska is cold and dark this time of year, which is enough to sabotage anybody's good mood. But there was more to it than that. With the children all out of the nest—and our oldest, Tamara, just married—I found myself wondering who I really was and where my life had gone. One afternoon I stood staring into the mirror, my face red and swollen from crying, calling out to the stranger in the glass, "Who are you? I don't know you."

During those bleak days, I buried myself at home. I vowed to get out of Alaska the next January, if that would keep the depression from happening again. Finally, with the arrival of out-of-town guests, I began to pick up my life once more.

Several months later, I listened to a "Celebrate Life" tape by Luci Swindoll. She advised, "Be involved. While you can, say yes to more things than you say no to." I re-inventoried my January melancholy and realized I had said yes to very little. I didn't meet with friends, complete any projects, work out at the gym, volunteer at church or reach out to anyone in any way. My life was one great big "no."

January is here again. This time around I'm going to try out a lot more yeses and see where that lands me. Maybe I won't need to leave the state. Maybe there is joy to be found in my own backyard. Even in January.

God of the changing seasons, help me to say yes a dozen times over—once for each month of the year. —CAROL KNAPP

5

I saw by night, and behold a man riding upon a red horse, and he stood among the myrtle trees....

—ZECHARIAH 1:8

I was running along Fifth Avenue in Manhattan. I had picked up a package from a friend at 50th Street and left myself too little time to catch the 5:20 at Grand Central. Around me people surged along, creating the typical turbulence of big-city bustle. Bumped and jostled, I began to feel angry. *How rude and hostile everyone seems. And I'm going to miss my train! Well, I can shove, too!* Growing ever more irritable, I stopped with the crowd at a red light.

Suddenly, a mounted police officer appeared. His chestnut horse, beautifully muscled, held its head high and looked at us with gentle eyes. The light changed. Nobody moved. We all stared as though we had never seen a horse, as though it were a creature from another planet. And indeed, it seemed almost like a messenger sent from above. Finally, a woman approached and patted the horse's neck. We all smiled, nodding to one another.

The horse stood quietly, accepting our praise and affection. I could feel the crowd's tension drain away. It didn't seem so important to catch that train...there would be others. We all wanted to stay awhile in this moment of grace. We wanted to experience the beauty of that who had stepped among us. How quickly our sour attitudes had changed! Friendly now, we moved along, polite, considerate, each changed by a moment's encounter.

Oh, Lord, help me to look beyond my petty concerns to the moments that inspire. —SUSAN SCHEFFLEIN

6

I will put a new spirit within you....   —EZEKIEL 11:19

The tree was undecorated, the last dried bits of mistletoe were swept from the foyer floor, and all the trappings of Christmas were back in the attic. It had been a long day, one I spent working hard and feeling sad that Christmas was over. With time enough to dash to the store for some quick dinner-fixings before David came home, I walked out to the garage.

My car Herbie had been sitting in the very same spot throughout the holidays. With all the rush of Christmas company and a quick trip to Cincinnati to visit David's family, I hadn't had an occasion to drive in weeks.

I got David's tin snips from his workbench and clipped the tired wreath wired to Herbie's front grill. Inside the car I found a Christmas cup lined with hot chocolate left over from the night we went caroling to the homes of several shut-in friends. I picked up a paper bowl from the floor that had held chicken salad I ate in the car the day I delivered groceries to my ninety-four-year-old friend Frances. When I looked down to see what was under my foot as I pumped Herbie's gas pedal, I discovered a bow from the packages I delivered to needy children at a rural school.

The last physical remains of Christmas, just tossed in the trash, bridged the gap between the wrappings that we had tied around the holidays and the real gift that had come straight from the heart of Christmas, the part that didn't have to end.

Herbie fairly purred as we rounded the corner and zipped out into the evening traffic. And I felt like purring, too, because the best part of Christmas was out here in the present and didn't have a thing to do with what I had packed away and left behind.

Father, on this Epiphany I thank You for the twelve days of Christmas, a perfect introduction to the opportunities of today.

—PAM KIDD

7

Now may our Lord Jesus Christ himself, and God our Father, who loved us and gave us eternal comfort and good hope through grace, comfort your hearts and establish them in every good work and word.

—II THESSALONIANS 2:16–17 (RSV)

David Allen is a man with cancer. He was told he had one year to live. But he continues in his dry cleaning business with a full-time workday.

Through the years David has helped friends and acquaintances with their personal hardships. He continues to do this. He calls himself a "silent evangelist" and finds many ways to give practical help to people in his community. For instance, he arranged music lessons for six children and provided pianos for some of them. When he learned that a family could not bury a relative because they could not afford to buy a cemetery plot, he saw to it that they got the money.

David is a man at peace with God. His philosophy is "If you give the world the best you have, the best will come back to you." David has already lived two years since the doctor gave him his one-year verdict. And he has many more years ahead of him. The Lord is blessing him as he gives to others.

Dear Lord, may I look for ways to help others today. Amen.

—RUTH STAFFORD PEALE

8

"For I was hungry and you gave me something to eat, I was thirsty and you gave me something to drink, I was a stranger and you invited me in." —MATTHEW 25:35 (NIV)

I'd become a volunteer hospice nurse to give patients the choice of living their last days at home. One icy night, I was called out to check on Mary, only to find her two adult sons in the midst of a heated argument over a financial matter. I managed some small talk, then excused myself to tend to their mother.

There I found Sarah, a lay hospice volunteer, trying to coax Mary into taking a few bites of her homemade chicken soup. Mary's breathing was labored and her pain intense. "Don't let them take me to the hospital, nurse," she pleaded. "I want to die right here, near Puddles." Puddles was her beloved beagle.

I gave Mary some pain medicine, then slipped out to the kitchen telephone to update her doctor. No sooner had I hung up the phone than one of her sons hurled a string of loud profanities at me "for being part of the whole bureaucratic system." I was mortified. But I answered their questions about their dying mother's care. That brought even more cutting remarks.

Two hours later, I'd had about all of the sons' verbal abuse I could take. "They can just find someone else to do this," I spouted.

"I was thinking the same thing earlier," Sarah admitted, "but then a little Voice inside me whispered, 'If that were Jesus in there, would you do it?'"

These days, when I'm tempted to throw in the towel because of the harsh words of a patient or colleague, I remember a lady who died at home in her own comfortable bed, her sons reunited by her side, her beloved beagle stretched out like an afghan at her feet. For, you see, that night I cared for Jesus in disguise, though I almost missed Him.

Jesus, help me to see You in those I am called to serve today.
—ROBERTA MESSNER

9

SATURDAY

We have confidence in the Lord....
—II THESSALONIANS 3:4

As a child, I had an insatiable curiosity. Whether riding my bike through city streets or scampering over rocks along a sun-drenched beach, I wondered what was waiting for me around the next corner. This set me on my way to many wonderful adventures, like the time I biked around an unfamiliar corner and came to a field where a baby calf had just been born. But more often than not, it got me into a lot of trouble.

One day I urged a childhood chum to follow me around "just one more bend of the cove" of our favorite beach. Within minutes we were trapped by the incoming tide. Terrified, we huddled at the foot of a cliff, our yells for help swallowed up by the crash of the waves. It was a good thing other friends came looking for us and rushed for the lifeguards.

As an adult, I am still curious. One afternoon my husband and I were just about to turn back from a long hike when I pointed to a ridge in the distance. "I wonder what's on the other side?" With a knowing sigh, John grabbed my hand and we trudged on. Imagine our thrill when we stood at the top and looked down into a valley brilliant with wildflowers.

Come January, I get jittery with curiosity. "I wish I had a futuristic spyglass to see what's around the corner for us this year," I told my husband over dinner.

"It's a good thing that you don't." He wagged his fork at me. "Leave well enough alone. God has a plan. Trust Him."

Moment by moment, through every day, I will trust You, Lord, knowing whatever plan You have for me, it is good. —FAY ANGUS

10
Thy word is truth.

"The Word of God for the people of God," our pastor says each Sunday at the conclusion of the New Testament reading. When I was a young mother, though, there was a time when the Bible seemed to me to be designed for people of a past age, a less busy culture. I still loved the familiar, ringing phrases of the King James Version I'd known since childhood, but the words didn't seem pertinent to my hectic world of children and work.

Then my friend Maria Hutley gave me *The Jerusalem Bible*. Each section began with an introduction that set the historical perspective, explained the literary form and summarized main themes. Footnotes clarified obscure passages and provided commentary on the text. Twenty years later, *Jerusalem* remains my choice for study and personal devotion, although I've used and learned from *The Living Bible*, *The Rainbow Study Bible*, *The New American Standard* and others.

Recently, I went through another dry spell. Scripture passages seemed stale no matter what version I used. When I mentioned it to Pastor Judee Ramsey, she showed me Eugene Peterson's paraphrase of the New Testament, *The Message*. "God's Word is unchanging, but our language isn't," she reminded me.

Take today's verse, for instance. Instead of terms like *doctrine* and *righteousness,* The Message uses plain language: "Every part of Scripture is God-breathed and useful one way or another—showing us truth, exposing our rebellion, correcting our mistakes, training us to live God's way."

Whether you're young or old, rich or poor, with a third-grade education or a doctorate, there is a translation or paraphrase of the Bible that will bring the Word to life and give guidance to your every step...and mine.

The Word of God for the people of God! Amen. —PENNEY SCHWAB

---

11   *MONDAY*

As each has received a gift, employ it for one another, as good stewards of God's varied grace. —I PETER 4:10 (RSV)

"We're adding a new mutual fund in February." My boss waited warily for my reaction.

"*What?*" My blood pressure skyrocketed. The first two months of the year we worked in a state of chronic exhaustion, burdened by year-end reporting. Adding a new fund was a major task—and adding one in February was absurd.

My boss winced. "Yesterday, without warning, the CEO announced to the board of directors that we're going to have one."

I sputtered in rage and disbelief. Did the company even *need* another fund? Was there a market for it? Couldn't the CEO have taken two minutes to talk to his staff about scheduling before promising a major project for the busiest time of the year? Furious, I stomped back to my office, threw on my coat and stalked out of the building to the church across the street.

"Is this really what You want me doing with the talents You've given me, Lord? Putting 'spin' on our CEO's whims?" I'd never figured out exactly what my job had to do with my faith, and the current situation made me wish (once again) that I did something that obviously helped people. I wished God were calling me to be a nurse or social worker. He wasn't, so I said a prayer and went back to the office.

Breaking the news about the fund to my staff was not easy. One person lingered behind after our meeting. "Julia," she said, "I want you to know I think you're doing a great job." It wasn't the reaction I was expecting.

"What makes you say that?" I asked.

"Oh, it's just that whenever we get yanked around, you try to soften the impact instead of yanking even harder. That makes it easier to remember that even if yanking is the norm, it's still not right."

I stopped to let the message sink in. Helping others meant I had to serve where God put me. My co-workers weren't hungry or poor, but they were often treated without much respect and they were downtrodden. There was something I could do about that.

Dear Lord, when my work seems to consist of doing useless things, help me to remember that my first job is to treat every person I meet today with love and charity. —JULIA ATTAWAY

12

This service that you perform is not only supplying the needs of God's people but is also overflowing in many expressions of thanks to God. —II CORINTHIANS 9:12 (NIV)

The most memorable event of the year is certainly not hard for me to identify. It was watching the wonderful family of Guideposts readers outdo themselves in labors of love. In July 1997, I wrote a short piece in *Guideposts* magazine that talked about my knitting for needy children. A sentence invited readers to write for a copy of the simple pattern I described. And they did—almost fourteen thousand of them! With the loyal help of colleagues and family, we sent out copies of the knitting pattern and the crochet version that had been created in response to an outcry from crocheters. (My husband even stuffed envelopes after supper and then went out and mailed them, filling up all three mailboxes in our neighborhood!)

Most of the requests contained the stamped, self-addressed envelope we'd asked for, but in addition almost all included notes and letters. One reader wrote from Illinois where, separated from her family, she was awaiting a double-lung transplant. "The project will help keep my mind and hands busy," she wrote, "and pass the long days away doing something for others.... God bless you." A woman from

South Carolina told me, "I am eighty-three years old and through the years I have knitted for three children, thirteen grandchildren and, so far, six great-grandchildren." Now she'd like to knit for less fortunate children.

One of the most moving letters was from a New Jersey correspondent who had written in response to an earlier knitting story I had written in *Daily Guideposts, 1996*. At that time she was struggling with lonely widowhood and long, empty days. Now she was reporting on the various knitting projects—including ours—that she had taken on: "Instead of dreading the long nights, it seems like I don't have enough hours in the day to do all that I would like to do."

Thank You, Father, Son and Holy Spirit, for all the wonderful and selfless people in Your human family. —BRIGITTE WEEKS

13

There are different kinds of service, but the same Lord. There are different kinds of working, but the same God works all of them.... —I CORINTHIANS 12:5-6 (NIV)

The thousands of envelopes stuffed with patterns spread out across the country from Alaska to Texas, and across the world from Canada to Japan. Almost before I had time to put away my letter opener, the packages began to arrive. There were large boxes from the knitting guild of St. John's. There was a special delivery envelope with a note pinned onto one sweater: "Is this one all right? Please let me know?" A letter without a package asked, "Can you send me a picture? I can't figure out the sleeves."

My assistant Anngel and I armed ourselves with box cutters and began to stack up the rainbow garments in large piles. My office got smaller with each day. Every visitor asked, "What are those?" and every visitor heard the tale.

Soon we acquired plastic sacks to ship the garments, fifty-five to a sack. They went to Oxfam in England, to a handicapped children's center in Harlem, to a reservation in Appalachia, to World Vision in Pittsburgh to send overseas—and still the packages keep coming. I never get tired of opening them and seeing such tangible evidence of the spirit of the Guideposts family.

Thelma Dye, director of a child development center in Harlem serving four hundred disadvantaged children, wrote to us when she received a shipment. "As we sorted through the three hundred-plus sweaters, we could not help but remark on the kindness and dedication that Guideposts, and the people inspired by Guideposts nationwide, demonstrated." It's not just the needy children who are warmed by the sweaters. The makers, the distributors, the recipients and the helpers all feel the unmistakable power of the prayers worked into every stitch.

Make use of all our talents, Lord, to reach out to others and to share our many blessings through the work of our fingers.

—*BRIGITTE WEEKS*

14

THURSDAY

The servant is not greater than his lord.... —*JOHN 15:20*

When I first got the idea of doing typing at home (it wasn't called "word processing" then, because nobody had computers), I was elated. No bosses to set my hours, no constant stream of "Oh, could you just do this one little extra job?" right when I was going to lunch. No "I need this fourteen-page memo in half an hour." Ha!

I was so eager to get work that I charged only two-thirds the going rate. I was so eager to keep clients that I took on everyone who called (and I lived near a college, so prior to exam week, there were a *lot* of late-night calls from students behind on their term papers). And I promised all sorts of starry-eyed deadlines: "Oh, sure, I can have that sixteen-page chemistry paper in three hours! No problem!" I would stay up all night, sometimes near tears, as I rushed to finish typing a term paper for someone who might then call me and say casually, "Oh, could you just mail that to me? My teacher changed the deadline. It's not a rush anymore." I'd grind my teeth and pull my hair, but aloud I'd merely say, "Sure."

When I was pouring out my troubles to my friend Lou Ann, she said, "Your problem is that you're working for a lunatic boss who doesn't know how to set limits!"

I protested, "But I don't have a boss! I'm working for myself!" Then I stopped and stared at her. She stared back at me. I wailed, "You

JANUARY 1999 · 21

mean, I need to set limits for *myself*?" Apparently, I did, if I didn't want to collapse.

It was a hard job learning to say, "I'm sorry, but Thursday is full. I can have your paper by next Monday." I nearly fell over when the customer said, "All right." I also gave myself a raise, so typing became more pleasant.

The next time I saw Lou Ann, I smiled and said, "I'm working for a lot nicer boss."

Today, God, help me to find a balance between my needs and the needs of those who look to me for help. —LINDA NEUKRUG

---

15   FRIDAY

I remembered God, and was troubled.... —PSALM 77:3

It was a holiday weekend, and I was eight years old. My family and I had traveled to my grandparents' cabin on Lake Weiss in Leesburg, Alabama. I'm sure that it was a time of fellowship and love. But when I think back to that particular holiday, I remember only one thing, and that memory fills my soul with sad regret.

Early in the day, I had spotted a couple of young men, who were neighbors of my grandparents, fishing from our pier. I grabbed my pole and walked down to the lake to join them. Our dock juts out into a beautiful cove, which happens to be a favorite spot for a lot of area fishermen, so I didn't think it was unusual when an old, dented, green johnboat puttered up into the cove a few minutes later.

As the boat came closer, I saw that it carried two older African American men. As the man in the front of the boat lowered his anchor, an ancient concrete block tied to a yellow rope, he looked full into my face, then smiled and waved.

"Hey, they don't have any business here in that ratty boat catchin' our fish," one of the neighbors said.

"Yeah, let's teach 'em a lesson," the other said.

"My pa told me this lake belonged to everyone," I said.

"Ah, what d'ya mean? These are our fish to catch, not theirs," the first man said.

I watched in silence as one of the neighbors pulled a pack of bottle rockets out of his tackle box. He lit a rocket and aimed it in the direction of the boat. It whistled over the water and exploded with a loud crack. I had admired these two men in the past, but now as I watched them laugh, I knew I would never think much of them again. But still I said nothing.

The men in the boat never said a word, but as the old man in front slowly began to pull up his anchor, he looked directly at me. His sad, hollow look told me he had been treated this way before. I wanted to call out, to apologize, to tell him that I wasn't like my neighbors, that I had been raised in a home where all people were counted as children of God. But I didn't, and soon they were gone.

I sat on the edge of that pier for a long time. Later, when I headed back up the hill toward the cabin, I felt timeworn and troubled. For the first time I knew how it felt to turn away from the face of God.

Father, as I remember Dr. Martin Luther King, Jr., forgive me for the times I turn from You, and give me the courage to stand strong for You. —BROCK KIDD

READER'S ROOM

Pausing momentarily to observe God's handiwork (a majestic blue jay, a three-quarter moon against a bright blue sky at 9:00 A.M., a dusting of snow or the softness of an evening rain), or noting a kind deed done (a smile that brightens a life, a friendly helper in a store, a couple holding hands at a movie, a faith shared, a good storyteller or a phone call expressing gratitude) helps me to focus on the love in life and less on fear.

—WILLIAM B. COX, VIRGINIA BEACH, VA

---

16 | SATURDAY
It is more blessed to give than to receive. —ACTS 20:35

Coming up the stairs to our apartment I could smell the tantalizing aroma of bacon. In the kitchen, as I kissed Carol, I looked down at the five pieces cooling on a paper towel. "We'll have to fight over these," I said wryly. In our house there are three of us who love bacon: Carol, I and our younger son Timothy.

"Bacon!" Timo said, following his nose into the kitchen. "I love bacon."

"But how are we going to divvy these up?" I asked him, turning the event into a bit of a math lesson. "Five pieces don't split evenly among three people."

He looked crestfallen.

So I said to my son, "I suppose I could give you two slices, and Mommy and I could have one and a half." I was willing to make the sacrifice. After all, I would only sprinkle the bacon bits on my baked potato, but for Timo, the two slices would be a main course. It's the sort of thing a parent does. "Do you agree?" I asked Carol. She nodded her head and put the two slices on Timo's plate.

"You'll have to do us a big, big favor someday," she said.

"I'm going to do you a big, big favor someday," Timo said, smiling as though he had a secret for me. I opened the refrigerator and poured the milk. But when I turned back to the counter I discovered an extra half slice of bacon on my plate and on Carol's. I looked down at my son, licking the bacon grease off one finger. "Timo, you didn't have to do that!" I exclaimed.

"I wanted to," he said.

And just then I understood better than words can express our pastor's recent message about stewardship. "Tithing," he'd said, "is a way of giving back to God what is His."

Good Lord, give me a giving heart.   —RICK HAMLIN

17

Remind the people...to be ready to do whatever is good.
—TITUS 3:1 (NIV)

Every Sunday our church bulletin is full of appeals to meet the needs of our congregation and community by serving meals at a charity dining room, helping with the youth group, fixing bicycles for a nearby school and, of course, teaching Sunday school. *I'd really like to help,* I'll think, but I never take much time to consider the idea before the need is filled.

One Sunday our pastor made a special plea for altar guild volunteers to help set up communion services. My first thought was, *I should do that, especially if they really need help.* But then came the questions: *What do I know about that? Our Sunday mornings are so hectic, when would I have time? Realistically, how could I do it?* Good questions all, so I let the thought pass. But as we drove home that morning I found out I'd been asking the wrong questions all along.

Sitting in the backseat, my son Ross, in his curious eight-year-old way, piped up with a new round of what we jokingly call the "What Ifs."

"What if our car could go as fast as an airplane?" Then he began to think up as many answers as possible, taking off on an imaginary journey that made anything seem possible.

What if? I thought again about our pastor's altar guild request, this time with a new set of questions. *What if I went to the training session to learn more about it? What if I volunteered just one Sunday a month?*

Thinking it through, trying to picture it fitting into my life instead of immediately rejecting it, the idea began to seem possible. So I signed up the following Sunday, and in the time since have discovered I actually look forward to this meditative time spent preparing our Lord's Supper for the congregation.

Stir my imagination, Lord, and show me how I might serve You.
—GINA BRIDGEMAN

18

MONDAY

Let the words of my mouth, and the meditation of my heart, be acceptable in thy sight, O Lord....—PSALM 19:14

My husband Larry and I own a custom woodworking business and sell more than four hundred doghouses each year. We enjoy meeting people from all walks of life and deeply appreciate every customer. Yet there are times when people have nothing good to say about our product, complaining about the color or size or the materials we use. On those days it seems as if most people are negative and insensitive.

But a couple of years ago, just before Christmas, a customer strolled into the shop brimming with energy and enthusiasm. She raved about the doghouses and complimented Larry on the high quality of his workmanship. Her kind words made us feel as if we were running an elite little shop on a street in Paris rather than a small woodworking business on a country road in North Carolina. And when Larry came home from delivering her doghouse, she sent with him a lovely thank-you note and a canister of Christmas tea.

What an incredible difference her attitude had made to our day! Even now, whenever we need a lift, we think of her. And she made me wonder what kind of impression I leave wherever I go. Am I remembered as a critic? Or do I leave people feeling glad that our paths have crossed?

Father, I never know in what way my life might touch another's. Help me to be an example of Your love. —LIBBIE ADAMS

19

TUESDAY

And he touched her hand, and the fever left her: and she arose, and ministered unto them. —MATTHEW 8:15

Elizabeth, Elizabeth, what happened?

You were an original, unique, there was no one like you, and now, at age eighty-one, you're a recluse, not having left your bed for six years. Only three people see you: the loyal woman who comes in once a day to clean and fix the small amount of food you eat; your son, my godson, who visits from California; and I. The other men and women who were close to you have all died. You have defied all attempts to let a doctor visit; all those plans to go to the West Coast you've canceled.

I see you only occasionally now, but I telephone you, or you phone me, once or twice or three times a day. You'll say, "I want to know how you are feeling," and I'll say, "I'm fine, how are you?" and you'll reply, "Fine," and I'll conclude, "Then that makes two of us."

I am resigned. I am resigned in all areas save one. Those efforts to bring God to your room have been tactfully deflected, but do you know what? There is hope. There is hope because I have been praying for you these many years, and I shall go on praying, and others who read this will, I dare say, pray for you, and you shall see the benefits.

When?

In God's time. In God's time.

For Elizabeth, and for all the homebound, I pray, I hope, for Your touch, dear God. —VAN VARNER

20

The Lord is nigh unto all them that call upon him....

—PSALM 145:18

Oh, no, not again! I'd thought when the doctor scheduled my second breast biopsy within a year. The first time I had been lucky. This time I wasn't so sure. Too many of my friends had developed cancer recently. Poor Kim had died.

As I lay in the pre-surgical area, now so dreadfully familiar, Rita, the nurse, smiled as she glided around my bed. She took my vital signs, snapped on my plastic ID bracelet and attached the patch that would reduce the side effects from the anesthesia.

Rita was a longtime friend from our church. Every morning she cycled for forty-five minutes to get to the early service, her two little sons tucked in a wheeled tandem. Seated in her pew, juggling her babies, plastic bags full of cereal and storybooks, she prayed fervently yet serenely. Best of all, her smile said, "Today is absolutely the best day of my life!" She smiled like that now.

Rita patted my arm. "Gail, would you like me to pray with you?" Words wouldn't come—I bit my lip and nodded. Still smiling, Rita clasped my hand, closed her eyes, and prayed that God would guide the surgeon's hand and keep me in His perfect care, no matter what. Her confidence assured me that I was in good hands—my Maker's, and my "fixers'" too. She clanked up the sides of the gurney and adjusted my hair net. I was smiling as we cruised into surgery.

I awoke about an hour later to good news: no cancer, no nausea. Yet even now, years later, the calming "side effects" of Rita's tender prayer still linger in my life.

Dear Father, thank You for Your Son, the Great Physician, and for all those You send to heal us, in body and soul.

—GAIL THORELL SCHILLING

21

"Whatever you did for one of the least of these brothers of mine, you did for me."

—MATTHEW 25:40 (NIV)

We still receive the monthly newsletter from the church we belonged to some years ago. It's interesting to read of its accomplishments, its concerns and new projects. As I skimmed over the newsletter the other day, my eye was caught by a familiar name, a "Thank you to Mr. and Mrs.—" for some office equipment they had donated to the church.

When I first heard that name, I was visiting with my friend Pam while our sons played together in her backyard. She told me about Richard, the young man who would be discharged from prison in a few weeks, and who was coming to live with them. Pam's husband Frank, a teacher at the university, had gotten acquainted with Richard through a correspondence course. Over several years their relationship deepened into a genuine friendship.

I remember wondering if Pam and Frank's decision was a good one. We had opened our home to a lot of people over the years, but none of them, as far as we knew, had prison records. "We realize there are some risks involved," Pam told me. "But we've met Richard. We've asked a lot of questions over there. And most importantly, we feel confident that God wants us to do this thing."

Richard joined the family in their tiny house on Wilson Street. He quickly settled into a job, and it wasn't long before he found his own place to live. We enjoyed seeing Richard's shy smile every Sunday morning. We rejoiced in his milestones: baptism; confirmation and joining the church; his wedding to Sarah. We were invited to the opening night of his art show at a local gallery. Now Richard and Sarah have an established business of their own, and they are contributing members of the local community and the church.

Thank you, Pam and Frank, for the important part you played in helping Richard turn his life around. Thank you for modeling Christ's love in your open home and open hearts. Your example reminds me how quick I am to make judgments about people, and how wrong I can be when I predict someone's future based on the mistakes of the past.

May I listen to Your leading, Lord, and be willing to let You do the judging.
—MARY JANE CLARK

22 FRIDAY

He restores my soul.... —PSALM 23:3 (NAS)

The red numbers on the clock radio said 5:00 A.M. "...and good morning, folks! It's a frosty thirty below out there today...."

I shuffled down the hall and turned up the thermostat. Working up a little heat of my own on the treadmill, I soon found myself grumbling to God as I plodded along. *Lord, I'm bored. I'm tired of winter, weary of this same old routine—eat, sleep, work, exercise....*

Suddenly, the power went off, plunging the house into total darkness. The treadmill stopped with a jerk. *Oh, great! I suppose this cold snap has blown a transformer again.* The treadmill coming to a halt epitomized life without electricity. No heat, no light, no radio. Not even toast and coffee to start the day. For breakfast I ate bread and water.

Water...plumbing...how long will the electricity be off? How soon will the plumbing freeze? The freezers thaw? Freezers! Cover them to keep cold...get some blankets...drag out the woolen comforters....

By this time my husband Leo was awake, too. We were down in the basement bundling up both freezers when the power surged back on. Lights shone brightly, appliances hummed softly, the kettle started to sing. Getting back on the treadmill felt so good.

Why do I seldom appreciate the comforts until the kilowatts quit?

God, thank You that there are no "power outages" with You. Your love warms me, Your Word feeds me, Your Spirit enlightens me. Help me plug into Your power. —ALMA BARKMAN

23 *Let not your heart be troubled....*

When loved ones die, we have a sense of loss. We know that we will have their companionship no longer. And it's easy to feel that their special qualities—their humor, wisdom, kindness, compassion—have vanished with them.

But sometimes memory can bring those qualities back, in unexpected ways.

In some old papers the other day I came across a letter written by one of my aunts more than half a century ago. This woman, who had already known more than her share of misfortune, had suffered a crushing blow when one of her children was killed in a tragic accident. To someone who had written her a letter of sympathy she replies, "Yes, you are right; I am deeply unhappy and distressed. But I try to remind myself that happiness is not the sum total of life. There are other important things and one of these, I think, is bearing pain bravely as one grows older."

There it was, the essence of this woman revealed in this quiet display of fortitude. I will try to remember her words as I grow older. And try, also, to pass along some of her courage to my own children.

Father, lend us Your strength in adversity always.

—*ARTHUR GORDON*

24

Let them now make intercession to the Lord....

—*JEREMIAH 27:18*

St. Mark's Church, Mount Kisco, New York, where my wife and I have belonged for forty years, happens to be located down the street from the village fire department. And it often seems to us that emergencies wait for Sunday morning. With devastating timing, the minister will reach the climax of the sermon when a window-rattling blast of the firehorn will drown him out. Long. Short. A brief silence. Then another teeth-jarring blare. The effect inside St. Mark's is always the same: paralysis of the service.

Different preachers have handled the intrusion in different ways. Some simply wait patiently until the interruption is over. One assistant rector, I remember, tried to outshout the horn. Another squeezed snatches of her sermon into the pauses.

One Sunday not long after our current rector's arrival, just as he began to preach, the deafening firehorn stopped him short. *How,* I wondered as the air vibrated to the din, *would Stephen handle this introduction to St. Mark's noisy neighbor?*

As the first blast quivered into silence he said, "Let's pray right now for whatever crisis lies behind this call for help."

I followed Stephen's lead: Instead of waiting out the interruptions with irritation, I pictured possible scenes—a burning house, an overturned oil truck on Interstate 684. I had no idea what the need was, only that someone was in trouble and that rescuers were being summoned to help. *Go with the emergency crew, Father. Give Your calm to anyone in danger.*

Intercession! What a creative response to interruptions, whatever form they take: a traffic tie-up, a power outage, a broken appointment, a snowstorm. Each one is a chance to assume our God-given role as intercessors.

Thank You, Father, for the interruptions in my agenda that make room for Yours.

—*JOHN SHERRILL*

25

Jesus Christ the same yesterday, and today, and for ever.
—HEBREWS 13:8

"We're changing everything," the car commercial bragged, and I wanted to shout, "Why? Was everything you made last year a mistake?"

Maybe the most revolutionary change of all would be to stop changing perfectly good things. I've become suspicious of bosses who are constantly tinkering with procedures, and I weary of books with the "change or die" theme. Oh, I'm all for improving things. It's just that many of the changes I see aren't really improvements and often only make things worse.

"I got this new coffeemaker," my wife sang out, ripping open the box. "It's supposed to be radically improved."

It wasn't. Quality was replaced with flimsy plastic. The new shape wouldn't fit under the shelf, and the cord was shortened. The brewing process was more awkward, too. Only the higher price was truly a radical change.

I know we have to change to be "competitive," but when the world is undergoing an earthquake of change, I want a few things to hold on to. When I heard that a minister friend was moving again, for the third time in seven years, I wanted to cry, thinking of Franklin's advice, "A tree oft transplanted seldom bears much fruit." On the other hand, when I read that the late James Michener always used a typewriter, I wanted to stand up and cheer!

So, as I face a new millennium, my hope is twofold: One, that I will have the courage to change when I should; but second, that I will have the courage to hold on to things that are worthwhile, in the face of derision or pressure. To drive that car a little longer. To hang on to the tenets of my faith and find new ways to express them. To stick with my beloved wife of thirty-four years, and buy her a coffeemaker that works.

In this world of quicksand, Lord, help me hold on to Your unchanging nature of love.
—DANIEL SCHANTZ

26

Hear my cry, O God; attend unto my prayer.

—PSALM 61:1

It was a bad day. A *really* bad day: tension headache; dirty house; work deadline; a class to teach that night.

With a sinking heart I remembered I'd promised to pick up a manuscript that morning from one of my students, an elderly woman who wanted my advice on a short story she had written for a contest. Begrudging the time it was taking, I drove to Ellen's house, which I had never visited before. It proved to be a homey place filled with her needlework, including an old-fashioned sampler on one wall: When your day is hemmed with prayer, it's less likely to unravel.

Following my glance, she said, "That message has gotten me through many a bad day."

So, had I stopped to pray that morning? No, all I'd done was wallow in misery.

I sat back and relaxed while Ellen fixed me a cup of tea. "Lord, take me into Your stillness," I prayed. The tension in my neck and shoulders gradually lessened.

As we sipped tea together, I answered some of Ellen's questions about her story, and in so doing I found the answer to a problem with my own work. By the time I left her house, thirty minutes later, the day had turned into a good one, after all.

Lord, any day is good when I hold You near. Amen.

—MADGE HARRAH

27

And now, dear lady, I am not writing you a new command but one we have had from the beginning. I ask that we love one another. *—II JOHN 5 (NIV)*

"Did you ever notice," my husband Bill said to me across the candlelit table, "that people who are on vacation talk to each other over meals more than they do when they eat out at home?"

My husband's observations always pique my curiosity, and I found myself mulling this one over in the weeks after we returned to wintry Maryland from a few precious days in Panama City, Florida. Farther away from home, couples do seem more responsive to each other when eating out. Maybe being in unfamiliar territory together brings out their old comradeship. I knew it was true for us. But how to keep that sense of adventure and renewal back home?

A couple of months later Brent Brooks, our ex-lawyer pastor, gave a series of sermons on marriage. In his four "A's," I had my clue:

1. *Awareness.* What is my spouse's greatest need right now? How can I help?
2. *Acceptance.* Accept my spouse as Christ has accepted me (Romans 15:7), idiosyncrasies and all!
3. *Adjustment.* The lifelong process of changing and being changed: "The best way to see someone else change is to change yourself," Brent said.
4. *Appreciation.* This means "to build up," "to increase in value"; to appreciate the similarities and differences Bill and I share.

The idea of loving someone by these four "A's" will work for any relationship. With whom are you struggling right now? How would becoming truly aware of them, accepting them just as they are, adjusting yourself instead of them or simply appreciating them change that relationship today?

Lord, help me to learn to love ___Paul___ *as Jesus has loved me.*
(FILL IN SOMEONE'S NAME)
—ROBERTA ROGERS

28

How we laughed and sang for joy. And the other nations said, "What amazing things the Lord has done for them."
—PSALM 126:2 (TLB)

Today, January 28, is National Kazoo Day, the purpose of which is to recognize the kazoo as a musical instrument that can be enjoyed by young and old alike. Of course, in order to celebrate this great and festive holiday, we adults must do something to promote it, right?

When my children were small, the junk drawer in the kitchen was always loaded with kazoos. One time when Michael was a teenager and grousing about something or other and his little brother Andrew was pouting about it being his bedtime and the girls (also teenagers) were arguing about something or other, I opened the junk drawer and pulled out a handful of kazoos. I started playing and marching around the kitchen, adding to the cacophony at hand. Before long, the whole gang had kazoos in their mouths, making silly music with me. The laughter that followed erased the bad moods and I've been a kazoo fan ever since.

Today, why don't you stop by a party-supply store and pick up enough kazoos for your entire family and a few extras for friends and relatives. When you're serving dessert tonight, place a kazoo on each person's plate and then watch the fun begin.

Your children may think you've suddenly become one rung short of a ladder, one card short of a deck, one slice short of a loaf, one cent short of a dime...never mind, that's another game you can play with your kids.

Lord, help me create memories for my children and grandchildren by finding ways to make them laugh. And thank You for making laughter infectious—I can always use a good laugh myself.

—PATRICIA LORENZ

29

FRIDAY

"Your young men will see visions, your old men will dream dreams." —ACTS 2:17 (NIV)

For eleven years, Eldon and Eileen Schertzs, a retired couple, came to Mendenhall, Mississippi, to do volunteer work for our ministry. Almost every year, they had to live in a different house and fix it up to be habitable. Their faithfulness and the great gifts their talents and enthusiasm brought us got me to thinking about how we could make the same opportunity available to others who did not have their house-fixing skills.

We decided to remodel a house in our community for retired volunteers to come and live in Mendenhall for short periods of time. We designed the house so that each bedroom had its own bathroom for privacy, but shared a central kitchen and living room.

Not long after the house was finished, a couple came from Colorado to help us, and I felt a great joy as I took them to the house and showed them their room. They stayed with us for two weeks on that first visit, and since then, they've been back with us again. I believe they'll be back many times as short-term missionaries.

A few years ago, I saw a program on TV about "The Graying of America." As the baby boomers reach their retirement years, more and more people will be looking for a chance to use their years of experience in ministering for others. There are many needs in all our communities that could use their help. I want to do everything I can to make sure that people with a heart to serve will find a place of service.

Lord, show me the best way I can help my neighbors.

30

God setteth the solitary in families.... —*PSALM 68:6*

My dad has had Alzheimer's disease for several years, and now he lives in a nursing home not far from my house. I see him often, and so do our friends and neighbors. But he missed our two dogs Suzy and Tara. When I mentioned it to one of the nurses, she said, "You can bring your dogs to visit—as long as they're well-behaved."

I was delighted. Since both dogs are big, I decided to take them one at a time, Suzy first. Suzy is a Rottweiler, and although she looks ferocious, she is the most loving, affectionate animal I have ever known. Smart, too. She had never been to the nursing home, but the moment I brought her out of my car on a leash, she seemed to know something special was about to happen.

As we approached the front door, I saw that it was blocked by a man who often parked his wheelchair there and made it difficult for others to pass. Many times I had said hello to him and tried to get a response, but never succeeded. All he did was glare at me. This time, however, he moved his wheelchair out of the way and grinned—not at me, but at Suzy. She stopped in front of him, and very slowly he reached out and rested his hand on her head.

"Hello," I said, figuring I might as well try again.

"Nice to see you," he murmured. "This your dog?"

"Yes," I said. "Her name is Suzy."

"I had a dog back home," he said.

He followed us inside to the reception room. His smile kept getting bigger as he watched Dad hug Suzy and saw her wiggle with excitement. Then, as Suzy lay down at Dad's feet, the man came closer and began to talk about his own dog.

I learned that the man's name was George and he had no family in the area. He had lived in the nursing home for several years and never had visitors. No wonder he glared at everyone! But animals don't care how people look. Somehow they sense who a person really is, deep down inside.

I decided I could learn something from my dogs, so now, when I take either of them to visit Dad, we also visit George. In fact, he's beginning to feel like one of the family.

Lord Jesus, You always see beyond the hostile glare. Teach me to look at others with Your eyes. —*PHYLLIS HOBE*

31

Not forsaking the assembling of ourselves together...but exhorting one another.... —*HEBREWS 10:25*

It is Sunday morning, and outside the wind howls and rattles the pane. I know without opening my eyes that the window will be covered with frost. I know that the wind-chill is below zero—way below zero. I snuggle deeper into my flannel sheets. At the moment, my bed feels more welcome than the idea of showering, bundling up, scraping the car windshield and going to church. Later I'll do some devotional reading in front of the fire or catch a sermon on TV.

But suddenly I remember the article I'd read while surfing the Internet the night before. It was all about diamonds. Did you know that diamonds are cut and polished and made less rough by rubbing against other diamonds? And as surely as I know it's cold outside, I know something else, too. Those folks at church who "rub me the wrong way"—the lady who always seems to scowl at my hats, the noisy child who sits near me every Sunday, the parking lot attendant who never lets me park near the door—are really polishing me, giving me a chance to let my Christianity shine.

I push back the sheets and dash to the shower, anxious for whatever polishing God has in store for me today.

I am Your jewel, Father. Polish me to perfection!
—*MARY LOU CARNEY*

MY FAITH JOURNEY

1 _____

2 _____

3 _____

4 _____

5 _____

6 _____

7 _____

8 _____

9 _____

10 _____

Beautiful sunny day, 20°. Rode to work w/Gayle. Paul picked me up and went to lunch, at our house. All prepared & opened, ate chicken.

11 Beautiful sunny day 50°. Very busy at work. Came home showered & watched soaps. Retired at 8:00.

12 Cloudy, dreary day 35°. Very busy at work. Came home & put Paul & my lounge chairs together. Butch called.

13 Snow, Rain, Sleet 20°. Icy roads, so I stayed home. Joyce called & said Bob called about soaps. Cleaned bedroom.

14 Heavy rain AM & sun PM. Paul & I went back to bed & slept till 10:30. We had pizza from pita bread for lunch.

15 Butch stopped over. I called Chantell. Beautiful sunny day 50°. Paul & I went to Shop Rite & for papers & coffee. We came home & I cooked & cleaned Tweety room. Cats shots.

16 Beautiful sunny day 55°. Chantell & Butch & Jan came over. I made meat loaf, baked potatoes & carrots.

17 Paul & I went for papers. Worked at old house. Rain, rain, wind, thunderstorm. 40°. Paul & I stayed in all day. Made sausage for lunch & ragu.

18 Beautiful sunny day 50°. Very busy at work. Came home & Paul & I showered, had soup & watched T.V.

19 Cloudy dreary day 45°. Very busy at work. Left at 2:00 - to take Paul to Dr. R. Surgery

20 on Feb. 9 at hospital. Got Mickey D's.

Missed Kids — Cloudy, dreary day 45°. Very busy as work. Did 2 hrs O.T. picked up Gladys at Solomon

21 Watched soaps, Paul optausled
Cloudy, dreary day, 50°. Rain & fog very busy at work. Vitamins

Missed Kids

22 came. Hosp called Paul & left message
Cloudy, rainy day 60°. Paul made gourmet breakfast. Deitch was here

Missed Kids

23 & Chantell & Jerry called. 5:00 Mass
Rain, Rain. Rain. 60°. Paul & I went to Shop Rite & for papers Koffee & Deitch Chantell

24 Read papers, laid down & went to Arthurs.
Cloudy, dreary day. Rain & snow PM 35°. Very busy at work. Went to

Missed Kids

25 Peters moms wake. Paul rode w/me
Beautiful sunny day 40°. Very busy at work. Chantell brought Kelsey

26 & Bailey to my office. She went to Hove.
Beautiful sunny day 50°. Very busy as work. Paul called

Missed Kids

27 lawyer about house deed.
Cloudy, dreary day 40°. Very busy as work. Paul & I worked

Missed Kids

28 down to old house & sorted.
Beautiful sunny day 35°. Very busy as work. Rode in w/ Joe

Missed Kids

29 Paul & I went to lawyer Jo house
Beautiful sunny day 35°. Kelsey came over & spent the day. We took her home & watched 9wety troue

30 Beautiful sunny day 35°. Paul & I stayed in bed till 9:00.

Missed Kids

31 Made scrambled eggs & bacon & cheese. We went to I G A, Bradlees, Shop Rite, Deli & Wawa. Never got home till 4:00. Made food.

February

He makes me lie down in green pastures....
—PSALM 23:2 (RSV)

S	M	T	W	T	F	S
	1	2	3	4	5	6
7	8	9	10	11	12	13
14	15	16	17	18	19	20
21	22	23	24	25	26	27
28						

1

For there is hope of a tree.... —JOB 14:7

Today is *Tu B'Shevat,* the Jewish Arbor Day, referred to as the New Year of the Trees. Every year, we're supposed to plant a tree to mark the day.

Two years ago, someone gave us a small cutting from a fig tree, and on Tu B'Shevat, we started rooting it, moving it to a small pot when the roots formed, then a larger pot and finally a monumental pot. Earlier this year, it was about seven feet tall, bristling with new growth and figs. But it was also root-bound in the pot, and we had no sunny place left in our garden or on our tree-shaded lawn in which to plant it.

I was wondering what we could possibly do with it when my friend Jan happened to tell me that she had grown up with a fig tree in her yard and had always wanted another one. I started to smile and said, "I've been raising one for you."

My husband Keith and I took it over to her house and stood the pot in the perfect place in her backyard. She inhaled its fragrance and tears formed in her eyes. "It smells like when I was little," she said, hugging us.

This year I can't wait to plant something else and find out who I'm raising it for.

Dear God, thank You for new growth, in my garden and in my heart. —RHODA BLECKER

LESSONS IN LISTENING

2

ASKING
You do not have, because you do not ask.

—JAMES 4:2 (RSV)

The first—and most embarrassing—discovery I made about why I don't hear God's instructions is that I haven't asked for them.

My friend Demos Shakarian learned this lesson the hard way. Demos was a California dairyman who spent seventy-five percent of his time volunteering for Christian causes. "I sort of took for granted," he told me, "that since I was attending to God's business, He would look after mine."

A dairyman's first priority is feeding his animals. With three thousand cows, Demos often bought grain "futures," committing his dairy to a specific price for feed long before harvesttime. When a bumper crop came in one year, grain prices plummeted to half what Demos had agreed to pay.

"I took delivery with a sick heart. It was a huge financial blow, when I was spending my time and money the way I thought God wanted me to." The words Demos addressed to God that night were more a complaint than a prayer: "'I sure wish You'd told me!'

"And as clear as though He'd spoken aloud," Demos said, "I heard Him answer: *I sure wish you'd asked me!*

"I realized then," Demos went on, "that I hadn't prayed at all before making that disastrous decision. I figured God knew my cows had to eat—why bother Him with the obvious?"

Why *do* we have to ask, since Jesus assures us, "Your Father knows what you need before you ask him" (Matthew 6:8, RSV)? Because, I've come to think, asking is entering into relationship—and relationship with Him is always God's purpose, beyond all the decisions, large and small, of our lives.

Before each decision today, Father, remind me that the journey with You is more important than the destination.

—ELIZABETH SHERRILL

3

See that no one pays back evil for evil, but always try to do good to each other and to everyone else.

—I THESSALONIANS 5:15 (TLB)

The temperature was five below zero. The icy wind caught my hat and sent it tumbling across the snow drifts. Now the car wouldn't start. Not a grind or a grumble; the battery was dead.

My head dropped to the steering wheel. I prayed for a way out of the cold mess. Finally, I got out of the car and raised the hood. A few minutes later a man walked over to my car.

"Battery dead?" he said with a smile.

"Yes, sir. I left the lights on," I said sheepishly.

"No problem. I've got jumper cables. I'll have you up and running in no time."

Within minutes the engine purred to life. I thanked the man and offered him some money. "No thanks. But maybe you can help somebody else someday."

The very next day I was in a shoe store at a nearby shopping mall. Over the store loudspeaker I heard, "If anyone in the store has jumper cables, there's a man on the far side of the parking lot who needs help."

I didn't want to leave the warm store, walk clear across the parking lot, and stand there in the icy cold while some stranger drained the electricity in my car and put it into his own. But then I remembered my cold, frightening experience the previous day. *Maybe you can help somebody else someday.*

When I reached the stranded car, the man's wife and three children were huddled inside trying to keep warm. The woman jumped out, shook my hand and asked if they could pay me for the use of my brand-new jumper cables, purchased that very morning. I smiled. "No, but maybe you can help somebody else someday."

"It's a deal!" she exclaimed as her husband started their car.

Lord, help me to keep the helping-chain going. If I'm tempted to become the broken link, give me a boost! —PATRICIA LORENZ

4

Where there is no vision, the people perish....
—PROVERBS 29:18

My wife Barbara and I were attending a health care conference on the island of Maui. We planned a trip by car to Hana, a scenic trip over a challenging road. Friends who live in Maui told us that Charles Lindbergh's grave was just a mile or so beyond Hana, and we decided to continue on to pay our respects to the great aviator.

Despite his fame, there were no signs pointing the way, and without directions from our friends we wouldn't have found it. The tiny cemetery overlooked the Pacific Ocean down a sandy lane behind a small church. Lindbergh had requested that he be buried in a hand-hewn eucalyptus casket in an unmarked grave. His widow honored his request for the casket but placed a simple marker on his grave. It gave only his name, the dates of his birth and death, and a verse from Psalm 139:9: "If I take the wings of the morning, and dwell in the uttermost parts of the sea." I stood quietly at the grave for a moment thinking of all the things that had been set in motion by his flight that had captured the world's imagination, and of all the doors that had been opened by his act of heroism so long ago.

Then I walked to the edge of the cemetery and stood gazing at the vastness of the Pacific Ocean. I was deeply touched and began thinking of the future, and of all the challenges that remain for us—problems in society that people think have no solutions, diseases for which we have yet to find cures and frontiers in every area of life that people now think impossible to cross. Then I remembered the next verse of that Psalm: "Even there shall thy hand lead me, and thy right hand shall hold me."

Dear God, help my faith in You to make me unafraid to try new things. —KENNETH CHAFIN

5

Lo, I have given thee a wise and an understanding heart.... —I KINGS 3:12

Many of you *Daily Guideposts* readers know that I am hearing-impaired and use a relay service for telephone communications. The hundreds of people who manage this twenty-four hour service are God's gift to me. They strive to have the deaf caller "hear" through the written word every sound that a hearing person would: dogs barking in the background; laughter; babies crying.

Recently, I was trying to contact a doctor's office about a misunderstanding on a medical report. I was nervous and the call assistant sensed it. She typed, "We are waiting. We are holding to music." Then she went on typing, "Oh, it's beautiful violin music.... It's a waltz! Why don't you take a spin around your room while we wait?"

"I'll do that," I voiced back to her. Quickly, I mentally donned a long, white ball gown, slipped into the arms of my imaginary partner and circled my bedroom, all the while keeping my eyes on the TDD (telephone device for the deaf) screen. A moment or two later, I saw the type moving and caught, "Doctor's office. How may I help you?"

When the conversation ended, I thanked the relay assistant for her calming suggestion. "It was a big help," I said.

"I'm glad," she typed. "That's what we're here for—to help."

Lord, thank You for the many wise and understanding hearts that dwell among us. —ELEANOR SASS

6

Forsake not the law of thy mother. —PROVERBS 1:8

When my sister Leila was ten years old and I was eight, we had a great adventure: browsing for two hours, unattended, through a Woolworth five-and-dime store. Mother was attending a meeting in a home three blocks away.

"You may walk to the house to meet me," she told us. "Be careful as you cross the streets, and don't run. Walk ladylike."

As we got out of the car in front of the store, she reminded us, "The meeting will be over at four-thirty. You are to be there at that time. Understand?"

"Yes, ma'am," we replied jointly.

"Four-thirty!" she repeated as she drove away, and we dashed across the sidewalk into a wonderland of lights, gadgets, toys and games.

Leila wore a watch and we checked it often, calculating how long it would take us to walk "ladylike" the three blocks. All too soon, it was time to stop feasting our eyes on the displayed wonders and begin our walk. Precisely at the appointed time, we rang the doorbell, and the hostess of the meeting invited us in. The meeting was over, and the ladies were having refreshments.

"You arrived just in time," the hostess told us, handing each of us a cup of punch.

"Mother said to be here at four-thirty," Leila said.

Smiling, the hostess turned to Mother. "They got here right at four-thirty," she said.

"I knew they would," Mother replied proudly. "I can always trust my girls."

That simple statement has never left me. I've conquered many temptations when I remembered those words. And as long as I have to make hard decisions, Mother's assurance of so long ago will continue guiding me to the right choices.

Thank You, God, for my mother. Help me never to betray her trust—or Yours—in me. Amen. —DRUE DUKE

7

"You are a gracious and compassionate God, slow to anger and abounding in love, a God who relents from sending calamity." —JONAH 4:2 (NIV)

It was impossible to teach my fourth-grade Bible school class with Sarah around. Sarah waved her hand eagerly in the air with nothing to say, just to be called upon. Her pencil lay silent on the table during workbook time while she tilted her folding chair until it nearly collapsed. She heckled and insulted our teenage helper. When the line of students went this way, she went that way. She refused to wear her name tag. She complained about the snack. My own silent complaints about Sarah mounted.

On Thursday when I counted heads in the hallway before we returned from craft class, Sarah was missing. I searched the craft room and the rest room. No Sarah. Anger tightened in my stomach as I sputtered to the class, "When I find Sarah, she's getting punished by not going to snack."

Sarah finally resurfaced at our classroom door five minutes later. I hustled her out into the hallway and scolded her. Her face crumpled. She wrung her hands and declared, "I'm sorry! I was really lost! I didn't know where you were!"

The anger in my stomach didn't believe Sarah, but I had no way of knowing whether or not she had been truly lost. I answered in a cold, stern tone, "I have no choice but to believe you."

Curious eyes were all over us when Sarah and I stepped back into the classroom. "Sarah was lost," I told them, "so she can go to snack." I went to the front of the room and paged awkwardly through my lesson about Jonah. As I retold the story, it suddenly sounded far from a children's story, for in the very end, when Jonah successfully gets the notorious Ninevites to repent, he promptly goes to pouting and complaining about the fact that God decided not to punish them. I had really wanted to punish Sarah; anger had complained that she had certainly earned it and deserved it. I had doubted and resisted her repentance. I was being just as disruptive to God's grace as Sarah had been to my classroom.

Lord, it's so terribly difficult to allow someone else to repent. Don't let me get swallowed up in enough anger to choke a whale. Please free me to love. —KAREN BARBER

8

When we cry, "Abba! Father!" it is the Spirit himself bearing witness with our spirit that we are children of God. —ROMANS 8:15–16 (RSV)

I'm at my dining table, surrounded by all the candles I could find, during the most violent blizzard to hit Nebraska in thirty years. Roaring fifty-mile-an-hour winds are beating against the house, rattling the storm windows, splitting branches from winter-brittle trees. All power is out, so not even the furnace will come on. It's four degrees below zero, with a wind-chill factor of sixty to eighty below. I've closed all the blinds and drapes to keep in as much heat as possible and I'm wearing three layers of clothes, but my hands, cheeks and nose are beginning to get cold.

About an hour ago, I had picked up the phone to call my grown children to make sure they were all safe at home and okay, but the phone was dead! Up to that point, I was rather enjoying the storm and the involuntary cutback to simplicity. But that loss of contact with the outside world made me feel alone, isolated, cut off. So I went to my prayer chair and called upon my heavenly Father to protect those I love, to guide all who are stranded safely home, and to provide warmth, shelter and food for those who are without them.

As I prayed, a great sense of connection with others by way of God came upon me, bringing with it a deep sense of peace and quiet protection. It's been a precious reminder to me that I'm never alone, and that there's always an open circuit to my heavenly Father. It's a circuit by which I can be instantly connected with those I love and with all the other "children of God" with whom I share this planet.

Abba! Father! Thank You for creating this family of children, and for being our always-available connecting circuit.

—MARILYN MORGAN HELLEBERG

9

And the ears of the deaf shall be unstopped.

—ISAIAH 35:5

The tiny, curtained cubicle in the doctor's office was freezing. I'd just had my mammogram. Till now, these hadn't worried me, but this year I was still reeling from the fact that my mother had had breast cancer. A friend had been diagnosed with early-stage cancer, too. And my own doctor was away, and this one seemed new—and brusque. So I sat in the cubicle and waited. And waited. And waited, getting more nervous as each moment passed. "Keep your gown on," the mammogram technician had instructed me earlier. "Doctor will be in to discuss your results shortly." *Why was he taking so long? What was wrong?*

Twenty minutes later, I finally pulled the curtain back and tapped a passing nurse with my sweaty-palmed hand. "Excuse me...if he's with another patient, that's fine...but I've been waiting for my results."

The young nurse's eyes widened. "Are you still here? Oh, I think he forgot you!"

In less than a minute, the doctor stuck his head in the curtain, snapped, "You're fine. You can get dressed and go," and strode off. I was fuming. *What nerve! He forgot me, and all I get is a two-second, brusque, "You're fine." And I waited so long, and it's cold in the paper gown, and all he says is "You're fine."*

I closed my eyes and stopped mid-thought. *What would my mother or my friend have given to hear those words, spoken brusquely, spoken in pig Latin, spoken at all?* I rolled the words around in my mind: *I'm fine. I'm fine. Thank You, God.*

Today, God, let me give up my petty grievances and rejoice in the good in my life.   —LINDA NEUKRUG

10

Jesus answered and said unto her...whosoever drinketh of the water that I shall give him shall never thirst....

—JOHN 4:13–14

One rainy morning, as my husband George was filling the percolator with water, he gazed out the window and marveled, "Isn't it wonderful how water falls from the sky, pure and clear? Then it seeps into the ground—into soil, clay, mud and sand. You would think it would be dirty from all its encounters by the time it finds its way into our kitchen." He plugged in the percolator, and soon the aroma of coffee filled the room.

"Yes, but the water is filtered as it flows," I said, "and then cleaned further by manmade treatment plants. By the time it reaches our faucet, it's as clean and pure as the day it fell, or as near to that as we can make it. Anyway, it's ready for us to drink."

George sat down and opened the Bible. Reading it aloud had become, like that first cup of coffee, the most cheerful, invigorating and encouraging way to start the day. He leafed carefully through it for a minute. We had gone to bed the night before troubled by a number of things: the loss of one of his patients; a problem with my work; a family misunderstanding. Now, pausing at the Sermon on the Mount, he read, "Blessed are the poor in spirit: for theirs is the kingdom of heaven. Blessed are they that mourn: for they shall be comforted. Blessed are the meek: for they shall inherit the earth" (Matthew 5:3-5).

George looked up with an expression of discovery. "You know, our minds are like that water! So often filled with muck and confusion as we try to find our way—regret, worry, self-pity, critical thoughts. The Bible is our filter. By reading the Bible, we can clear and purify our thoughts."

Thank You, God, for the Bible. Help me to remember to turn to it whenever I'm troubled or confused. —MARJORIE HOLMES

11 THURSDAY

Over all the glory there will be a canopy.... It will be for a shade by day from the heat, and for a refuge and a shelter from the storm and rain. —ISAIAH 4:5–6 (RSV)

It was one of those days when storms raged outside and inside of me. Outside, a blue norther was settling in. The wind was picking up, and the temperature was dropping. Deep within me, I felt a tempest of anxiety and depression, the result of too much work without rest. I yearned to hear a gentle voice from God, to be reassured of His guidance and presence. I put on my running shoes, picked up a small New

Testament and slipped it into my jacket pocket, and set out to run my blues away.

I decided to jog around a small, picturesque lake, one of my favorite routes. The strong wind was kicking up short, choppy waves, and the gray sky threatened rain. Usually wood ducks skirted the sandy shore, bobbing and quacking at one another. But today they were nowhere to be seen. *Where do ducks go when it storms?* I wondered.

Finally tiring, I stopped and pulled out my New Testament. The brisk gale blew its thin pages back and forth. I looked around for a windbreak, a place to sit down, and saw a thick clump of trees nestled in a shallow cove by the water. Entering the leafy shelter, I leaned back against an oak. Dozens of ducks huddled together in front of me in the cove. They, too, had sought shelter from the storm. They knew where to find still water.

I sat down under the oak tree and read from my New Testament. Quietly I savored the safety and security found in the Scriptures— the shelter that God provides for all of us in the midst of storms.

Father, thank You for always being with me in Your Word.
—*SCOTT WALKER*

12

"Those who are wise will shine like the brightness of the heavens, and those who lead many to righteousness, like the stars for ever and ever." —DANIEL 12:3 (NIV)

A friend was lamenting the lack of leadership in the country. "We should be doing better with health care, the environment, feeding the hungry...." I couldn't disagree, but reminded him of an old political truism: People only get the leadership they demand. Sometimes that means taking leadership roles ourselves.

How so? By agreeing to *lead* the stewardship committee; by agreeing to *lead* the class; by agreeing to *lead* the PTA; by agreeing to *lead* a neighborhood action group. Leadership doesn't require enormous intellect, dazzling talent or superhuman strength, only commitment and a willingness to give of our God-given gifts.

There is a cemetery off the coast of Normandy in Caen, France, where many RAF pilots are buried. They died during the early, crucial air battles of World War II. One of the graves bears this great definition of leadership: "Leadership is wisdom, courage and carelessness of self." God honors people who are careless givers of themselves.

Free our spirits, God, our hands unbind,
Give us hearts loving, a serving mind.

—FRED BAUER

13

For today the Lord will appear unto you.—LEVITICUS 9:4

For a long time my husband Alex and I wanted to try cross-country skiing but felt intimidated. We simply are not very athletic. Finally a friend said, "Really, it's as easy as walking. Go for it." So we are going for it.

We carry our skis to the start of the trail, then try to lock our boots in them and almost fall over. Perched on the thin skis, I feel very unstable and almost wish I'd stayed by the fire in the lodge. But soon Tom, our instructor, has us pushing and gliding along. He cheers us on, "That's it! You're doing great!"

Then he points us in the direction of another trail. I gasp. "You're leaving us on our own?"

He insists. "You've got the techniques down fine. This is an easy trail."

Push, glide. One arm and foot reaching ahead, then the other. Soon, we enter a lush stretch of forest. I glide along, exhilarated. What a wonderful way to be outside and see winter's beauty! I savor the fresh air, the snow-drenched trees sparkling like glitter in the sunshine. *Oh, no, a little hill! How do I get up if I fall?... I did it! I sailed down without falling!*

We pass a family repositioning a child in a sled. My mind races ahead. *We could do this with the kids! I wonder if we can pull Mark in a sled? Can we find another free weekend to take them? I wonder how hard the trails are at home. Where can we get equipment?*

Then I catch myself. *How easily I jump out of the joy of the present. Stop anticipating, fretting about the future. Come back, fully experience "now."* A lush grove of evergreens, the peaceful joy of a steady gliding rhythm—even falling, then shaking with laughter as we try to help each other up. This beauty. The thrill of learning a new skill.

Thank You, God, for beckoning me into the beauty right here and now.

—MARY BROWN

14

May he grant you your heart's desire and fulfill all your plans.
—*PSALM 20:4 (TLB)*

It was Valentine's Day, and I was feeling lonely. Valentine's Day had always been my favorite holiday, but in the five years since my divorce I had dreaded its arrival. So why was I in a store filled with bright red "I Love You" cards, Victorian lace and softly scented candles?

I stood in the aisle of the shop and looked around. People were busy selecting last-minute gifts and cards for their sweethearts. I decided to leave, but as I walked down the aisle, something caught my eye. It was a clear plastic dome filled with white, finely grained sand. I stopped and picked it up. The sand poured quickly through a pattern of holes and became a perfectly shaped heart. I turned it over. The sand then poured through another set of holes and formed the words *I Love You.*

"It's beautiful," I whispered, longing to have someone for whom to buy it. I prayed that God would send someone for me, someone with whom I could share my life.

Then I recalled a sermon I'd heard as a child. Our minister had talked about having faith that God will answer our prayers. We'd had no rain for more than four weeks and a dry, still, hot Louisiana was almost unbearable. The congregation had been joining hands at the end of each service to pray for rain. One Sunday the pastor stopped the prayer, looked around for a moment and quietly asked, "Who brought an umbrella to church today? It's no use praying for something that we don't believe will happen." So I bought the little dome to give one day to my own sweetheart.

After two more Valentine's Days alone, I finally gave the gift I'd bought on faith to a wonderful man named Roy. Two years later, he became my husband.

Lord, You want to give me my heart's desire. Help me to wait for Your perfect timing.
—*MELODY BONNETTE*

15

Let every soul be subject unto the higher powers....
—*ROMANS 13:1*

This is the two hundredth year since the death of George Washington. I suppose there will be much made of the commander of the triumphal forces of our Revolution and first President, yet he remains for most people a rather elusive, somewhat cold hero. He was not a Lincoln who stirred the emotions of the self-made man. He was wealthy and self-sufficient, and yet, to quote Dixon Wecter in a book called *The Hero in America,* he resembled "the average man, raised to the highest power by will and duty."

That was Wecter's view of him, and Wecter was a professor of mine at the University of California who provided hours of spirited talk on any number of topics, yes, including Washington.

Washington was not an exceptional speaker, had none of the gifts usually associated with a leader, and yet he had an infinite integrity that transcended any task. In spite of his acts of soldiering, in which he gained the respect of his men and fellow countrymen, and in spite of his eight years in the presidency, in which he carefully avoided all the lures of dictatorship and set the style we know today, he retained as his great passion a love of the soil. "Agriculture has ever been the most favorite amusement of my life," he wrote. Mount Vernon was the focus of his life and the things he did there, planting and reaping, riding to hounds, hunting, acting in amateur theatricals, dancing with uncommon stamina, all these things were paramount in his mind. To Mount Vernon he returned as a private citizen, a country gentleman, yet done to the "highest power," as in everything set before him.

I have, we have reason to mark this day. Thank You, God, for giving us a great American. —VAN VARNER

READER'S ROOM

I have been teaching a study on the Book of Hebrews this winter at our church. The writer of Hebrews encourages his readers to persevere. My husband and I are going through some serious challenges. The biggest challenge is to let go of my anger. God is reminding me that His love is stronger than any emotion I feel. This isn't easy for me. Yet God's love surrounds me in such a way that I know it is possible.

—JUDY LOVITT, COEUR D'ALENE, ID

16

Show yourself...a model of good deeds....

—*TITUS 2:7 (RSV)*

I signed up for duty at a children's hospital in Manhattan with hopes of saving the world—only to discover I was the world's worst volunteer. Every Tuesday night, I joined twenty other women to lead craft time for young kids who lived at the hospital year round. My sheltered, Alabama childhood had certainly not prepared me to work with city kids from broken homes. I colored and painted with them, but their emotional outbreaks and battles for our attention made me a nervous wreck. I didn't know how to reach out to them—even hugging was against the rules because most of the children had been abused. After a few months of failing to connect, I was just about ready to give up. Surely someone else could love them better than I.

On what was to have been my last night, eight-year-old Victor wanted help drawing a tiger. "Please, somebody," he pleaded, as one by one the volunteers turned him down. "How about you?" He stood right in front of me with a brown crayon. I didn't want him to be disappointed, but it was only fair to warn him: "It won't be perfect, Victor."

He frowned and pointed right between my eyes. "Nothing in life is perfect, but you have to try." I looked at that child, whose life had been anything but perfect, and knew he was right. I might never be the best volunteer, but I could be a willing one. So I tried. And for weeks to come, a goofy tiger with a lopsided grin hung over my favorite second-grader's bed.

Lord, I know I'm not perfect, but with my trust in You, I'll try.

—*ALLISON SAMPLE*

17

One thing I know, that, whereas I was blind, now I see.

—*JOHN 9:25*

For years my ophthalmologist insisted I was too old for contacts. When we moved, I asked my new doctor about them. This incredibly young man smiled and replied, "Good idea!"

In a few moments, a whole new world opened up for me as his assistant placed soft contacts in my eyes. I ran to the window and looked down into the parking lot, easily picking out my car. I could almost read the license plate! Glancing joyfully at the wall, I read my doctor's diplomas without squinting. I almost danced a jig as I left his office wearing my new contacts, glasses in my purse. All the way home I smiled, nearly laughing out loud as I read the street names effortlessly. *How marvelous to see clearly, Lord!* I prayed.

I thought He spoke to me before the light turned green. *I'm glad you have new contacts and can see. Don't forget about seeing spiritual things clearly, too. When your feelings were hurt recently and you and your friend became estranged, when you were openly critical of that relative and stubbornly refused to apologize, you were blind to the spiritual consequences of what you were doing. When you give in to your feelings of pride or envy or anger, you turn away from Me. Read My Word, talk to Me, listen for My voice, so that you can see clearly into the unseen world where you fight your spiritual battles every day. Keep your eyes on Me, and My grace will give you victory.*

God of sight, on this Ash Wednesday, enable me to see clearly into my own heart.
— MARION BOND WEST

18 THURSDAY

Thy gentleness hath made me great. —PSALM 18:35

When I was in the fifth grade, my classmates and I were not doing so well in geography, and we expected a major reprimand.

Instead, the teacher brought to class a large wooden puzzle of the United States. He never said a word about it; he just placed it on a table by the window. After lunch, we began to toy with it, timidly at first, then eagerly. It was homemade of fine, laminated birch, about three by four feet. The fragrance of the wood reminded me of my uncle's cabin in Minnesota, surrounded by white birches.

We took turns putting the puzzle together. Then my friend Butch suggested we divide into teams and have competitions putting it together. So it became a regular lunch-hour contest, as fierce as any football game. In order to win, we had to work together and we had to refer to our geography book.

It was amazing, after that, how often we knew what the teacher was talking about when he referred to Boise, Idaho, or Mystic, Connecticut, or Narragansett, Rhode Island.

I'm grateful for that gentle, wise teacher and for all the others who have taken the softer, more indirect approach with me: the boss who took me to lunch, instead of taking me to task...the way my wife quietly slips a paper towel under my coffee cup, instead of lecturing me about spills...the student who comes privately to my office after class to tell me I made a factual mistake, instead of embarrassing me in front of the whole class.

Easy does it better, and I hope to find alternative ways to handle those tense and awkward situations when I would like to use a club on someone.

Father, with all Your power and authority, You are as gentle as a grandfather. Make me gentle like You. —DANIEL SCHANTZ

19

Fear not them which kill the body, but are not able to kill the soul.... —MATTHEW 10:28

When I tell people my mother suffers from Alzheimer's, they invariably ask if she still recognizes me. I am relieved to say she does, for now, though this will probably not continue to be the case. Yet the question I increasingly ask myself is: Do I recognize her?

This was a woman who continued to jog well into her seventies. Her favorite pastimes included shoveling snow and mowing the yard. She relished telling you she had never been sick a day in her life, and on the rare occasions when she admitted that a cold might be coming on, she liked to combat it by scrubbing the kitchen floor, as if hard work was the only tonic to malaise. You suspected she didn't quite understand people who got sick.

When the time came to take away her driver's license, I will never forget my brother and sister and I standing guiltily around Mom's kitchen table while she shook her head defiantly, much too stubborn and proud to cry *or* plead—after all who were we, her children, to tell her what she couldn't do? After that, she walked the three miles to church nearly every morning. She counted the money from the collection basket, though someone always quietly recounted it after Mom began slipping. For a long time she was the church librarian, though again, in later years, she had trouble reshelving the books correctly and had to be checked.

My mother will still tell you she has never been sick a day in her life. She told me that very same thing this morning, in fact, from the hospital where she had been taken when she couldn't get out of bed. She is failing physically now. The ravages of osteoporosis, a stubborn intestinal disorder, high blood pressure—these are the wolves that circle her. At eighty-five and barely able to understand what is happening and why she is in pain, Estelle Grinnan is not the person I once recognized as my mother.

But then there is that strange but nonetheless resounding declaration of health despite the tubing that invades her, the cumbersome back brace that is supposed to relieve the pressure on her crushed vertebrae, the X rays and blood tests and CAT scans and sonograms, the whole unnerving high-tech arsenal of modern medicine. There is, after all, somewhere in all of that corporeal wreckage of a long life well-lived, a woman who has never been sick a day in her life.

Lord, at the end of our journey, we are still the people You made us. —EDWARD GRINNAN

20 SATURDAY

"Along unfamiliar paths I will guide them; I will turn the darkness into light before them and make the rough places smooth...." —ISAIAH 42:16 (NIV)

I took my seat in the middle section of a small local theater, but my mind was not on the performance about to begin. Pesky worries whirled around in my head. *Should I take early retirement from my part-time nursing job?* Recently, I'd felt pressure from the administration. *But how will I support myself then? To make ends meet, I will have to move. Where to?* I shivered at the thought of leaving the security of friends and family. So many life-changing decisions at a time when I felt weak and vulnerable.

The theater darkened. The curtains on the stage parted. A beam of light coming from the control room behind me illuminated the stage.

Lord, light up my life like that, I thought. *I need more light to make wise decisions.*

Halfway through the first scene, an usher came down the aisle, guiding two latecomers. The flashlight he held formed a small circle of light at their feet. Slowly, he moved ahead to the appropriate row; then he shone the light onto two vacant seats. He waited patiently until the man and woman sat down. Then he turned off the flash-light and walked quietly back to the entrance.

That's how I lead you! The thought was crystal clear, as though I heard God speaking. *As you read My Word and obey it, you'll have enough light to know what step to take next. And then there'll be more light for the next step, and the next. Trust Me. Have I not promised to get you safely to the right place?*

Thankfully, I relaxed and enjoyed the rest of the play.

Lord Jesus, thank You for the light of Your presence.
— *HELEN GRACE LESCHEID*

21

SUNDAY

Give therefore thy servant an understanding heart....
— *I KINGS 3:9*

After church, Don, one of our vestry members, asked me, "Oscar, will you accept the job of chief usher?" A little reluctantly, I said yes. "By the way, you'll be the greeter, too!" Don added. In our church, the greeter is responsible for talking to visitors to make them feel welcome. Feeling I was getting more than I bargained for, I gulped.

My first newcomer was Ralph, a tall, gray-haired gentleman. "I'm returning to church after twenty-five years," Ralph told me. "I hope I can understand the service." I welcomed him and thanked him for choosing our church for his return.

We all tried to help Ralph follow the service and make him feel at home. He attended faithfully for several months, but then he disappeared. I wondered where he had gone. After a few weeks, Ralph returned. I was delighted to see him, and I told him so as I shook his hand warmly.

He stood back as if he hadn't heard me. Then he looked down at me and said, "I was gone for weeks and no one called to see if I was living or dead!"

Ralph's angry words struck home. I didn't even know his telephone number! I was acting as if Christian fellowship were only a one-hour, Sunday-morning event. But it isn't; it's something that's only real if it reaches beyond the walls of the church. It can't be reduced to a warm smile and a firm handshake.

Ralph's words opened a door for me. Since then, when I miss seeing someone in church, I call to see if anything is the matter. And when the absence is prolonged, I make sure to keep in touch. Doing little things like these can help a church family glow with warmth and love.

Father, let me be a real brother or sister to my brothers and sisters in Christ. —OSCAR GREENE

SIX FOR WORKING, ONE FOR REST

As we look forward to the wonderful things God has in store for us, it's a good idea every now and then to pause and look back at where we've been and at the ways God has led us through the years. For many of us, the path we've traveled is the unfolding of what the Lord gave us in our childhood, through the words and examples of our mothers and fathers. This week, we invite you to join Isabel Wolseley as she returns to the roots of her own spiritual journey in the routines of her growing-up years during the Great Depression. —THE EDITORS

22 MONDAY

WASH DAY

And ye shall wash your clothes...and ye shall be clean....
—NUMBERS 31:24

During my growing-up years, all our activities were crammed into seven pigeonholes, each labeled with a weekday name. If it was Monday, it was Wash Day.

Monday mornings my mother raced every other woman in the neighborhood to be the first getting out her family's laundry. If any clothesline didn't have wash flapping in the Kansas wind by the time we kids left for school, it was a sure sign someone in that household must be "down sick."

Back then, Mondays didn't mean emptying clothes from the hamper into an automatic machine, pushing a button and forgetting the matter, either. No, Mondays meant shaving homemade lye soap into copper boilers filled with water lugged from windmills and heated over fires. If I whined about helping, Mom simply answered with the not exactly scriptural "cleanliness is next to godliness," and continued her usual wash day instructions:

"Take that stick and punch the clothes up and down so the soap gets through them."

"Make sure the overall buttons are flat before they go through the wringers." "Watch your fingers!" "Don't throw away the cold wash water—pour it on my verbenas."

I used Mom's old Maytag during my first years of marriage. When we replaced it, we saved its square aluminum lid. It made a dandy pancake griddle. We saved her copper wash boiler, too, to sit in retirement in our family room holding magazines.

As for me, Mondays mean "Wash Day" even yet. And each time I sort the family laundry, I remember a particular Monday from long ago. I'd questioned a shirt Mom had put on the pile, saying, "I don't think it's dirty enough to wash."

"Let's wash it, Isabel," she replied. "If there's any doubt about it, it's dirty."

Father, help me to keep my souls as clean as my shirts.

—ISABEL WOLSELEY

23

IRONING DAY
Six days shalt thou labour, and do all thy work.

—EXODUS 20:9

The early 1930s were the Dust Bowl years in the country's midsection where we lived. We had no rain for months on end. Then a plague of grasshoppers—worse, we thought, than old Pharaoh ever had to face—swarmed into the Plains states. After devouring every snippet of growth the drought hadn't claimed, they lined themselves on the north sides of telephone poles and fence posts for shade. With no foliage blocking the way, hot south winds—fueled by a red, Frisbeelike sun—rolled tumbleweeds across a terrain so flat we could have seen Tulsa and points south had they not been hidden by rust-colored clouds.

Even though dust, fine as face powder, sifted beneath closed windows and left mini-drifts on sills, whenever the second day of the week came around, my mother ironed. It was Tuesday, after all.

Each Tuesday Mom ran to heat the irons on the kerosene stove, which covered them with black smudge. She ran to wipe them clean. She ran the now-cooled iron back to the stove. She ran back with a hot replacement. She ran in a circle with the stove, the sink and Dad's white shirts on its circumference.

When I got to be Mom's age, I had an electric iron to end Tuesday drudgery, yet my overflowing ironing basket was seldom empty. But I rescued one of Mom's venerable sadirons—all four-plus pounds of it. It's a quaint doorstop in my home. Nothing beats it for cracking nuts. And it continues as a spiritual reminder....

At each Tuesday's close, Mom tucked a damp strand of hair back into her bun and wiped her forehead with a corner of her apron. "There!" she'd say in satisfaction, patting the rows of starched, ironed garments hooked on chair backs. "The Lord keeps us clean on the inside and He expects me to keep my family clean on the outside. He has to work twenty-four hours. I'm done for the day!"

Thank You, Father, for ironing out the "wrinkles" that creep into my life each day.
—ISABEL WOLSELEY

24

WEDNESDAY

BAKING DAY
She took some dough, kneaded it, made the bread in his sight and baked it.
—II SAMUEL 13:8 (NIV)

Wednesday meant Baking Day during my growing-up years.

Only a huge aluminum dishpan could hold the twenty-four cups of flour my mother scooped into it with a chipped ironstone mug, plus the quart of scalded milk, salt, a little sugar, some potato-water starter, and have enough room left—after ten minutes of hand-kneading—for rising dough.

Several hours later Mom plopped the spongy batch onto a floured board and sliced it into eight chunks. Marble-sized pieces pinched from the first lump went three at a time into muffin-tin cups. "Your cloverleaf rolls are so light I could use them to powder my back," someone said. The second chunk—patted into a flat rectangle, sprinkled with cinnamon sugar, raisins and nuts—was rolled and sliced. "Let me have the uneven ends," I teased. Although the sugar gritted with each bite, I ate the raw, sweetened dough.

Mom smoothed the other six chunks into cocoon shapes, buttered their tops and slid them into waiting pans. Several hours later, well-tanned loaves pulled from the oven wafted a wonderful, bakerylike smell. The fattest of the lot was set aside as "the Lord's loaf." During Depression days, food was hard to come by, but "Someone needs it worse than we," the folks said. "God will show us who."

"Homemade bread should be eaten while it's hot and crusty" was an unwritten law at our house. Besides, we couldn't wait until suppertime. Grace came first, then stirring the jug so it wouldn't be mostly cream, Mom poured milk for me and coffee for herself and Dad. Over chunks of hot crusty bread slathered with homemade butter and strawberry jam, conversation began: "Anything new at school today?"

Wednesday Baking Day ended with Wednesday night's Bible Study and Prayer Meeting. Everyone attended the services. That's where "the Lord's loaf" went, too.

My bread doesn't measure up to Mom's, so I share other things with those the Lord points out. After all, troubles always lessen over a slice of hot apple pie or fresh peach cobbler topped with cream.

Jesus, You're the "bread of life." Remind me to keep sharing that bread with those who don't know its satisfying taste.

—ISABEL WOLSELEY

25

CLEANING DAY
Thus saith the Lord, Set thine house in order....
—II KINGS 20:1

"Cleaning Day is the worst one of the week!" I'd complain every Thursday. My opinion didn't "carry water" with my folks, who usually mixed metaphors by adding, "Getting you to do something is like pulling teeth."

"But I mopped this floor just last week."

"When you live on a farm, it should be mopped every day. Besides, company's coming."

"Who?"

"Your aunt and uncle."

I groaned. This aunt was "Gertrude" to Uncle Dave, but "Gertie"—or "The Best Housekeeper in Town"—to everyone else. Their upcoming visit precipitated frenzied woodwork-wiping, window-washing and lace-curtain-stretching. Dad freshly blackened the coal stove, then pulled up the carpet, dragged it outside, draped it over the clothesline and whacked it nearly threadbare.

"Cleaning is a waste of good time," I muttered while kneeling next to a scrub brush and soap pail on the now-bare floor.

Mom broke into my thoughts. "Some day you'll have your own place. You'll want to make your husband proud he has an orderly house to come home to." Then, she added gently, "Cleaning it is a wife's duty."

"Not for me. When I grow up, I'm never going to clean. Spider webs and dirt can keep growing for all I care."

Marriage, two sons and six grandchildren later, I've eaten those words over and over. I've learned something else, too, during the intervening years. The place where my family and I live is not the only home in need of continual cleaning.

My heart's home is where You wish to live, dear Father. Keep it clean by the power of Your Spirit. —ISABEL WOLSELEY

---

26 | FRIDAY

MENDING AND SEWING DAY
She seeketh wool, and flax, and worketh willingly with her hands. —PROVERBS 31:13

Mending and Sewing Day ranked with Cleaning Day on my list of loathsome chores. For my mother, mending and sewing were not chores, but skills every young lady should acquire. I was a slow learner.

"Fancywork" was something all women did during my childhood. Fancying meant embroidering curlicues, French knots or daisy-filled baskets on sheets, pillowcases, bureau runners, tablecloths, napkins and doilies. Even on underwear.

I was about eight when Mom handed me a dish towel with a dotted, ironed-on design in one corner, placed a basket filled with colored skeins of thread between us and said, "It's time you learned to embroider." Countless needle pricks, groans and a month later, I finally finished the word *Monday* and beneath it, a cat doing laundry.

My feeling of relief didn't last long. Mom brought out a second towel with *Tuesday* and the same cat ironing. Five more weekday names and five more cats on five more dish towels followed.

When I protested, Mom merely quoted, "Satan finds mischief for idle hands," and found something else for me to do...like making bud vases from bottles and curtain-tieback butterflies from clothespins.

Nowadays, my mending basket sits in the closet, along with the hope that I'd get to its contents sometime before our sons finished college. Mom may not have succeeded in making me a seamstress, but she did teach me a principle I followed with my own children, grandchildren and small neighbors: Youngsters kept busy seldom have time to find trouble.

Lord, help me to focus on the tasks You've given me to do.
—*ISABEL WOLSELEY*

27

GO TO TOWN DAY
And having food and raiment let us be therewith content.
—*I TIMOTHY 6:8*

During the Great Depression, most everyone bartered for their needs. My folks traded homemade butter for flour and sugar; crates of eggs for livestock feed. Every Saturday morning our dairy products went into the Model A's backseat, the three of us in the front. Going to Town (the map called it McPherson) meant an exciting excursion. Saturdays included window-shopping (about all anyone could afford) and time for socializing with others who came to town.

On the way, we stopped at Dad's parents' to "see if Pa and Ma need anything." I savored the sugar cookies Grandma pulled from a pig-shaped jar. After arriving in town and delivering our butter and eggs, Mom headed for the dry goods store to look at dress patterns while Dad went to the feed mill. I targeted the drugstore alternately to ogle Lady Esther face powder, Tangee lipstick—and Vincent, the soda jerker, so tall, dark and handsome he made me swoon. Later, friends joined us to people-watch on Main Street (we waved to those we knew), count fireflies (we called them lightning bugs) and listen as the locusts began their *zooree, zooree* at dusk.

Eight dignified bongs from the courthouse clock signaled curfew for us farm folk. We headed home, empty-handed except for the staples we'd gone for and a dripping fifty-pound chunk of ice tied to a bumper.

"We have food in the house and clothes on our backs," Dad often said. "And we're healthy. That's a lot to be thankful for."

Heavenly Father, You've provided my family and me with enough to eat, enough to wear and extras too numerous to count. Thank You. —ISABEL WOLSELEY

28 SUNDAY

CHURCH AND DAY OF REST
Remember the sabbath day, to keep it holy.
—EXODUS 20:8

Except for gathering eggs and milking cows, no work was done on Sunday at our house. Most of our neighbors kept Sunday the same way. I can still recall the first time I saw someone doing otherwise. One Sunday while driving to church, we noticed a farmer plowing his field. After a few seconds of shocked silence, Dad excused the man. "He must have forgotten it's Sunday."

Doing homework, attending a movie, participating in or attending sporting events—"There are six other days for that," Dad said. "It's not appropriate on Sunday."

"Sunday best" was what we wore to church. Mother never had to wonder what she'd wear; she had only one "good" dress. There was no decision for Dad, either: a blue serge suit. Mom pressed it from the inside, especially the pants so the seat wouldn't shine.

At church I sat between Dad and Mom on the walnut pews, listening to the choir, looking at the stained-glass windows and thinking about the Bible stories they depicted. One morning when the pastor's sermon seemed unbearably long—I was five or six at the time—I persisted in whispering, "When can we go home?" Finally, my mild-mannered father had enough. Grabbing my hand, he marched me outside and gave me the most withering scolding I'd ever had.

Time always looks forward, never back, so I no longer keep all of the rules I learned in my childhood. But I've always kept one rule Dad taught me: Church and rest on one day give strength for the following six.

Setting aside one day a week, Father, as You have asked, is my way especially to honor You. —ISABEL WOLSELEY

Missed Kids Beautiful sunny day 40°. very busy
at work. Paul + I got in
a big dispute about him calling
Malones office in Bol D. about med bills

1
Rain, Rain, Rain 50°. very busy at work.
Compiling figures for Lou from reports.

2
Balmy. Paul got a haircut.

Missed Kids Beautiful sunny day 50°. very busy at
work. Paul washed bed things +

3
hung them out. wonderful.

Missed Kids Cloudy, dreary day 50°. Very busy at
work. Went to Medical Unit to see

4
about Pauls hosp. bills.

Missed Kids Beautiful sunny day 40°. Very busy
at work. Writing letters for monthly

5
report. Watched kids for Chantell + Bob.

Missed Kids Cloudy + dreary day, come rain 40°.
Paul + I had lunch + took a nap.
Butch stopped by. Went to 5:00 Mass.

6
Cloudy, rainy day 75° Paul + I went
for papers + times to get a cell phone

7
at 12:00 we went back to Chantells

Missed Kids Snow, rain, slush, then? left for
work at 4:00. It was 34°. worked
on report for Pat on O.T.

8
Cloudy, dreary day 40°. Paul + I got
to the Hosp. at 8:30. He did fine

9
with his tests. We got home at 3:00.

Missed Kids Beautiful sunny day 50°. very busy
at work. Dr. K called. Paul has

10
a 70% blockage in bottom ends heart

Missed Kids Beautiful sunny day 50°. Very busy
at work. Cried all day in my

11
sleeplessness for Paul. 4 day off.

Missed Kids Sunny AM + cloudy + rain PM, 60°.
washed clothes in basement. Paul
+ I went for papers. Watched T.V.

12
Beautiful sunny day 30°. Butch
stopped over. We went to Mass

13
Beautiful sunny day 25°. Paul gave
me great big sweety card for

14
Valentine Day. We took a nap +
went to Debbies Wedding +
reception. Had a wonderful
Valentine Day.

Missed kids Beautiful sunny day 40°. Paul + I went to Target for cat food + phone cover. Came home + took a nap. Chantell...

15

Missed kids Beautiful sunny day 50°. Very busy as work Paul + I took off was till 5:30. Chantell called.

16

Missed kids Cloudy dreary day 45°. Busy at work. Did this O.T. A.M. Paul + I didn't go for ashes.

17

Missed kids Rain + cloudy 40° Very busy as work. Called Ann Ruth. Watched soaps.

18

Missed kids Cloudy AM + Sunny PM 45°. Went to Diane McGuires Meeting with Flody + Carol Conklin at 10:00.

19

Beautiful sunny day 35°. Paul + I slept most of day. We went to Rays + picked up the kids.

20

Beautiful sunny cold day 30°. Beverly + Kelsey spent the night. Clay, Deborah + Tom. Pa...

21

Missed kids Beautiful sunny cold day 20° very busy as work. Called...

22

Missed kids Beautiful sunny cold day 32° very busy as work. Had phone duty. Yuk! Used cell phone to call Paul.

23

Missed kids Beautiful sunny day 40° very busy as work. Deborah called. Lady gone when we called back.

24

Missed kids Beautiful sunny day 30°. Started work as 5:00 + left as 12:00. Called Deborah + Flossy w/Paul.

25

Missed kids Beautiful sunny day. Worked till 9:00. Took Paul for blood work + called Deborah + Flossy. Catheryn for Thur-May.

26

Missed kids Cloudy dreary day 30°. Paul + I got up as 10:00. Made ham + cheese egg buns for...day 5:00 P.M...

27

Missed kids Cloudy rainy day 45°. I may... Ham + cheese + egg for breakfast. Paul + I went for paper + coffee. Relaxed w/papers. Watched TV. Fixed curtains. Had dinner... for supper.

28

March

He leads me beside still waters.
—PSALM 23:2 (RSV)

S	M	T	W	T	F	S
	1	2	3	4	5	6
7	8	9	10	11	12	13
14	15	16	17	18	19	20
21	22	23	24	25	26	27
28	29	30	31			

LESSONS IN LISTENING

MONDAY

1

QUIET WITHOUT, QUIET WITHIN
But I have calmed and quieted my soul....

—PSALM 131:2 (RSV)

Twenty-five kindergartners make a lot of noise. On the mornings when I helped out at our son Scott's school, I'd notice my voice rising louder and louder over the din. That wasn't the teacher's way! A veteran of thirty years' experience, Mrs. Dietz would step to the front of the room and make her announcements in a whisper.

"If we're not very, very quiet," the soft voice would begin, "we won't hear what Mrs. Dietz is saying, will we?"

Near her, a few children, straining to hear, would shush others, shouters would be poked, and a wondrous hush would descend on the room as Mrs. Dietz whispered the names of the orange juice captains or the words of a new song. Because she spoke so quietly, the children's listening had a special quality. An alert, breathless attentiveness lest the barely audible message be missed.

When, years later, I began praying for guidance, I thought of Mrs. Dietz and that boisterous classroom. God will not raise His voice to be heard above the racket of my life. He wants me to shut off the TV, lay down the newspaper, let the phone ring. He calls me to a room alone, then waits for the inner commotion, too, to subside. He will not shout down my preoccupations, the conversations in my head. Like Mrs. Dietz, He speaks more softly than them all, until one by one they cease their chatter.

Then, quiet without, quiet within, I listen for the still, small voice that spoke the world into being.

Help me carve a quiet time from this active day, Father, when I can listen for the whispers of Your love. —ELIZABETH SHERRILL

2

This is my comfort in my affliction.... —PSALM 119:50

The word "comfort" is scattered all through the Bible, as well it should be, because there are times when all of us need it. Especially when a loved one dies.

Recently an eighty-four-year-old friend named Edna Hawkins sent me a note from Smyrna, Georgia, where she lives. "Here's something I found on a tombstone in a North Carolina cemetery," she writes.

> Spring will come again to the valley.
> Flowers will grow on the mountains.
> And the Shepherd will return for His sheep.

Just twenty-one words. I don't know who wrote them. But it seems to me that there is an enormous comfort in them. My friend recognized this, and passed them along to me. So now I am passing them along to you.

Lord, teach us to comfort the afflicted in any way we can.
—ARTHUR GORDON

3

The prayer of faith shall save the sick.... —JAMES 5:15

When I was helping the late poet Helen Steiner Rice write her autobiography many years ago, she told me something that I've never forgotten. "What happens to you in life, Fred," she counseled, "is not as important as your attitude toward it."

Her words came back to me in the winter of 1996 when I was diagnosed with non-Hodgkin's lymphoma. My first thought upon hearing the doctor's verdict was, *I am going to die—soon.* My chest tightened and my heart raced. My second thought, a calming one, was, *Your life is still in God's hands, the same as it was when He gave you your first breath. Nothing can separate you from His love.*

And it was that faith and positive mindset—along with the prayers of many others—that sustained me through the chemotherapy. As I am writing this, my cancer is in remission, the length or permanence of which I do not know. What I do know is that Mrs. Rice was right about the importance of attitude. There are many things that we cannot control, but with God's help we can control our thoughts, and with Him triumph over anything.

When troubles mount and worries grow large,
Remind me, Lord, of Who's in charge.

—FRED BAUER

4

In him is no darkness at all. —I JOHN 1:5

"Why can't I *be* good?" I asked out loud one morning at breakfast. Sitting across the table from me, my husband David smiled.

"What do you mean, hon?" he asked, half distracted by the paper he was reading.

"Well, I just can't seem to let bad things go," I answered. "Like this new project at church. Nearly everyone is enthusiastic about it, but all I can think about is the one man who can't say anything good about it."

"Don't be so hard on yourself, Pam," David answered. "I'll bet God appreciates the fact that you struggle with your shortcomings."

Later, sitting in my little home office, still fretting about that man at church, I fiddled with a box of paper clips, sharpened some pencils and then rummaged through my desk. Shoved back into the deep recesses of the drawer was a pair of toy eyeglasses, obviously misplaced by Brock or Keri some years before. I pulled the glasses out and before I could even think about it, I put them on.

The effect was dazzling. The glasses had light-refracting lenses that sent splashes of color out from any object I focused my eyes on. My coffee cup became a Fourth-of-July fireworks show, and the clock on the windowsill shimmered like crystal.

Earlier David had suggested that God might see hope in my struggles to become a better person. And if God looks at me in such a positive light, might I not try to do the same? I refocused on the church naysayer, until that moment the bane of my existence. I remembered his kindness when my father died, the way he pitched in to help load a truck with supplies for hurricane victims. I recalled his recent job loss and the financial problems he must be experiencing.

I carefully put my new glasses near the pencil holder on top of my desk. If I really wanted to break the habit of thinking hateful thoughts, those light-refracting lenses could come in mighty handy. From now on, I planned to do my best to look at others through God-glasses.

Father, through Your eyes, the light of goodness always overcomes the dark. —PAM KIDD

5

"Strike the rock, and water will come out of it for the people to drink." —EXODUS 17:6 (NIV)

When I was a little girl, our only source of water was a hand pump outside the back-porch door. So when my father decided to dig a new well and install an electric pump to bring water into our kitchen, it was a very big deal.

I still remember my excitement when the well men arrived with their big drills. Day after day they drilled, pulling up piles of clay-colored dirt. Once or twice the dirt was moist, but my father never hesitated in his directions: "Go deeper." Even when they did hit water, my father wasn't satisfied. "Deeper," was all he said.

Then, one morning they hit rock. And cold, clear water bubbled up from it. Our well was completed. And from that day on, we had the clearest, coldest water I've ever tasted.

I think about that well sometimes when I find myself doing less than my rock-bottom best. I take the back row in aerobics class and cheat on some of the moves. I skim my morning devotions, already thinking about projects at work. I only half-listen when my husband Gary talks about his worries over his dad's failing health.

Go deeper. So I'll lift my legs a little higher in aerobics class. Read my Bible passages out loud. Share the burden of Gary's worries. Because I know that in life, as in well-digging, success comes only when I dedicate myself to the task, settling for nothing less than the best God has for me. Even if that means drilling through layers of laziness or self-centeredness. Even if it means taking the front row in aerobics.

Keep me from shallow living, Lord. Let me drink deeply from Your well of self-discipline. —MARY LOU CARNEY

6

An athlete goes to all this trouble just to win a blue ribbon or a silver cup, but we do it for a heavenly reward that never disappears. —I CORINTHIANS 9:25 (TLB)

Despite a lifelong, total lack of athletic ability (I was chosen last for every single baseball game in grade school and played junior-high basketball only if every other guard fouled out), I *love* watching sports! Football, baseball, basketball, track—I could stay glued to the television for hours watching marvelous athletes kick, hit, shoot and run.

Over the last few years, though, the behavior of many star athletes has stolen some of the pleasure from sports. There are exceptions, of course. Western Kansas's own Steve Tasker of the Buffalo Bills is a devout Christian on and off the football field. But too often, the newsmakers are the baseball player who spits at an umpire, basketball players who can't give an interview without profanity and football "hold-outs" who won't suit up without zillion-dollar contracts.

So, although I watch, I feel a little guilty for supporting professional sports. I had the TV on when Cynthia Cooper led the Houston Comets to the first ever Women's National Basketball Association Championship in 1997. Since Cynthia was also named the Most Valuable Player, I expected the usual "I am great" speech during the postgame show. Instead, Cynthia's first words were a spontaneous and sincere expression of gratitude to God: "Thank You, Jesus! Give God *all* the glory!"

The next time an athlete misbehaves, I'll remember Cynthia. And I'll be cheering—and praying—for her as she uses her talent and her voice for the Lord.

Thank You, Jesus! And thank you, Cynthia, for your example of superb athletic talent and your joyful testimony to our shared faith.
—PENNEY SCHWAB

7

But the fruit of the Spirit is love, joy, peace, patience, kindness, goodness, faithfulness, gentleness, self-control; against such there is no law. —GALATIANS 5:22–23 (RSV)

When I was a child, my sisters and I loved creative art projects, and often we worked with our pencils and scissors late into the evening.

One night our father joined our circle. He wouldn't tell us what he was making, and we were intrigued by the white placards on which he printed words like *love, goodness, patience.* We were as curious as cats over his tiny ball bearings, clipped to strings of fishing line, to say nothing of his dismantled hangers, cut various lengths and straightened with his needle-nose pliers. When he started to assemble things, it was my younger sister Tresa who guessed, "A mobile!"

"Do you know what kind of mobile?" my father asked, sporting a grin uniquely his own while hanging the mobile from our ceiling light.

I suddenly recognized the fruits of the Spirit! God's gifts to us! And each night throughout the year I went to bed watching the words turn in the cold draft and dark shadows of nightfall.

Forty years have gone by, and the old mobile is long lost. But the words still come to mind—particularly when life's colder and darker moments wash over me. When angry, or in trouble and turmoil, sometimes even unkind and spiteful, I need only to hearken back to Dad's mobile to discover anew God's gifts that are mine. And find all over again His love, joy, peace, patience, kindness, goodness, faithfulness, gentleness and self-control.

When I feel out of sorts and destructive, God, please help me to remember Your precious gifts, gifts that transform.

—BRENDA WILBEE

8

Behold, God is my salvation; I will trust, and not be afraid.... —ISAIAH 12:2

I'd walked almost all the way home when with a jolt of panic I realized I'd left my apartment keys in my desk drawer at work. My wife Julee was out of town. *Oh, no....* It was starting to drizzle, and I had no interest in trekking back to my office. Then it occurred to me that my upstairs neighbor Anna kept an extra set of our keys for emergencies. Ricardo, our super, had a master set. And Ari, our next-door neighbor, still had the key we gave him when he watered our plants last time we were on vacation.

Suddenly, it struck me: *An awful lot of people can get into our place.* For instance, our new cleaning woman, Eva, and our previous one, Emily, who brought Eva over from their mutual homeland, Poland, when Emily finally got a job in her original field, biomedical technology. Then there was our dog walker, Sarajane, a veterinary student from England who worked at our vet's office, and her backup, Cara, an aspiring artist. There was Louie, Julee's musician friend, who sometimes stopped in to practice on our piano when no one was around. And Amanda, who occasionally availed herself of our spare bedroom when she was in town from Massachusetts. The more I thought about it, the more names came to mind of people who could let themselves into my home any time they pleased. We'd been utterly profligate in handing out keys.

Was this such a bad thing? I wondered.

Perhaps. But I thought not. Every single person who had a key, I trusted completely. *What a terrible world this would be,* I decided as I walked up my street, *if I couldn't trust people.*

Anna and Ari were out to dinner (they'd left a note asking me to join them), and Ricardo was running an errand. Fortunately, Ricardo's sister Maria, newly arrived from the Dominican Republic, just happened to have let herself into his place with *her* extra set of keys, so when I knocked on the door she was able to show me where her brother kept mine.

Lord, thank You for making people trustworthy, and trusting.

—EDWARD GRINNAN

9

The man who uses well what he is given shall be given more....
—MATTHEW 25:29 (TLB)

During my fifteen years as a radio copywriter, I wrote more than forty thousand radio commercials and learned that it's possible to say a lot in very few words. Sometimes you can get your message across in ten seconds.

Remembering that one day, I decided to try an experiment. My son Andrew had left his room a mess again. Instead of my usual five-minute "messy room" tirade, I delivered my message in ten seconds flat. Andrew got the point. Later that evening, he beamed as I inspected his room. "So, Mom, how do you like my room now?"

I congratulated him, praised him and pointed out how nice it was that he'd finally found an organized home for some of his latest acquisitions. Now Andrew didn't seem to mind my wordiness a bit.

When you're correcting a child, fewer words work best. Less is definitely more. But when it's time for some positive strokes, the more the merrier.

Lord, when I'm upset, help me keep my words brief—and let me save my wordiness for praising. —PATRICIA LORENZ

10 *"Listen to Me, you stubborn-minded...."*

WEDNESDAY

—ISAIAH 46:12 (NAS)

When I'm talking to my two grown daughters on the phone, I often hear them complain to their children, "Don't touch me," or "Quit watching me," or "Stop chewing the phone cord." I remember how much my children resented my phone conversations when they were young.

Once, one of my daughters went to a neighbor's house, picked up the phone and asked the operator to interrupt my conversation with an emergency call. My daughter then got on the line to ask where my orange lipstick was. Another child made a huge poster with red marker that read "Listen to me, Mother!" and held it up high when I'd been talking too long on the phone. My husband could also get bent out of shape by my long phone calls. Suddenly, Jerry needed me to help him find a ten-year-old shirt or the posthole digger. Even our cat would hop up on the kitchen table and glare at me as I talked on the phone.

Then one day, I was attending a women's Bible study on Proverbs 31 taught by a godly older woman. "Try not to talk on the phone when your husband and children need you," she said. "Learn to listen to your family."

That very night, just as the six of us sat down for supper, the phone rang. The twins poured milk on each other, and my husband suddenly needed to know where the Christmas-tree stand was. The critical cat hopped up on the table nonchalantly and began drinking the spilled milk. I decided to try something new. "I'm so sorry," I told the caller, "but I can't talk to you now. May I call you back?"

Order and peace swept through our chaotic kitchen like a gentle spring breeze. "What were you saying, Jeremy?" I asked my son, giving him my full attention.

He sat up very straight, beamed and announced, "I got chosen room monitor at school today!"

Today, Abba, I thank You for always listening to me. Amen.

—MARION BOND WEST

11

THURSDAY

If I speak in the tongues of men and of angels, but have not love, I am only a resounding gong or a clanging cymbal. —I CORINTHIANS 13:1 (NIV)

Some years ago, I developed a large tumor that caused my left eye to bulge and droop. I hid behind a pair of brown eyeglasses that had been molded to fit the contour of the tumor.

I was referred to a surgeon, who glanced at my chart as he dashed through a list of questions. Without ever making eye contact, he proceeded to snap photos of my "problem" as he instructed me to make various facial contortions. He selected a photo, and after circling the area he would be operating on with a red grease pencil, he tacked it onto his bulletin board alongside other photos of patients with facial disfigurements. I was so mortified that I nearly sideswiped another vehicle as I drove home.

While the surgeon had impeccable credentials and spoke in impressive medical jargon, my sagging spirit led me to seek a second opinion. This surgeon, too, needed photographs, but rather than just focusing her camera on my deficiencies, she took the time to make a heart-to-heart connection. "We'll be planning your operation in the days ahead, Roberta," Dr. Foster explained, "and I want to have a picture of you to carry in my pocket. That way, when I think about your surgery, you'll be right here with me."

I learned an unforgettable lesson that afternoon, and I often call it to mind when things get harried: When dealing with people, I can focus on the problem, or I can focus on the person. It seems like a small choice, but it makes all the difference in the world.

Dear Lord, You were the greatest "people person" Who ever walked this earth. Teach me Your loving ways. —ROBERTA MESSNER

12

God is faithful, and he will not let you be tempted beyond your strength, but with the temptation he will also provide the way of escape, that you may be able to endure it. —*I CORINTHIANS 10:13 (RSV)*

Why can't I have a year without problems? I asked myself. *Or at least a month without any hassles.*

Life has not been smooth-going lately, either for me or for my church. In February our pastor was ill for a month and then was transferred in June; our new pastor has a very different style. Our elderly members are experiencing more health problems, and I'm not doing too well with the bookkeeping aspects of being treasurer. At home, with dry rot and termites precipitating an orgy of remodeling, I've lived for months in an upset house, a garden full of timber and a disrupted routine, while trying to cope with work deadlines.

The other day, though, I got an answer to my question from my favorite ring, a solid green opal with lots of fire. As I looked at it, I thought about the fact that I have worn the ring almost every day for twenty years. It's gardened with me, gotten dirty, washed dishes in very hot water, painted rooms—all contrary to conventional opal wisdom.

For a few months some years ago when I decided to wear a different ring, the opal rested in my jewelry box, away from the possibility of damage. Not long after I took it out and resumed wearing it, I was shocked to discover that a great slice had been chipped off one side. I had to have the ring redesigned to cover up the flaw.

What had happened? When I wore the ring every day, though the surface got a bit rough, the constant contact with the oils from my skin gave the opal resilience to stand up to shocks. Without it, the opal dried out.

So that's why You keep the problems coming, Lord, to strengthen my spirit and to keep me turning to You for help. Please continue to give me resilience so that Your light can shine through.
—*MARY RUTH HOWES*

13

Lay not up for yourselves treasures upon earth....

—*MATTHEW 6:19*

Ever wonder what happens to people who have a lot of talent yet never make it to the top? Well, I know one of them.

A few months ago I came across a notice on our library bulletin board. It announced a new Saturday-morning program for children, featuring a storyteller named Eleanor Booth. "I know her!" I said to my friend. "We were in high school together."

Even as a teenager, Eleanor seemed destined for stardom. She loved to act and had the lead in every school play. She was beautiful, too. We all expected to see her name up in lights someday, but she went on to college, got married, had a child, and then I lost track of her. That was a long time ago.

Naturally I was curious, so I went to the first storytelling hour. The room was so crowded that some of the parents and children sat on the floor. When Eleanor was introduced, I saw that she was still lovely—a tall, slim woman who moved like a dancer. And for the next hour she took us all on a journey to a magical world of children, talking trees, singing waterfalls and exciting chases up and down mountains. She acted out every part, lowering her voice to a growl for the villains and chirping birdcalls that sounded like the real thing. She made us see the story and the characters in it, and when she finished we all stood and cheered.

"Thank you," she whispered. Except for being older, she looked exactly the way she did when she used to take a bow after a school play—happy and a bit surprised by all the fuss.

She was surrounded by excited children asking questions, so I waited to say hello. But I could see that Eleanor hadn't missed out on anything by missing the big time. She used her God-given talent to make people happy. And maybe that's why God gives us our talents—not to put our names up in lights, but to bring light into the lives of others.

Thank You for my gifts, Lord, and give me opportunities to share them.

—*PHYLLIS HOBE*

14

He that giveth, let him do it with simplicity....
—ROMANS 12:8

Not long ago someone asked me to name my all-time favorite present. I quickly thought past fishing poles, footballs and even a shiny blue bicycle the year I turned seven.

It was March 14, 1979, and my grandparents had driven over to Nashville from Chattanooga to spend the day with me. I woke up to my grandfather's voice booming, "Good morning, buddy! How'd the birthday boy sleep last night?"

Soon I was downstairs examining the presents that were stacked near the table. I couldn't wait to rip them open and pillage my newly acquired loot! But breakfast came first. We were gathered around the table, and I was busy peeling my hard-boiled egg (Mom had drawn a happy face on the egg and scribbled "Happy Birthday" across its shell) before I noticed that my father was missing.

"Where's Dad?" I asked.

"I guess he's working," Mom answered. "You know how busy he is."

It was true that my father, a minister, worked long hours and was gone a lot. But this wasn't like him, missing a big event like my birthday breakfast. About halfway through the meal, Dad walked in the room. He handed me a white envelope.

I tore it open, noticing that the flap was still wet. Inside was a small booklet about the size of a business card. It contained fifteen pages, all stapled together. He kept the paper he used for his sermons in a drawer where he stashed the packs of chewing gum that he offered to my sister Keri and me when we came into his study to visit. The little booklet had a faint spearmint smell, and its edges were rough and hand-cut.

I read the first page: "Brock's Coupon Book. Happy Birthday! Love, Dad." Inside, the next page read, "Good for one Saturday trip to the fishing pond." The next, "Good for one afterschool backyard football game." Page after page, all of my favorite activities were there.

My favorite present? The simple sensation that I felt on the morning of my seventh birthday: My father loves me!

God, today I thank You for the simplest gifts, the ones that show the hugeness of Your love. —BROCK KIDD

READER'S ROOM

Looking back at March wonders, I see I am aware of God's hand on me each day and night. It is indeed spring in Oklahoma. Tulips, jonquils, pear trees, forsythia all in beautiful bloom, I am aware of His creation and glory. My children celebrated my seventy-second birthday March 8. I noticed each day I had written a praise note. These mementos will be something special to me in the days ahead.

—*JUANITA GILL, SHAWNEE, OK*

---

15 MONDAY

Let us not become weary in doing good, for at the proper time we will reap a harvest if we do not give up.
—GALATIANS 6:9 (NIV)

Almost every morning at 5:55 A.M., I come out of my apartment building and cross the street to the gym, which opens at 6:00. When I began this routine, I noticed that every day a stout, older woman was always standing in just the same place, very straight, on the sidewalk, just to the right of the door. *Perhaps she's waiting for a ride,* I thought. New to Manhattan apartment living, I flashed her a bright smile. No response—in fact, she seemed to direct a scowl in my direction. *I'm not wasting any more smiles on you,* I thought to myself as I hurried on my way. This sour behavior continued for several months. I would come out of the building and glance at the woman. No reaction, and I'd walk briskly by.

Finally, one day, my husband was out of town, so the early dog-walking fell to me. I came out of the building right at 6:00 A.M. Our seventeen-year-old dog tottered stiffly behind me, dragging reluctantly on her leash. The stone-faced woman was in her usual spot. She looked at me in my scruffy sweatpants and the dog with her tangled fur over her now-blind eyes, and she smiled at us. I was astonished, but I managed to recover just enough to smile back. Somehow, the ancient dog and the sleepy walker had connected with that solitary woman in a way that the energetic passerby never had.

These days, I not only smile at my fellow early riser; I've progressed to "Good morning" and receive a greeting in return. Next time I come across a grumpy stranger, I won't give up so quickly.

Let me always reach out to those around me, God. Your time is too precious to waste on imagined slights. —BRIGITTE WEEKS

16 TUESDAY
Therefore I will look unto the Lord.... —MICAH 7:7

I did something today that I dread doing: I went to the doctor for my annual physical. I procrastinate even making the appointment, and when I do, it's mostly out of guilt and fear, because we all know that once we reach a certain age, an annual physical is advised. Making the appointment reminds me that I've reached that certain age.

I woke up today feeling apprehensive. I didn't eat breakfast because of the weigh-in. Instead of taking the elevator, I walked up the three flights of stairs to the office. When it came time to step on the scales, I quickly removed my shoes, watch and earrings, but still I winced at the results, fearing the nurse might demand to see my driver's license, just to see how badly I lied about my weight.

Next came the finger-prick for blood. I watched the nurse take out the pricker, squeeze my finger and pause. In that split second, I anticipated agonizing pain, and sure enough—*ouch!* With a Band-Aid wrapped around my throbbing finger, I was ushered into a little examining room. The nurse told me to remove my clothes and put on this teensy triangular piece of cloth, and then she left me alone. A few minutes later, I sat perched on the edge of the examining table, with nothing to do but think about how much I dreaded the next part of the examination. I leaned back on my elbows, looked up at the ceiling and then laughed out loud. There was a drawing of a silly looking worm, laid out stiff as a board, with a grimace on its face. Underneath was just one word: *Relax.*

The ceiling picture helped me lighten up, but it also made me realize that I needed to change my focus. I'd been looking *down* at everything I dreaded—the scales, the finger-pricking, the teensy triangle of cloth. In the midst of my angst, I'd forgotten to look *up,* which is where I'd find the strength to relax.

Relax. I know the Word comes from You, Father. Thank You.
—CAROL KUYKENDALL

17

Some of the Pharisees in the crowd said to Jesus, "Teacher, rebuke your disciples!" "I tell you," he replied, "if they keep quiet, the stones will cry out."
—LUKE 19:39–40 (NIV)

To most of us in his eighth-grade English class, Mr. Daugherty was the most exciting adult we had ever met. Just out of school himself, Mr. Daugherty seemed hardly older than we were. He was plainly in love with words, with their uncanny power to open the mind and move the emotions. And he had the ability to communicate that love to us. In Mr. Daugherty's class, poems and novels and plays and stories weren't just assignments to be read over grudgingly between games and TV shows; they were invitations to live more fully, magical objects that could reveal intricate patterns of meaning and beauty within the ordinary-seeming events of life.

Most afternoons, after classes were over, some of us would stop by Mr. Daugherty's homeroom for a half-hour's conversation. We'd talk about what we'd been reading, in class or at home, about the news of the day, and about our own struggles with parents and teachers. One day, in one of our after-school discussions, Mr. Daugherty started telling us about the importance of faith to his parents and their attempts to communicate their faith to him. "I don't believe in God anymore," Mr. Daugherty concluded, "but I just can't seem to get that man on the cross out of my mind."

Now, I was thirteen, and I thought I knew it all. And one of the things I knew was that religion was for the weak. But something about Mr. Daugherty's remark worked its way down under the skin of my cynicism. I began to read the Scriptures, seeking to learn more about the Jesus Who so haunted Mr. Daugherty. And when I finally had my own encounter with the Lord, it wasn't the vision of His glory that humbled my pride, but the battered and broken figure of the "man on the cross."

Lord, You brought the gospel to the Irish people through the preaching of St. Patrick; bring all those who have testified to You, however unknowingly, into Your eternal kingdom.
—ANDREW ATTAWAY

18

Will what is molded say to its molder, "Why have you made me thus?" —ROMANS 9:20 (RSV)

While waiting for my son Ross at the library, I picked up a book and started reading about James Naismith. In the 1880s, he spent three years in a seminary but never became a pastor. He earned a medical degree but never practiced. As a teacher at the YMCA Training School in Springfield, Massachusetts, he invented a game he hoped would hold his students' interest during the long winter months in the gym. With a soccer ball and a couple of peach baskets nailed to the balcony above the hardwood floor, Dr. Naismith invented basketball and changed the world of sports.

I'm intrigued by his story for a couple of reasons. One, he didn't become what he set out to be; his life moved in an entirely different direction from what he had planned. I can't help but think of the direction my own life has taken. I'm not starring in a Broadway musical or hosting a morning talk show. Those were dreams for me at one time, as I studied singing, then later began a career in TV news. But God led me in other directions. Some days I wonder what might have been, but I can't say I'm disappointed. God knew marriage and children were in my dreams, too, and those have come true beautifully. Now my stage is the church's fellowship hall, and I host some lively Cub Scout den meetings.

Still, as I'm midway along life's adventure, I'm trying to imagine where God's plan for me is headed. That's where the second and even more intriguing aspect of Dr. Naismith's story comes to mind. When "The Father of Basketball" died in 1939 at age seventy-eight, he had no idea what he had created. The game's phenomenal appeal was still decades away. Like Dr. Naismith, I may never know how what I've done on earth reaches into the future, but God does. On days when I can't see beyond the end of my driveway, I'm comforted by this: God knows well the road I'm on because He set me on it, and He knows where I'm heading because He's leading me there.

God, light my way along Your path so that all I do leads me toward the destination You have in mind. —GINA BRIDGEMAN

19

Are not two sparrows sold for a farthing? and one of them shall not fall on the ground without your Father.

—MATTHEW 10:29

I must confess I'm used to having my husband make all our travel arrangements. That's why, when I recently had to make a trip to Washington, D.C., on my own, I was a little apprehensive.

"Sue, there's nothing to it," Ernie said. "You get on the train at Penn Station and you get out at Union Station." It certainly sounded easy. But still, I wondered if I would end up in Chicago.

Ernie dropped me off at Penn Station, and I hurried into the vast terminal with its crowds of people rushing back and forth. As I waited for my train, I tried to think of soothing passages from the Bible. "His eye is on the sparrow" kept popping into my head. In the midst of so many people, God had an eye on each of us.

When I had calmed myself enough to sit back and look around, I noticed a friend standing in the distance. "What are you doing here?" I asked, running up to him.

"I'm taking the 10:30 train to Baltimore," he replied.

"How amazing. I'm taking the same train to Washington."

"How about a sandwich?" he asked as we sat down together on the train.

I accepted his offer with pleasure. When he left the train at Baltimore, I continued confidently on my way, marveling all the while at God's provision for a lonely traveler.

Lord, thank You for traveling with me, every step of the way.

—SUSAN SCHEFFLEIN

20

Not my will, but thine, be done.　　—LUKE 22:42

"I don't think the Easter lily we bought last year is going to bloom again this Easter," I said to my husband Roy. Easter was two weeks away, and all of our children would be home. I had hoped the lily would flower in time to adorn our fireplace hearth. It was a family tradition to keep last year's Easter lily in hopes that it would blossom once again. This year didn't look very promising.

I was not handling my disappointment very well. It wasn't just the stubborn Easter lily that concerned me. Our oldest daughter Misty was getting married in August to a young man she had only known a short while. Our daughter Kristen had arrived home from college with a drastic new hair color. Our seventeen-year-old son Christopher was far more interested in playing with his rock band than in school. Our youngest son's best friend had moved away, and Kevin didn't seem to be doing anything to make new friends for the summer.

It was two months after Easter before our lily finally blossomed, one flower at a time, until there were four beautiful blooms.

"It's just like our four children, isn't it?" Roy mused, as we admired God's handiwork. "We just need to step back and allow them to develop in their own time, to be whomever God has meant them to be."

My husband was right. Just as my Easter lily had bloomed when it was ready, my children would do the same.

God, give me the patience to do what I can and leave the rest to You. —MELODY BONNETTE

21
Mercy triumphs over judgment! —JAMES 2:13 (NIV)

SUNDAY

My wife Rosie and I were driving to a speaking engagement at a church not far from where Rosie grew up. It was a wonderful opportunity for me; I would be the first African American to speak at this church. The pastor had become my friend, and he wanted the people in his church to learn about our ministry.

As we drove along, Rosie said, "Dolphus, this is the town where I was taken to a doctor for the first time. I was an eleventh-grade student then, and the experience really scared me. I wish you hadn't accepted the invitation to speak here." I was nervous enough about speaking at the church, and Rosie's words made me uneasy.

By the time we got to within a few blocks of the church, Rosie's pulse was racing. "I don't know what good can possibly come out of our being here. I wish we could just turn the car around and go home!"

When we drove up, the pastor and some of the members of the congregation were waiting outside for us. We were warmly greeted, and when it was time for me to speak, I felt an incredible sense of freedom. Afterward, in the fellowship hall, I could feel the love of Christ through the love the people showed us.

As we drove back to Mendenhall, Rosie was thoughtful. "You know," she said, "when we drove into town, all I could think of was my bad experience here. I wasn't willing to live in the present. I wasn't ready for God to do something really new here. But He didn't care if I was ready. He just wanted me to feel His love."

Lord, teach me today to let go of the past and experience Your love.
—DOLPHUS WEARY

22 MONDAY
"The time of the singing of birds has come...."
—SONG OF SOLOMON 2:12 (TLB)

One day, twenty years ago, jostled about by a family of four getting ready for school and work, I felt overwhelmed, trapped by the myriad responsibilities of motherhood. And then, among the sounds of alarm clocks ringing, showers running, children squabbling and dishes clattering, I heard a robin sing. I still remember that melody filtering through the cracks of that hectic spring morning, challenging me to slow down, relax, enjoy life more.

A robin's song spoke of spring rains, clean air and lilac blooms, a brook running meekly within its banks, earthworms surfacing in the garden, fish swimming upstream. It meant water bugs sprinting on the surface of the river and fiddlehead ferns uncurling along the banks. A robin's song meant apple blossoms white and pink as sugared popcorn, and a nest with four blue eggs holding promises of new life.

Today, the house seems almost deathly still, the brooding silence broken only by the monotonous ticking of the clock. I feel lonely, unmotivated, depressed—until a robin's song penetrates the quiet. That cheerful sound means it is time to resume daily walks, take the fishing tackle out of storage, build a trellis, round up the garden tools.

The label on a packet of flower seeds boasts "spring's best promise." How dare they plagiarize a robin's song!

God, thank You for that harbinger of joy that tells my soul "the winter is past, the rain is over and gone."
—ALMA BARKMAN

23 *Your lips have spoken lies....*

—ISAIAH 59:3

I was having trouble with the A-drive of my new laptop and had brought it in for analysis by my computer mentor and friend Sven Jarvis. Sven has spent years struggling with these wonderful-awful machines, and I was sure he could help.

But even Sven was stumped by the problem. Perhaps, he said, the trouble was with the diskette I had been using. Sven took the disk out of my laptop, put it into his own equipment and hit the Enter key. Suddenly, a voice boomed out, filling his entire shop.

You have made a fatal error. Nothing can be done!

Dismayed, I stared at my friend, but he was unconcerned. Then he explained that his computer will talk to you when you do something wrong. "You learn, though, not to panic," Sven said. "The computer gives false messages all the time."

So often, when I blunder, I can hear a voice inside telling me I've made a fatal error and nothing can be done. I can be frightened into immobility unless, like Sven, I know better. My errors are *not* fatal; they are opportunities for Jesus to redeem.

Father, help me to discern voices that are bringing messages that do not come from You.
　　　　　　　　　　　　　　　　　　　—JOHN SHERRILL

24 *He will be the sure foundation for your times, a rich store of salvation and wisdom and knowledge; the fear of the Lord is the key to this treasure.*

—ISAIAH 33:6 (NIV)

When my dad was dying, I wondered how my mom would react after his death. In her eighties, would she choose to move on, or would she be unable to adjust to his loss after more than fifty years of marriage?

The first months were a struggle, but then Mom did something new: She went to a women's retreat at her church. I talked to her after she got back.

"We each had to bring some small item and tell why it symbolized our life at this moment. I took my key chain," she said to me. "I showed them the car keys and said that they symbolized a new independence. I told them how I had to start driving all over again after

Daddy died. He had done all the driving for ten years! I still don't like driving much, but I can get to the store and church by myself at least.

"And I showed them the house key and told them how hard and sad it was to come back to an empty house. I told them that this key also was a bit scary to me since I am probably going to have to sell this house. I wondered what door key will replace it."

Mom made her choice to move on. She sold the house, and within another year became president of the residents' committee at an active retirement complex. In facing reality through the eyes of faith, she had found the keys to surviving her great loss.

Lord, when I face great loss, help me to remember Mom's keys to survival. Help me to grieve, to accept and then to move on.

—ROBERTA ROGERS

25 THURSDAY

Honor all men. Love the brotherhood. Fear God....

—I PETER 2:17

Easter Eve and only a few minutes after we put the children to bed I could hear William coughing in his upper bunk. The night before, he had an upset stomach, and he had slept all day, dragging himself listlessly from bed to sofa and back to bed again. Carol had taken his temperature several times, and by dinner it was back to normal, but there was no telling how he'd feel tomorrow and if he'd be able to go to church with us.

"Kids bounce back fast," I reassured Carol.

"We'd never be able to get a sitter for tomorrow," she said. "It's Easter Sunday."

"If I have to, I could stay home."

"But you need to sing in the choir. I'll stay home."

We were carrying on this way, competing in a husband-and-wife stakes for martyrdom, when I answered the phone. It was a neighbor of ours, a Jewish friend with two young children. Carol and she had been talking earlier about William's bug. "I forgot to tell Carol," Annie now said, "that if you need me, I'd be glad to baby-sit for you tomorrow."

"That's very kind," I replied, wondering how we could accept this offer.

"Look," she went on, "it's your big holiday. I wouldn't want you to miss it."

"Thanks," I said. "We'll call you in the morning."

As it turned out, we didn't need Annie's help that next day, but when the Jewish high holidays came in the autumn I thought of her. She had showed enormous respect for my spiritual needs. At Yom Kippur and Rosh Hashanah, I would have to look for ways to help her or Cliff or Lois or Fred or any of my Jewish neighbors. It's the right thing to do.

Dear Lord, show me how I can serve the spiritual needs of my neighbors and friends. —RICK HAMLIN

26

FRIDAY

"What joys await the sower and the reaper, both together!" —JOHN 4:36 (TLB)

In late March of every year, our small town of Sierra Madre turns purple to celebrate a Wisteria Festival. Tucked into the foothills of Southern California, we boast (according to the *Guinness Book of World Records*) the world's largest blossoming plant: a wisteria vine that drapes over one and a half million lavender blossoms in a fragrant canopy covering nearly an acre of land.

This year I visited the vine. With reverence, I wore purple. During "Wisteria Week" even the local newspaper prints in purple. It is a time of wonder and reflection.

The astonishing fact is that it all began in 1894 when Alice Brugman wanted a fast-growing flowering vine to cover her front porch. She purchased a wisteria seedling in a one-gallon container for seventy-five cents, and diligently planted and nurtured it.

Today the vine is awesome magnificence! The tiny seedling sown more than one hundred years ago now spreads five hundred-foot-long branches that during the growing season, horticulturists figure, shoot out at the rate of about twenty-six inches in forty-eight hours. That one-gallon plant is now a hefty two hundred and fifty-two tons.

Little did Alice know what a joyful legacy we would all reap from her small seedling.

For all those who have sown seeds of beauty in our lives, Lord, thank You. —FAY ANGUS

THROUGH THE VALLEY

27 *Faith is being sure of what we hope for and certain of what we do not see.* —HEBREWS 11:1 (NIV)

When I read the story of Holy Week, I see a cast of characters in various stages of belief or unbelief, who are trying to reconcile Jesus' claims and miracles with the contradictions before their eyes. Finally, in the blackness of Good Friday, it was the scoffers whose reality prevailed. "He saved others, Himself He cannot save." They buried Jesus and, to a large extent, their faith and their hopes with Him.

I wouldn't have doubted, I always said from my armchair, the end of the story in the Bible on my lap. But when my own unfinished story descended into darkness, I found those same Holy Week characters alive inside me, crying out to see God when despair was all that seemed real.

I was sitting in my living room in South Salem, New York. We were in a severe financial crunch and would have to sell our beloved home of eighteen years. And Whitney and I had just placed our daughter in a rehab center for drug and alcohol addiction. Her situation and ours looked hopeless. I sat on the sofa, feet pressing the hardwood floor, begging God to give me faith. A thought pushed up through the depths of me like a sapling through concrete: *Use the faith you have.*

That floored me. *If I have faith, where is it?* I opened my Bible to the passage in Matthew where Jesus talks about the lilies of the field, because it had always comforted me. But that night I saw the lilies not as gleaming white goblets on stems, but as drab bulbs pushed into the earth like dead things—which, of course, is when they begin to live. Therein lies the power and despair of Holy Week: silent and powerless, resting in the earth, holding on to an unseen hope. Living from moment to moment. Because that's where God is.

Lord, thank You for strength in weakness. —SHARI SMYTH

28

Peace I leave with you, my peace I give unto you: not as the world giveth, give I unto you.... —JOHN 14:27

The rumor rose with the sun and the surging crowd. It fanned across the rocky slopes where the pilgrims camped. It burned through the tiny villages. It roared into Jerusalem. King David's heir was on His way to free them from the Romans. From crushing taxes. From grinding poverty. Hearts and feet set out to make Him king, snapping palms and ripping cloaks in a frenzy of hope. The crowd crowned Him, throwing everything but themselves in His way. But His heartbroken, unkingly cry on the brow of the Mount of Olives fell on ears that couldn't hear. "If today you had known the things that make for peace," He said. His tears were lost in the donkey's neck.

Our gentle gray barn nestles into a dome of blue sky. I stand on the deck, as I've done most mornings for the past eighteen years, snatching some quiet with God. Lately, I've been clinging stubbornly to a hope that is slowly dying. "This house—these four acres of paradise house. I can never sell it," I whisper. "I've found too much happiness and peace in this spot to leave it behind."

Yet, what if Jesus were to come down my street, past the pristine fields and pond? What if He were to stop by the stone wall, look through the lilac bushes at me, His eyes holding eternity, and beckon me on and away? I close my eyes against it. The swimming darkness forms a picture: a spread of land, a house to which I've glued myself and which—dare I say it—I almost worship.

"Real paradise is within you," I hear Him whisper.

Here on the deck, the sheen of dew on the railing and grass, I open my fists and let go to the Prince of Peace.

Lord, thank You for loving me enough to bring down my idols.
—SHARI SMYTH

29

Jesus said...."She has done a beautiful thing to me." —MARK 14:6 (RSV)

The woman slipped through the crowded room and knelt, waist-length hair cascading over the floor. Breaking the seal on a costly jar of perfume, she poured it over her Lord. The practical people in the crowd breathed its fragrance with a collective gasp. "Why this waste?" But Jesus held up her gift.

Hair, beard and clothes dripping, He promised its aroma would last to the end of time, spreading to the edges of the world on the message of the Gospel.

Its fragrance reaches me on a stormy morning as I drag about, readying the house for prospective buyers. Added to the weight I'm carrying is an agitated phone call from my daughter. She isn't doing well in rehab. "Mom, I'm scared, and I hurt really bad," she said, her voice small and deflated. "I want to come home."

I take a deep breath and say the hardest thing in the world: "You can't."

I ask the therapist, "Is she going to make it?"

"At this point, it's up to her," she tells me honestly.

The storm darkens. A gust of wind sends sheets of rain shivering down the window of the breakfast room. Dragging my mop across the floor, I look out to see the tall trees that shade and shield the pasture. Their branches wave back and forth, calling me to join them in praising God. My hands start to go up. The practical in me gasps. *Silly. Waste of time.*

But like the long-ago woman whose love would not be confined by such boundaries, I persevere. Hands in the air, I sway with the trees in a symphony of praise to God. Time stops. The plodding heaviness, the fear, is being pulled out through my outstretched fingertips. Back at work, joy is my strength.

Lord, help me to remember that the shortest route to Your presence is worship. —SHARI SMYTH

30

For where your treasure is, there will your heart be also.
—MATTHEW 6:21

A poor widow stood in line at the temple treasury. She watched the wealthy carelessly drop bags of shekels into the chest. It was her turn. Plink, plink. Two small coins left her palm, disappearing into the vault. She scurried off, having given the last of her money to God. Jesus stepped forward. Crooking a finger at His wowed-by-the-rich disciples, He told them that the widow had given more than all the others because she had given everything she had.

Somehow, I hear awe in His voice.

One self-pitying Sunday, the tithe envelope grudgingly parts from my palm. I've fallen into a slough over a stack of medical bills that have eaten much of the profit from the sale of our house. And there are still more bills. My peripheral vision goes hunting and finds what it seeks: others who have it better. *Life—God—isn't fair.* Here on this hard church pew, my mind goes back and forth from God to those others, from the move we're making to the bills still left to pay to the tithe we can't afford.

We stand and sing "Praise God from Whom All Blessings Flow." The overflowing offering plates are left at the altar. The minister stands and reads his text: Mark 12:41–44. The poor widow. His eyes roam the well-fed, well-dressed congregation. Including me. I duck my head in shame and hide.

But the widow's example reaches me. It pulls me up with a yearning to be like her. She who'd have starved rather than withhold from God points to our Lord: He Who left the splendor of heaven so that I could one day live there; He Who became poor so that I might be rich; He Who endured the crown of thorns so that I might be crowned with glory. From me He asks so little, and values it so much.

Lord, help me to offer back to You what You have given me.

—SHARI SMYTH

31
"I am among you as one who serves." —LUKE 22:27 (RSV)

It was a borrowed upstairs room in Jerusalem. A simple room with rough planking bathed in lantern light, and a dinner table set for thirteen friends. Jesus, His death imminent, broke the bread with callused carpenter's hands. "This is my body," He said to numb silence. From a clay pitcher He poured wine and held it to the light. "This is my blood." Then He took a basin of water and stooped to lift the foot of a disciple.

Bread. Wine. Water to wash feet. Things as ordinary as the disciples themselves turned holy.

Her name is Kathleen, and she lives on Bittersweet Lane in Wilton, Connecticut. Many times I'd driven that road, with its name that twines opposites, to Kathleen's house. This would be my last visit before our move to Tennessee.

I parked my car in her circular drive and rushed from the cold to the warmth of Kathleen's kitchen. I washed my hands at her sink, then moved to the antique table under the ticking clock. She served me coffee and her unbeatable sugar cookies. I dunked one, thick and sweet, in the steaming brew. We ate and talked in a pool of sunlight.

"You know what I dread most about moving?" I said to this woman who's had more than her share of sadness.

"What?" she asked, setting down her mug.

"Walking out of my house and closing the door for the last time."

"It's time to give you your going-away present then," she said, and I knew even before she reached into her apron pocket what it would be.

A feather. This time a brown one. Fingering its airy softness, I remembered the first time she'd given me one. "Feathers remind me that in order to fly, the spirit must remain light," she'd said. "So I've learned to lay my burdens on God."

The afternoon receded, dragging the light with it. Time to go. As I pulled on my coat, I hugged Kathleen and thanked her. "For what?" she asked.

For cookies. Coffee. Conversation. For friendship and feathers to warm my journey south. Ordinary things turned holy because they were given with love.

Lord, tune my ears, sharpen my eyes to hear and see You in the most ordinary disguise.　　　　　　　　—SHARI SMYTH

MY FAITH JOURNEY

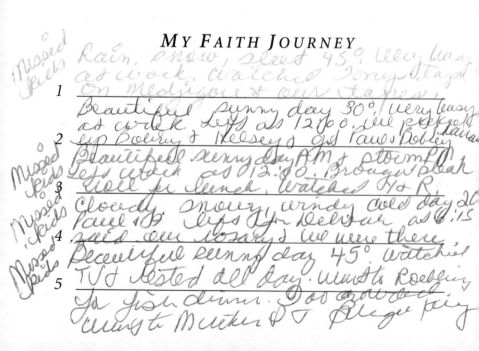

Rainy day 45°. I made scrambled eggs
for breakfast.

MARCH 1999 Paul & I took
Woody to Chesterfield for rabies shot.

6 Butch stopped by. Bob. Went to 5:00 Mass.

Missed Kids

Beautiful sunny frigid day 0° with
wind chill. Paul & I went to Shop Rite
7 & IGA & got papers. I made clam pie.

Missed Kids

Beautiful sunny cold day 35°. Very
busy as work. Working 2 hrs O.T.
8 Paul made stuffed cabbage.

Missed Kids

Beautiful cloudy day 35°.
Very busy as work. I talked to
9 Bobby & Kelsey on the phone.

Missed Kids

Cloudy day 40°. Very busy as work.
Worked 2 hrs O.T. Dr. K. office
10 called Paul & said ok to buy drugs.

Missed Kids

Beautiful sunny day 30°. Very busy
as work. Paul called Deborah & the
11 said to see Dr. K not Lederman.

Missed Kids

Cloudy snow flurry day 30°. Cleaned
out desk as work. Had clam
12 pie for supper. Called Shirley H.B.

Missed Kids

Beautiful sunny day 45°. Paul & I went
to Kohls & Mall for vitamins. Phone cease
13 for Bobby birthday present.

Missed Kids

Northeast snow storm. Paul & I
went to IGA & wawa as 7:00.
14 Relaxed all day. Turkey dinner

Missed Kids

Cloudy dreary day. 4 inches snow.
Roads clear. Parking lots snow
15 Clear. Made bacon Dr. K. did I call

Missed Kids

Beautiful sunny day 50°. Very
busy as work 2 hr O.T. Came
16 home & went to dump w/ Paul.

Missed Kids

Beautiful sunny day 38°. Very busy
as work. Worked 2 hrs O.T.
17 To Pats party. Watched soaps.

Missed Kids

Beautiful sunny day 90°. very busy
as work. Came home & wrote out
18 bills & we took them to P.O. Called
Chantell. Grandparents day tomorrow
Paul washed bed things & made meal.
He's such a sweetheart

Beautiful sunny day 50°. Took VAC day. Paul + ___ ___ to school w/ Bailey + Kelsey for grandparents Day. ___ to Medford for license

19 + called Dr. K. Kids spend night

Beautiful sunny day 52°. Kelsey + I moved daffodils from old house washed bed clothes. Kids spend night

20

Cloudy rainy day 40°. I went to A.P. + ___ + got papers. Made ham + pork roast. Aunt + Kelsey competition

21

Missed kids

Rain A.M. Then P.M. 45° day busy at work. Worked 4 hrs. ___ took Joyce home.

22

Beautiful sunny day 50°. Very busy at work. Worked 4 hrs O.T.

23 Chantel + kids were here.

Missed kids

Cloudy dreary rainy day 45° very busy at work. Left at 1:30 + Paul

24 went to see Dr. K. at 3:00.

Missed kids

Beautiful sunny day 50°. very busy at work. Called Dr. Buccino +

25 Dr. K. Watched soaps. Called Butch

Beautiful sunny day 45° very busy at work. Baileys first birthday.

26 Fish fry in Allentown.

Missed kids

Beautiful sunny day. Paul + I went to old house for daffodils + tulips + hyacinths + ___. Church at 5:00.

27

Missed Kelsey

Rainy damp day 40°. Paul + I went for papers. Called

28 Chantel + Butch. Oyster dinner New Egypt

Beautiful sunny day 60°. very busy at work. I have a ___. Met Paul at Mall w/ Chantel + kids

29

Missed kids

Beautiful sunny day 60°. Stayed home from work. Stayed in bed

30 most of day. Butch stopped by

Missed kids

Beautiful sunny day 70°. Paul went to Bruces. Blood clot in

31 leg. I went to Dr. K. asthmatic bronchitis - ate went to ShopRite. Came home ate + went to bed. Called Pat.

April

He restores my soul....
—PSALM 23:3 (RSV)

S	M	T	W	T	F	S
				1	2	3
4	5	6	7	8	9	10
11	12	13	14	15	16	17
18	19	20	21	22	23	24
25	26	27	28	29	30	

1

A broken and contrite heart, O God, you will not despise.
—PSALM 51:17 (NIV)

Whether reclining at supper, or as Mark has it, sauntering Jerusalem's dark, narrow streets toward Gethsemane, Peter at some point bragged to all around him that he'd die with Jesus. Gently Jesus warned him: "Before the cock crows you will deny me thrice." "Never," Peter shouted. Turning away from the truth reflected in Jesus' eyes, Peter swaggered into the night to become the coward he so despised.

A sliver of dawn finds Peter, a scared shadow, by the fire in the courtyard. The rooster stretches awake and crows. Peter, busy saving his neck, misses it. Never mind, Peter. You get a second chance. Shrill and sure it comes again. The shadow crumples.

Across the crowded courtyard, Jesus, His face tender, searches out Peter—coward, denier, liar. Whatever names the weeping Peter now begins to call himself, Jesus has given him another—Peter, the rock. The rock he can now become because he's faced his darkness.

Such a yawningly familiar tale...yet it slept in me, the less-than-perfect mother whose faults had contributed to her daughter's addiction. My own childhood, so broken and wanting, had caught up with me through my sweet daughter. Things I passed on to her because I couldn't or wouldn't face them earlier. Together, in family counseling, we will.

For generations my family has struggled to keep the lid on depression. I learned to keep the secret, to pretend that everything was fine so I wouldn't have to face my own depression. By the time I sought help, I'd taught my daughter to deal with life as I had.

I ask her forgiveness. It's an emotional moment. She has already faced her darkness; I, mine. Turning in faith, we will grow, pushing up through the dirt. I see a stirring of spiritual life in her. She wants to get well. She knows only God can heal her.

Lord, give me the humility to weep for my sins like Peter, then accept Your forgiveness.
—SHARI SMYTH

2

Surely he has borne our griefs and carried our sorrows....
—ISAIAH 53:4 (RSV)

What a difference a week makes. As I drag myself toward the Cross, I feel a sudden, cold draft from hell. It's the loneliness. Jesus, barely recognizable, has been abandoned—even, at the last, by His Father. So I, too, turn from the horror and find myself face to face with an old widow, puffy red eyes and ashen face distorted in grief. Oh, Mary, thank you for sticking it out, not just as His mother, but as an example of faith to all grieving mothers down the years.

I curled in a red vinyl hospital chair, blue-jeaned knees against my chest, watching my daughter under the bedcovers. She was sleeping with tubes in her arms, dark hair spilling over the pillow, so thin she hardly seemed to be there.

"She's lucky she's alive and there's no damage to her major organs," the doctor had told me earlier. After three months of struggling with sobriety, she'd binged on drugs and alcohol. Whitney and I had rushed her to the hospital. Now he was at work. I was alone with memories only a mother knows. Carrying her. Birthing her. Nursing her late at night when the house was quiet and I'd given her to God. Watching her grow into a child with bobbing curls. Tending her dolls and later her pony with a simple faith that God would take care of all.

The covers stirred. I knelt by her bedside and watched her awaken, enormous dark eyes searching for, then finding me. "I'm sorry, Mom," she said, shame filling her face. Never had I felt so helpless, wanting to take her shame, her sickness upon me.

I can't bear it, I cried inwardly.

From across the centuries I felt the touch of another mother, reminding me that she'd watched as her Son bore the shame and sin of the world. I felt her whisper, *You can bear it because He bore it for you.*

I hugged my daughter, feeling the awesome strength of love. Bigger than any addiction, deeper than any shame.

My daughter hugged me back. Tubes and all.

Thank You, Lord, for a love that will not let me go. —SHARI SMYTH

3

"My prayer is not that you take them out of the world but that you protect them from the evil one."

—JOHN 17:15 (NIV)

Jesus tried to prepare His disciples for the longest Saturday of their lives. He told them He'd be gone. He told them they'd be grieving, while the world rejoiced. "But your grief will turn to joy," He'd promised. Over and over, like a good teacher, He'd told them these things in different ways. In Gethsemane,

He'd urged them to pray "that you fall not into temptation." But exhausted and sorrowful, they couldn't. So Jesus prayed for them. And all during that long Saturday when they huddled behind locked doors, weak, scattered and unbelieving, they were held in the grip of Jesus' prayer.

It was December. Moving day was weeks away. I was living with boxes, in a twilight zone of not here, not there. I was numb, hurtling toward the unknown. What was out there for Whitney and me, for my daughter in rehab? Waiting in the dark.

On one sleet-ridden day, I sat in a pool of lamplight on the dusty floor of our attic, sifting through memories of our four children, now grown and scattered. In addition to our daughter in rehab, there was a daughter in Oregon, a daughter in Hawaii and a son in Maine. "Don't worry, Mom. We'll come visit," they promised. Among their treasures I found a few old Sunday school pages, Bible scenes with childish crayon scribbles that rendered them priceless.

I traced a yearning finger over an orange Jesus motioning a purple Zacchaeus from a sycamore tree. A red Jesus, arms and lap full of multicolored children; His timber-brown hair brushing little, uplifted faces; His eyes, even through the crayon, shining with love. Then I catch my breath. A praying Jesus, scribbled in black, kneeling at a rock, crayoned dots of red for the blood He sweated. Nearby are the sorrow-laden, sleeping disciples, ghostly white, with no color. I feel myself one of them—blank and unable to pray. Yet I am held in the grip of Jesus' prayer, of His praying for me still. I am protected.

Lord, help me to pray always. But when I can't, cover me with Your prayer. —SHARI SMYTH

4

EASTER SUNDAY

"Your grief will turn to joy." —JOHN 16:20 (NIV)

Perhaps she was going mad again. Mary Magdalene, who'd once been healed of seven demons, stood alone in the garden, trying to make sense of it all. With her own eyes, she'd seen Him buried, the stone sealed shut. Now she crossed the wet earth and bent to the gaping mouth of the tomb. She was weeping uncontrollably, seeming not to see the dazzling light of the two angels sitting inside. "They've taken away my Lord, and I don't know where they've put Him," she said between her sobs.

From behind her, a footfall. She whirled around, blinded by her tears. Must be the gardener, *she thought. "Sir, if you have carried Him away, tell me where you have put Him," she begged. Instead, He spoke her name. "Mary."*

A river of joy rushed through her. "Rabboni!" she cried in recognition. He Who'd once called her from madness now called her into ultimate reality: the glory of the risen Christ.

Our new church in our new state was dressed in lilies, arrayed in the glory of Solomon. Pastor Kidd, in his white stole, announced, "The Lord is risen!"

"Please give me faith," I'd begged on that night in South Salem, New York. And God had said, *Use the faith you have.*

Impossible, I'd thought. But here I was.

We moved to Tennessee in winter, chased by spring, a spring I viewed from the porch of our new cedar house, perfect for rockers. Our finances have turned around. Best of all, my daughter has graduated from rehab. She's working and saving money to go to school to become a therapist. As I sit here next to Whitney on this Easter, I think of her visit a few weeks back. We were approaching the church door a few minutes late and heard the strains of "Amazing Grace." Face radiant, she grabbed my arm. "Mom, that's my favorite song because of what I was and what I am now." We both cried.

Resurrection life is planted deep in our souls. The same power that raised Jesus from the dead pushes us up to new life. But first, we must die in whatever dirt we find ourselves in, and reach out and wait for God.

Living Lord, thank You for the gift of Your risen life.

—*SHARI SMYTH*

LESSONS IN LISTENING

5

HEARING MYSELF
Happy is the man who listens to me, watching daily at my gates....　　—*PROVERBS 8:34 (RSV)*

When I first began seeking guidance, I'd ask God only about "big" things—a move, a job change, buying a home. I've learned over the years, though, that He wants me to ask regularly, daily, to make discerning His will a habit.

The reason, I think, is that it takes practice to distinguish God's voice from my own notions. The makers of voice-recognition security systems tell us that each of us has a "voice print" as individual as a fingerprint. By pausing to pray over everyday choices I'm learning to recognize my voice print. Plans that begin *I-can-easily* probably aren't from God! I-can-easily take on this extra project...go there and get back in time...do this job all by myself—till I end up rushed and anxious.

One hectic day recently, a friend telephoned to ask me to pray for her son, hospitalized with AIDS. We'd prayed many times during his long illness, and I only half-listened as she described the latest crisis. Behind on a deadline as usual, I held the phone between cheek and shoulder and kept working at my desk as she talked. Doubtless I murmured words of concern. But I did not say the God-given thing, the thing He might have given me to say, had I had time to hear.

My friend's son died that night. And I, who might have helped her prepare, had been busy.

God's voice never tells me *you-can-easily*, never asks me to crowd many things into the day. His voice tells me, *Set priorities. Ask for help. Say no.* My day, when I let Him guide me, has room for obedience...has time for the phone call that wasn't part of my plans, but of His.

Teach me to know my own voice, Father, so that I can listen better for Yours.   —ELIZABETH SHERRILL

EDITOR'S NOTE: Where has God been leading you this year? Take a few minutes to look over your monthly "My Faith Journey," and let us know some of the ways you've learned to listen for His guidance and direction. Send your letter to *Daily Guideposts* Reader's Room, Guideposts Books, 16 E. 34th St., New York, NY 10016. We'll share some of your letters in *Daily Guideposts, 2001.*

6

For, lo, the winter is past, the rain is over and gone.
—SONG OF SOLOMON 2:11

T. S. Eliot may have had his reasons for thinking April was the cruelest month, but I always associate it with one glorious occurrence—Opening Day, when major league baseball gets its long, lumbering season under way, a season that will reach from the spring buds to the greening of summer grass through the kaleidoscopic fall. Baseball is one of life's great constants.

Baseball seems to follow me. I watched the historically dramatic game five of the 1975 World Series crowded around a fuzzy TV set in a tiny fishing village in Ecuador. I remember my mom sending me the Detroit sports pages when I went east to school so I could keep up with my beloved Tigers. I remember being an impoverished freelance writer in New York, making my way up to Yankee Stadium in the Bronx, too broke to buy an Opening Day ticket but still wanting to eat a hot dog and watch the fans stream into the famed ballpark on a windy April afternoon.

My most vivid memory, though, is of one soft summer evening when I was a college student working as a deckhand on one of the big boats that haul iron ore across the Great Lakes. My ship, the *Roache,* was drifting down the Detroit River headed for Lake Erie from Lake Superior. Sitting on a hatch cover, I felt a restless yearning as the Motor City skyline swept past. I'd been on the boat for most of the summer, and I missed home. I missed the Tigers.

Tiger Stadium stood not far from the river. The lights were on. The evening was perfectly still and the *Roache*'s captain had cut the engines back because of the swift current. All at once I heard the stadium crowd roar, though it sounded more like a sigh at that distance, and a speck of white, like a tiny moon, arced above the rim of the stadium, through the wash of lights and high into the dusk, hanging suspended for an instant in the sapphire sky before falling back to earth, a routine fly ball. For that instant I felt a part of the crowd instead of alone on the deck of a freighter bound for Cleveland, and it felt good.

Every April on Opening Day I remember that ball looping into a soft summer sky. God gives us many challenges in life, and sees us through many winters. But He also gives us baseball.

Thank You, Father, for the promise of spring. —EDWARD GRINNAN

7

"I will give you the treasures of darkness, riches stored in secret places...." —ISAIAH 45:3 (NIV)

A blizzard scooped up snow from the Ukrainian steppes and hurled it against the small windowpanes of my childhood home. But inside our small kitchen, my mother had prepared a happy Easter surprise. An awestruck six-year-old, I gazed at the red, blue, green and yellow Easter eggs nestled among a forest of rye shoots, five inches high, growing in a rusty old dishpan.

Not until I was an adult did I grasp the significance of my mother's creativity. During the early 1940s, I was too young to be worried by the privations that World War II had brought into our lives. Food was scarce. Carefully Mother rationed potatoes, beets and flour. Fuel was almost gone. The dried cow dung and cornstalks carefully gathered in fall were almost used up. Such luxuries as egg coloring could not be found. Mother had used boiled onion skins for yellow, cooked moss for green, a bleeding piece of red fabric for red and a few drops of ink for dark blue. Despite our hardships, she had created a joyous Easter celebration for us children.

Two years later, my mother and we four children fled from our home in eastern Europe. We survived the war and eventually immigrated to Canada. In time, life became easier; we no longer had to worry about food and fuel and egg coloring.

But the joy of that Easter celebration in war-torn Ukraine has remained with me through the decades. At times, the chaos of my own life threatens to overwhelm me, and it's hard to see how I'm going to keep going. Then I remember Mother and the maxim she lived by: In a world of chaos, find a corner where you still have control and fill it with beauty—then share it with others.

Lord Jesus, help me find the treasure of joy You've scattered throughout this day. —HELEN GRACE LESCHEID

8 THURSDAY

Let all the earth keep silence before him.
—HABAKKUK 2:20

It was toward evening when we spotted him, inching his way across a busy riverside highway. The huge snapping turtle must have been sixteen to eighteen inches in diameter. My wife Shirley was driving, and she was the one who reported the lumbering creature in the opposite lane.

"Quick, turn around and go back before someone hits it!" I instructed. At the next turnoff, Shirley wheeled the car around and we headed back. "A turtle that big could be twenty-five or thirty years old," I ventured. When we came upon it from the other direction, it was near the center of the road. Miraculously, it was still whole.

"Turn on your hazard lights and stop. I'll try to get it out of danger," I said, jumping from the car. When I reached the turtle, I tried to turn it in the direction from which it had come, but the menacing snap of its big mouth at my moccasined foot let me know we had different goals.

By now traffic was building behind our car and Shirley called for me to hurry. Again I nudged it with my foot and again it snapped, adding a mad hiss just in case I didn't get the message. That's when I reached down and grabbed it by its tail. Though it tried to resist with its clawed feet and struggled to bite me, I was at the right end. In a matter of seconds, I had dragged it to the shoulder. "Go back to the river," I scolded.

Back in the car, Shirley laughed at my rescue effort. "It didn't want to cooperate, did it?"

"No, I couldn't make it understand what was best for it."

"Just like God trying to get through to us sometimes," she mused.

"That's a pretty big sermon from a snapping turtle," I joked. But, unlike many sermons, I still remember it.

> *Train me, Lord, to be quiet and still,*
> *Listening each day to know Your will.*

—*FRED BAUER*

9

"Whose confidence is fragile, And whose trust a spider's web." —*JOB 8:14 (NAS)*

As I planted the garden, the weather was unseasonably cold, the soil lumpy. And, oh, my aching back! Gardening under such conditions was not just a workout for my muscles; sowing tiny seeds in the hardened ground was a real test of faith.

But as I worked, I noticed the hollyhock plants leafing out along the foundation on the east side of our bungalow. Last year, a summer storm had bent one of the hollyhocks almost double. I expected the plant to die, but within a very few days the crippled stem was mysteriously standing upright again. The strong multiple strands of a spider's web had drawn the broken hollyhock back up into position and anchored it to the foundation of the house. With its injured stalk supported by this silken splint, the hollyhock soon recovered, its pink blossoms eventually inching up its entire length.

The memory of that spider's web supporting a tall hollyhock reminded me that even fragile faith can be effective. I resumed my planting. *This garden shows very little promise now, Lord, but these are mountain-moving mustard seeds of faith I'm sowing here.*

Lord, I believe, but help my unbelief.   —ALMA BARKMAN

Long before the movie Titanic, *Van Varner loved the great ships. Last year he had the opportunity to sail on two of the classic old liners. Whenever you see this little ship in the months ahead, you'll be able to sail along with Van as he learns life-lessons on God's great oceans.*   —THE EDITORS

10

The sea is his, and he made it....   —PSALM 95:5

 I might just as well admit it: I'm a ship freak. Passenger ships, mainly. I belong to a number of societies that discuss everything from the appointments of the latest cruise vessels to what it was like to be in steerage in 1910 to who has the best collection of Cunard passenger lists. There are special events, like the day we traipsed about New York looking at objects saved from *Normandie* before she burned and capsized. That meant everything from an apartment on 90th Street filled with fantastic memorabilia to the huge bronze doors that were once the gates to the smoking room and are now the main entrance to Our Lady of Lebanon Maronite Catholic Church in Brooklyn.

I also like to be a passenger, and I have sailed since the days of transatlantic crossings when your friends could come aboard to see you off in style. Waving good-bye was sad, because you were leaving pals as you ventured into the unknown. It didn't matter that there wasn't much chance of its really being the unknown; you felt it.

I have been adapting slowly to cruise ships now, though I still hold on to every vestige of the ships that were. This year I've concentrated on the queen, SS *Rotterdam* (you won't find the *S* for steam on many ships; diesel it is now). I took her twice, once for the last leg of her world cruise and once on her final Holland-America voyage.

I guess that you can't be a ship freak without delving into the past, and I never have been to a compulsory boat drill when, tying on the life preserver, I haven't thought of *Titanic*, of *Andrea Doria*. It makes you wonder about feeling the unknown, about the greatness of the oceans and the smallness of yourself. But for all the vastness out here, God is near.

You, God, are never nearer than when I am at sea. Is that the reason I'm a ship freak? —VAN VARNER

11

SUNDAY

For whom the Lord loveth he chasteneth....

—HEBREWS 12:6

When my twin sons were youngsters, there seemed to be no way to get them to be genuinely sorry when they misbehaved. Restrictions, threats, spankings, even crying myself seemed to have no effect. So I asked God to show me a better way to discipline them.

One day after they'd fought over a tube of toothpaste (there was blood), I began to practice what I thought God was showing me. "Jon and Jeremy," I said, "sit down and put into writing exactly what happened. Then you can get up." After prolonged wailing and shouts of "You're not being fair!" they bent over their papers and began to write quietly. Over the next few months they wrote about being sorry for making fun of someone, why it was wrong to steal a friend's apple, why shoving other children was inappropriate.

One Sunday when they were about ten, Jon threw small wads of paper during church. I assigned him an essay on any Scripture he chose. After procrastinating as long as he could and breaking several pencil points, he lowered his head and began to write in his careless scrawl:

Jesus said whom shall ever believe in me shall not perish but have everlasting life. John 3:16. Jesus died on a Cross for our sins so we would not have to go to hell. They put Him on a Cross and put spikes through His hands and feet.

And He died for three days, then He arose from the grave! Right now Jesus is preparing a place for us in heaven. Jesus is sitting on the right hand of God. If you don't know Jesus, I will tell you how to get saved. All you have to do is ask Him into your heart and if you really mean it He will come in....

When he finally handed me his essay, he was blinking hard to prevent the tears from spilling from his eyes. He had earned his first A-plus for an essay, and my newfound, deep respect. And the next Sunday, he paid a lot better attention in church.

Father, I long to learn and practice more of Your ways.
—MARION BOND WEST

12 MONDAY
Thou hast enlarged me when I was in distress....
—PSALM 4:1

Getting the first olive out of the bottle makes the others come more easily, and solving one problem, I discovered, can lead to the solution of others.

My wife Sharon was figuring our income taxes. It was a three-day ordeal, made worse because she was overworked at her school job. At last she was done, and her mood was giddy. "Let me go over these figures with you," she sang, spreading the papers out on the desk. A piece of paper fluttered to the floor.

"What's this?" she wondered, reaching for it. She stared at it, then her face paled. "Oh, no! Another W2! I missed a W2, and all these figures are wrong! I'll have to start all over again!"

For several minutes she retraced her steps, then the tears began to flow. Since she seldom ever cries, I knew she was totally discouraged.

"Let's go for a drive," I suggested. After thirty-four years of marriage, I know it takes time to settle down this redhead.

For an hour we cruised slowly through the countryside. Sharon opened up about other things that were wrong in her life: relationships; school problems; even things from twenty years ago that had never been resolved. It was a healthy purge of festering emotions, and it brought several issues into focus. Sharing with her made me feel closer and gave me ideas how I could be a better husband. On the way home, her mind shifted to solutions. "Next year I'll put those W2s in a special place, and tomorrow I'm going to call the principal and get some things ironed out."

What started out as a disaster became a springboard for change, and I plan to look for such opportunities the next time I "hit the wall."

God, when my situation seems like the last straw, make it a first step.
—DANIEL SCHANTZ

13 *A time to be born, and a time to die....*

TUESDAY

—*ECCLESIASTES 3:2*

"Hi, Mom. I just thought I'd let you know that Cheryl's in labor." My son Paul sounded quite nonchalant on the phone, but after all, this would be their seventh child. I arrived at the hospital only five minutes after little Haley Sierra was born, and was greeted by my beaming firstborn son, who was now anything but nonchalant. "Just look at her, Mom—isn't she the most beautiful baby you ever saw? Perfect in every way!" She was. She really was. But, of course, I've felt that way about each one. The excitement and sense of wonder at the birth of a baby never diminishes. What a miracle a new life is!

In the twenty years I've been writing for *Daily Guideposts*, I've shared the stories of the births of my eight grandchildren, each time finding some special meaning I thought you might apply to your own life. Every birth has had its own uniqueness. Yet a mysterious thread has been weaving in and out among the members of our extended family, a thread I've not told about before. It's this. It often happens that soon after the death of an elder family member, a new baby arrives. Grandmother Morgan died just before Karen was born; John was born shortly after my father died; Joshua, our first grandchild, arrived a few days after the death of my husband's father; Saralisa was born shortly after her paternal grandmother died; and little Haley's maternal grandfather died only a few days before she was born.

So what do I make of this? I don't think it's cause and effect (though at the time my father died, while I was pregnant with John, a friend consoled me by saying, "Your dad is with God, picking out just the right little angel to send into your family."). For me, the message has always been: *Every ending is also a beginning.* Whenever I find myself grieving a loss—a friend moving away, a cherished possession stolen, a death in the family—I see the faces of all those beautiful babies, and I give thanks for new beginnings, yet unseen, that are just a life-breath away.

Thank You, Great Creator of all life. Thank You for the continual promise of new beginnings. —*MARILYN MORGAN HELLEBERG*

14

WEDNESDAY

If ye abide in me, and my words abide in you, ye shall ask what ye will, and it shall be done unto you. —JOHN 15:7

My subject for the talk was prayer. A hundred and fifty women were seated in an unfamiliar church waiting for me to give them whatever spiritual wisdom I might have gleaned. I had only ten minutes on the program, and I was completely preoccupied with thinking about how my usual forty-five-minute speech could be condensed to fit. Should I talk about the Psalms? Should I mention praying the hymns as I sing them? Would I describe my father's rambling dinner-table graces?

I put my hand in my coat pocket to pull out my note cards. Not there. I plunged my hands in my trouser pockets. Nothing. I fumbled through the bag next to me. Nothing there either. Maybe I'd left them in the car. There was no time to check now; I was being introduced. I had to go on.

Bounding up to the lectern, I began, speaking a mile a minute off the top of my head. And then suddenly I drew a blank. I couldn't think of what to say. My mind was empty. I had no idea what should come next. I looked out at my listeners, who looked back at me, and then I looked down, hoping the floor would give me some answers. Finally, I said the only words that came to me: "Let us pray." For a moment the room was deadly silent. "Amen," I said at last. A little calmer, I resumed my speech.

"You were wonderful!" said one woman afterward, shaking my hand. "And so clever, too. What a powerful demonstration of prayer you gave."

"Nothing could have been better than for us to have a chance to pray together in silence," said another woman. "We were all praying for you."

"Thanks," I said, smiling. "I needed it!"

Thank You, Lord, for this time of silence that I give to You.

—*RICK HAMLIN*

15

THURSDAY

O Lord...we all are the work of thy hand. —ISAIAH 64:8

When I was in college, I worked with one of the campus theater groups and took theater courses along with the English classes that were part of my major. The course in stage lighting turned out to be especially meaningful, though it was also very frustrating. The professor told us a great many of the "what" facts about electricity (what an *ohm* or an *amp* was) and some of the "how" facts (complete a circuit using conductors), but he could never answer any of my "why does it work that way?" questions.

"It just does," he said repeatedly.

One of the exercises he assigned was to choose a spot on the campus and study it at different times of day to see what difference the changing sunlight made. A line of flowers edged the walkway outside my dorm, and I studied it for several weeks. I saw how light brightened and intensified the colors, or softened and muted them, sharpened and then blurred shadows. I identified new growth, mourned the fading of an especially beautiful bloom. It was absolutely normal, and it was extraordinary.

Months later, I realized I couldn't explain the "why" of the flowers any more than Dr. Thayer could explain the "why" of electricity. I'd thought he was only teaching me stage lighting, but actually he was teaching me faith. We may never know why it works, or why it makes the ordinary appear so extraordinary. It just does.

When I need answers, dear God, help me to remember that all questions lead to You. —RHODA BLECKER

READER'S ROOM

On Good Friday, I took two small hyacinth plants to the cemetery and placed them on my parents' graves. The hyacinth plants were in tight buds. The day following Easter was blustery with a heavy blanket of snow, so I expected the plants to be blown away. The following Saturday I returned to the cemetery and found the hyacinths in full bloom—protected and cared for by our loving Lord Jesus. —JEAN B. LORY, ALLENTOWN, PA

16

FRIDAY

Blessing, and glory, and wisdom, and thanksgiving, and honour, and power, and might, be unto our God for ever and ever. Amen. —REVELATION 7:12

While waiting for a friend to come through surgery at our local hospital, I decided to get a snack at the cafeteria. Coming down in the elevator, I ran into the hospital pathologist, a man who was a deacon at our church and someone whom I much admired.

"Great to see you," he grinned as he shook my hand warmly. "Stop with me as I drop this file off at the lab, then I'll join you for coffee." Suddenly, I found myself in the dazzling white and gleaming stainless steel of a pathology lab. The doctor gave me a brief tour, pausing to demonstrate the high-tech machines in which, in a fraction of a second, a biopsy specimen can be frozen, dissected and placed under an electronic microscope for projection onto a large screen for scanning.

On the way down to the cafeteria he chatted about the courses he would be teaching at the University of Southern California that week; the exciting progress of medical research; and the awesome responsibility of the life and death decisions made by a pathologist.

As we had our coffee, I asked him, "In all your family, church and professional involvement, what do you consider your primary focus?"

He slowly removed his glasses and wiped them with a napkin. Then, looking at me with soul-searching intensity, he quietly said, "The purpose of my life and my primary focus is to glorify God and to love Him forever."

I was not ready for that. "I thought certainly the purpose of your medical career would be to find a cure for disease," I sputtered, "or to train up young doctors in the healing art of medicine, or to alleviate human suffering."

"All true," he smiled, "but everything I do pyramids down from my primary purpose—to glorify God."

May Christ be glorified through the simplicity of my life, dear Lord. Each task I undertake, I consecrate to You. —FAY ANGUS

17

There was a wedding in Cana of Galilee...and Jesus also was invited, and His disciples.... —JOHN 2:1–2 (NAS)

Central Texas is not known for torrential rainfall. But tonight it gushed eight inches in three hours, flooding streets, gorging streams, endangering homes and livestock.

Tonight was also the evening of Allison and Don's wedding. Carefully made plans, refined for months, were washed away by the rain. The reception was to have been outside under bright Texas stars, with us seated beneath a lovely white canopy. Moments before the wedding, the raging wind collapsed the canopy, crushing the wedding cake and blowing the white tablecloths around like the sails of a schooner. Despite the disastrous weather, the wedding had to go on.

As the organ prelude began and echoed across the empty pews, I put my arms around the bride's dazed mother to comfort her. Mustering her courage, she said, "I know that nobody in their right mind will get out in this storm. But our family's here, and that's what matters."

Thirty minutes later, as the processional began and I entered the sanctuary, my mouth fell open in amazement. The church was packed with people. More than eight hundred folks had braved the treacherous streets and dangerous winds to demonstrate their love and support for Allison and Don. As Allison glided down the aisle on the arm of her beaming father, I wasn't the only one blinking away tears.

Sometimes it takes a storm to help us realize what's important in life. Perhaps that's why the loveliest wedding I've ever attended was this one, where so many things went wrong, but all the things that counted went right.

Dear God, thank You for the friends who love us. —SCOTT WALKER

18

SUNDAY

I am come that they might have life, and...have it more abundantly. —JOHN 10:10

It was the day before Easter, and I was on a train from Fort Worth to Houston to fill in for a pastor who was recovering from a heart attack. I had prepared a standard Easter sermon—the certainty and centrality of the Resurrection, the reality that created the church and our hope for life after death.

Somewhere between Cleburne and College Station the train slowed to a crawl to let a northbound train pass, and I looked out of the window at a small farmhouse with its swaybacked barn. What caught my attention were three gravestones in the yard by a flowerbed. As the train picked up speed that scene stayed in my mind and I wondered what stories went with those stones—who was buried there and who tended the graves so lovingly.

As I thought about that private burial place, I was reminded that there are more kinds of death than physical dying that each of us experiences—death to friendships, to marriages, to belief in people, to integrity, to ambition and even to hope. In those private places of the heart, each of us tends graves where we have buried things that were precious and whose loss we grieve often all by ourselves. I wondered what Easter had to do with all these deaths.

During the rest of the trip and that night in the hotel, I reworked my sermon for the next day. What I had already prepared was true and was the basis for our Christian hope, so I made it the introduction to a more relevant message for myself and for those who would hear me. Easter is not just remembering our hope for life after the grave. It is a celebration of the fact that the living Christ comes to us in all the deaths we experience in this world and seeks to bring us life.

Father, thank You for the hope that brings the promise of real life both here and hereafter. —KENNETH CHAFIN

19

MONDAY

"Take courage! It is I. Don't be afraid."
—MARK 6:50 (NIV)

I was physically and emotionally exhausted by 10:00 P.M. on moving day. My husband Gordon offered to stay behind to see the last items loaded onto the van while I got a head start with our six-year-old son John on the hundred-and-twenty-mile drive to our new home.

It was an emotional battle to start up the minivan and back out of our familiar driveway for the last time, hauling household chemicals that the movers would not transport. Just before I reached the interstate, I rounded a corner and heard an ominous hiss coming from somewhere inside the van. Fearing that something was about to explode, I swerved into a parking lot and screamed at John to get out of the car. I flung open the trunk and pawed through boxes of paints and cleaning supplies. At last I discovered the culprit—the vacuum cleaner wand had fallen on top of a spray bottle of carpet cleaner.

Shaking, I sank back into the car seat. Just then I saw a flash of lightning in the direction I would be heading. *I can't do this,* I thought. *I especially can't drive through a thunderstorm this late at night.* I gripped the steering wheel until my hands ached as I pulled back onto the interstate.

The lightning became more visible as we sped into the countryside away from the interchange lights, but the darkness brought out something that the lights had hidden. Hovering just outside the top of my left-hand window was a single star. In the light of it, four ancient words spoken on another stormy night invaded my mind: *Courage. It is I.*

I took in a deep breath and repeated, "Courage. It is I." Each time I repeated it, I emphasized a different word, and the meaning grew. *"Courage.* It is I." (Karen, take heart.) "Courage. It *is* I." (This whole move is in My hands, a process that I will complete.) "Courage. It is *I."* (I am here now, and I go before you.)

At 1:00 A.M. we finally arrived at the hotel, having gone through only a brief ten-minute period of mild rain. I found the Bible in the nightstand drawer and searched until I found the words, "Courage. It is I." Then, with a grateful heart, I closed the Bible and my exhausted eyes.

Father, this stormy journey is awfully dark. Help me to know that You are really here. —KAREN BARBER

20 _____ TUESDAY
But if we hope for what we do not see, we wait for it with patience. —ROMANS 8:25 (RSV)

Another wedding invitation had arrived from the South. As I headed to the post office to mail my regrets and a silver serving spoon, I wondered when my turn for marriage would come. Most of my college friends were celebrating third and fourth anniversaries. Some had babies. What about me? "How much longer?" I asked God.

It was the same question that had wearied my parents during my childhood on our annual eight-hour drive from north Alabama to the Gulf of Mexico. Ten miles from our driveway I was ready to jump out of the station wagon and feel sand between my toes. So I nagged my mom all the way to the coast. "Have we gone halfway? Are we there yet?" Mom suggested I entertain myself. I tried to play the alphabet game or read a book, but they soon lost their charm.

After more than a decade, dating was getting old, too. Fun, yes, but hard work and heartache were part of the long haul. I began to wonder: *Am I really getting closer to a lasting relationship?*

My family always made it to the beach by supper time, I remembered as I posted my package. Above the creaking mail-bin door I thought I heard God say, "You'll make it, too. You're just not there yet."

Grant me patience, Lord, when my dreams feel far away, and help me to enjoy the ride. —ALLISON SAMPLE

21 WEDNESDAY
[Jesus] said to the man, "Reach out your hand." He did, and instantly his hand was healed! —MARK 3:5 (TLB)

We were seated around the table in the boardroom of the Medford Savings Bank. As secretary of the board, my chair was next to that of our president and CEO. At one point during the meeting, he pushed his papers aside and said, "You probably know that John, our vice-president, hasn't been at the bank lately. I'm sorry to have to tell you that he has leukemia. There's little hope that he will recover." The president fell silent and bowed his head. His shoulders shook as he fought off the tears.

As I watched him, I realized that a gentle touch on the shoulder might comfort and help. But it's never been easy for me to show my feelings, and I was afraid that a touch might be interpreted as disrespectful. So I sat there in frozen dignity and did nothing. The inches between the president and me might as well have been miles.

One evening a short while later, I attended a meeting of our church vestry. Our senior warden, a surgeon, talked to us about how he brought his faith into his work. "Most of the patients who come to me don't know me; they're referred to me by colleagues," he said. "They're facing surgery, and they're placing their lives in my hands. They're frightened. I've found that if I put a hand on their shoulder as we talk, they're comforted. Five minutes before we were strangers. But after that simple touch, there is trust."

I remembered his words sometime later when I served as an usher at the funeral of the wife of the former rector of our church. After the service, he slipped out of the church through the door where I was standing. His shoulders sagged, and he was weeping. This time I didn't worry about maintaining my reserve. I reached out and touched his shoulder.

Lord, help me to see that it's a privilege to reach out and comfort another in Your name. —OSCAR GREENE

22 — THURSDAY

"Go, walk through the length and breadth of the land, for I am giving it to you." —GENESIS 13:17 (NIV)

My little girl Maria and I were waiting for my mom to finish a doctor's appointment, and rather than try to keep a lively toddler busy in the waiting room, I took her for a walk. We wandered across the street to a church with a huge, wide lawn. Maria ran as fast as she could up the grassy hills, then rolled down, smiling and laughing.

Just then a woman began walking toward us from the church office. *Uh-oh!* I thought. *Did I overlook a "Keep Off the Grass" sign?*

"You know," she said as she reached us, smiling at my little girl, "I've worked here quite awhile and I've never seen anyone play on this lawn. I think it's because we're a church, and people think they have to show reverence for the whole place, even the grass."

The woman was correct. If Maria hadn't been with me that day, I would have walked on the sidewalk and appreciated that lush green lawn only from afar. But Maria had the right idea. I can't imagine God intended His great natural wonders merely to inspire reverence and awe. So to the popular slogan, "Reduce, reuse, recycle," I'm adding another word, *realize.* For me that means getting up close to realize fully the world's wonder and appreciate its treasures.

Here are some new ways to celebrate this Earth Day: Stick your nose in a flower; lie down in wet grass; get some dirt under your fingernails; bury your toes in the sand; play in the water; bite into a fresh apple and let the juice run down your chin. Care for the earth in the simplest way: Spend some time with it.

Giver of all life, help me to embrace Your earth like a little child, with more enthusiasm than reverence and more love than awe.
—GINA BRIDGEMAN

23 — FRIDAY

Judge not according to the appearance.... —JOHN 7:24

Overhung with maple, oak and birch, the Massabesic River gently winds through my New Hampshire hometown until it broadens by the dam in Auburn center. Here, local anglers rest against the massive granite wheel from an eighteenth-century gristmill as they watch their bobbers for jerky clues of pickerel and horned pout in the cola-colored depths. Only the most nimble fishermen venture out on the lip of the dam, close to the dark water, which cascades about three feet to the deep pool below. Since the river feeds into the regional water supply, fishing is permitted but swimming is not.

One spring evening when I was about sixteen, as my parents and I watched television, our neighbors turned into our dirt driveway. Mom hurried out to greet them. Even before I reached the porch I could hear her normally soft voice become agitated and high-pitched: "...Too early to go swimming yet! Even your shoes!..."

My brother Dennis, then about fourteen, sat drenched in the back of the pickup. Water dripped from his hair and squelched from his sneakers. He grinned and ate chocolate cake from a piece of waxed paper.

Oh, boy, I thought, *you're in big trouble now.* Since Dad worked for the water department, we figured he'd lose his job if we kids were ever caught swimming in the Massabesic.

Our neighbor ignored our grim reactions. His six-year-old was soaked, too. "Dennis just saved our little son." We stopped our critical chorus mid-breath. "Roger was trying to fish from the dam and slipped. We didn't know it happened, but Dennis was riding by on his bike and saw him fall under the waterfall. He jumped in and pulled him out. And all I have to give him is this cake."

Mom sighed and smiled indulgently, and I gazed with bewildered respect at my brother. He just grinned and licked frosting off his fingers.

Heavenly Father, let me always look for the big picture while You do the judging. Amen. —GAIL THORELL SCHILLING

24

Then will I sprinkle clean water upon you, and ye shall be clean.... —EZEKIEL 36:25

I was digging through my under-stove cabinets to get out a cookie sheet. I was to bake hermits for a potluck lunch for a sick friend. I pulled out a Bundt pan I hadn't used in five years, a heart-shaped cake dish (ditto), a popover pan I hadn't used in three years and a glass vase I'd searched for on my anniversary. Then I yanked out two glass cake pans (I've used metal for half a decade), four Pyrex custard cups and a bottle of shampoo (don't ask—I have *no idea* how that got in there). Sitting amidst the pile, I found the cookie sheet. *I don't feel in the mood to bake now,* I thought, and brought a big bag of Oreos to the party.

When I told her the story, the hostess laughed. "When I got sick, I had to do something about clutter. So I took all the stuff that was in my cabinet and put it in a box outside on my porch. Then, whenever I needed something, I went outside and retrieved it."

I don't have a porch, but I got a big box and threw everything from under the stove in there. At the end of three months, I had used just one cookie sheet, two round cake pans and a baking dish, along with a couple of pots and pans from my cabinet. I felt cleansed.

Then I got an idea: Wouldn't it be wonderful if I could "clear out" my brain, too? That grudge against Barbara for taking credit for my work—did I really need it? It was years old. That anger at June for always being late? June is June, foibles and all. And that gloating that I'd placed first in the company Scrabble game—all right, I'd leave that, also.

God, help me to clear out my mental "cabinet" of grudges, hurts or overenthusiastic pats on my own back! —LINDA NEUKRUG

25

SUNDAY

A man's mind plans his way, but the Lord directs his steps. —PROVERBS 16:9 (RSV)

Many years ago, when Norman Vincent Peale was pastor of Marble Collegiate Church on Fifth Avenue in New York City, a gentleman started coming to the Sunday morning service, sitting in a pew about eight or ten rows from the back. He never talked with the ushers or with anyone around him. And when the service was over, he left the church without lingering to chat. The ushers were interested in finding a way to make him feel more at home. Finally they approached him, and learned that he was a lawyer, considered one of the most brilliant in the city, and a bachelor. He had been to every church on Fifth Avenue, attending each one for only a few Sundays. But he flourished in the friendly atmosphere at Marble Collegiate, and in time he became an elder.

Then one year Norman and I took a tour party of about twelve hundred people to Hawaii. We persuaded the lawyer to go with us. One evening I was planning the seating arrangements for dinner at our hotel. I had invited a good friend from San Francisco, a beautiful woman, to sit at our table. Who could I find to put next to her? Our lawyer friend came to mind.

And do you know what happened? He fell for her! They were married, he moved to California, and they enjoyed a rich, rewarding life together.

I often speak on the subject "God Has a Plan for Your Life." I believe that this story was God's plan for two wonderful people.

Lord, may I live so aware of Your constant presence that all my actions are directed by You. —RUTH STAFFORD PEALE

26

MONDAY

Seek ye first the Kingdom of God.... —MATTHEW 6:33

Grandpa died when I was twelve. As the family gathered in the church basement before the funeral, my father and uncles talked to us about how Grandpa always put God first, and how he demonstrated his faith in action. They reminded us of his loving concern for others, how as proprietor of the general store he often extended credit to needy families, how he worked to develop the local timber industry that provided supplemental income for farmers struggling on the marginally productive land.

Several years ago when I was visiting my Uncle Vincent's house, I noticed a Bible verse hanging on the wall in a narrow bamboo frame: "Seek ye first the kingdom of God and His righteousness, and all these things shall be added unto you."

"Didn't that used to hang on the wall behind Grandpa's desk?" I asked my uncle. "Yes," he replied, obviously pleased as I recounted my daily childhood visits to Grandpa's office. Impulsively, Uncle Vincent reached up and plucked it from its nail on the wall. "I'd be happy for you to have this if you want it."

When we removed the old frame and glass, we discovered that it was a beautiful piece of calligraphy, hand-lettered in black ink with small flourishes of gold and silver. Now it hangs in a prominent place in our living room. We enjoy its beauty, but more than that, it's a message to all who see it. And it's a regular reminder to me of the lasting influence a grandparent can have on a child's heart and life.

I thank You today, heavenly Father, for grandparents. May their influence be loving, lasting and sweet. —MARY JANE CLARK

27 TUESDAY

A time to get, and a time to lose; a time to keep, and a time to cast away.
—ECCLESIASTES 3:6

I once lost a valuable coral-and-silver bracelet at a concert in a large auditorium. I went back the next day and searched the auditorium and the parking lot, but I didn't find the bracelet, nor did it ever turn up at the lost-and-found.

When I bemoaned my loss to my friend Elsie, she said, "Nothing is ever lost. *You* don't have the bracelet anymore, but somebody does. Bless that person and let the bracelet go."

Following her suggestion, I thought of the bracelet on another woman's arm and said a short prayer: "Lord, let that woman wear the bracelet in health and joy." A weight lifted from my heart, replaced by a feeling of peace.

Releasing loss and moving ahead—a good way to enter the new millennium.

Father God, Ruler of the universe, I release all my losses to You as I proceed toward the future. Amen. —MADGE HARRAH

28 WEDNESDAY

Thou shalt relieve him: yea, though he be a stranger....
—LEVITICUS 25:35

It happened on a rainy morning. Since my dog Wally hates to go out in the rain, we were taking a fast walk around our block when I noticed an ambulance and a patrol car, lights flashing, at the crosswalk. I also noticed my neighbor Mark with his dog Daisy, a cairn terrier who dislikes the rain even more than Wally. I could see an elderly woman lying on her back and assumed that the medical attendants were reluctant to move her until they had finished their examination. A policeman was crouched beside her, taking notes.

"Oh, dear," I said to Mark, "I wish there were something we could do." Then I turned to head for my apartment building with Wally in the lead.

"Wait," Mark said. "I think there *is* something we could do," and he moved to position his opened umbrella over the woman and the medical attendant. He looked at me and nodded in the direction of the police officer. I got the message and moved to hold my umbrella over him.

Looking down, I saw that Daisy and Wally were both sitting quietly, almost as if they knew what was needed of them. Mark noticed it, too, and said, "Good girl, Daisy."

"Good boy, Wally," I said.

And there we four stood with the rain pouring down until the attendants lifted the woman into the ambulance and the police officer finished writing. "Thank you," he said. "Thank you."

Both our dogs wagged their tails.

Lord, help me to be open to ways in which I can be useful.

—*ELEANOR SASS*

29

Lift up now thine eyes....

THURSDAY

—*GENESIS 13:14*

Each morning, I set aside time to pray. And because I pray best away from looming chores and ringing phones, I usually take a long walk as I bring the concerns of my family and friends to God.

But even at my best, it's often hard for me to keep my focus on praying. A shiny new car passes and I start fretting about the new tires we need to buy, or I pass a perfectly manicured lawn and worry about finding time to weed our overgrown flowerbeds.

But there was one stretch on my prayer route where I really hummed. I turned a corner and saw a hill in the distance. As I caught sight of it, my spirits soared and the rest of the way home my prayer was focused.

So you can imagine how I felt the day I rounded the corner and heard the grind of earthmovers. To my horror, I saw a bulldozer ripping the trees off my lovely hill. In the next few days construction started, and finally big houses began springing up—the kind of houses that seemed to shout, *"More! Bigger! Better!"*

God, I fussed, *why did You let this happen? I'm trying so hard to center myself, and to use this time to pray for others, and now every morning I have to fight off feelings of jealousy and discontent.*

A funny thing happened then: I looked up to prove my point and found my eyes resting on another hill. Farther out in the distance, it was higher and more lovely than my original prayer hill. I had never even noticed it there, acting as a backdrop for the smaller hill. And all I had to do was lift my eyes a little higher to where it had been waiting all along.

Father, how patiently You wait for me to lift my eyes above those earthly barriers that separate me from Your help. Help me to keep looking up. —PAM KIDD

30

Stand still, and consider the wondrous works of God.
—JOB 37:14

I'd hit my late-afternoon slump. After peering at a computer screen for hours, my brain and body needed a recharge, so I put on my jogging shoes and headed out the front door.

"Where you going?" asked Schuyler, my five-year-old nephew who lives next door.

"To find some endorphins," I told him, thinking of the feel-good chemicals released in our bodies when we get vigorous exercise.

"Can I come?" he asked, and before I could answer, he raced off to "tell my mom." Unfortunately, that was the last time he moved quickly for the next hour. We'd barely started off when he squatted down to study an ordinary-looking brown rock buried in the driveway. "What are we looking for? 'Dorphins'?"

"Endorphins, Sky. They make us feel happy inside when we go for a fast walk."

"I know that," he said simply as he kicked the rock. "My friend collects rocks."

"Oh," I said, reaching for his hand. "Let's get going, Sky."

At the end of the driveway he stopped again. "Way cool!" he exclaimed, sounding like his older brother as he reached for an odd-shaped piece of bark hidden in the weeds. "Looks kinda like a boat." I nodded even though it didn't look a thing like a boat to me.

"Sky, we need to go faster or we won't find the endorphins."

"Why?" he asked simply as he kicked over another stone. "Wow!" he said, squatting down again. I looked at his "wow" and saw a shiny, black, fat beetle scurrying off into the tall grass. Already, I'd started revising my expectations for this walk.

"You make great discoveries when you look under rocks, Sky," I said.

"I know that."

An hour later, we returned from a very short, slow walk around a familiar neighborhood, but I had to admit I felt recharged. "Thanks for sharing your discoveries with me," I told Sky as we reached the split in our driveways.

He merely nodded as he walked away, and then stopped. "Hey," he said, "did we find any 'dorphins'?"

"Nope, but guess what? I discovered that I didn't really need any today."

"I know that," he said. And then he ran home.

Father, thank You for giving me more than one way to get recharged.
—CAROL KUYKENDALL

MY FAITH JOURNEY

Missed kids

1 Cloudy, rainy day 50°. Called kid to april fool, no answer. Walked soaps + went for papers. Made spagetti.

Missed kids

2 Beautiful sunny day 70°. Paul + I went to acme + IGA for ham, shrimp + crab legs. We did a 2 dinap + did daffodils from old chouse.

Missed kids

3 Beautiful, sunny day 60°. Paul + I went to old chouse to get more lilacs, daffodils + forsythia. Butch + Emma. Aunt...

4 Cloudy dreary day 70°. Paul had crabs for lunch + made a pig of himself. We went to Chantells for Easter Dinner.

Missed kids

5 Beautiful sunny day 60°. Very busy at work. Stopped taking antibotic. Paul's sister Irene called + ...

Missed kids

6 Beautiful sunny day 70°. Very busy at work. Paul called Irene + created a rukus again. I cried all night. He also went to the dump without me.

7 — Missed Kids — Beautiful sunny day 70°. Worked 4 hrs. O.T. Real tired. Came home & showered & watched Y & R & G.H. Paul retired at 7:30.

8 — Missed Kids — Beautiful sunny day 70°. Very busy at work. Called Chantell from work. Went for dinner & Bobby's Birthday.

9 — Missed Kids — Rain, Rain, Rain. 45°. Very busy at work. No O.T. Came home & Paul & I took a 2 hr nap. He's got what I had.

10 — Missed Kids — Beautiful sunny day 70°. Paul & I had breakfast & started daffodils at 10:00. Chatted w/ Joyce, Mary & Christa, ming Florence

11 — Missed Kids — Cloudy rainy day 45°. Paul & I went to I 60 A for papers & Wawa for coffee. Called Chantell & Butch & Terry.

12 — Missed Kids — Rain AM. Sun PM. Worked 4 night. Paul & I went to Home Depot. Mickey's & bed by 8:30. Exhausted.

13 — Missed Kids — Beautiful sunny day 50°. Very busy at work. Came home at 2:30. Hernia paining me. Worked 2 hrs OT AM.

14 — Missed Kids — Beautiful sunny day 60°. Very busy at work. Worked 2 hrs O.T. Came home & made spagetti. Paul's hurt his back.

15 — Missed Kids — Beautiful sunny day 60°. Very busy at work. Worked 4 hrs O.T. BB made mistake on report & I redid it

16 — Missed Kids — Rain Rain Rain 50°. Very busy at work. Came home ate & showered & went to bed. Exhausted!

17 — Beautiful sunny day. Rep & I went to J-Bee open house for Bobby's. Kelsey we walked a mile.

18 — Beautiful sunny day 50°. Paul & I went to sleep late & Wawa. We had potatoes & eggs for breakfast. At noon we went to Bobby's baseball game. Kelsey also had a game. Chantell made Turkey dinner. Butch came over.

Missed kids Beautiful partley cloudy day.
Worked 5:00 - 12:00. Came
home etc. I took nap + Paul
19 I went to see Main Esperanza.

Missed kids Rainy day 50°. Very busy at work
worked from 5:00 - 12:00. Paul +
20 I picked up Toni + went see Main Esperanza

Missed kids Beautiful sunny day 60°. Paul + I
went to Medford + got his blood
21 work done. We went to Target + K-Mart.

Missed kids Rainy cloudy day AM + Sun PM
60°. Very busy as work. Worked
22 4 hrs O.T. Chantell called.

Missed kids Cloudy, rainy day. 50°. Very busy
as work. After work Paul + I went
23 to John Deere + got a battery for mower.

Beautiful sunny day 60°. Washed
+ hung and clothes. Took Bobby
24 to his Baseball game chil Kelsey completed

Beautiful sunny day 60°. Paul + I
took Bobby to his baseball game
25 Kelsey came home w/us. Exhausted.

Missed kids Beautiful sunny day 70° very busy
as work. Did 1 hr O.T. Paul
26 finally mowed the lawn.

Missed kids Beautiful sunny day 60°. Very busy
as work. Worked 4 hrs OT. in
27 Paul made roast beef, carrots + potatoes crock

Missed kids Beautiful sunny day 65°. Very
busy as work. Worked 4 hrs O-
28 Paul met me as Shop Kitt.

Missed kids Beautiful sunny day 65°. Very busy as
work. Did 4 hrs O.T. Came home +
29 relaxed. Watched soaps.

Missed kids Beautiful sunny day 65°. Paul +
I went to Dr. X + then to the sho
30 Sandy took Jo Paul + Jolly. We got
home as 6:30 + Butch + Jim saw
ours. We retired as 9:00.

May

*He leads me in paths of righteousness
for his name's sake.*

—*PSALM 23:3 (RSV)*

S	M	T	W	T	F	S
						1
2	3	4	5	6	7	8
9	10	11	12	13	14	15
16	17	18	19	20	21	22
23	24	25	26	27	28	29
30	31					

LESSONS IN LISTENING

1

DISCERNING THE DECEIVER
"The devil....is a liar and the father of lies."

—*JOHN 8:44 (RSV)*

An idea comes. Is it from God? From my own head? Or is there a third possibility?

At a PTA meeting when our daughter Liz was in middle school, a diffident, little inner voice kept me from standing up to protest a funding cut in the music program. *We are new to the community. I don't understand finances. My opinion wouldn't count for much.* Later the teacher whose program was cut told Liz, "If just one person had spoken up in support, the board might have reconsidered."

I had undervalued my worth. And sometimes I *over*value it. Last week at our local drugstore there was a long line of kids waiting to pay for candy. Reasons at once sprang to my mind why I should not have to wait. *I'm an adult. I have a long list of things to do. My time is valuable. My prescription is worth more to the store than a candy sale.* So when the druggist signaled me to step to the front of the line, I did.

Many times when faced with a choice, I'm aware of a voice that is not God's. "The devil" is the name the Bible uses here for the force that from the beginning has specialized in wrong choices. Unlike God's consistent Word, the devil shifts its tone. Where I'm insecure, it belittles. *Why should the* PTA *listen to you?* Where I'm egotistical, it flatters. *Your time is too important to waste.* And I listen, because it's *partly* right. It's true that I'm inadequate. It's true that time is precious. But these are only half-truths, and they lead to counterfeit guidance.

How does God deal with the same truths? To my insecurity He says, *Yes, you're inadequate, and it doesn't matter. In My strength you can stand up at the PTA. You can do all I give you to do.* To my self-centeredness He says, *Yes, you are important, valuable, precious. And so is each one of these children standing so patiently in line.*

Next time, wait your turn.

Father of truth, make me alert today to the small half-truth that can be twisted into a big lie. —ELIZABETH SHERRILL

2 SUNDAY

For every creature of God is good.... —I TIMOTHY 4:4

We all know about the great happenings that Easter commemorates and are eternally grateful for them. But sometimes a small happening can make this radiant day even brighter.

Early last Easter Sunday morning, coming home from jogging, our next-door neighbor told us a sad little tale of an opossum struck by a car not far from our house. He said the opossum was dead, but some of her babies seemed to be alive, so he had flagged down a passing patrol car and reported the incident.

When my wife Pam and I went to see if we could be of help, we found that the policeman had parked his car so that traffic was deflected around the scene. Three baby opossums were dead, but eight were very much alive, small furry creatures with sharp noses and pointed ears and bright little eyes. The patrolman put on some gloves and helped free them from the mother's pouch. When they were safe inside a box we had brought, he asked us for a shovel so that he could dig a grave for the others.

All this took a good deal of time and a lot of caring from a man whose love of animals and respect for life made him stop when he might easily have 'passed by on the other side.' Today, four weeks later, the opossum babies are growing fast in foster homes, waiting for the day when they can be returned to the wild.

Easter: a time of life and hope and joy so vast that I like to think there is room in it even for a handful of small furry creatures who owe their lives to the compassion and kindness of a Good Samaritan in blue.

Father, make us kind to all living things, especially those that are helpless. —ARTHUR GORDON

3 MONDAY

When times are good, be happy; but when times are bad,
consider: God has made the one as well as the other....
—ECCLESIASTES 7:14 (NIV)

My husband Alex introduced a little tool to help our family dinner conversations get past "How was your day?" "Okay." Alex said, "Let's each tell the best and worst thing that happened today."

Eight-year-old Elizabeth exclaimed, "The best thing was that we had cupcakes for David's birthday!" After thinking a few minutes, she said the worst was having to sit at their desks the first five minutes of recess because some kids in the class had misbehaved.

Each night this "best and worst" focus has given us new glimpses into each other's days. But tonight I sat down to dinner exhausted. My son Mark had jumped off his changing table last night, screaming in pain when he crash-landed on the floor. "Well, of course, the worst was that Mark broke his arm." I sighed, thinking of him crying during our trips to the doctor, the X-ray lab and finally an orthopedic specialist. "The best? Gee, I don't think anything good happened today.... Well, the best is that Mark wasn't hurt worse, and the doctor said he will heal quickly."

As I cleaned up the kitchen, my back ached from carrying Mark. I thought grimly, *No, this was mainly a day of "worsts."* But then I smiled, remembering how Mark had dozed in my arms this morning, something this active three-year-old hasn't done in many months. Yes, we had to wait until late afternoon and drive an hour to the specialist, but thankfully Alex could take us. Mark fell asleep during the long car ride, enabling Alex and me to talk all the way—about the accident, the children, our parenting—the kind of a long, uninterrupted, thoughtful conversation parents of young children rarely get.

Why, the unpleasant challenges of the day had yielded unexpected gifts.

Dear God, help me to see Your goodness and find blessings in the
burdens of this day.
—MARY BROWN

4

The name of the Lord is a strong tower; The righteous runs into it and is safe. —PROVERBS 18:10 (NAS)

Missouri has more churches than it has mules. Even the smallest village will have two or three houses of worship, even if it doesn't have a single store. Many of the towns have biblical names, like Bethany, Beulah, Goshen and Mt. Moriah.

Church chimes send hymns wafting through the streets of our town of Moberly all week long, and some of our streets bear names like Corinth, Wisdom, Samson and Ruth.

When I fan through the phone book I come across hundreds of names like Peter and Andrew, James and John, Paul and Silas, Timothy and Mark, Joseph and Daniel, Sarah and Abraham.

When I go into my college classroom I teach students named Esther, Candace, Tabitha, Mary and Deborah; Jordan, Stephen, Thomas, David and Nathaniel.

Alisa Kigar, our college PR person, is building a new home in the little town of Bible Grove. Two of the workers are named Elijah and Jacob, and her contractor is an Amish man named Noah. "At least the roof won't leak," she says confidently.

All these biblical names are a constant reminder to me that this country was built on faith in God, not on wealth, talent or technology. So real was this faith that people named their children, towns and streets after their Bible heroes. When I see the big names in America today—Hollywood, Wall Street, Silicon Valley—I am underwhelmed. Most of them are symbols of money, sex and power.

So each morning, when I arrive at my office, I put my head down on my desk and pray for my country:

Lord, I know that the secret of greatness is with You and not with humankind. Keep this country in touch with its power Source. Mend her flaws, and inspire me to be a godly citizen to Your glory. Amen. —DANIEL SCHANTZ

5

"I will show you compassion...." —JEREMIAH 42:12 (NIV)

A student had left a tiny frog in my desk drawer! I'd heard about playing pranks on substitutes, but this was the first time it had happened to me, and I was angry. Seeing my anger, Craig confessed. And now I was going to give him a big-time scolding, when I suddenly remembered another scared student.

My friend Carole and I were watering bushes in her garden one day when our high school Spanish teacher walked past as he did every day after school. Honestly, we didn't *mean* to squirt him—but squirt him we did. Then I was terrified; he was not the kind of man who liked a joke. In fact, he was my only teacher with a Ph.D. We had to call him Professor Wald. He was also the only teacher who called us by our last names. When he called on us, he insisted we stand. He made us memorize poetry. In Spanish. (I can still recite "Cultivo Una Rosa Blanca.") In short, he was tough. And I'd hosed him down! I felt sick.

Afraid to tell my mother, I stayed up all that night, tossing and turning in bed. The scenarios that replayed in my head varied, but all were horrifying: Would he send me to the principal? Have me expelled? Perhaps he'd make me stand up and embarrass me in front of my class by having me explain what I did—in Spanish. My stomach hurt.

He did none of those things. When I crept bleary-eyed into *clase Español* the next morning, he waited until I was walking by his desk and murmured, *"Buenos dias, Señorita Neukrug.* The weather is *muy seco* [very dry] today, no?" There was a twinkle in his eye—the first and last time I ever saw one there—then he was back to being the tough Professor Wald. But most amazing, he never mentioned the incident again!

If the stern professor could show compassion for a scared student, how could I do less? I looked straight at Craig. "Ribbet!" I said. "Now on to our lesson on the past tense."

Today, God, help me to show compassion—and humor—when it's deserved, and maybe even when it isn't. Nobody's perfect except You.
—LINDA NEUKRUG

6 THURSDAY

I was sick, and ye visited me.... —MATTHEW 25:36

Visiting a nursing home had always been difficult for me. I'd stop by to deliver flowers, messages and gifts, but to stay for more than a few minutes was more than I could do. I felt helpless to take away the pain or lessen the loneliness the residents felt. And the prospect of one day being a nursing-home resident myself frightened me.

Then my friend Sue, who'd been a vibrant and active woman all her life, became gravely ill and had to enter a nursing home. I visited her often, but I was never "living room comfortable." Sue was too sick to chat, and I worried that my visits weren't helping her. I discussed my problem with Dorothy, a friend at church. "Sometimes you can't do much for the person you're visiting," Dorothy said, "But you can often do wonders for the family or the other patients in the room."

The next time I visited Sue I was more relaxed. She wasn't able to talk much, but her roommate was. I listened as the lady shared her joyful memories of friends and loved ones. As she talked, the years seemed to vanish from her face, and my eyes glistened with tears. She was so pleased!

When I got up to leave, she squeezed my hand warmly and said, "Thank you for chatting with me. It meant so much to me. Sometimes I've wondered if anyone cared."

Dorothy's words had helped me to look beyond my own fears and find a way to help someone else.

Thank You, Lord, for showing me that caring is never wasted.

—OSCAR GREENE

7 *Consider the lilies of the field...they toil not, neither do they spin.* —MATTHEW 6:28

I drove with my friend Kate along the back roads toward Cold Spring, a little town in upstate New York. It was May, and after a long, gray winter, I looked forward to getting away from the office and a project I was having difficulty completing. Suddenly, I heard Kate squeal, "Stop the car!"

"What's the matter?" I asked abruptly, stepping on the brakes. Feeling annoyed, I watched her jump out and run back the way we had come. Fortunately, there was no traffic. She returned bearing armfuls of pungent lilacs still damp from a morning rain.

"Smell these," she cried, waving them under my nose. "Aren't they wonderful?" The car filled to bursting with the scent of flowers. Suddenly, I noticed the new life blossoming all around us. Kate thrust a bouquet into my hands, sprinkling me with a residue of rain.

"They were just growing along the side of the road," she said, "waiting for us like notes from God. Each one makes me feel how much God loves us."

I laughed and apologized. "Oh, Kate, I'm sorry I was so fretful with you. Thanks for blasting me out of my blahs. I'll put these on my desk as a reminder. Who knows? Maybe I'll even finish my project this spring." I gave Kate a hug, crushing the pale blossoms against her cheek, laughing as she laughed, with the pure joy of being alive.

Dear Father, help me to rejoice in the beauty around me and sing out with joy. —SUSAN SCHEFFLEIN

8 SATURDAY

Work hard and cheerfully at all you do....
—COLOSSIANS 3:23 (TLB)

Last Saturday, Julee and I were coming into our lobby with our dogs from their walk when Julee spotted the mailman and made a beeline for our box, Sally the cocker spaniel in tow. I quickly followed, tugging my Lab retriever Marty behind me.

You see, one of the various ways my talented wife earns a living is by lending her voice to commercial jingles and voice-overs. I always get a thrill when I realize that it is Julee's voice on television singing about a skin-care cream or purring about some sensational new candy bar. For Julee, though, the thrill comes when the residual checks appear intermittently in our mailbox. This makes retrieving the mail a rousing proposition.

A lot of this work Julee does on faith, auditioning and making unpaid demos for many more spots than she ever gets. Sure things become busts, hopeless projects suddenly blossom, and old commercials are unexpectedly resurrected and aired. Julee's grown simply to trust the process, with all its uncertainties and surprises. "If I do all the hard 'front end' work," she explains, "the rewards will take care of themselves over the long haul."

That approach is something I apply to my prayer life. I like to think that I have a kind of spiritual mailbox where God's blessings arrive. I can't always predict what they'll be or when they'll appear in my life, but the dividends of prayer are continuous as long as I am patient and am willing to do the daily "front end" work.

I looked down at Marty who was grinning like a fool and trying to get the mailman to shake his paw. Julee extracted a bluish envelope from our box, carefully tore the seal with her fingernail, peeked inside and smiled. "Take you to lunch," she said.

God, Your blessings always arrive. Teach me to be patient and wait for them, and never to tire of looking. —EDWARD GRINNAN

9

SUNDAY

Remember the days of old.... —DEUTERONOMY 32:7

Observing my daughters Julie and Jennifer mothering their children, I sometimes feel guilty about myself as a mother. I didn't teach my girls much about cooking or cleaning, and zero about sewing. I guess our home was sort of—messy. My fondest memories of their childhood are of taking them to the places I loved: libraries, ten-cent stores (particularly the paper-doll counter), animal pounds, antique shops.

One Mother's Day I was feeling particularly inadequate, wishing I'd given my daughters more instruction as they were growing up. Then, hesitantly, I opened the card on a gift from my oldest daughter.

Hi, Mom!

Oh, the smell of an antique shop! Memories of sharing a love of something in common. You taught me to love awesome things—books, conversations, old things, unique qualities in others, calico cats. Today in an antique shop, I remembered how you pointed out dusty treasures to me when I was small. Thank you for teaching me to see beauty in hidden places. Otherwise, I guess I might have thought dusting the furniture was important! I can't imagine life without you.

So grateful,
Julie

Her gift was paper dolls from the antique shop—rare ones from the 1940s. Looking around, I noticed that the furniture still needed dusting. Nevertheless, I sat down cross-legged in the living room and tried all of the wonderful, long-ago dresses on my brand-new antique paper dolls. I felt like a child again. And for sure, I felt a whole lot better about myself as a mother.

One of Your finest gifts to us, Father, is our memories. Amen.
—MARION BOND WEST

10

But he saith unto them, It is I; be not afraid.

—*JOHN 6:20*

Last spring, my wife Rosie flew to Memphis to visit our daughter Danita. It's a flight that normally takes an hour. On this particular day, however, it took close to three hours. There was a storm in the area, and the plane had to be rerouted twice to try and fly around it.

From the moment the plane took off, Rosie had the feeling that it was going to be an unusual flight, so she began to pray. As the plane repeatedly ran into turbulence, she started praying harder. Finally, as the pilot began trying to fly around the storm, Rosie began to have some really serious conversations with the Lord.

The flight attendants had not been able to serve beverages for the first two hours. When the turbulence subsided, they began to serve. They had only served about six rows when the FASTEN SEAT BELTS signs came on and the pilot instructed the flight attendants to be seated immediately. "Within five minutes we hit something extremely hard," Rosie said, "and the glasses and beverages began to fly everywhere. People were really shaken up. I asked the Lord to take care of the family if I didn't make it.

"Then I felt the Lord telling me, 'Look at your hands. What do you see?' My hands were pressed together, with the fingers interlocked tightly and the right thumb pressed down over the left. When I looked down, I saw that my thumbs formed a cross. Then I felt the Lord saying, 'Whenever the turbulence gets so heavy that you think you can't go on, just look to the cross.'"

When the plane finally landed, Rosie's hands were still clasped together, and her eyes were on that cross.

Jesus, in good times and hard times, let me look to Your Cross and lay all my cares on You. —*DOLPHUS WEARY*

11

You care for the land and water it; you enrich it abundantly.... —*PSALM 65:9 (NIV)*

I'm always surprised at what comes up in my small backyard garden, as well as in my front-yard flower bed. Each spring I sow seeds and wait for small green shoots to appear. Usually, there are a lot more than I planted! Many I know are outright weeds, and I feel no compunction in pulling them. But there are always some I don't recognize. When that happens, I let them grow, waiting to see what I'm going to get.

So each year I have wonderful surprises. The first year I gardened, I let some unknown shoots grow to maturity and had a wonderful crop of goldenrod! One year I had three marvelous foxgloves in my front garden, which delighted me with their great purple flowers. Another year I had a blue delphinium growing among my vegetables. In the corner of one bed, I have a flourishing stand of red clover that continues to delight me because I never mow it down. This year two strange plants that came up last year produced pink flowers. And now the flowers are turning into silver dollars, those amazing, paper-thin ovals beloved by decorators.

Where do the surprises come from? Goldenrod and red clover, I suspect, were blown in by the wind. The silver dollar plants came from seeds I threw out a year or two ago after a friend gave me a bunch for my house. But I've also got cosmos growing up, which I don't remember planting.

My garden continues to speak to me, not only of God's love and care for all growing things, but also of the wonderful surprise and variety of His workings. I wonder what surprises God has in store for my life this year.

Father God, I trust Your love and care, and look forward with anticipation to whatever unexpected events You send my way.

—MARY RUTH HOWES

12

A time to laugh....

WEDNESDAY

—ECCLESIASTES 3:4

It was my flub of the century. Tossing and turning through one of those restless nights when I couldn't sleep, I decided to get up, make myself a nice hot pot of tea and redeem the time by catching up on all the household bills that had stacked up. Bleary-eyed, but with checkbook in hand, I felt virtuous that 3:00 A.M. insomnia wasn't going to get the better of me. Stamps on the envelopes, the chore done, I crawled back into bed and quickly fell asleep.

A month later I faced the shocking results. When I went to pay the

utility bills, I found a credit balance from the electric company of
$996.00; from the gas company, $928.76; our local water department, $811.46, and so on down the line—enormous credits every-
where. In the muddleheadedness of my middle-of-the-night caper, I
had written checks for the balance in our bank account instead of the
amount due! You could hear my shriek through the neighborhood.
John came running, and after his initial shock, he started to laugh.
"Well, I guess this makes anything I do wrong pretty tame in comparison!"

"Oh, darling, what'll we do? Our account must be *way* overdrawn."

"Relax. Just call up the bank and the various companies and explain what happened. It'll be okay."

It was eventually, but only after I felt the humiliating brunt of the
incredulous "You did what?" phone calls and days spent rushing
around to local offices to pick up the refund checks.

I still wince when writing out checks and verify them umpteen
times, but I no longer brood over my less-than-perfect performance.
Instead I laugh, and have great fun telling the joke on myself!

I'm grateful, Lord, for the gift of laughter—especially at myself.

—FAY ANGUS

13 THURSDAY
*"I have loved you with an everlasting love....I will build
you up again....Again you will take up your tambourines
and go out to dance with the joyful."*

—JEREMIAH 31:3–4 (NIV)

My grandmother is quite a woman. Though slight and not quite five
feet tall, she was always the one pulling us children along at break-
neck speed. I won't tell you how old she is—I'm not even supposed
to know. Her answer to that question has always been, "Well, I'm
ancient."

But all this changed one day when she was defrosting her freezer.
As an activity it seems harmless enough, but she slipped and broke her
back. Eventually, we flew her down from Washington to California for
treatment and surgery. It was frightening to see her, so small in the
giant hospital bed. She looked so tired; I had never seen Grandma truly
helpless before. But this woman, eighty-something, was determined

to walk again, to be independent. We were all skeptical, and we moved her to our house. The family room turned into a hospital room, with our dachshund keeping vigil.

It took months of dedication on everyone's part, but one spring night, we saw it was going to work. I was sitting with Grandma, watching a TV game show, when, taking advantage of a chance for mischief, I reached out and tickled her feet. To my surprise, her foot twitched, and she giggled and scolded me. "Hey! What do you think you're doing?" This was the first sign of reflexes since the accident. How beautiful that it came with a laugh, a smile and a loving touch!

Grandma is once again running around. She doesn't quite hit ninety miles an hour anymore, but her cane is usually standing in a corner somewhere, getting dusty.

Father in Heaven, thank You for the strength and determination to pursue a miracle.   —KJERSTIN EASTON

14

Dear friend, I pray that you may enjoy good health and that all may go well with you, even as your soul is getting along well.   —III JOHN 2 (NIV)

At the age of six, I began reading the King James Bible. Two chapters a day, every day. It was one of Mother's rules. I came to think of the Bible as a necessary and important part of the day, sort of "vitamins for the soul." Now that I'm grown—and busy—I don't always take time for two chapters a day, every day. And if I don't have time to read two full chapters, I'm tempted to skip my Bible reading altogether. But something my friend Katie said the other day changed my perspective on this.

I have been buying vitamin supplements from Katie for almost a year. "You know," I confessed, "I know I don't take these as often as I should."

I braced for a lecture, expecting her to tell me how good these pills were, what a positive effect they could have on my overall health. Instead, she just smiled and said, "Well, they'll help you in direct proportion to how often you use them."

Katie's words don't apply just to vitamins. God's Word, too, is available to me on a daily basis. I can read a little; I can read a little more; I can read a lot. It's there, waiting to help me—in direct proportion to how I use it.

Remind me, Father, that there is no health outside of regular communion with You. Supplement my busy life with Your patience and Your strength. —MARY LOU CARNEY

15
SATURDAY

By their fruits ye shall know them. —MATTHEW 7:20

It's been more than a dozen years since I helped lead the youth group at church, but what I clearly remember from the experience was how ill-prepared I was, how awkward I felt with the kids and how certain I was that they took nothing away from our weekly gatherings. I can recall skits that never quite came off, and art projects that left glue and pen markings all over the table, and discussion groups that ended with my breaking up fights between the boys. The only things that went smoothly were a party when we acted out Bible stories and the play about Noah we performed in church to rousing applause. But overall, I wouldn't have given myself high ratings.

Then just the other day I ran into one of my alumni, a woman in her mid-twenties who was now working with the youth at her church. A bit discouraged about her efforts, she said, "I wish you'd come talk to our staff. You could tell us some of the things you did when you ran the youth group at church."

"What?" I said, aghast.

"I loved that group when I was a kid," Judy said. "It was so well run. We had a great time, and I remember learning a lot. We played great games, had good parties and the skits we did were incredible."

I was stunned. It was as though we were remembering two different experiences. Where I had stored up dozens of instances of failure, Judy had remembered only successes.

"Judy," I said with more confidence than I would have guessed, "stick with it. I'm sure things are going better than you realize. I'd be glad to come and talk with your staff. You just might not know how well you're doing."

At least not for a dozen years.

Lord, show me what I can do today to encourage one of Your children. —RICK HAMLIN

READER'S ROOM

I led a group of singers with piano accompaniment for the devotion in two county retired teachers' meetings. Eight former teachers sang in the first group on January 13. The group increased to fourteen at the March 10 meeting. Although the group was mixed racially, the unity for Christ was incredible. *Amens* followed the rendition of "Blessed Assurance" and "How Great Thou Art." I am happy to experience a little of heaven here on earth before the glad reunion day with Christ and His saints. —*ALLENE DEWEESE, FLORENCE, SC*

SUNDAY

16

The Lord make you to increase and abound in love one toward another.... —*I THESSALONIANS 3:12*

"So, how's that new woman Mary who joined your prayer class?" my husband David asked me one morning as we enjoyed our coffee.

"Well, she's—she's okay."

Actually, the sentence that formed in my head, then met resistance before it cleared my lips, went more like this: "Oh, she just came and used our class to get on our prayer list. As soon as her prayer was answered, she disappeared."

I sat in the silence as David riffled through the paper, feeling amazed with myself. I had actually managed to stifle my inclination to be judgmental. I didn't particularly like the woman, and all along I had felt that she was using our church family for a quick fix. But I didn't say it.

Maybe all my praying to be a better person was actually working! Our Sunday prayer class is based on the teachings of *Prayer Can Change Your Life* by Dr. William R. Parker and Elaine St. Johns. The book urges us to accept God's unconditional love for ourselves, then to reach out to others with this same, idealistic kind of loving. If we are able to do that, we can move past those awful tendencies to judge and criticize and even hate.

Later, on my morning walk, I found myself praying. *Well, God, a tiny victory is better than none at all, isn't it? Hey, if I keep working at this, do You think I might actually come to the place where I no longer have to suppress my hard words because I'm seeing the best in others as You so patiently see the best in me?*

Don't give up on me, Father. Because I'm not going to give up on me either. —PAM KIDD

EDITOR'S NOTE: If you would like to order *Prayer Can Change Your Life* by Dr. William R. Parker and Elaine St. Johns, please write to *Prayer Can Change Your Life*, Guideposts, PO Box 569, Brewster, NY 10509.

17

MONDAY

"Write this down, for what I tell you is trustworthy and true." —REVELATION 21:5 (TLB)

I'm not sure if it's because I wrote radio commercials that forced me to get a whole message across in thirty seconds of precious air time, or if it's because I just like bits of wisdom that come in small packages, but I've been a collector of sayings all my life. I snip them out of magazines, newsletters and church bulletins, and keep them in a folder. Sometimes I memorize them so I can pass them on to my children. Often I'll tape them to the front of the envelope of a letter I'm sending to the older children, hoping that all the mail carriers from here to there will enjoy the words of wisdom as well. They're also taped to my computer and on the walls of my home office.

Here are a few examples of my favorites.

We don't laugh because we feel good.
We feel good because we laugh.

No matter how long you nurse a grudge, it won't get better.

If you must speak ill of another, do not speak it;
write it in the sand near the water's edge.

Age is a matter of mind; if you don't mind, it doesn't matter.

Over the years I've learned that other people's wisdom in the form of sayings helps me, as a parent, make a point without belaboring the issue. When Andrew missed getting his swim team letter his sophomore year by three points, I taped this one on his mirror; "Success is not permanent...and neither is failure." To encourage my daughter Julia to take good care of herself and her daughter while Julia was struggling through her divorce, I sent this one: "In life, the destination will take care of itself if the journey is done well."

Lord, thank You for the wise words of others that help me keep an optimistic spirit and be a better parent. —PATRICIA LORENZ

18

Without controversy great is the mystery of godliness....
—I TIMOTHY 3:16

I reached for my passport and presented it gingerly to the woman behind the check-in counter. It was ripped so that the U and the S no longer read "USA," the picture of me was mauled, and the entire booklet looked like a loose-leaf gone wrong.

"Oh, oh, what's this?" came the not unexpected reply. I did my best to explain that it had just happened last night, and there wasn't time for me to do anything about it. "I don't know," she said, perplexed. I *had* to get on the plane to Vancouver, Canada, otherwise the SS *Rotterdam* might sail without me. The next highest in command came over. The two of them conferred. I waited. And prayed.

"Okay, though I don't know about the Canadian officials," he said, giving me a go-through, but reluctantly. At least I'd get out of the country, but what would the Canadians do? Send me back? Maybe, I vacillated. I said a little prayer as I got on the plane.

"What's this?" the Canadian immigration officer said as he handled the mess I offered. I did my best to minimize the destruction. In the end, he passed me in, but not without an unsaid benediction about crazy Americans.

"What's this?" said the man at the U.S. Immigration, and I, on firm home turf, listened to a dressing down, after which I promised to get a new passport as soon as possible.

When I got home, I showed the cause of the trouble to the one who had caused the trouble. "Look here, Shep, if you had gnawed more of my picture and gotten to the signature, it might have cost me the trip. Why this, the *only* thing you have ever chewed?"

A look of total innocence. And I....

It's a mystery, Lord. Just how much do dogs know? —VAN VARNER

19

"How long will you refuse to humble yourself before me?..."
                                                —EXODUS 10:3 (NIV)

When I went back to work several years ago after staying home to raise our children, one of my greatest challenges was learning to master the machines in the office, such as the copier, postage meter, phone system and, of course, all the computer programs. My children had already told me I was "technologically challenged" because of my total dependence on them to run the VCR and the CD player, and even to set the digital clock in my car. But at my job as a vice president of MOPS (Mothers of Preschoolers International), I was on my own, and I wanted to appear confident and competent, which I was not. So I had a problem.

Somewhere in my desk, I had manuals explaining how to use all these machines, but when I got frustrated, I didn't reach for a manual or ask for help. I started pushing buttons, hoping I'd miraculously hit upon something that would make the machine do what I needed. All too often, I cut off the person on the other end of the line; I jammed the copier; I froze up the computer.

One day I sat at my computer, madly moving the mouse around, hitting random icons and muttering threats to the screen, which had ceased responding. A co-worker heard me. "Why don't you let me help you?" she asked as she pulled up a chair and peered at my screen.

While she unfroze my computer, her gentle question slowly began to unfreeze something in me. The answer was suddenly clear: I didn't ask anyone for help because I didn't want to appear "technologically challenged." I wanted to appear capable, confident, competent. But there's something worse than being "technologically challenged." And that's being too proud to admit my need for help.

Father, I need You, and I need the honest humility to admit I need others, too.
                                                —CAROL KUYKENDALL

20

For by him were all things created, that are in heaven, and that are in earth...all things were created by him, and for him.
                                                —COLOSSIANS 1:16

I got my love of flowers from my mom, whose yard seems always to have something blooming. So in all the places my wife Barbara and

I have lived, I've planted irises, mums, hollyhocks and all sorts of annuals. But I'd never worked with peonies until we moved to Upland Road in Kentucky, where there was a large bed of them by a little rock wall in the front yard. That first spring I watched the lush green foliage grow and followed with interest the huge buds as they developed, anticipating the large, double-flowered blossoms. Then, just when they seemed ready to burst open, I was alarmed to find that the buds were crawling with ants.

That morning my neighbor was working in her flower bed, so I asked her what was the best way to get rid of the ants. She grinned and said, "You don't want to get rid of them. If you do, the peonies won't bloom."

She explained that the ants depended on the peonies for food. The flowers depended on the ants to eat away the green, waxy substance that encased the buds so they could bloom. With a certain skepticism, I decided to wait and see what would happen. My neighbor was right. It wasn't long before the peonies began opening, and the ants were nowhere to be seen.

We've enjoyed the beautiful pink and white peonies for several springs now. Each time I see them I recognize new ways in which plants and animals and people are interdependent. That's how God created it, and it's something I need to celebrate and value.

Father, teach me how to live in peace and harmony with all of Your creation. —KENNETH CHAFIN

21 FRIDAY
For God hath not given us the spirit of fear; but of power, and of love, and of a sound mind. —II TIMOTHY 1:7

Years ago, Mother answered a knock on our door in Macon, Georgia. A tall black woman grinned at her and said, "My name is Annie. The man at the grocery store said you needed somebody to keep your house tidy and clothes washed."

My sister Leila and I were in elementary school, and with another baby on the way, Mother had said she needed someone to help her.

"Where do you live?" Mother asked.

"I've been staying with my sister Ellen and her husband, Mr. Bounds. He died last year."

With some questioning, Mother learned that the Bounds family—mother, father and five children—had been sharecroppers at

Bolingbroke, a farming community fifteen miles north of Macon. Annie had walked partway, then caught a wagon ride.

Mother asked, "If I hire you, where will you live?"

"With you," Annie stated, "if I'm to do a good job."

Annie soon became part of our household. The room next to the kitchen became a bedroom for her. She was devoutly Christian, devoted to her duties and pretty soon loved all of us. It was a happy arrangement until Annie grew very depressed, worrying about her sister Ellen.

So on Sunday afternoon, Daddy took all of us in the car and drove, the first of many times, to the small frame house where the Boundses had always lived. Such a joyous reunion of two sisters! We all visited together, and Ellen served lemonade. Her children were grown and gone, she told us. But one son, John, came home weekends.

"He has a good job," she explained, "but he has to stay close to it weekdays."

Seeing no other buildings in sight, Daddy asked, "You stay here alone? Aren't you afraid?"

"Afraid? No, sir!" Ellen said emphatically. "I'm never alone. Jesus is here with me!"

Dear Lord, when fear assails me, help me to remember Ellen's words and know that, truly, I am never alone. Amen.

—DRUE DUKE

22 *God hath power to help....*
SATURDAY
—II CHRONICLES 25:8

For the last couple of years at Pentecost, I have participated with the nuns at my monastery in drawing cards representing the gifts of the Holy Spirit, qualities that are supposed to help guide our lives in the coming year. The seven qualities we choose from are understanding, piety, wisdom, fortitude, knowledge, counsel and fear of the Lord.

Last year, I drew the "Fortitude" card and left it pinned on my bulletin board so that I could see it when things got tough. But about halfway through the year, one of my workplace friends, Gene, hit a really rough time, and I thought he needed it more, so I took it down and gave it to him.

Later in the year, I went through some hard times, and I started withdrawing, as I do, so that I would not subject others to my troubles. Gene was shrewd enough to see what I wasn't saying and came to my office. He handed me back the "Fortitude" card and said, "If I had a card that said 'Faith,' I would give you that one, too."

He was right: Depression is only losing faith. Things improved very, very slowly, but I knew they would, because Gene had given me one visible and one invisible card, and they were both right.

All I need to do is turn to You, dear God, in my darkest hour. Let faith and fortitude be my guides. —RHODA BLECKER

23 SUNDAY

And suddenly a sound came from heaven like the rush of a mighty wind.... —ACTS 2:2 (RSV)

About thirty miles north of Nairobi, Kenya, is a small community called Kijabe, the Place of the Winds. It is perched on the escarpment wall overlooking the Great Rift Valley. When I lived in East Africa, one of my assignments was to write about the work at the mission hospital there for donors in the United States. The views from Kijabe are extraordinary, and I always enjoyed my visits there.

One afternoon the nursing director and I were trying to concentrate on a quiet task together when the wind became particularly gusty, blowing our papers around. "Wind can be so unsettling," I remarked as Norma got up to close the windows.

"Yes, but I think maybe that's its job here on earth—to rearrange things," she replied. With the windows closed we were nearly oblivious to the wind. It howled around the buildings as we carried on with our task.

Later, thinking about what Norma had said, I remembered how the Holy Spirit came with the sound of the wind at Pentecost. The Spirit came to rearrange people's lives, changing their priorities and reordering history. For the people who were there, nothing was ever the same again.

Am I open to that Power in my life? Or do I close my soul up tight at the prospect of change? Am I willing to let God the Holy Spirit blow out the cobwebs and reorder my comfortable routines?

Holy Spirit, I want to keep open the windows of my heart and let You rearrange my thinking and my doing. —MARY JANE CLARK

24

To this end we always pray for you....

—II THESSALONIANS 1:11 (RSV)

When I discovered gardening (and combined it with my Scottish heritage of thrift), I accidentally discovered a special way to pray for my children. Instead of throwing out their old boots, I turned them into planting pots. Several pairs now sit cheerfully on the steps around my deck and door. Pansies, chrysanthemums, lobelia, marigolds, impatiens.

Here are Phil's size-thirteen hiking boots. *Dear God, help Phil at the university today. Keep his mind alert for the quiz on Friday.* I come to his old high-tops. For some reason I remember when he'd folded his six-foot-four-inch frame into two plastic laundry baskets. *Thank You for Phil's silliness!* Heather's boots have curled up at the toes from the rain; they look like elf shoes. *Help Heather in her job hunt. Guide her to something meaningful and worthy of her intelligence.*

I'm almost done...but someone's missing. My youngest, Blake, won't give me his boots. He wears them full of holes and falling apart. One pair he painted silver. He wore these shoes to emcee his sister's wedding last year, dancing the Macarena on the tabletops. *Thank You for Blake, who keeps us laughing. Please be with him today in the callbacks for his school play!*

I put away my watering can and prayed:

Be with all my children, God. Help them to be everything You've meant them to be. Fulfill in them every good resolve and work of faith by Your power, so that Your name be glorified. Amen.

—BRENDA WILBEE

25

You guide me with your counsel.... —PSALM 73:24 (NIV)

My friend Jeanie's father died after a lengthy illness. Jeanie had always been close to her father, and I knew this would be a difficult time for her. I decided to send flowers to the memorial service, but as I reached for the phone to call the florist, I stopped. I had the distinct impression not to order flowers. "Lord," I prayed, "show me how I can comfort my friend."

The following day I passed an open-air produce market and my thoughts returned to Jeanie. *What is it, Lord? Should I send a basket of fruit?* I tried to dismiss the thought. It didn't seem appropriate. The idea, though, refused to go away.

The next day I returned to the produce market. As I walked through the aisles, the pungent fragrance of ripe peaches, sweet strawberries and tangy oranges filled my nostrils. I purchased a large wicker basket and filled it with fresh fruit for Jeanie. A fragrant breeze blew through the aisles, and I felt my spirit lift. I prayed that this gift of God's goodness would lift her spirit as well.

I received a note from Jeanie a few days later. "During my dad's last days he spoke of picking peaches. As I held his hands, I thought of our life together. Dad was a chef, and each week when I was growing up, a produce man would leave fresh fruit in a box on our porch— juicy oranges, sweet apples and fragrant peaches. Your gift of fresh fruit was more than a coincidence, it was a sign from my dad."

Thank You Lord, for Your gentle guidance.   —MELODY BONNETTE

26 *He shall not fail nor be discouraged....*

WEDNESDAY
—ISAIAH 42:4

Shortly before I graduated from college, I learned that my best friend and classmate wouldn't be graduating with me. Margaret had good grades in every subject except chemistry, and she had flunked her final exam. Science courses didn't come easily to her, but I knew how hard she had worked to master chemistry, and my heart ached for her when she gave me the bad news.

"Guess what?" she said, holding back her tears. "They said I can't get my degree, but I can go to the class dinner if I want to."

The class dinner was a fun event, the highlight of the senior year, and without thinking I said, "Then you're going?"

"Of course not!" Margaret said, and now she was crying. "What have I got to celebrate?" She turned and ran down the hall.

Without my friend to share in the celebration, I couldn't look forward to the class dinner. I wasn't even excited about graduating. I didn't see Margaret for several days, and when I called her she always made an excuse to avoid getting together.

I went to the class dinner determined to smile so I wouldn't spoil anyone else's good time. As I approached the gymnasium, I could hear the laughter from inside and it lifted my spirits a little. Then

I saw someone standing by the front door, waving to me. It was Margaret!

"I thought you'd never get here," she said, grinning and pulling me toward the door. When she saw the look on my face, she said, "I decided that I'm not going to let one course turn me into a failure. I don't think that's what God has in mind for me."

"What are you going to do?" I asked.

"I'll take the course again," she said. "As many times as I have to."

She meant what she said. She took chemistry twice before she passed, but finally she got her degree. Then she got a master's degree and went on to teach children with learning disabilities.

Margaret taught me a lot about persistence. It's not just our stubbornness that makes us keep trying. It's our faith that failure isn't what God has in mind for us.

When I run into obstacles, dear Lord, help me to look for ways around them. —PHYLLIS HOBE

27

And I will pray the Father, and he shall give you another Comforter, that he may abide with you forever.

—JOHN 14:16

I glanced at the clock on the bedside table. The bright orange numbers read 3:25 A.M. Slipping quietly from the bedroom so as not to disturb my husband Larry, I moved silently into the living room. My thoughts seemed almost as dark as the shadows I found there, and my hand moved automatically to the switch on the floor lamp. I was tired, but my mind wouldn't let me rest, and I lay down on the couch, mulling over the affairs of the day.

My son Jeff was in a struggle to pull his life back together following a recent divorce, and I keenly felt his pain and loneliness. My parents, who own a large turkey farm, seemed always to have too much work to do, and not enough time to do it. Neither had been well, and I was concerned about their health. I was also concerned for my poor mother-in-law, who had been in the grip of a serious depression that had affected her entire family. Tonight I couldn't help but wonder what the future held for these people I loved.

As those dark thoughts clamored in my mind they seemed to chill the very air around me. Glancing up behind me on the couch, I spotted the soft throw that is always folded there. *Pull the comforter over you,* I said to myself. But as I reached up to tug at the throw, I was suddenly struck by the phrase I had just used. Why, of course! What other possible answer could there be for any of life's problems than to pull the Comforter over me?

Snuggled inside the folds of the warm throw, I finally closed my eyes. I could rest now. I had been reminded that the affairs of the day, as well as the people I love, were also resting...safe in the arms of the Comforter.

Father, when I rest in You, my yoke is indeed easy, and my burdens are light. —LIBBIE ADAMS

28 FRIDAY

Each one had a harp and they were holding golden bowls full of incense, which are the prayers of the saints.
—REVELATION 5:8 (NIV)

Recently my cousin Mary Sue phoned to tell me, "Mother died last night."

I was devastated. Aunt Sue was no ordinary aunt. She was a woman of prayer who prayed for me—by name—every single night.

Years ago an elderly neighbor—"Old Brother Joe" everyone called him—had done the same for me. But Joe, too, had died. Then, two years ago, another blow: Mom's death. I still tell myself, *I'll ask Mom to pray with me about that,* before suddenly remembering I no longer can.

With both Old Brother Joe and Mom gone, only Aunt Sue was left to pray for me faithfully and daily. Now Mary Sue's call...I panicked. "What am I going to do?" I wailed over the phone, more concerned with my own plight than with hers.

Surprisingly, it was Mary Sue who comforted me instead of the other way around. "I believe prayers go on and on," she answered. "They never die."

At first I thought her words were too good to be true—until I remembered Revelation 5:8. Aunt Sue lived to be a hundred and three, Mom past ninety-seven, Joe into his late eighties. If all the prayers of those three are in golden bowls, think how many they must fill! I, too, must have started filling bowls years ago when I first began praying for my sons, my grandchildren, and my other relatives and friends. Yes, and even a great-grandchild now on the way.

Heavenly Father, how wonderful that prayers, old or new, are still at work. —ISABEL WOLSELEY

29

Behold, as the eyes of servants look to the hand of their master.... —PSALM 123:2 (RSV)

The retriever scrambled up onto the bank of the lake near our home in Chappaqua, New York, carrying a stick she had just brought back to shore. I watched as she dropped her prize at her owner's feet, shook water all over him and waited, tail wagging, as he praised her. "Good girl, Martha!"

"Want to see something interesting?" he said to me. He handed me a stick. "When I tell you, throw this into the lake, close to my dog."

Martha's master hurled his own stick far out into the lake. As before, the dog jumped in and began to swim. "Now!" said the owner to me. "Throw your stick just in front of her."

I did. The stick landed a few feet in front of Martha, to her right. She swam toward it and then, with the incredible sense of smell of retrievers, she discovered that this was not the stick her master had thrown. She corrected her course and continued straight for the assignment he had given her.

I hope for the same kind of faithfulness—never to be distracted, but to head only for the goal given to me by my Master.

Father, how often in the simplest scenes do You show me how You would like me to work with You. —JOHN SHERRILL

30

He forgave us all our sins, having canceled the written code, with its regulations...he took it away, nailing it to the cross. —COLOSSIANS 2:13-14 (NIV)

Not a Memorial Day goes by that I don't pause to remember Jim, a Vietnam veteran with post-traumatic stress disorder and depression. Jim served two tours of duty in Vietnam when he was in his late teens, but it was the memory of one particularly horrible night in Southeast Asia that refused to let his mind rest. His best buddy Frank was shot in the chest and bled to death in his arms, despite all Jim's efforts to save his life.

"I haven't been able to enjoy a single moment since then," Jim told me, his vacant eyes fixed on the gray linoleum floor. "What's there to celebrate? Christmas, Easter, my birthday...they're all just another day to me." Another day filled with intrusive thoughts, reliving

Frank's death in agonizing detail. Another night filled with the dreams of a soldier who blamed himself for his best friend's death.

But then a meeting with Frank's mother changed everything for Jim. "Frank's daddy and I loved him better than anything in the whole world," she told him. "But we knew he would want us to move on with our lives, not spend the rest of our days on might-have-beens. We've released him to the good Lord, Jim, and, oh, how he'd want you to do the same!"

That chance encounter set Jim on the road to a freedom he hadn't known since Vietnam. That day, Jim began to ask God to help him forgive himself for Frank's death. Eventually he was able to let go of the survivor guilt that had held him in bondage for nearly thirty years.

It was a great gift to be able to watch Jim begin to celebrate life again. And as I did, I said a prayer of thanksgiving for Jim and Frank to the One Whose victory makes us truly free.

Thank You, Lord, for the lessons in freedom our brave ones have taught us. —ROBERTA MESSNER

31 *He that is faithful in that which is least is faithful also in much....* —LUKE 16:10

I scanned the sordid headlines as I waited in the grocery checkout line. Scandal. Corruption. Deceit in high places. *Aren't there any honest people left in this world?* I wondered glumly. At least I felt secure shopping at Mr. D's, my favorite market, where the clerks gave me smiles and the bakery attendants gave my children free cookies.

The cashier with the crew cut shook his head and grinned the way he had the week I had left my checkbook at home, twice. "Okay, Allen. What's up?" I teased.

I was the last in line, so he paused. "This is incredible. Do you see that white-haired man just going out?" I saw the slightly stooped gentleman in a cardigan who had been ahead of me in line, slowly weaving through the Memorial Day crowd. I nodded.

"Well, he told me he had come all the way down from Buffalo to decorate his wife's grave. That alone is amazing—it's two hundred and fifty miles. Anyway, he had come in here to buy a floral arrangement, but he never found what he wanted. He picked up a cookie in the bakery, then absentmindedly left the store to shop somewhere else. Only after he had found his flowers and gone to the cemetery did he remember the cookie. He came all the way back here to pay me thirty-five cents! That guy made my day!"

As Alan sacked my order, I gazed at the elderly widower who had finally shuffled through the glass doors. I probably won't read "EXTRA! EXTRA! Man Pays for Cookie" in the newspaper, but I know he's out there somewhere—and so are thousands more just like him.

Lord, help me to take the time to be scrupulously honest in all my dealings with my fellow human beings. Amen.

—*GAIL THORELL SCHILLING*

MY FAITH JOURNEY

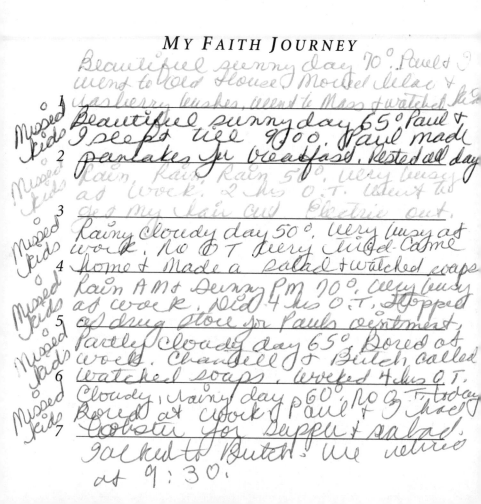

8 — Missed kids. Beautiful sunny partly cloudy day 70°. Paul & I cleaned. We went to 5:00 Mass & Freehold Mall & dinner.

9 — Beautiful sunny day 70°. Wonderful Mother's Day. Brunch as country club w/ kids & supper at Butch & Jan's.

10 — Missed kids. Beautiful sunny day. Very busy at work. Did 3 hrs. O.T. Kelsey in May crowning. Chantell didn't tell me.

11 — Beautiful sunny day 73°. Left work at 12:00 & had spaghetti w/ Paul. Picked up kids & went for haircuts. Visited Terry.

12 — Missed kids. Beautiful sunny day 75°. Took A/L day & Paul & I went to the shore. We had one of the most wonderful times ever.

13 — Missed kids. Cloudy rainy day 50°. Very busy at work. Couldn't see my desk from being out yesterday. 2 hrs O.T.

14 — Missed kids. Beautiful sunny day 60°. Very busy at work. Did 4 hrs O.T. Came home ate, showered & went to bed.

15 — Missed kids. Beautiful sunny day 70°. Paul & I went to Angies & got a remote control fan. The Peterson wedding.

16 — Missed kids. Beautiful sunny day 70°. Paul & I went to shop Rites & Caldor. We came home & read papers & washed.

17 — Missed kids. Beautiful sunny day 70°. Very busy at work. Came home showered, watched programs & relaxed.

18 — Missed kids. Partly cloudy day 60°. Very busy at work. Rain P.M. Paul took Butch to go his motorcycle & never told me!

19 — Missed kids. Rain, Rain, Rain 63°. Bored at work. Only worked 2 hrs O.T. Computer down & of course BB had me work for her. Showered & watched soaps. Retired at 8:00.

MAY 1999

20 Missed kids — Beautiful sunny day 70°. Bored as work. Worked 4 hrs O.T. Paul & I went to Cherry Hill 2 days to get fans & K-Mart for shoes

21 Missed kids — Beautiful sunny day 80°. Paul & I went to Cape May Point. We had lousy dinner. Got home 6:30

22 Missed kids — Beautiful sunny day 80°. Paul & I went to St. Pat open House & spent $140.00 & Paul finally saw my office

23 Rain, Rain, Rain 76°. Paul & I got papers at Wawa & coffee & breakfast. Chantel & Bob's kids & Butch & Jan were here

24 Missed kids — Rain, Rain, Rain 60°. very busy at work. Worked 5-12 & came home took a nap & Paul & I went to old house

25 Missed kids — Beautiful sunny day 70°. Bored at work. Worked 5:90-12:00. went to get trundle bed & Sam's

26 Missed kids — Beautiful sunny day 100°. Worked 5:00-12:00. Paul called me at work. Old House demolished at 4:00.

27 Missed kids — Beautiful sunny day 70°. Paul & I watched items from old house put on truck. went to Country Club of Julian

28 Beautiful sunny day 70°. Paul & I went to get my radius at 8:00 A.M. & Then to Ballup school play.

29 Missed kids — Beautiful sunny day 80°. Steve took me to Rancocas Indian Festival in Mt. Holly. 5:00 Mass & Pizza

30 Missed kids — Beautiful sunny day 90°. Gary came over w/ this little girl. Justin, Aunt Ruth stopped & Butch & Jan

31 Missed kids — Beautiful sunny day 90°. Paul & I did some cleaning up. We watched soaps. I made veg. bee soup. called Butch & Jan. went for papers. showered & retired at 8:00.

June

*Even though I walk through the valley
of the shadow of death, I fear
no evil; for thou art with me....*
—PSALM 23:4 (RSV)

S	M	T	W	T	F	S
		1	2	3	4	5
6	7	8	9	10	11	12
13	14	15	16	17	18	19
20	21	22	23	24	25	26
27	28	29	30			

LESSONS IN LISTENING

1

HOLDING BACK
Trust in the Lord with all thine heart; and lean not unto thine own understanding. —PROVERBS 3:5

Suppose I've remembered to ask God for guidance, learned to recognize those persuasive voices that are not His, been quiet and listened—and still I hear nothing at all? That's when I wonder if I've put my fingers in my ears by placing some area of my life off-limits. *Thy will be done—but please, dear God, don't ask me to...* Give up chocolate. Work at the rummage sale. Live in the inner city. In other words, God doesn't know what will give me joy. Only *I* do.

As a young girl in England, Pam Rosewell asked God to use her as He would—with three reservations. *I don't want to leave home. And you know I could never speak in public. And above all, please don't ask me to remain single!* With these safeguards in place, Pam did find ways to serve God, but never, she told me, with absolute certainty that she was doing what He intended.

It was only when she removed all restrictions from her prayers that God's guidance grew crystal clear. When I met Pam, all three of her fears had come to pass. As Corrie ten Boom's companion, she was traveling with the Dutch evangelist all over the world, speaking at Corrie's side before throngs of people, her footloose ministry ruling out any chance of marriage. I had never met a more fulfilled and joyful person.

Why don't I hear God when I put a DON'T TOUCH label on some part of my life? I think it's a fundamental fact about the process of hearing: I can't cover my ears to block out one sound without shutting out all.

And my friend Pam? She ministered with Corrie until the older woman's death in 1983. And afterward, the husband God had for her, the one she never would have met back in England, was waiting for her in Texas, where Carey and Pam Moore make their home today.

What parts of my life, Father, am I holding back from You? Give me today such trust in You that I know my true joy is waiting in the center of Your will. —ELIZABETH SHERRILL

2

The voice of the Lord is upon the waters.... —PSALM 29:3

After a day of backbreaking, fruitless work on our ailing car, I was sore, tired and despairing. I settled into a bathtub full of hot water and stayed there until my sanity returned, an hour later.

It was so healing that it set me to thinking about other times when I have been helped by water. Perhaps one of them will work for you.

- *Tears:* I spent six hundred dollars trying to save an important tooth, then the dentist gave up: "I can't save it, after all." I shuffled outside, sat down and mourned another loss of middle age. These losses are real; they must be mourned or they will fester.
- *Sweat:* Faculty meetings tie me in knots. When I get home from work, only one thing will untie the tangles: hard physical labor. Cleaning the garage, pruning trees or a hard ride on my bike— it doesn't matter. The sweat is like a healing ointment, and I wonder if many of the woes of this sedentary society could not be better treated by sweat than by drugs.
- *Waves:* Oceans are a long way away from us here in the Midwest, but our nearby Sugar Creek Lake is a bewitching place to visit in the early morning mists. Sometimes I go there to pray. The cool mists and gentle waves are like heavenly caresses.
- *Drink:* The fast-food restaurant offered many choices: soft drinks; tea and coffee; punch and lemonade. All nice, but expensive and full of sugar and caffeine. My father's words came to mind: "When you are really thirsty, nothing beats water." More and more I choose it.
- *Rain:* When storms roll in, I stop what I'm doing and plunge out into the downpour with my red umbrella. Sometimes I take off my shoes and wade through puddles with the neighbor children.

- *Baptism:* I was just a boy when my own father baptized me in a creek near Versailles, Indiana. Getting right with God was the perfect start for life.

Lord, You covered the earth with water. Teach me to use it wisely.
—*DANIEL SCHANTZ*

3

Observe these things without preferring one before another, doing nothing by partiality. —*I TIMOTHY 5:21*

I was sitting in my office with a colleague, when Mr. Gaines appeared at my door. "Hello, Brock, do you have just a minute?"

"Sure, Mr. Gaines, come on in." Mr. Gaines had a question about a very small investment he was considering. Then he was gone.

My older, wiser, richer colleague reared back in his chair and laughed. "Brock, there's no way you'll get ahead in this business unless you save your time for important clients. You've got to learn to seek out the people who really matter if you want to be a success in the real world."

As a financial consultant, I am paid by commission and my time is valuable. Maybe my colleague was right. If I didn't concentrate on clients who make significant investments, I'd never make it to the top.

The next week I had the opportunity to call on the chief financial officer of an influential Nashville company. "Mr. Jackson, I would like the opportunity to present a financial plan for you," I said on the phone. "If I could just have an hour of your time—"

"Brock, do you know how many brokers call me each week?"

"Mr. Jackson, if you would just meet me for lunch at Fauntleroys at noon next Thursday."

"Well, that is near my office. Okay. But remember, I'm on a tight schedule."

The restaurant was tough to get into, so I breathed a sigh of relief when our reservation was made. On the appointed day, I confidently walked up to the front desk. "Reservation for two under Kidd."

"I'm sorry, sir," said the hostess as she ran her finger down two pages of names. "We don't have your name down, and there is an hour wait for walk-ins."

I panicked and staggered outside to get some air. Just then I saw a long black car pull up. It was Mr. Jackson. "Hello, Brock. Is our table ready?"

"Mr. Jackson, our reser—" Suddenly, the restaurant door swung open behind me.

"Mr. Kidd, it's wonderful to see you again. Come in, please." It was none other than Mr. Gaines—the maitre d' at Fauntleroys. He winked and continued. "We have a special table for you and your guest." I felt like hugging him right there.

That day, my career took a turn for the better. Not only because Mr. Jackson became a client, but because I learned again what I had first learned as a small boy in Sunday school: In the real world, every man, woman and child matters.

Dear God, help me to remember what's really important in this life.
—BROCK KIDD

4

Return unto thy rest, O my soul; for the Lord hath dealt bountifully with thee. —PSALM 116:7

For more than fourteen years, the first two weeks of June have been set solidly on our calendar. This is when time stands still for John and me. We escape from clocks and schedules and take a refreshing, restorative vacation in an old cabin high in the mountains of Southern California.

Breakfast is anytime. Four A.M., if we're awake. Sometimes we go out and eat it under the stars, no longer having to fight the night because of an early-morning appointment, but free to embrace the darkness and listen to the plaintive hooting of an owl or the rustle of some small creature in the underbrush. We watch the first soft light of day whisper through the pines and bring the stream alive, then we hold hands and say small prayers of gladness. When we're drowsy, it's back to bed to snooze through lunch, or sleep till who-cares-when.

I have sat wrapped snug in a much-worn comforter, my hands warmed around a cup of steaming coffee, while snow (yes, snow in June!) piled around about me and put crowns of white on sumac leaves and the fragile shoots of an unfurling fern. "You'll catch your death of cold," my husband warns.

"Worth it!" I reply.

I have packed him a snack and watched him trudge, alone with his thoughts, down a rough dirt road. "Take it slow and easy in this altitude," I caution.

"Pshaw!" he mutters.

This is our rest, our hearts' ease, our oasis for the soul.

> *For getaway places, and times set apart,*
> *for the healing of nature on my tired-out heart,*
> *I give You blessed thanks, dear Lord.*

—FAY ANGUS

5 SATURDAY
Love does not demand its own way....
—I CORINTHIANS 13:5 (TLB)

For thirty-five years my husband Don wanted to take a raft trip down the Colorado River. For thirty-four of those years I came up with excellent excuses: the children were too young; I was starting college; I was too busy at work; it was too expensive. The real reason was that it didn't sound like fun. Sleeping on the ground, bathing in the river and drying my clothes on rocks was *not* my idea of a good time.

Then last year Don made nonrefundable trip reservations for four (he persuaded my sister Amanda and her husband Tim to go along)—without consulting me. It was a rotten, low-down, underhanded, sneaky, selfish thing to do. I let Don (and everyone else) know it at every opportunity.

Two days before we were scheduled to leave, my daughter Rebecca stopped by my office. "Don't spoil this trip for Dad," she ordered.

"What about me?" I shot back. "This is his dream, not mine."

"Mom, you're an important part of his dream," she said softly. "So promise."

I promised. And keeping that promise wasn't as difficult as I'd thought, because the trip was (I still don't like to admit it) fun! I loved rafting down the rapids, and sleeping on the ground gave us a panoramic view of the night sky. We hiked to the ruins of an ancient Anasazi village, saw petrographs (pictures carved into the rock) and swam in the crystal falls of Havasu Creek. And for the first time in years, my sister and I had uninterrupted time to visit.

Don and I will never have exactly the same tastes in vacations, or even the same ideas about our life together. Sometimes, though, God's richest blessings come through our willingness to be an active part of someone else's dream. I hope I remember and act on that knowledge during the next thirty-five years of married life.

Thank You, Lord, for the special blessing of marriage.
—PENNEY SCHWAB

6 ── SUNDAY
Tell your sons about it, And let your sons tell their sons, And their sons the next generation. —JOEL 1:3 (NAS)

During my devotional time yesterday morning, I remembered the first time I truly enjoyed reading the Bible. I was ten years old and attending Brent School, an Episcopal boarding school, while my parents were missionaries in the Philippines. Bible was not my favorite class. Twice a week my classmates and I would be herded to the chapel, where Father Leroy Cox faced the daunting task of filling us with biblical knowledge.

One day I was sitting in class, bored silly as usual, when Father Cox began to talk about the apostle Peter: how he had betrayed Jesus, repented in tears and later died for his faith. I was mesmerized. For the first time the Bible came alive for me. It was a pivotal moment that led to a lifetime of Bible study.

As I reflected on this memory, I began to wonder what had become of Father Cox. On impulse, I telephoned the national headquarters of the Episcopal Church and learned that he was living in retirement in Oregon. I decided to call him and tell him how he had shaped my life.

It had been thirty-five years since we had last seen one another, and I was sure he wouldn't remember me. But he did. It took him a moment, but he finally said, "Yeah, you were the kid with the red hair. Always pretty lively, I remember."

Helping someone to love and study the Bible is the gift of a lifetime. It's a wonderful way to provide direction—and healing—in the life of someone you love.

Father, thank You for all those who have taught me to read Your Word. —SCOTT WALKER

7

"By faith in the name of Jesus, this man whom you see and know was made strong...." —ACTS 3:16 (NIV)

In the mornings I always make time to marinate in the whirlpool at my health club for a few minutes before showering and heading to the office. It's my reward for dragging myself out of bed and doing my workout. I'm there more mornings than not. Today an older woman I often see at the gym smiled and said, "I admire your discipline!"

Initially, I wanted to deflect her compliment and say something like, "Oh, I wish I could get here *every* day," as if what I do isn't enough. But then I thought, *No, my exercise regimen is part of one of the biggest changes in my life, and I should be proud.*

When I was younger I treated my body like a rental car—that is, I didn't feel very responsible toward it. I smoked and drank heavily and slept little and lived fast. It wasn't a lifestyle conducive to long-term physical health, as several doctors pointed out to me. "Everyone who needs to stop drinking does, sooner or later," one said. "It's just nice still to be alive when you do."

I can attest to that. But knowing my lifestyle was taking a terminal toll on my body wasn't enough to get me to stop. I finally admitted defeat and acknowledged that only a power greater than myself, God, could restore me to mental, spiritual and physical health. Only when I realized that my soul was connected to my physical being was I able to begin taking care of myself. Eventually I started an exercise program, which I have stuck to for years now. But discipline? Discipline had little to do with it. If all it took was discipline, I could have shaped up my life without God.

No wonder, then, that I hesitated to accept the woman's compliment. Still, I thought, there's nothing wrong with giving myself a *little* credit. After all, I already do, almost every morning, by treating myself to the whirlpool. Giving myself a pat on the back, I've found, takes a bit of discipline, too.

God, You give us bodies as well as souls so that we may serve you better. I'm glad You helped me learn to take care of mine.

—EDWARD GRINNAN

8

It is fine to be zealous...and to be so always and not just when I am with you. —GALATIANS 4:18 (NIV)

I was quite disappointed that "First-Grade Field Day" wasn't rained out, because there were a thousand and one places I would have rather been that morning than doing my parental duty of helping out. I had a two-day business trip coming up the next day, a dinner party on Friday night and only one more week of freedom before the kids were underfoot for the summer.

I was assigned the obstacle course. My main job was to watch a coiled fabric play tunnel through which the children had to crawl before jumping over a low bar. Most of them dove into the tunnel with such force that the whole thing nearly slid off the mat and into the mud, and I had to straighten the tunnel after every assault. I certainly didn't think that this was a worthwhile pursuit, and I counted the minutes until it would all be over. Unfortunately, I soon found out that there were worse jobs than tunnel keeper when the volunteer from the starting line suggested we trade places. Not only was it impossible to keep the children behind the starting line until tagged by their teammates, but their excited yells were above the ear-shattering level.

Finally, the last class was finished. I rushed into the gymnasium to put away the tunnel, intent on not wasting another moment of my precious time. As I sprinted toward the exit, I noticed a huge computer banner taped up over the doorway: IF YOU HAD FUN, YOU WON. I halted and read the words again. Although the teacher who made the banner was probably trying to keep the students from letting competition ruin their experience, a larger life message came through loud and clear. *Karen, you didn't run on the obstacle course today, but you still lost out at "First-Grade Field Day." You could have found something to enjoy about it. Isn't it time that you do something about your long history of doing the right thing with the wrong attitude?*

When I got home, I had to make the brownies for the Cub Scout picnic. *Oh, no, another kids' picnic,* I started to think. But then a little rhyme skipped through my mind. *If you had fun, you won.* I leaned over and smelled the chocolate. It smelled heavenly.

Father, today let my heart and body become the best of traveling companions, ending up in the same place at the same time.

—KAREN BARBER

9

In your thinking be adults. —*1 CORINTHIANS 14:20 (NIV)*

When I graduated from college, a bank was giving out a "free" Polaroid camera if you applied for your first credit card. Sure that this would make me a grown-up, I eagerly autographed the credit application. A year later, I was buried in impulse buys and late charges.

I called the credit card company to say that I would be late—yet again—and for some reason, I mentioned that I thought having a credit card would make me feel like a grown-up. The motherly sounding woman on the other end of the phone must have heard the anguish in my voice, for she said kindly, "Hon, it's not *getting* bills that makes you a grown-up—it's *paying* them!"

I laughed, but I also stuck my credit card in the bottom of my sock drawer, not to be used until I was really an adult. I cut back on my shopping, made regular payments and felt much better when I saw my balance going down each month.

But even though I've been real grown-up for a long time now, sometimes I still see a pair of shoes that makes me want to blow my budget.

God, today, help me to make the responsible decision in all my daily affairs. Help me to be a grown-up! —LINDA NEUKRUG

10

O Lord, open thou my lips; and my mouth shall show forth thy praise. —*PSALM 51:15*

After Duffy, our border collie, died at age fifteen, Shirley and I went without a dog for better than a year. Then we began looking for something in the terrier category. Heidi, a German schnauzer, had been one of our favorites, and we thought something like her would be nice. Maybe a mutt from a dog shelter. But nothing turned up.

Then we heard about a four-year-old Welsh terrier, a downsized Airedale that was available for adoption, and it was love at first sight. Teddy, as we renamed him (ungroomed, he looked like a teddy bear), was perfect. Well, as perfect as dogs get. He had some habits that we didn't care for (like jumping on sofas and beds), and we set out to determine if we could teach an old dog new tricks.

That's when I got out a rag-eared copy of Barbara Woodhouse's classic *No Bad Dogs*. Her philosophy is that with clear commands, patience, persistence and lots of praise any dog can be taught to mind. And amazingly, in a few weeks, Teddy had learned that chairs and beds are for people, and though he has moments of amnesia, he remembers most of the time.

Too bad I didn't have Mrs. Woodhouse's book when I was raising four children. The principles are the same: make sure your wishes are stated simply and clearly; be patient but persistent in seeing that orders are carried out; and praise to the high heavens when the subject gets it right. That's the most important part.

In retrospect, if I had it to do over, I'd praise my kids more and faultfind less. Any relationship, including our relationship with God, could do with a little less complaining and a lot more praising.

When I bristle with cold words deflating,
Lord, help me find warm ones more elevating.

—FRED BAUER

11 FRIDAY
Stand fast, and hold the traditions which ye have been taught.... —II THESSALONIANS 2:15

On June 14, 1997, our grandson Jeremy graduated from high school in Londonderry, New Hampshire. Ruby and I attended this special event, and as I watched Jeremy cross the open-air stage to receive his diploma, my mind raced backward to my own graduation from high school some sixty years before.

Like Jeremy, I was the only African American in my class. But my class numbered thirty-two, while Jeremy's totaled 392. Our graduation was held indoors at seven in the evening. As our class walked onto the stage in the school gym, a violent thunderstorm swept in from the west. Lightning flashed and knifed through the sky, and the breaking thunder echoed through the auditorium. The storm felt like an omen. We were in the grip of the Great Depression; within four years, the clouds of conflict would gather, and we would be fighting the Second World War. Our families would know separation and heartache, the joys of reunion and the sorrows of loss. That great conflagration would be followed by a long cold war, the threat of nuclear destruction and two costly "hot" wars in faraway places. But our future also held triumphs: computers and transistors, space satellites and moon walks, a resolve to heal our divisions.

My thoughts returned to the warm afternoon and to Jeremy, receiving his diploma in the bright sunshine. Our Lord had seen me through it all, and He would take care of Jeremy, too. In my heart was sixty years of proof.

Lord Jesus, thank You for the love that has seen me through the years.　—OSCAR GREENE

12

SATURDAY

O magnify the Lord with me, and let us exalt his name together. —PSALM 34:3

I saw a flurry of activity in an open grassy field in the valley a couple of miles from our house early one bright Saturday morning. Panel trucks appeared, and people scurried about, and finally a huge, white tent started to take shape. Curiosity got the better of me, so I set up our telescope and zoomed in on the field. I saw pots of flowers arrive. Rolls of white carpet. Tables and white tablecloths. Catering trucks. And finally guests, including the guest of honor, wearing a long white dress.

The telescope made the difference. Without it, I would have known something was going on out there in that field, but that's about it. With it, I magnified the scene and focused on the details, which helped me experience the event in a personal way. As I put away the telescope, I wondered if that is what Mary meant when she said, "My soul magnifies the Lord." Her soul became like a telescope, focused intently on God, which magnified His magnificence and the details of His character. As her soul magnified Him, she experienced His closeness in a new and personal way.

How could my soul *magnify* the Lord?

Maybe I could use my eyes and mind and heart like a telescope, to zoom in on the details of just one passage of Scripture. Maybe I could study just one facet of God's character, like His faithfulness, and see how it is consistently demonstrated in a single book of the Bible. Or maybe I could sit quietly and ponder the ways He showed His faithfulness to me in the last week.

Like Mary, I can *magnify* the Lord by focusing on Him.

Jesus, as I seek to magnify You, I pray that Your presence and truth will grow larger and more real in my heart. —CAROL KUYKENDALL

13

With all lowliness and meekness, with longsuffering, forbearing one another in love. —*EPHESIANS 4:2*

"I don't think I've ever told you about a team of horses my papa had when I was a child," my mother wrote a few years ago. Mom was born in 1898. She was talking about a *long* time ago. Her neat, cursive writing continued.

"Blind Billie was one of many horses Papa kept on our farm. I never knew how he came to be blind, I merely accepted him that way. Billie's teammate was named Daisy.

"When the horses came in from the fields each evening, they rushed to the water tank. Billie always got crowded back until the others had their fill. But Daisy faithfully stood by, waiting until he could drink, then follow her into the barn."

This sounds a lot like what's happening in our home. My husband's eyes are failing. Lately I've noticed Roland has been unsure of his footing. And he often says, "Go ahead, I'm right behind you," when we're in crowds. I kept reading Mom's account.

"Once in awhile Billie loitered too long in the corral and Daisy went through the gate without him. When he was left alone, Billie showed his fear. He tossed his head, reared up and whinnied."

So that's why Roland makes a fuss about my leaving the house without him...he's afraid.

Mom's story continued, "When Daisy saw Billie could not find the gate, she slowly and patiently went back to the corral, walked near him, and he happily followed her again."

Daisy had what I need more of. Patience.

Mom didn't out-and-out say so, but I sensed her reason for writing me was to tell me more than just a story about a team of horses. Especially when her horse story concluded, "I learned more about love and loyalty from Blind Billie and Daisy than any other way in all my long life."

You never said our lives would be carefree, Father, and coping with new circumstances is frightening. Yet You promise always to light the way. —*ISABEL WOLSELEY*

TRIAL BY FIRE

In June 1997, south-central Alaska was ravaged by the Miller's Reach Fire. "Is Carol Knapp all right?" Daily Guideposts readers who knew Carol lived in the area asked us. "How did she get through the fire?" This week, Carol will take us with her to that time of testing, fear and sorrow—and of renewed faith in the mercy of God. —THE EDITORS

14

MONDAY

DAY 1

So I find it to be a law that when I want to do right, evil lies close at hand. —ROMANS 7:21 (RSV)

It was a beautiful June evening, the sky still bright with Alaska's summer insomnia. Riding down the highway toward Big Lake about 8:00 P.M., my husband Terry and I noticed a narrow column of smoke cutting cleanly above the trees. We hadn't gone far along Miller's Reach Road when a man approached us on a four-wheeler, warning that flames were blowing in our direction. A sixty-acre blaze thought to be under control the night before, fanned by capricious winds, had kicked to life again. On the ten-mile jaunt home, Big Lake's volunteer fire department raced past us, sirens screaming.

An hour later I was stunned to see huge mushrooming clouds of creamy smoke rearing against the vivid sky. "What is happening?" I asked anxiously. Terry and I drove in search of answers. We encountered a roadblock near the high school, seven miles away. Firefighters were frantically soaking its cedar-shake roof, preparing to defend the multimillion-dollar structure from one-hundred-fifty-foot flames that were marching inexorably toward Big Lake.

Several thousand families were scattered for miles across this large, heavily wooded recreational area located in south-central Alaska. Now, suddenly, it appeared as if the stands of spruce and birch trees—our highly prized neighbors—had unwittingly become the enemy. We rode home to watch and wait—and hose down our roof.

The Miller's Reach Fire, as it came to be known, was left to smolder unattended and grew to monstrous proportions. I've watched this same thing happen in my own life. A flare of resentment...a flash of ego...a flicker of temptation...careless fires that I fail to douse completely and eventually rage out of control.

Lord, quench the embers of selfishness that smolder in my heart.

—CAROL KNAPP

15

DAY 2

TUESDAY

Blessed is he whom thou dost choose and bring near....We shall be satisfied with the goodness of thy house....

—PSALM 65:4 (RSV)

Smoke filled the air, smudging the last bit of color from the sky like a dirty eraser. By 11:00 P.M., the fire had jumped Big Lake Road three miles away, heading ominously in our direction. Offers of horse trailers and pickup trucks jammed the airwaves as people raced to assist dog mushers and others in getting their animals out. Sixty scorched acres had become fifteen hundred.

Soon the muffled drone of a bullhorn drifted through the trees. Alaska State Troopers were ordering us to evacuate. I slipped into our bedroom alone, knowing exactly what I would take. I had learned a tough lesson from the recent tragedy of our relatives Jim and Lynndeen Knapp. A freak winter electrical fire had destroyed their lovely home. All the records of their past had been obliterated. They began to compile a heart-wrenching oral history, trying to remember where they had been and what they had done. Now ready to rebuild, they had nothing familiar with which to adorn their new home.

As I reached for my Bible—the one I had read and underlined for twenty-five years—I understood I was being asked to give up my home and all it represented. At the same moment, Jesus was there. I heard the echo of His imperishable promise, "In my Father's house are many rooms" (John 14:2, RSV).

My house was very likely about to burn up, but the fire's paralyzing power to destroy had diminished. Whatever else I might take with me this night, I already had what I needed most.

Jesus, You are the same "yesterday and today and forever." Be my past, my present and my future.

—CAROL KNAPP

16

DAY 3

And Jesus said to them, "...Have you never read, 'Out of the mouths of babes and sucklings thou hast brought perfect praise'?"

—MATTHEW 21:16 (RSV)

Shortly after midnight we pulled out of our dirt drive, towing our small travel trailer. We had decided to wait out the fire at the alpaca farm of our friends Janet and Jim, another ten miles south on Stefan Lake. But unrelenting sun, low humidity and howling winds transformed fifteen hundred ravaged acres into ten thousand within twenty-four hours. Tanker planes had difficulty accurately releasing their red-dyed fire retardant. Firefighters fought madly with chain saws, axes, shovels and hoses. Helicopters, continually refilling their bright orange buckets from local lakes and ponds, dumped thousands of gallons of water from the air.

Nothing slowed the burning frenzy. It appeared to be wrapping around our friends' farm. By late afternoon we began furiously loading alpacas, even fitting pregnant mothers and newborns into the back of a sport utility vehicle.

While Terry and Jim hosed down the farm buildings one last time, Janet and I—and the children—gathered in a circle in her kitchen to pray. Holding hands, we spoke from our hearts as never before. Andy, just eight, squeezed his eyes shut and uttered his plea with a child's faith, "Stick by us, Lord, like You always stick by us."

It was hot and dusty as we took the last open route out of Big Lake. Driving through heavy smoke we arrived in the neighboring town of Wasilla, fifteen miles east, where we stayed in the homes of fellow church members. The situation looked grim; aerial views on television showed the whole area in flames.

Still, I slept soundly that night with a little boy's perfect praise playing through my head.

Sometimes it takes a child, Lord, to help us see Your goodness.

—CAROL KNAPP

17

DAY 4

Three things are never satisfied; four never say, "Enough": Sheol, the barren womb, the earth ever thirsty for water, and the fire.... —PROVERBS 30:15-16 (RSV)

Houses were going down hourly. Gigantic smoke plumes ascended fifteen thousand feet. This day the fire tripled in size, devouring thirty thousand acres. Would it never end?

When the telephone rang, we were eating a late breakfast. It was our friend Sharon calling from her cellular phone. She had entered Big Lake through an Army National Guard "backdoor" checkpoint. Our house was still standing. Terry slumped over his plate, tears of relief pouring from his eyes. Words failed us. We had been spared.

That afternoon, shortly before the checkpoint closed again, we edged past it into our subdivision. Big Lake still sizzled. An Alaska native firefighting crew was attacking hot spots. One home had been lost—a retired couple's, where our daughter had delivered pizzas. Flames had crept right up to another place. Out of our dining room window I saw smoke curling through the trees.

The main thrust of the fire had missed us by about a hundred yards, but I was still worried. *Maybe our house isn't out of danger. Perhaps I'd better rescue more keepsakes. My recipe box—how stupid to have forgotten that!* Terry patiently carted things to the car. Finally he said, "Enough."

At the base of our hill, we paused to thank the firefighters. We learned that the fire had roared past the night we evacuated, then spun back around in the freakish winds late the next afternoon, as if to clean its plate.

That's when it narrowly missed us—when we had sought refuge in prayer in a farm kitchen. I looked over my shoulder at the extra stuff I had emptied from our house—just in case—and I had the grace to feel ashamed.

Had I wanted to second-guess my Provider?

Jesus, when I bring my doubts to You, You give me renewed faith in return. —CAROL KNAPP

18

DAY 5

Thou hast kept count of my tossings; put thou my tears in thy bottle!... —PSALM 56:8 (RSV)

They let us go home permanently on the fifth day. Our salvation came in the clouds that moved over Big Lake, raising the humidity and aiding the heroic efforts of twelve hundred stubborn firefighters. After zigzagging destruction across fifty-seven square miles, shutting down an eleven-mile stretch of strategic highway and twice menacing Alaska Railroad passenger trains, the Miller's Reach Fire was over. Its southern flank had come within a quarter-mile of Janet and Jim's alpaca farm.

Returning home, we drove down road after road searching out our friends, afraid to look. The flames had played a hideous game of hide-and-seek.

Edie, a single mother, stood in the ruin of her little basement home clutching a ceramic plaque that had somehow survived. I stepped closer to read it and then wished I hadn't. It said, BLESS This HOUSE. Gordie and Simone—I'd been at their wedding—lost all their new things. Pauline's husband hadn't been buried a week, and now her place was gone. "Well, I don't have to pack," she said. Ken Hughes, a missionary bush pilot, had watched his uninsured hangar and shop go up in smoke. We were grief-stricken for everyone—three hundred and fifty families in all—who came home to rubble.

There were happy endings, too. Lou and Elsa, immigrants from the Czech Republic, ran from the woods, coated in grime, shouting, "Come and see!" There stood their house, everything around it black. Four times burning trees collapsed on seventy-eight-year-old Vivian's roof, and four times someone pulled them off. Euphoria engulfed us whenever a house we thought for sure must be gone turned out to be there.

Along the highway a local restaurant—hoping for rain—displayed a sign, LORD SHED A TEAR FOR US. I read the message differently. Jesus, when He walked the earth, wept. I believe He still weeps for our pain. Why? Because I felt His tears for Big Lake, though not a single raindrop fell.

Suffering Savior, You share in every tear we shed. —CAROL KNAPP

19 SATURDAY

DAY 6
The Spirit of the Lord God is upon me, because the Lord has anointed me...to give them a garland instead of ashes.... —ISAIAH 61:1, 3 (RSV)

Before the wildfire, I had a favorite country road—Hollywood—where I always walked. Privately, I called it my "Emmaus Road" because, like the two travelers en route to Emmaus, whom the risen Christ had joined, I often felt my "heart burn within me as Jesus talked with me by the way and opened to me the scriptures" (Luke 24:32, RSV). Now I summoned the courage to retrace my fond country meanderings.

Groves of stark, black skeletons stood where there should have been trees. In other spots, withered brown leaves drooped from scorched limbs. Truck beds crammed with charred debris rolled by, as people trekked to the landfill. Even the spring sweetness was sucked from the air, so that I tried to not take a deep breath. I almost turned around, except that I heard dogs barking up ahead at the Humane Society.

The fire had leveled the place, but already they'd moved the animals back into outdoor pens. Their yowling was so welcome, it sounded like a canine choir! Farther along, I discovered a glimmer of purple—a single wild iris, growing on a lone tuft of grass in the singed marsh. Then, across a burned meadow, I spotted a sandhill crane, standing shyly on its long thin legs. Hope surged with each fresh glimpse of life, bringing a new jauntiness to my step. A car passed. The driver waved, glad to see me back on the road. Suddenly, I realized that for the people who regularly traveled Hollywood Road, I was also a sign of returning life.

The fire had not destroyed everything. Hope was alive in the dogs awaiting adoption, the fragile iris blooming, the solitary crane and even myself out walking. Jesus, in His compassion making all things new, would see to the greening of the land. As for the rest, by stepping forward in vigor and faith, we could each have a place in making Big Lake beautiful again.

I turned toward home, keenly aware of a familiar sensation. My heart burned within me once more.

Who but You, Risen Lord, can give me new life? —CAROL KNAPP

20

For the Lord is good; his mercy is everlasting; and his truth endureth to all generations.   —PSALM 100:5

A welcome cold front blew in for Father's Day, and the air was sparkling, dry and clear. The last games of the boys' baseball season were in the morning after church. I packed a bag with gloves, water bottles, pretzels and part of the Sunday paper, just in case. Also a bottle of sunscreen. Will had a poison ivy blister on the bottom of his foot and was bench-bound for his game, but Timothy was raring to go; he had slept in his uniform to be ready. I pitched Timo's game (at his age level, parents pitch) and found myself mumbling a prayer as each kid came up, "Jesus Christ, have mercy upon me. Have mercy upon the parents who want their child to do well."

Neta hit a single, Marla batted one runner in, Jeremiah hit a grounder and, most miraculously, Sam actually made it to first base. For the first time ever in any of these games, the catcher caught a pop fly, looking stunned at the ball in his glove. I marveled that the kids had learned so much about baseball in two months. Afterward, the teams gathered in the outfield for their season-end trophies, glittering chunks of plastic that were pure gold for the proud players. Everyone got an award—in our league everyone wins—and for the closing everyone sang, "Take Me Out to the Ball Game," as stirring as a hymn.

In the afternoon I vacuumed the house, went for a jog, finally read the paper (the children curiously silent until I realized this quiet time was part of their gift), and then we packed a supper for a picnic. Outside, the sun, nearing the solstice, refused to set and it was past bedtime when we came in, but still time to read one more chapter of Narnia. As I was putting the boys to bed, I asked Timothy, teasingly, what it was that he had given me for Father's Day. Not missing a beat, he replied, "A wonderful day." It was, indeed, a wonderful day.

Lord, I sing praises for the blessings of this day. —RICK HAMLIN

21

MONDAY

Be subject to one another in the fear of Christ.
—EPHESIANS 5:21 (NAS)

Barbara and I met as seminary students, fell in love, and married the following summer. We had lots in common but were naive about how our different families and cultures had shaped us—she was from Georgia, I, from Oklahoma.

Not long after we married, Barbara cooked a small picnic ham. With Sunday lunch and a few sandwiches, it was soon reduced to the bone with just a little ham left on it.

I remarked, "My mother would cook that bone with a big pot of beans and serve it with corn bread."

To my surprise she said, "That's exactly what my mother would do," and made plans to prepare it the next day. When I left for class she reminded me of the supper menu, and in the afternoon I called to get a report. She told me that I would like the aroma in our apartment. I could hardly wait.

The minute I opened the door I knew that something was terribly wrong. The air did not smell like pinto beans cooking. Barbara saw the disappointment in my face and asked, "Is something wrong?"

Without thinking, I blurted out, "When I say beans, I mean *pinto beans.*"

With the same intensity she responded, "And when I say beans, I mean *green beans.*" We looked at each other and burst out laughing.

That was over four decades ago, and we are still discovering interesting and wonderful differences in each other. And by the way, she likes the way I cook pintos, and I've learned how good green beans are, cooked with a ham bone.

Dear God, help me to be more sensitive to the differences in people that make them so special. —KENNETH CHAFIN

22

Like newborn babes, long for the pure milk of the word, that by it you may grow.... —*I PETER 2:2 (NAS)*

My friend Susan phoned and asked, "I'm looking after some animals for friends on vacation. Want to go help me feed a newborn calf whose mama died?" I had no idea how I could help, but I love animals, so I eagerly agreed.

At first, it appeared that Buttercup, a buff-colored Beef Master calf, was dead. He lay sprawled out awkwardly in his pen, obviously dehydrated. Two golden retrievers stood by him, still and silent. Buttercup had been given to his new owners just a day before their departure. They hadn't been able to get him to drink from a bottle, so they used a feeding tube. "We're supposed to stick this rubber hose down his throat and pour the formula directly into his stomach through the funnel," Susan told me. She didn't look convinced that either of us could do it.

My husband Gene, who'd raised cows, came to our rescue. "You have to let him taste the milk on your fingers and teach him to suck from the bottle. It just takes patience." Gene got down on his knees and talked gently to the weak calf. He instructed Susan and me to straddle Buttercup carefully and hold him up. After awhile we were ready to give up, but Gene persisted.

"Just taste it, Buttercup," Susan and I wailed. And then Buttercup curled his pink tongue around the nipple and sucked long and hard, getting white, frothy foam all over his mouth, which the dogs eagerly and tenderly licked away. Buttercup downed three bottles and bumped against a startled Susan to ask for more of the good stuff.

Suddenly, I remembered the long-ago faithful friends who had tried to help me to have a real encounter with the Lord. Like Buttercup, I had resisted. But when I finally tasted the goodness of God, I drank deeply—and became a new Marion, a new wife, a new mother in Him.

Oh, I do thank You, Father, for tenacious friends. Amen.

—*MARION BOND WEST*

23

Thou rulest the raging of the sea: when the waves thereof arise, thou stillest them. —*PSALM 89:9*

 SS *Rotterdam* was three days from New York when I got my wish: stormy weather. This was the last time she would have the opportunity to show off in the North Atlantic she had been built for, and I relished it. Up early in a rocky cabin, I looked out at a gray, rainy day, with fierce winds and the sea boiling furiously. I could hardly wait to go on deck, to walk blithely past the warning signs—then a minute of fresh air and I was back inside. The Lido's breakfast, normally busy, was not, and when it was time for the dining room to open, the Indonesian staff welcomed me as somebody daring. Why, shucks, I remembered being in a storm at sea when they shut down the kitchens entirely and just threw a sandwich into your stateroom.

The day went on. Few passengers were about. It was announced that we were in a gale, just short of a hurricane. The evening's show—Shirley Jones—was canceled, along with other activities. I wandered and read and wandered some more. Word came that the best spot to see the thirty-five to forty-foot waves was in the card room, and they were right. What power! What beauty as the ship came down and the waves came up, splashing, again and then again.

Preparing for dinner, I was just fixing my tie when, suddenly, I was hurled across the room, hitting the bureau. I wondered, as I lay on the floor amid scattered papers, if I was hurt. I wasn't. But it was enough to make me think of other people aboard who might have suffered worse than I.

I went to dinner that night chastened, a little less romantic, yet still in love with the sea. Going through my head were the words to the old hymn:

When the world is tossing me, Like a ship upon the sea;
Thou who rulest wind and water, Stand by me (Stand by me).

—*VAN VARNER*

24

For I have learned to be content whatever the circumstances. —PHILIPPIANS 4:11 (NIV)

"It was one of life's great moments," Dad said, recalling an afternoon some sixty years before when the lady who lived next door took a bunch of the neighborhood boys on their once-a-year outing to Sportsman's Park to watch the St. Louis Cardinals play. "The Widow Lady," as the kids called her, gave each boy a nickel, enough to buy an ice cream on a stick, and each devoured it before it melted in the hot summer sun.

"Then when you finished the ice cream, you checked the stick, and if it said FREE, you got another one." My dad's eyes brimmed with excitement. "I still remember the day I got that extra one. Now that was one of life's great moments."

Considering all my dad has accomplished, I wondered why he remembered that day so well. "At that moment, I was completely happy being right where I was," he said.

How often can I say that? With all my blessings, I still seem to be habitually looking toward some future time. "I'll be glad when things settle down after the holidays," I'll say, or "We'll do it when the kids are older," or "When I lose ten pounds...." Meanwhile, life's great moments are marching past, and I'm not even watching the parade. Even prayer can become too much asking and not enough thanking for gifts already bestowed.

Expecting the spectacular, maybe I'm missing the sublime, the little gifts from heaven that fill my days: the feeling of well-being after a brisk walk; the pleasure of a new recipe turning out just right; the joy on my children's faces when I've come up with the perfect surprise. Perhaps my dad is on to something. Life's great moments aren't in the satisfaction of great things achieved, but in the pure contentment of small pleasures enjoyed now, to the fullest.

Today I offer a simple thank You, Lord, for all You have given me.
—GINA BRIDGEMAN

25

He revealeth the deep and secret things.... —DANIEL 2:22

My husband David and I were traveling by car in rural Ohio. We were lost. In the backseat, Brock was one unhappy camper. If we asked him a question that begged for a "yes" answer, he gave us a "no." He had plastered the backseat with damp, squishy crackers, spilled his juice and ripped a page from his favorite book.

In the front seat, David was agitated because we were lost. He was hungry, and we couldn't find a restaurant. He was irritated because Brock was behaving badly. Then lo and behold, up ahead, we saw a town.

It was a magazine-cover example of small-town America, with a stately, whitewashed courthouse on a trim, green town square. But by the time we found ourselves circling the square for the third time, looking for a restaurant, its loveliness was fading. Like a broken record, Brock was singing "I'm hungry," and there was no food in sight.

"Stop and let me run into this jewelry store for directions," I said.

I pushed through the door and walked in. "Be with you in a minute," the clerk called from the back.

While I waited, I looked into the glass-topped counter. A strange-looking ring caught my eye. "What's that?" I asked the clerk, who was now standing in front of me.

He pulled out the ring and showed it to me. Mounted in the loveliest gold filigree was the ugliest rock I had ever seen, rough and misshapen. I was mystified. The clerk laughed. "You are holding probably the finest diamond in this town in your hand," he said. "It just hasn't been cut yet."

When I slipped back inside the car, I wasn't the same wife and mother I'd been a few minutes earlier. I would never again look at a cracker-crusted child or a tired, grumpy husband and not remember the life-lesson God sent to me in that little Ohio town. We are all uncut diamonds of one grade or another. The secret is in looking past the surface and coaxing out the rainbows that wait inside.

Father, You are a perfect diamond and Your brilliance is within us all. Help me to see.   —PAM KIDD

26

And in thee shall all families of the earth be blessed.
—GENESIS 12:3

There are six weeks during June and early July when we celebrate a family birthday every weekend. The parties are held at my house because it's the only one that's big enough for all fifteen of us to sit down together. Today it was Josh's special time.

We're nearing the end of the series, and I have to admit to some weariness. That's probably what brought on my impulsive suggestion that we have just one big party next year, celebrating them all at once. But I caught the shadow that passed across my son's face and quickly changed my mind. Life's not easy for Paul and Cheryl, with seven children and barely enough coming in each month to take care of necessities. Most of the time, they're all working very hard to make ends meet. There's not much time for frivolity and celebration.

Today we've laughed together, shared pizza, ice cream and birthday cake, and seventeen-year-old Josh has been reminded of how very special he is. The whole gang has gone to the school yard across the street now, except for two-year-old Joseph, who has curled up in Grandma's lap and fallen asleep. There's a wastebasket stuffed with gift wrap in the middle of the room; cake plates and licked-off candles on the table; helium balloons that have slipped out of small hands clinging to the ceiling; and lemonade glasses on all the end tables. But I know one sleepy boy and one tired grandma who can't think of a thing in the world they'd rather be doing.

Today, Lord, I give thanks for the very great blessing of a loving family. Let me always remember that every child is special in Your eyes.   —MARILYN MORGAN HELLEBERG

27

In the morning will I direct my prayer unto thee, and will look up.   —PSALM 5:3

My husband Larry and I, along with our daughter Meghan, her husband Pete and their daughter Kayla, not yet two, visited the Atomic Museum in Albuquerque, New Mexico. Pete was eager to show Kayla the planes that were on display outside the museum, but Kayla was more interested in the display grounds' two-feet-tall floodlights, now turned off for the day.

"She can't see the planes," I said to Pete. "They're just too big."

Kayla ran under the belly of a plane, headed for another floodlight. She glanced up and slid to a halt with a gasp, her eyes round, her mouth an O of surprise. Then she flung out her arms like wings.

"She sees it!" I cried. "At last, she sees it!" We all laughed at Kayla's astonishment.

Several days later, I was overwhelmed by the tasks that had piled up in my life—bills to pay, errands to run, phone calls to make, letters to write. Looking up to the ceiling, I flung my arms wide. "Okay, God, I know You're there, but sometimes I get so focused on the small things that I forget to look up. Please help me keep my eyes on the bigger picture that includes Your love and support."

I seemed to hear a chuckle and the words, "At last, she sees it!"

Lord, as I move forward through this day, I will set my eyes on You.
—MADGE HARRAH

28

He set my feet on a rock and gave me a firm place to stand.
—PSALM 40:2 (NIV)

Growing up on a farm, it seemed I was always having to cross the creek that ran through our property. Take a jar of fresh water to Daddy, working in the back cornfield. Go get the cows. Pick a daisy bouquet for the supper table. Visit my favorite apple tree.

My path across that rushing water was a series of rocks, placed just right for my small strides. Big, flat rocks that felt safe and smooth beneath my bare feet. Only once did I ever slip on those rocks, crashing into the creek and cutting my foot on a jagged stone. That was the time I looked not at the rocks, but at the water.

Sometimes life swirls around me. Deadlines to meet. Concerns about my almost-grown kids. Quarrels at work. And when I concentrate just on the problems, I find myself sinking. But when I concentrate on the solid things in life—my husband's devotion, my children's good judgment, the power of apologies, God's unchanging love—I begin to walk with a firmer step. And like those childhood rocks, the path becomes safe and smooth.

Oh, Father, You are the bridge across every trouble—one small step at a time.
—MARY LOU CARNEY

29

I thank my God every time I remember you. In all my prayers for all of you, I always pray with joy.

—PHILIPPIANS 1:3-4 (NIV)

Every night after work last summer I tried to make it to the hospital to see Ken, an elderly friend of mine who had suffered a stroke. He was in his nineties and now could barely speak or feed himself. In addition to all these sorrows, he was blind—a man who had spent his entire professional life with the printed word couldn't even read.

One evening I had walked home from the office, and on my feet were an especially unattractive pair of sneakers, which had long ago given up the battle with the dirt of Manhattan streets. *No point in putting on the bright red pumps that I wore in the office and are now sitting in my backpack,* I thought. *After all, Ken can't see my shoes.* But then, in a flash of anger against his present fate and my memories of his elegance, wit and love of festive occasions, I threw the sneakers under the bed and put on the red shoes. Then I renewed my lipstick, combed my hair and set off for the hospital.

When I arrived, I chatted to Ken about trivia, not even sure if he could hear me. Running out of things to say but not wanting to sit in silence, I said, "And, Ken, I have on my red dress and the new pair of red shoes I just bought to go with them. I wanted to look my very best to visit you." As I said these words, quite unmistakably he squeezed my hand as if he agreed.

Not long after, God gave Ken rest from his sufferings, but every time I wear that pair of red shoes I remember that night in the hospital, my friend and the pressure of his fingers on mine.

Thank You, Lord, for the memories of love and friendship that add sweetness to our days. —BRIGITTE WEEKS

30

Forgive...the trespass of thy brethren.... —GENESIS 50:17

I was feeling very bitter a few summers ago during a visit to my brother in Washington, D.C. I had just discovered that a trusted friend had been trying to stir up resentment against me to make herself look better. I couldn't get over her betrayal. I made the usual tourist stops, seeing the sights, but my heart wasn't in it. I kept thinking how much I wanted to punish my friend for what she had done.

One day, as I walked in the National Gallery, I came upon a room of sixteenth-century Dutch paintings and noticed several Vermeers. In one of them, a young woman held a scale in her right hand. Behind her on the wall of her room hung a representation of the Last Judgment showing the agony of souls condemned to hell. In my bitterness, I thought of my friend.

My eyes moved slowly upward to the face of the woman in Vermeer's painting. It was suffused with grace and soft light as she gently lifted the scale. I wanted so much to have the sweet peace reflected in her face. Then I saw that it came from the Christ portrayed behind her. Her face told me that she judged with love and understanding.

Suddenly, the light from the window in the painting seemed to flow into me. I felt the most tremendous weight lifting from my heart. Tears filled my eyes as my anger and resentment drained away. A guard approached and handed me a tissue. "It's a beautiful painting, miss, isn't it?" he asked. I smiled back at him, unable to reply.

Father, help me to put away my harsh judgments and know the sweet blessing of Your forgiveness. —SUSAN SCHEFFLEIN

MY FAITH JOURNEY

Missed kids Beautiful sunny day HHH 90° very busy at work. Worked 3 hrs O.T. Working on old house lot today.

Missed kids Beautiful sunny day 87° very busy at work. Paul Room Called from Jans house in Florence.

Missed kids Beautiful sunny day 80° very busy at work. Worked 4 hrs O.T.

I called Chantell, aunt Ruth + Connie Thaddour. Only Connie answered I did bills. Paul + I ate lunch at 11:30.

Beautiful sunny day. 80°. We
went to Kelsey school
play. They all came home sick
Brian's, Pat & Me so Play. All
4 came down. Pat & Norm came over. Butch & Dan

Missed Kids

Beautiful sunny day 80°. Paul
& I walked to aed Chester, Aunt
Ethel. We too I had dinner
5 on my homemade turkey soup.

Beautiful sunny day 80°.
Paul & I went shopping.
6 Picked up Bobby. Chantel & kids came over late

Missed Kids

Beautiful sunny day HHH 94°.
Left work at 1:30, to go to Dr's.
7 Spider bite on my back came out. Butch

Missed Kids

Beautiful sunny day HHH 95°.
Worked 5:00-12:00 & we took
8 Bobby for his haircut & M.V. Medford again

Missed Kids

Beautiful sunny day HHH 90°.
Very busy at work. Big oak
9 tree came down. Worked 3 hr O.T.

Missed Kids

Beautiful partly cloudy day 80°.
Busy at work. Worked 4 hr
10 O.T. Walked down to old house.

Missed Kids

Beautiful sunny day 80°. very
busy at work. Did 3 hr O.T.
11 Paul & I showered & watched T.V.

Missed Kids

Cloudy comfortable day. Relaxed
all day. Chantel called &
Butch came over. We went
12 to 5:00 Mass. I G A &
Shop Rite. Watched TV
retired at 11:00.

Cloudy, rainy day 75°. We went to
QB + Micumael + saw Chantell + kids
then Aunjus + meely for my birthday.

13 We all went to Arthurs w/Butch + Jen too.

Cloudy, rainy day 80°. HHH.
Worked 3 hrs O.T. New O T
14 FA project 1000 misses to check.

Beautiful sunny day 80°. Very
busy as work on FA Miss project.
Worked 4 hrs O.T. came home
15 + Paul + I showered + watched soaps

Cloudy, dreary day 70°. Very busy
at work. Did 2 hrs O.T. I finished
the FA project by 11:00. Took 3 hr nap
walked to old house.
16 me. Bob home from work at 11:00.

Cloudy, dreary, rainy day 70°. HBD.
Paul + I had lunch + took a
17 nap till 3:00. Went to Island Beach STPk.

Beautiful sunny day 75°. Very busy
as work. No O.T. today. Came home
+ laid down w/ Paul till 6:00.
18 Chantell called. Butch was here today

Beautiful sunny day 75°. I took a
2 hr AM nap. Paul + I walked
down to old house + took pictures.
19 Went to Kelsey Matal. W/ mom + dad.

Cloudy, rainy day 70°. Paul + I
went to 8:30 Mass. Got papers
+ ran to shop rite. Chantell + Bob
20 + kids dropped off flowers + cake.

Cloudy, rainy day 70°. Worked
4 hrs O.T. Paul made turkey
21 poopie for supper. It was
delicious. We retired at
8:00.

Missed kids — Beautiful sunny day 80°. Very busy at O.T. Paul made spagetti for
22 supper. We showed & watched soaps

Missed kids — Beautiful sunny day 85°. Very busy at work. Worked 4 hrs.
23 Came home showed & watched soaps

Missed kids — Beautiful sunny day 90°. Very busy at work. Worked 4 hrs.
24 Came home showed & watched soaps.

Missed kids — Beautiful sunny day 90°. Very busy at work. Worked 4 hrs. Paul & I showed & had
25 pasta salad & watched soaps

Missed kids — Beautiful sunny day 90°. Paul & I went to Delaware & Pa. for lottery ticket. We got hoagies
26 from Hoagie Factory. Delicious.

Missed kids — Beautiful sunny day HHH 95. Paul & I relaxed w/ papers
27 Walked through woods. Relaxed

Missed kids — Partly cloudy day HHH 95°. Did 2 hrs O.T. Mass for Danah.
28 Bobby, Kelsy, Chantell called.

Missed kids — Cloudy, dreary day 95° HHH no rain. Did 4 hrs O.T. Brought Joey home. Watched soaps. Margaret
29 called

Missed kids — Cloudy dreary day less HHH. Bobby has Chicken pox. I called
30 Chantell to tell her Happy Anniversary. Worked 4 days O.T. Bonnies Bakes flown at work.

July

Thy rod and thy staff, they comfort me.

—PSALM 23:4 (RSV)

S	M	T	W	T	F	S
				1	2	3
4	5	6	7	8	9	10
11	12	13	14	15	16	17
18	19	20	21	22	23	24
25	26	27	28	29	30	31

LESSONS IN LISTENING

1	THURSDAY

STARTING WITH THANKS
Let us come before his presence with thanksgiving....
—PSALM 95:2

In the 1960s my husband John and I went to Africa as teachers—and learned far more than we taught. Especially about guidance! With so much that was unfamiliar, our year there became a twelve-month crash course in learning to listen.

One darkening afternoon as thunderclouds built up over the Nile, we were driving across a log-and-dirt bridge over a ravine when the car lurched to the left and stopped. John climbed gingerly out. "The back tire's gone through the bridge," he reported. I shepherded our three small children to solid ground while John jacked up the car. "Look for logs to cover the hole," he told us. But in that bush country, fifteen minutes of searching produced nothing but slender branches that dropped straight through into the draw.

What to do? We were ten miles from the village where we were to stay; on the dirt track behind us we'd passed a single car in six hours. We couldn't spend the night out of the car—this was lion country. We couldn't stay in it for fear the rest of the bridge would go when the rain came.

And so, as we did many times a day, we asked God what to do. "Let's start with thanksgiving," John said, recalling a principle learned from an African pastor: *Thank God before the answer comes.* We thanked Him that He had the perfect answer to the problem. Then we simply waited. And in the calm that followed, the simple solution burst on us both. The spare tire! John took it from the trunk and found that it exactly straddled the hole. He let the jacked-up wheel down and drove off the bridge as the equatorial rainstorm struck.

Was it God or common sense? Certainly it was a logical solution—but logic usually deserts me when I'm anxious, and giving thanks is the best anxiety antidote I know. From that day on, I've started every prayer for guidance with the words we used on that bridge:

Thank You, Father, that the plan for handling this situation is complete right now in Your sight. —ELIZABETH SHERRILL

2

FRIDAY

"Look at the birds of the air...." —MATTHEW 6:26 (NIV)

When we arrived at the farm for our summer vacation, the first thing I did was put up the front porch swing. As I began to work, I noticed a nest of mud and straw at the end of the porch that had to be the work of barn swallows. That afternoon, we heard twittering and the sound of wings on the porch; we looked out to see an adult swallow perched on the side of the nest, where three huge mouths supported by tiny fuzzy necks were vying for the food.

My wife Barbara and I decided to ban ourselves from the porch, lest we frighten the parents into abandoning the nest, and to watch the baby swallows develop. From daylight till dark the swallows could be seen flying back and forth over the pasture catching flying insects and depositing their catch deep in the throats of their charges. It was like watching parents try to match the appetites of three always-hungry teenage boys.

Within days there wasn't room for all three inside the nest, so they took turns holding on to the edge, whirring their wings like an airplane at the end of the runway waiting for clearance from the tower. When the day came for the young to leave the nest, their parents flew close to the nest with food in their mouths and then flew away. First one bird took off, then a second. It took a little more coaxing for the third. It reminded me of all of us who have wanted desperately to be on our own but who were reluctant to leave home. When the last swallow took off, I stood in the front room and applauded! Imagine—from a tiny egg to a magnificent flying acrobat in just over a month.

How God must love us to surround us with so many wonderful things!

Dear God, grant me open eyes with which to see and celebrate the wonders of Your creation. —KENNETH CHAFIN

3

"And he has blessed you this day." —EXODUS 32:29 (NIV)

I was working at my desk this morning, anxiously awaiting the results of my mother's ultrasound, when a *Daily Guideposts* reader, Michelle Grebel, telephoned from Valley City, North Dakota. "I just read your devotional about your dog Spanky," she said, "and I wanted to let you know you're my 'God-Find' for today." I soon learned that every day Michelle asks the Lord to help her discover a "God-Find," then she tracks them down and tells them how they've blessed her life.

It took four long-distance calls for Michelle to locate me. When I asked her to tell me more about "God-Finds," Michelle explained that they don't have to be something that knocks you over. "A 'God-Find' is anything that lets you see God at work in your life. It can be something like taking your dog for a walk and noticing all the wonderful things God has provided for us. It really helps focus your attitude and is such a neat way to tell people about God," she said.

Whenever Michelle has a down day, instead of plummeting into despair, she reaches for her "God-Find" book. Over and over again, it reaffirms that whatever happens, God will be there with her and help her through it.

Intrigued by Michelle's idea, I reached for the scratch pad on my desk and jotted down my very first God-Find: Michelle Grebel. Then, finding it impossible to stop with just one, I added the doctor who ordered Mother's ultrasound. I smiled, remembering how Dr. Huckaby had treated us as if we were the only people in the world. Then the stranger in the hospital waiting room who offered her prayers joined the names on my growing list.

Why don't you begin a search for "God-Finds" today? Your "God-Find" book will become a treasured reference whenever you need a reminder that God is working on your behalf.

Thank You, dear Lord, for our wonderful family of Daily Guideposts *readers, knitted together by Your love.*

—ROBERTA MESSNER

4

Where the Spirit of the Lord is, there is liberty.
—II CORINTHIANS 3:17

Our old neighborhood in Brooklyn thought it really knew how to celebrate the Fourth of July—fireworks, and plenty of them. The unofficial (and illegal) detonations began in the early morning. By evening, when the block parties were going full blast, a pall of smoke hung over the brownstone-lined streets and the smell of gunpowder overpowered the aroma of hamburgers and hot dogs cooking over charcoal.

The *rat-tat-tat-tat-tat* of strings of small firecrackers alternated with the *ssszzz* of bottle rockets, the *plonk* of Roman candles, the sharp *bang* of cherry bombs and the reverberating *boom* of big silver salutes. The intervals between explosions were filled with the constant, piercing whine of car alarms, jarred into life by the fireworks assault.

Inside our third-floor apartment, my wife Julia and I tried to go about our day. In the kitchen, Dad sat hunched over in a chair well away from the windows. "I haven't heard anything like this since the war—since the Anzio beachhead," he said.

Under the kitchen table, our cat tried to curl up into a tiny ball, her paws over her ears. *Our* ears were still ringing at one o'clock in the morning, when the fusillade had died down to an occasional, sporadic report. "Honey," Julia said to me just before we sank into a troubled sleep, "we've got to go away for the Fourth next year!"

And we did. That next Fourth we spent in Ocean Grove, a charming Victorian community on the New Jersey shore that began as a Methodist camp meeting more than a hundred years ago. We enjoyed an old-fashioned parade down Main Avenue, a professional (and legal) fireworks show and, most of all, we showed our thankfulness to God, the Giver and Sustainer of our freedom, by worshiping Him at morning and evening services. For as John Adams suggested 223 years ago, Independence Day "ought to be commemorated as the day of deliverance, by solemn acts of devotion to God Almighty."

Dear God, let us celebrate our Independence Day joyfully but soberly, giving You the glory. —ANDREW ATTAWAY

5

God is our refuge and strength, a very present help in trouble. —PSALM 46:1

My friend Bonnie and I decided to see something of the Olympic Peninsula, the only real rain forest in the continental United States. We were not surprised that it was raining when we arrived at the Lake Quinalt Lodge. While she wanted to stay warm and dry at the lodge,

I wanted to go for a hike. I put on my rain suit and an extra pair of socks, and went out on the clearly marked trail that made a three-mile loop through the trees and back to the hotel.

Despite the rain and the grayness of the day, I was enjoying the hike. I thought it was almost over when I found myself at a signboard that said, "You are here," and showed a red dot at the beginning of a side trail that made a longer loop back to the hotel. I had been moving very well, and I was reluctant just to leave the misty trees, so I turned off the main trail. I would, I thought, get back to the hotel in plenty of time for dinner.

An hour or so later, when my trail dead-ended at a raging stream I couldn't possibly cross, I realized I was not where I was supposed to be. I didn't know how late it had gotten, and I didn't have a flashlight. If night fell, I would just have to stand still and hope someone found me. Knowing that searchers would have a better chance of finding me on the main trail, I turned around and nearly ran back. It took another hour, and I was praying between gasps for breath the whole time. Eventually, I found myself back at the signboard and map. Now I could see a third trail, a spur, some distance away from the red dot, that went 2.5 miles out to a dead end. That was obviously the one I'd taken.

I got back to the hotel just before dark, soaking wet but grateful. I had learned a valuable lesson: Sometimes someone moves the "You are here" dot, and it can take a lot of common sense and prayer to get you back.

When I am lost, God, You are the beacon that leads me home.

—RHODA BLECKER

6

"I am the light of the world. Whoever follows me will never walk in darkness, but will have the light of life."

—JOHN 8:12 (NIV)

Her porch, overgrown with vines, sagged and creaked as I walked across it and stepped into a dark Victorian parlor crammed with heavy furniture. I was eighteen and had accepted a summer job taking care of Mrs. Martin, an elderly woman from our church. Though I'd never met her, she was rumored to be "difficult."

Mrs. Martin's daughter-in-law ushered me into the front bedroom. Mrs. Martin was propped up in her bed, arms clamped across her bosom, mouth drawn tight as the drapes. She didn't like the sun pouring in, I learned in the next few days. It ruined the furniture. Nor did she like "today's youth." They were disrespectful and had it too easy. Me, for example—why hadn't I learned to poach an egg properly, make a bed or polish silver?

Three days later, I was chained to one of Mrs. Martin's awful moods when the doorbell rang. There stood Deacon Moore, beaming like a lighthouse. Across the years, he had lost a wife and son in an accident, and there'd been other tragedies as well. But at eighty-four, he carried himself young.

I brought Deacon Moore through to the front bedroom, where Mrs. Martin, robe buttoned to her throat, hunkered in semidarkness. "How are you today, Mrs. Martin?" he began.

When she stopped her litany of complaints long enough to take a breath, he held up his hand. In a voice as close to stern as Deacon Moore could get, he said, "Mrs. Martin, when life hands you a hardship, you can focus on the awfulness or you can focus on God, Who allowed it. Either way, you'll come through it. Because we *do,* you know. But one way, you'll be imprinted with the hardship, the other, with God."

I spent the summer trying to focus on God, and I came through. And perhaps that was one of the reasons I was put there. Because across thirty-five years, that light from Deacon Moore has gotten me through darker storms than Mrs. Martin.

Lord, for myself and for those coming after me, may I blaze a trail of light that leads to You. —SHARI SMYTH

7

"Just as a hen gathers her brood under her wings...."
—LUKE 13:34 (NAS)

I remember my mother slipping some duck eggs under a hen one summer. The hen never surmised that she had hatched ducklings until the day her mottled babies took to the river.

Eventually, there was only one duckling left, but the old hen was determined to mother that one duckling as long as possible. Despite its protests, she tried to sit on it to protect it long after it was a fully grown duck, and farmyard visitors often chuckled over that "two-story bird."

As my own family matured, letting go of our three sons was hard enough, but parting with our only daughter Gae was even worse. I tried to influence her as long as possible, but one day when I took exception to the music she enjoyed and then turned around and criticized her style of clothes, she reacted to my nagging by exclaiming, "Mom, would you just quit sitting on me all the time!"

Her words brought back memories of that overprotective old hen. Acknowledging that Gae was developing into an independent young woman with tastes very different from my own, I had to learn to *mother* her, not *smother* her.

The nest has been empty ever since my "bird of a different feather" found her wings, but in letting her go, we came closer together.

Father, help me to nurture—not nag—those I love.

—ALMA BARKMAN

8

THURSDAY

He heareth the cry of the afflicted.   —JOB 34:28

My dad's doctor had told me that Alzheimer's disease might change Dad's personality, and finally it was happening. Dad had always been a kind, generous, helpful man, but now he was becoming suspicious and angry. The staff at the nursing home understood and were patient with his outbursts, but I couldn't accept the change in his behavior. He just wasn't the man I had known.

Dad was especially resentful toward his new roommate. Alvin was too weak to do anything but sit in his wheelchair with his head bent forward. He didn't look up or talk, and my dad insisted that Alvin was ignoring him. When I tried to explain why Alvin didn't talk, Dad turned away and said, "He's pretending! He's not sick!" He didn't seem to care whether Alvin could hear him.

One day I brought a little box of candy with me. It was a brand my dad used to buy for my mother, and I hoped it would remind him of happier times. As soon as he saw it, he smiled, and for a few minutes he reminisced about the old days. Then he removed the wrapping and opened the box. There were six different kinds of chocolate-covered candies in it, and I recognized one as my dad's favorite. He reached for it—and stopped.

Alvin was in his wheelchair on the other side of the room, head bent and silent as usual, and Dad suddenly wheeled himself over to him. I didn't know what he was going to do, so I followed along behind him. Dad parked his chair in front of Alvin's and held out the box of candy. "Alvin!" he said, rather sharply, and Alvin's head came up.

"Would you like a piece of candy?" Dad said in the gentlest way. It seemed to take Alvin forever to reach for the box, and his fingers were clumsy. Dad picked out his favorite piece and put it in Alvin's open hand. A tired smile came over Alvin's face as he put the candy in his mouth. "Thank you," he mumbled.

"Here, have another one," Dad said, holding out the box. This time Alvin picked up a candy by himself, and Dad's eyes were bright with encouragement. "He's a nice guy," he said, turning to me. "He just needs a little help."

Quietly I thanked God for showing me that the man I always knew and loved was still there. I think he was also assuring me that no illness on this earth can destroy the goodness in a person.

Thank You, Lord Jesus, for the comfort and love You give me when others seem far away. —PHYLLIS HOBE

9 FRIDAY

But the men of Israel encouraged one another and again took up their positions.... —JUDGES 20:22 (NIV)

We drove slowly through an African wild game reserve on our three-hour night ride, with four volunteers patiently holding spotlights and carefully scanning the trees and brush for any flash of eyes. Having already spent the day driving and searching for animals, many of us found it hard to keep looking. Suddenly, someone called out, "Eyes on the right!"

Our ranger Dan Pretorius stopped the car and identified the animal as a side-striped jackal, a very rare animal to see here. "That was well spotted!" he exclaimed.

As the ride grew longer and colder, Dan sustained us with a steady stream of encouragement. Whether it was the frequent rabbits, a small duiker or the eyes of a little night owl, he praised every sighting.

After two hours, my eight-year-old daughter Elizabeth asked, "When will we get back to camp? How much longer?" Before I could answer, someone spotted an elephant on the left of the road, devouring a tree. While we watched, Elizabeth glanced to the right and exclaimed, "Impala!"

"Well spotted, Elizabeth," Dan announced. She grinned with pride.

As we bumped along, getting more tired and colder, Dan's constant praise kept us searching for and finding the treasures out there at night. Elizabeth was no longer impatient to get back but eagerly searching. I thought of our current work with her on not whining or arguing. I needed to do some more careful spotting myself and watch for the times she didn't challenge, the times she cheerfully complied, and praise her.

Father, in my parenting—and in all my relationships—help me to be a vigilant encourager. —MARY BROWN

10

Inasmuch as ye have done it unto one of the least of these my brethren.... —MATTHEW 25:40

When my wife Pam and I drove into the parking lot, a mud-splattered, red pickup truck was in the space next to ours. The hood was raised, and the owner was leaning over the engine. "Car trouble?" I asked sympathetically.

He was a black-haired young farmer with sunburned forearms and astonishingly blue eyes. "Nope," he said, "it's time for Snowball's lunch, that's all." He pointed to a cardboard box at his feet and in it I saw a tiny white kitten, so young that its eyes were still closed. "We've had a long ride into town and I've had her milk on ice. I have to warm it up, so I put it on the hot engine manifold for a few minutes." He pointed and I saw a small nursing bottle, like a doll's toy, complete with nipple.

"Where did you find her?" I asked, faintly amazed.

"Didn't exactly find her," he said. "We have some stray cats around our barn, mostly pretty wild. This kitten's mother came right up and put her down by my feet. Then she ran away. I guess she thought I'd take care of her baby for her."

"White cats are sometimes deaf," Pam told him. "Perhaps this one's mother knew it was handicapped."

"Maybe so," the farmer said cheerfully. "But she'll be all right once we get her started."

We left him there with the kitten drinking thirstily. "That man is an angel," Pam said. "And the kitten's mother knew it."

"An angel with blue eyes and a red pickup truck?"

"It's not what angels look like," Pam said serenely. "It's what they do."

Father, teach us to reach out to all small helpless things.

—ARTHUR GORDON

11

O taste and see that the Lord is good....   —PSALM 34:8

One quart of strawberries, washed and stemmed. It was early in the season for strawberries and these were beauties: full, thick, fat, all the more tantalizing for the cold, rainy weather outside. Carol had bought them for a Sunday lunch with friends because they looked so good, but even sugar sprinkled on top couldn't disguise their main flaw: They were tart, tangy, almost bitter. "I hate to throw them away," she said in disappointment.

"They'd probably be perfect for jam," I said. When my mom made jam she used to say that tart berries were the best. I recalled huge flats of berries that stained our fingers pink, and huge pots bubbling on the stove, the canning jars banging against each other in boiling water. Mom's maternal grandparents had immigrated to Los Angeles from England, and about the only thing they brought with them to this new, dusty land was a recipe for strawberry jam.

"Well, if you want to make some," my wife said, "then go ahead."

And so I did, that very night. I poured the berries into a big pot and dumped in loads of sugar plus a smidgen of lemon juice. Then I stirred. And I stirred. I thought of what it must have been like to arrive in Los Angeles in 1888, and I thought of Mom, who had revived the jam-making tradition after a thirty-year lapse. I thought of the friends who had come over for lunch (picking sparingly at the strawberries), and I thought of my wife who had been so disappointed by her rash, early-in-the-season purchase. As I stirred and skimmed the pink foam from the top—just as the recipe said—I said a prayer for my wife and friends, then I poured the heavy thick goo into a jar. My first batch of strawberry jam. From something bitter to something sweet. All it took was a little work—and a prayer.

From my bitterest disappointments, Lord, let me find Your sweetness.   —RICK HAMLIN

12

O Lord, revive thy work in the midst of the years....

—*HABAKKUK 3:2*

My thirty-year-old son Jeremy has a small landscaping business, and he's done well with it. He's always loved hard work outside; when he was a little fellow, he enjoyed helping his father keep up the yard. But after the job was done, he'd run into the house, leaving dirt and debris wherever he went. Instead of praising him for his work, I'd scold him for the messes he made.

Now Jeremy had come out to help my husband Gene cut down some diseased pine trees, and I could see from the kitchen window that it was a long, hot, dirty task. I was making lemonade for them when Jeremy came through the back door. "Man, it's hot out there. Got anything cold to drink?" When he saw the lemonade, he said, "Hey, thanks, Mom!"

Suddenly, he glanced down at the shiny, white kitchen floor. My gaze followed his. He'd brought in mud, leaves, dried bark and all the grubby stuff he'd walked in while cutting down the trees. We both stared for a long, silent moment. Then he looked at me with a stunned expression. "Aren't you going to holler or fuss? I should have cleaned my feet. Look at this mess!"

I began picking leaves off his shirt as though they were miniature trophies. "Oh, Jeremy, look at all the hard work you're doing. We're so grateful for your help. If your daddy were alive, he'd be so proud of you.... I'm so proud of you."

His puzzled expression melted into a slow, deliberate smile that broadened into joy as we hugged each other. "This is really something, Mama. I made all this mess, and you don't even care!" He went back outside carrying the lemonade, whistling now, as I picked pieces of bark from my blouse. And as I began cleaning up the kitchen floor, I was still smiling.

Oh, Lord, even when it's late, I'm so grateful for the chance to make amends. Amen.   —*MARION BOND WEST*

13

Thou wilt keep him in perfect peace, whose mind is stayed on thee....   —*ISAIAH 26:3*

Not long ago I visited a farm friend in Ohio, not far from where I grew up. Like his father and grandfather before him, he is a superb farmer, knowledgeable, creative, hardworking. His machinery is well maintained, his fences in good repair, his barns and house painted, his fields productive.

"Farming has changed a great deal, I know, but what does it take to be a successful farmer today?" I asked him. "What is your secret?"

"Just like my forebears: I plant the seeds, God grows them," he answered simply. I had expected to hear about farm economics, crop rotation, perseverance in bad growing years, but he had reduced the complicated business of farming to a simple maxim.

St. Augustine had good insight on the division of labor between God and His children when he wrote that we should work as if everything depended on our efforts and pray as if everything depended on the Almighty.

I think Augustine's advice is particularly apropos for teachers, parents, healers, ministers and everyone who serves others in Christ's name. Our job is to do the planting and trust God to do the rest.

> *God, teach us to be planters of seeds,*
> *Tillers of prayers, fillers of needs.*

—*FRED BAUER*

14

Then he opened their minds to understand at last these many Scriptures! —*LUKE 24:45 (TLB)*

There's an old saying that goes, "I hear and I forget. I see and I remember. I do and I understand."

One hot summer day during the early eighties, my nine-year-old son Michael ran into the house out of breath. "Mom! There's a new water slide at the park! It's really fast, and there's a tunnel and everything!"

I'd never seen or heard of a water slide before, and what he was trying to describe was as foreign to me as molecular biology. But a few days later Michael and I went to the water slide together. We both screamed with delight as we plopped down on our bellies at the top and experienced heart-stopping speed as we slid down the wet, four-story-tall slide with its bobsledlike tunnels and hairpin turns. Suddenly, I understood what Michael had been trying to tell me and, to tell the truth, I couldn't wait to understand it again.

Before that experience I'd been afraid of two things, giving up my old typewriter and joining the computer age, and taking a trip by myself. After that experience with Michael, I decided I shouldn't be afraid to try anything new. After all, I might like it as much as I liked the water slide! And you know what? I did! I've been computer literate since 1982. And I've taken many trips by myself, and every one was a fabulous experience.

Lord, help me to get the most out of this wonderful life You've created by being a "doer," not just a listener or a watcher.

—PATRICIA LORENZ

15 THURSDAY

My soul doth magnify the Lord, And my spirit hath rejoiced in God my Saviour. —LUKE 1:46–47

It is after dinner on board SS *Rotterdam* as it cruises to Lisbon. We are far out in the Mediterranean Sea, with the last land sighted when we slipped between Sardinia and Corsica. That seemed ages ago, for now we are free, with no lights of land in sight whatsoever. I lean over the rail and ponder the ocean.

The ship has taken the bone in its mouth, I muse romantically, using an old term for the white water that is created when the bow is slicing its way through the sea.

A young couple comes by. "That Hale-Bopp comet is quite a sight," they tell me enthusiastically. "Better go forward now."

"Thanks," I reply, though the idea of seeing the comet doesn't thrill me. I had ventured into South Africa for Halley's in 1985 and lay deep in the bush for hours. I saw it, all right, but it was disappointing, just a shimmer of brightness. And the tail—well, I couldn't say for sure that I saw the tail.

I reach the farthest point on the promenade deck where the sky is most visible. A passenger is there with a pair of binoculars, but no aid to the eye is necessary. Above me is a moon as full as possible, playing its light on the whiteness of the ship around us, and to its left is a burst of brilliance. Can it be so much larger than Halley's? I gaze at the nucleus as it spreads its luminous way across the heavens, and the tail—this one I definitely see—is full, and my imagination takes over, and the tail swoops down and carries me away.

The man and I remain there, unspeaking, for I don't know how long. We are two specks on a vast ocean, magnifying heaven.

God, for that evening of majesty, thank You. —VAN VARNER

READER'S ROOM

Some of my everyday wonders: Memory can bring someone close. When you have God, loneliness is just a word. Fear can be cleansed by God. —MARGARET MCABEE, PORTLAND, IN

16

FRIDAY

...The shadow of a great rock in a thirsty land.
—ISAIAH 32:2 (NIV)

I love flowers. But when Gary and I built our house in what used to be a wheat field, I faced a dilemma: too much sun. No trees provided the shade I needed for the kinds of annuals I wanted to grow: delicate petunias, salmon-colored impatiens, begonias. Try as I might, I could not get them to grow around my mailbox or in the flowerbeds I put in the backyard. Even with daily watering, the constant, harsh sun proved too much for them.

Then I noticed that the big rock Gary had placed at the end of our driveway—a huge boulder left from the excavation work—provided a patch of shade every afternoon. So I made a new flowerbed around the rock. And—joy!—the flowers that had floundered in the full sun began to blossom here in the shade of the rock.

I'm like those flowers, too. Often I find myself feeling parched and withered. Too many committee meetings, too many projects, too many late-night work sessions. So instead of blooming, I wither under the harsh light of fatigue and overcommitment. That's when I seek the shadow of God's quiet strength, drawing close, becoming still before Him. I read the book of Psalms. I walk in the woods. I set my priorities with prayer. And soon, prompted by His agenda, nestled in His shade, I begin to thrive.

You are my refuge, Father, in a land of heat and hurry. I want to grow near You! —MARY LOU CARNEY

17

SATURDAY

Let us eat, and be merry: For this my son...was lost, and is found.... —LUKE 15:23–24

Our church choir was having its annual summer outing. Thirty of us had gathered for a day in the sun and an evening cookout. There was a beach about two hundred yards from the house we were visiting, and throughout the afternoon, the children enjoyed themselves in the water.

As the lobsters were being put in the pot and the chicken was being placed on the grill, one of the mothers noticed that her four-year-old son Mark was missing. We all stopped what we were doing and began searching the area around the house. We knocked on doors, scoured the woods and talked to the neighbors. No one had seen Mark. Then we began to comb the beach. By now, Mark had been missing for two hours. The crashing waves seemed menacing; I began to fear the worst. As I walked along, I prayed, *Lord, I'm scared. Please help us find our Mark!*

We decided to contact the police. As we were walking to the police station, a patrol car pulled up beside us. A young policeman smiled up at us and said. "You folks look worried. By any chance, are you looking for a little boy? We found him wandering on the beach about a mile from here. He didn't know where he was visiting, but he knew his name and he knew that he was lost. He's down at the station, but I'm afraid that three dishes of ice cream have spoiled his supper."

We took Mark back to the house with great rejoicing. Our hearts overflowing with thanks, we said grace and began our postponed meal. As I filled my plate, I added a prayer of my own:

Father, You watch over us wherever we wander. If I should stray, bring me back safely to Your loving arms. —OSCAR GREENE

18

SUNDAY

Incline your ear, and come unto me: hear, and your soul shall live.... —ISAIAH 55:3

The whimper-whine started at the second line of the first hymn. Elizabeth wanted attention. I took a deep breath and put down my hymnal. It was going to be a difficult Sunday. Andrew was away on business, I was tired, and the humidity was competing with the temperature to see which could climb higher.

With one hand I stroked Elizabeth's cheek. With the other I tried to contain eleven-month-old John, who when he wasn't trying to disassemble everything in the pew rack, periodically made a break for the aisle. The huge fans buzzed, the pastor spoke with a heavy accent, and the acoustics made the Bible readings sound like muffled instructions on where to leave the ransom money. I couldn't understand a word of what was going on. I stormed heaven with a hundred one-second prayers for patience, but the distractions were so big and so many that eventually I gave up.

There's no way I'm going to get anything out of this today, I thought with a sigh. What should I do? Stay, and go insane? Go home? I shut my eyes, trying to think. Almost immediately I knew I'd been focusing entirely on the wrong thing. I needed to think about what I could put *into* the service instead of what I could get *out* of it. Bowing my head, I said a quick and simple prayer, telling my Lord that as a gift of love I was bringing Him the most precious gift He had given me: my children.

John and Elizabeth instantly sensed the difference in Mommy's approach to church. John bounced to the music of the next hymn. Elizabeth knelt when everyone else did. And then, miraculously, Elizabeth did something she'd only ever done once before: She said the Lord's Prayer along with everyone else. I don't know how she knew that it was time to say it, given the cacophony in the church. But then, perhaps I needed my own lesson in paying attention to what was important.

Heavenly Father, help me to come to you because I love You, not only because I want You to do something for me. —JULIA ATTAWAY

19

As cold waters to a thirsty soul, so is good news....
—PROVERBS 25:25

A chime sounded on my PC, alerting me to an interoffice e-mail just received. I found a message from someone named Lisette, addressed to every on-line employee in the company, announcing that she was back at work. With a flick of my mouse I relegated the message to my electronic wastepaper basket and went back to work.

I had no idea who Lisette was. There are a good three hundred and fifty people in this organization, the great majority of them situated in an exurban complex sixty miles upstate from the New York City office where I labor. We all get together every summer in an anonymous throng for the company picnic, and until recently that had been pretty much the extent of our interactions. Lately, though, like many organizations, we've forged electronic ties through e-mail, voice mail, computer faxes and who knows what next. We are just a few simple keystrokes from becoming on-line buddies—a prospect, I admit, that does not naturally appeal to my somewhat solitary nature.

Oddly enough, though, as the afternoon slipped by, I found my thoughts slipping back to Lisette. Where had she been? Maternity leave? Sabbatical? Honeymoon? Illness? I had no idea what her job was, but I began feeling relieved that we had her back, flattered that she'd seen fit to let me know and a touch guilty I'd so cavalierly dismissed her message.

Later that day I picked up the phone and called my new friend and found out a little more about what she does and where she had been (it was just a brief vacation). Fittingly, her position involves corporate communications. She'd certainly done a good job with me.

Lord, let me not forget that I need to stay in touch—not just with You but with the others You bring into my path.

—EDWARD GRINNAN

20

TUESDAY

Be strong and of a good courage, fear not...for the Lord thy God...go with thee.... —DEUTERONOMY 31:6

When I was growing up in eastern North Carolina, my grandmother had a huge wisteria bush in her front yard. During hot summer days, the bees buzzed thick and swiftly around the luscious lavender blossoms, setting here and there to feast on the sweet nectar. I was terrified of the bees and stayed well away, often running up on the porch if I thought they were after me.

Then one memorable day, Grandmother marched right up to the bush among the swarming bees. She selected the most perfect clusters, breaking them easily with her experienced hands. I watched in horror, terrified she'd be stung. But the bees darted here and there, all around Grandmother's head, and not one stung her.

Years later, I came to understand that Grandmother had not taken dominion over the bees; she had taken dominion over her fear. And although it hasn't been easy, her example has helped me take control of my own fear.

Last week, as I sat under a shade tree reading, a large, brown wasp soared from the sky in a circle, then gently touched down on my arm. I remained very still, waiting until it had rested, then it took flight and was gone. Somehow I think Grandmother would have been proud of me.

Father, all kinds of things cause me fear, but in Your presence I find courage. —*LIBBIE ADAMS*

21 WEDNESDAY
To all perfection I see a limit.... —*PSALM 119:96 (NIV)*

Busy packing for a two-week visit with my husband Paul's parents in Ohio, I was feeling the pressure of last-minute details.

"Let's try not to forget anything important," I called out to my son Ross, glancing into his room as I passed. Then I saw his packing method, tossing items into his suitcase any way they fit.

"Honey, here," I said, refolding shirts and shorts to repack them *my* way. "Try to fit things in neatly: shirts like this, stuff socks down the side, shorts—"

"Mom," he interrupted, "does everything have to be perfect?"

"Well, uh, no. Is that what you think?" I stumbled, stunned by what his honest question had revealed about me. I told him to finish the job the way he wanted, but as I left his room I began turning his question over in my mind. *Am I passing on to my children the childhood perfectionism I thought I'd conquered? Doesn't God want me at least to try to be perfect?*

I found an answer several days later in an unlikely place: the Merry-Go-Round Museum in Sandusky, Ohio. Among the exhibits was an old carousel horse, painted bright red and blue with shiny stones on its saddle and bridle. When the guide told us to look at the horse's other side, we were surprised to see very simple painting with no decoration at all.

"This is called the romance side," he said, pointing to the front. "On many of the older carousels, they fancied up the side people saw, then painted the other side very simply."

The plain side was inconsequential compared with the beauty of the ride, the thrill of the music. The craftsmen knew what was important. Did I? That day I promised myself to focus on the "romance" side of my daily life, the things that matter in God's eyes, such as teaching my children right from wrong, honoring others and loving Him. The little things nobody cares about, like how to pack a suitcase, I must learn to let go.

Dear God, help me to see what matters most, and to set free the rest.

—GINA BRIDGEMAN

22

THURSDAY

You shall walk after the Lord your God, and fear him, and keep his commandments, and obey his voice....

—DEUTERONOMY 13:4

During our trip down the Colorado River, the raft tied up often for hikes into back canyons where we could see things not visible from the boat. The first hike was only a mile, but I quickly discovered that scrambling over rocks in one-hundred-degree heat was nothing like an evening stroll on the flat Kansas prairie. I was at the back of the group; by the time I caught up with the leaders, Irv, our guide, was already moving ahead. An hour later I was exhausted, but my sister Amanda wasn't even breathing hard. "How do you do it?" I asked. "I'm not *that* much older than you!"

"I stay close to the guide," she told me. "When it's steep or there's loose rock, I put my feet exactly where Irv puts his. He sets the best pace for the terrain, and I have to keep up so I won't hold up others. Best of all, when he stops to check on stragglers like you, I get a rest break." The next morning I was the first hiker in line. Amanda was right: Whether I was climbing over rocks, picking my way through cactus and creosote, or sloshing through a stream, hiking was easiest when I was close to the guide.

Amanda's advice is good for my Christian walk, too. Many times in the Gospels, Jesus commands, "Follow Me." Peter reminds us that Christ left an example, so we could "follow in his steps" (I Peter 2:21, RSV). My Grand Canyon hikes were rewarded with a glimpse of a mountain sheep or a spectacular view of a waterfall. I have Christ's promise that my spiritual walk will yield the eternal privilege of walking with Him through eternity.

All along my pilgrim journey, Savior, let me walk with Thee.

—PENNEY SCHWAB

23

The Lord is my helper, and I will not fear what man shall do unto me. —HEBREWS 13:6

Our friend Chip is a volunteer with the local fire department. He was telling us one day about some of his experiences and the training course he had just completed.

"I really admire you volunteers and your ability to deal with emergencies," I told him. "I know I could *never* do that." And then I told him a story about trying to rescue my toddler son who had fallen into the deep end of a swimming pool. Instead of running around the pool's edge to where he was, I immediately jumped in where I was standing, and then struggled to wade through the shallow water trying to reach him. Fortunately, someone else ran around to the deep end, reached in and scooped him up.

"Don't worry," Chip replied. "You'd be surprised how common that kind of reaction is. We want to do something to help, and we just jump in. That's why they put us through so much training. In fact, just last week they taught us to STOP before we act. Sit down (at least mentally), Think (and take a deep breath), Observe the situation, and Plan how to deal with it."

I don't often find myself in true emergency situations. But I'm thinking that a slightly modified version of STOP could prove helpful in my everyday life: when I find myself caught in a cycle of worry; when I'm tempted to make decisions for my husband or grown-up kids; when I want to step in and try to "fix" something for someone I love. Usually when I feel an urgency just to do something—anything!—too often I jump in and do or say the wrong thing. Maybe I'll try this instead:

Stop
Think
Observe
Pray

When I face troubles or difficulties, Lord, help me thoughtfully to place the situation in Your strong and loving hands before I act.
—MARY JANE CLARK

24

"Woe to those who are at ease in Zion...."

—AMOS 6:1 (RSV)

Here's a mystery: The sweetest memories of my life are from my childhood, yet never was I more outside "the comfort zone" than in my youth.

At my best friend's farm, near Harlan, Indiana, we played softball barefoot in a field of coarse grass mixed with straw stubble and sticky alfalfa. Our feet were rubbed raw, and our legs swollen with bee stings and chigger welts. Sticky foam made by spittlebugs in the alfalfa clung to our legs like ointment, our only relief. And yet the sound of a softball smacking against a wooden Louisville Slugger bat is still the most beautiful music in the world.

Sometimes we sat all day on the steep banks of the muddy St. Joe River, fishing for catfish. Surrounded by cans of smelly worms, rusty tackle boxes and tangled lines, we were in paradise. At the end of the day we were so exhausted and thirsty that only visions of pink lemonade enabled us to make the four-mile trek to the house.

In winter we played basketball in an unheated barn. Ten-below winds blew feathers of snow through the sideboards, and falling to the floorboards was like falling on a glacier. But Michael Jordan has never played a more exciting game of ball.

Nowadays I am a middle-aged comfort seeker: "Let's not go to that concert in the park. It's too hot and crowded, and there's no place to park. Let's just stay home and watch TV."

I may be more comfortable, but I must be missing out on some treasures, hidden in fields of stubble. I've decided that from now on I'm going to choose my activities on the basis of their worth, and not for their ease. But first I'm going to make a pitcher of pink lemonade.

Lord, You wove pain and pleasure together in a fabric. Help me not to expect one without the other. —DANIEL SCHANTZ

25

Thou art the same, and thy years shall have no end.

—PSALM 102:27

This year I was asked to help celebrate the one hundredth anniversary of the church in my hometown, Storm Lake, Iowa. I was baptized there when it was still a little building down by the railroad tracks. My mother played the piano, sang in the choir and taught a Sunday school class there for more than fifty years, until the day she died. By that time, we had all worked very hard to build a wonderful new building, and we no longer felt inferior to the other churches in their modern buildings with clocks and chimes. I'll never forget the day the church was dedicated, the music and the beat of drums as we marched down the hill singing "Onward Christian Soldiers."

The town is still so beautiful, with its magnificent trees and miles of shining blue lake, where some of us learned to swim almost as soon as we could walk. The first thing we'd do after church on Sunday was get into our bathing suits and race down to Sunset Park and dive in. The house on Cedar Street where I was born still stands, as does the house where my parents met for the first time. They didn't have much money but, oh, how they loved each other and their children and this once-small town.

Like everything in this passing world, Storm Lake has changed. Most of the familiar landmarks are gone. But people still gather in the "new" church on Sunday, and while the messengers—Pastor Gary Hollers and his wife, a dynamic pair—are different, the message is the same. And people still go swimming in the lake on Sunday afternoon. Who could ask for more?

Thank You, Lord, for Your Word, a rock to cling to in this changing world. —MARJORIE HOLMES

26

"Thy face, Lord, do I seek." Hide not thy face from me....
—PSALM 27:8-9 (RSV)

Feeling frazzled and exhausted, I leaned back in a chair beside the motel swimming pool and watched while three of our grandchildren—boisterous with relief at being freed after a long, hot day with Larry and me in the car—frolicked in the water. They began a game of "Marco Polo," similar to Blind Man's Bluff. The child who is "It" closes his or her eyes and repeatedly yells "Marco"; the other children must answer "Polo" as they try to elude It's attempts to catch them, sometimes by swimming away underwater.

When it was nine-year-old Cheyanne's turn to be It, she became increasingly frustrated over her inability to catch the others. Finally, she opened her eyes and yelled, "Hey, you guys, quit hiding from me!"

Cody called back, "Chill out, Chey, it's just a game! We're supposed to hide."

Later, as we prepared for bed, I found myself worrying about the rest of the trip. Could the children tolerate more long days on the road? Could Larry and I?

At that moment Cheyanne pulled a Gideon Bible from the nightstand drawer. "Look what I found!" she exclaimed. Then she added with conviction, "When I call to God, *He* doesn't play games and hide from me!"

God, I'm calling Your name. I place my trust in Your loving presence, which is always within my reach. Amen. —MADGE HARRAH

27

Let all the inhabitants of the world stand in awe of him.
—PSALM 33:8

In midsummer 1988, I joined a team of *tortuga* taggers. *Tortuga* is the Spanish word for turtle. Our group at the Caribbean Conservation Corporation's green turtle station in Costa Rica patrolled the beach every evening, looking for female green turtles to intercept after they'd finished laying their eggs (sometimes as many as two hundred) in the sand. We'd record their tag numbers in our little books or give them a new number if they didn't have one. Those tags help to monitor the turtles' migratory patterns and nesting behaviors. I kept my own personal list just for the fun of it.

I'm still a supporter, so I'm on their mailing list. The other day I received an update, a report on a turtle tagged in 1988. *That was the summer I was there!* I thought as I headed for my desk. Buried under the clutter of bills and unanswered correspondence I found my personal "turtle diary." Flipping through the pages, I found the number—25400! She had been back to nest at least four times since I placed the tag on her. On each occasion, her hatchlings emerged sixty days later and made their way to the sea. *Wow!* I thought. *She's braved fishing nets, oil spills, dredging operations all those years. How marvelous! How awesome!*

I stopped to thank God for His love lavished on a turtle.

Oh, Lord, how great Thou art! —ELEANOR SASS

28

Clothe yourselves with compassion, kindness, humility, gentleness and patience. —COLOSSIANS 3:12 (NIV)

Our son Ryan was nearing his tenth birthday, and he still hadn't learned how to swim. We were on a short vacation, staying at a friend's house that had a swimming pool. One morning, Ryan was playing in the shallow part of the pool. I was anxious to teach him to swim, so when he asked me to join him in the water, I did.

I held Ryan on top of the water so he could practice floating, but he was frightened, thinking that I might let him go. I told him to stop worrying and relax, but he still floundered in the water. Every time I spoke to him, I seemed to make him more and more nervous. Finally, Ryan looked at me and said, "Dad, I'm sorry I haven't been listening to you. I'm really scared, but I'll try again. I'm sorry." Then I realized that Ryan's fear of the water wasn't the real problem; he was afraid of *me*. I was issuing a lot of instructions, but I certainly wasn't doing a good job of teaching Ryan to swim. I decided to try a gentler approach.

For the next thirty minutes, I just had fun in the water with Ryan and encouraged him to relax. Then we started playing a game: How long could Ryan stay above water without touching the bottom? As I counted, he managed to stay up for five, then ten and, finally, thirty seconds. He was beginning to feel confident in the water, and enjoyment had replaced his anxiety.

As we headed back to the house, it seemed to me that we had both made good starts that morning. Ryan was well on his way to learning to swim, and I was on the road to learning the value of patience.

Lord, help me to teach as You did, with gentleness of heart.

—DOLPHUS WEARY

29

Rejoice with me; for I have found the piece which I had lost. —LUKE 15:9

It's just a plain, little, black-handled knife. In a yard sale, you wouldn't pay a dime for it. But that little knife was the first bit of "housekeeping" Bob and I bought more than fifty years ago, and for sentimental reasons, it is priceless to me. Yesterday a neighbor brought us a bushel of ripe peaches from the trees in her yard, and I pitched in, using the little knife, to peel them for our freezer. I worked long and hard and was totally exhausted by the time I dumped the peelings in the backyard garbage can.

A little while ago I needed to cut up some celery and reached in the drawer for my special knife. It wasn't there! I took everything out of the drawer to no avail. *Perhaps I dropped it into another drawer,* I thought, but a full search produced no little knife. Then a fearful thought: *I threw it away with the peelings! Nothing to do but look through the garbage can.*

If you've never done that, I don't advise trying it. Or if you have, you know what it took for me to root through that debris.

Then there it was! The small blade twinkled brilliantly as the sun hit it. I was so excited I yelled aloud, "I found it! I saved it!"

A hot shower followed my ordeal. Then I closed myself in my study to have a visit with my God. A wonderfully new understanding of His love poured through me. When I was lost in the mire of sin, He sought me and found me. And He washed me fully clean, as I shall now wash my little knife.

Dear Father, I'll use that knife again and again. Please accept my gratitude for Your love, and use me as often as You will. Amen.

—DRUE DUKE

30 Let patience have her perfect work.... —JAMES 1:4

It had been a long week. As I cleared my desk, my temples were throbbing with a sinus headache. All I wanted to do was go home and take a nap. Then the phone rang.

My wife Beth's voice was excited. "Scott, one of Luke's friends has given him three tickets to the Rangers game tonight in Dallas. Luke and his friend Jake are dying to go. If you leave now, you can make it on time. Can you take them?"

My blood pressure shot up—way up! The last thing I wanted to do was drive two hours to Dallas, sit through a baseball game and get home long after midnight. But how do you say no to twelve-year-olds with free tickets?

An hour and a half later, we were approaching a bridge ten miles from the ballpark when a truck jackknifed up ahead of us. Traffic backed up for miles. We were stuck, with no option but to sit it out. I clicked on the radio. The game was well under way, and the Rangers were getting a shellacking. Then the little voices from the backseat rose to a crescendo:

"Dad, I've gotta go to the bathroom!"

"I'm hungry!"

"When are we going to get there?"

"Can't we just walk?"

My headache was spiking. And *I* needed that bathroom, too.

As the eighth inning started, the traffic began to move. We got to the stadium by the bottom of the ninth inning, in time to see the last three Rangers batters strike out. By the time I had fought my way through the parking lot traffic and was headed home to Waco, Luke and his friend Jake were asleep. *What a wasted night!* I fumed.

But within a week, Luke and I were laughing about our great fiasco. And with every laugh, it became apparent that the night, with all its frustrations, hadn't been wasted. It had become a memory, shared between us, that will cause eyes to sparkle and smiles to glisten for years to come.

Dear God, please give me the gift of patience—and the reward of laughter.   —SCOTT WALKER

31

My soul thirsteth for God, for the living God....

—PSALM 42:2

"Let's go sit by a stream somewhere," my husband Lynn suggested late one Saturday afternoon. I'd been working for hours on a project, trying to squeeze the right words out of the thoughts in my head. I wanted to be done, but I felt too weary and depleted to finish.

That's why Lynn suggested the "time-out" by the stream. Since we both grew up in Colorado, we've come to rely on the sound and sight of a rushing mountain stream for rejuvenation. So we grabbed a couple of sweatshirts, turned on the telephone answering machine, hopped in the car and stopped at a take-out place to get a bag of Mexican food for a picnic dinner. Then off we went, in search of a stream.

We headed up a nearby canyon where the rushing water runs alongside the road, and pulled into one of the first parking areas with no cars. We found a picnic table right by the water and spread out our fast-food feast. After eating, we simply sat and listened and drank in the sound and sight of that rushing water. By the time the shadows began to disappear into the gathering dusk, I felt renewed.

What is it about a mountain stream that replenishes me when I feel depleted? It reminds me that God is the endless source of the love that flows into my life and touches all the dry places in my thirsty soul. It washes away the sludge of stuff that clogs my brain and slows my thinking. God's creation is filled with other reminders of Himself that replenish people in dry times. For some, it's the ocean, or a sunrise, or the formation of a flock of birds flying in the sky. As we headed back down the mountain, I knew I'd be able to finish my project with renewed strength.

Father, I'm so thankful You have tucked reminders of Yourself into Your creation. Let me take a "time-out" to soak them all in.

—*CAROL KUYKENDALL*

MY FAITH JOURNEY

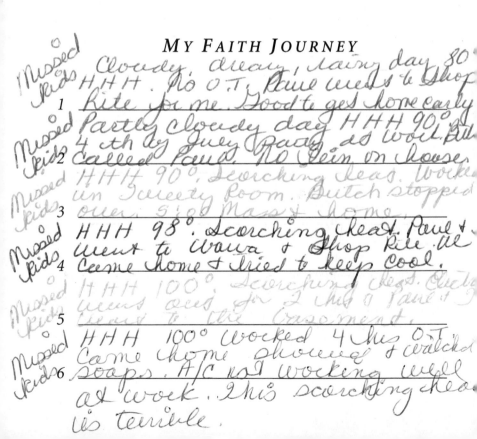

Missed kids HHH 100°. Electric went out about 2:30 + came back on at 5:30. Couldn't go to work till 6:00 as

7 garage door wouldn't open.

Missed kids Beautiful sunny day 90°. No humidity worked 3 hrs OT. Showed + watched

8 soaps + ate hamburgers.

Missed kids Beautiful sunny day 90°. Worked 4 hr OT. Paul & I went for a walk after

9 I called Chantell. Shower + soaps

Missed kids Beautiful sunny day 90°. Paul & cleaned the living room. Butch

10 stopped by. 5:00 Mrs. Shirley called

Missed kids Beautiful sunny day 85°. Paul + I went for papers + # 6 A + Broilers.

11 Relaxed all day. Shirley & Heather came down

Missed kids Beautiful cloudy day AM & 80° sunny PM. Got up late & had

12 breakfast at work. Paul & I

Missed kids Beautiful sunny day 80°. Worked 4 hrs OT. Paul went to records at

13 house yesterday & got Mom's will for me.

Missed kids Beautiful sunny day 80°. Boredat work. Did 4 hrs OT. Paul & I and

14 walked & showed & had tomato.

Missed kids Beautiful sunny day 85°. I took off for Paul & my 36th anniversary. Took

15 a 2 hr nap & we went to seaside.

Missed kids Beautiful sunny humid day 90°. very busy at work. Chantell called.

16 We walked 2 hours almost.

Missed kids Beautiful sunny day 90°. HHH My Paul & I went to 5:00 Mass. My

17 cousin Joyce came to visit

HHH 100°. Paul & I went for the papers & stayed in the A/C all

18 day. Butch + Chantell + kids stopped

Missed kids HHH 100°. Worked 4 hrs OT. Paul & I walked as rain made it a little cooler. Showed

19 & watched soaps. Irma helped for supper.

Missed kids

20 Beautiful sunny day 90° a little rain & less humidy. I did 4 hr O.T. Paul & I took a walk & showered & watched soap. Bad Day!

Missed kids

21 Beautiful sunny day HHH. Rode quite leg humid 85° very busy at work. Walked w/ Paul

Missed kids

22 Beautiful HHH day 85° very busy at work. Paul got Jill's Major & flounder on sale

Missed kids

23 Beautiful sunny day HHH 94°. Bored at work. Paul made corn fritters. Called Chantell on way home

Missed kids

24 Beautiful sunny day 95° HHH. Chantell came over & we took kids to see Barry Boy of Negie Tales

Missed kids

25 Beautiful sunny day 95° less humid PM. Bobbey called to say his daddy caught fish

Missed kids

26 Beautiful sunny day 95° so humid. Worked 4 hr O.T. Walked w/ Paul.

27 Beautiful sunny day. Came home at 12:00 & HHH. Ride weeks to Kansas. Raised the troopers show today AM

28 Beautiful sunny day 98° very busy HH at work. Claudle Julie w/ Bobley. Kelsey made no cookies

Missed kids

29 Beautiful sunny day 95° HHH. Worked 2 hrs O.T. Picking up Paul & went for burrito.

Missed kids

30 Beautiful sunny day HHH 95° called Chantell on my way home from work & sang H.B.

31 Beautiful sunny day 95°. Paul & I went to see where Brian lives in Medford. We stopped & Aunt Ruth & went to 5:00 Mass & then to Chantell's to watch the kids till 12:30 AM.

August

*Thou preparest a table before me in the
presence of my enemies....*
—PSALM 23:5 (RSV)

S	M	T	W	T	F	S
1	2	3	4	5	6	7
8	9	10	11	12	13	14
15	16	17	18	19	20	21
22	23	24	25	26	27	28
29	30	31				

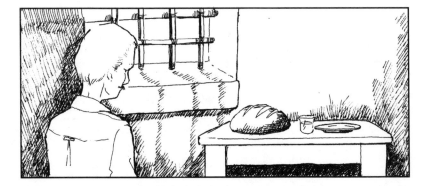

LESSONS IN LISTENING

1

SUNDAY

COINCIDENCE: PROVIDENTIAL SURPRISES
My times are in thy hand.... —PSALM 31:15

Before we set out for Africa my husband John and I had sent letters offering a writing course to more than twenty schools, trusting that God would lead us to those where He wanted us. One letter had gone to a friend of John's parents, a man John *thought* he remembered vaguely from childhood. Dr. Morton Hanna, John's mother believed, was currently teaching at a seminary in Kenya. A reply came: Dr. Hanna had indeed been at the seminary, but had recently left. We thought no more about it.

Our flight to Africa stopped in Rome, where I'd wrung a promise from the three children to sit wiggleless through an opera. Alas, we arrived to discover that the great Rome opera house was closed in August. The only musical performance anywhere was in a tiny theater way out in the suburbs.

The horseshoe-shaped room was so small that we looked directly into the faces of the audience on the other side. John, I noticed, kept staring at someone. "I know I've met that man somewhere," he said at intermission. Since John fought in Italy during the war he thought it must be an acquaintance from that time. Summoning his best Italian, he made his way around the horseshoe and introduced himself.

It was Morton Hanna, vacationing in Rome on his way home from Kenya. Dr. Hanna wrote the next day to set up a month-long writing class at the seminary—without question the most fruitful one of the entire year. And John and I added to our growing kit of guidance tools, *coincidence.*

Events that converge. Mere happenstance? Or is coincidence "the universe caught in the act of rhyming," a drumroll from the great Conductor: *Stop, look, listen! You, too, have a part in the universal hymn.*

Make me alert, Father, to Your harmony in the world today.
—ELIZABETH SHERRILL

2

Behold, I stand at the door, and knock: if any man hear my voice, and open the door, I will come in to him, and will sup with him.... —REVELATION 3:20

Last summer, in my part-time work as a stylist for home-decorating magazines, I visited a grand Victorian mansion. While the photographer set up his equipment, the homeowners took me on a tour of the house. "Don't open that door," the lady of the house warned me with a nervous chuckle when I stopped to admire a grapevine wreath on a closet door. "That's where we throw all our junk." Ironically, the wreath encircled a white picket fence with a miniature "Welcome" sign on an open garden gate.

When we passed the bedrooms occupied by the two daughters in the family, doors were suddenly slammed shut. "Your magazine wouldn't be interested in anything in there," the husband explained. "You know...teenagers. The usual rock-star posters."

As I scouted the grounds, I found a charming little potting shed behind a fragrant herb garden. "Our readers are going to love this," I said to the caretaker. "I'll bet there are all kinds of treasures inside."

"That's where I work," he said apologetically, shooing me instead toward the impeccably kept rose garden. "Too dirty for your camera's eye."

Later that day, as I styled the sparkling kitchen with food and flowers and other extra touches, I thought about my relationship with the Lord. How many parts of my life had I declared off-limits lately because I feared what junk or dirt He might discover behind closed doors? Truth was, deep down I knew I needed to change my approach to a difficult co-worker, and the situation was uncomfortable enough as it was. If I invited the Lord in, there was no telling what He might ask me to do.

As I arranged a bowl of sunflowers in a white ironstone pitcher, I felt a familiar gentle knocking. "I want to share everything with You," I prayed. "Even the secret places."

Abba, Father, You long to sup with me in the secret spaces, too. Come into my heart anew this day. —ROBERTA MESSNER

3

The Father that dwelleth in me, he doeth the works.

—JOHN 14:10

Apprehension tagged along with us to the hospital. My eighty-seven-year-old mother needed another bone scan. A year earlier, the breast cancer she had been treated for thirteen years ago had reappeared in her spine. The oral medication that had worked so beautifully was no longer effective. Mother had emphatically declined chemotherapy. Now the doctors were not at all optimistic, and neither was I.

Finally, after what seemed like an hour of waiting, they called Mother in for the test. She greeted the young man who came for her with cheerfulness and with polite, chatty conversation. My husband Gene and I stayed in the tiny, magazine-cluttered waiting area. We didn't try to talk. After a long wait, another man brought Mother back to us, and then motioned for me to step outside into the hall. After locking eyes with Gene for a moment, I walked into the hall, braced for the very worst news.

"Is your mother taking chemotherapy?" he asked cautiously. I assured him that she wasn't and didn't intend to. "That's what she told us, but we thought maybe she was...confused...or...."

"My mother's mind is sharper than mine." *Why was he hesitating? Why doesn't he just get it over with?*

Still looking very serious, he whispered solemnly, carefully choosing his words. "There's been a dramatic...ah...reduction in the disease. We've never seen anything quite like this. I just couldn't let you leave without some encouragement."

At last he smiled, and I wasn't afraid to look directly into his eyes.

Oh, my Father, will I ever learn that You are continually doing new and marvelous things? —MARION BOND WEST

4

Open thou mine eyes, that I may behold wondrous things.... —PSALM 119:18

My father and I had just arrived in Tellico, Tennessee. We were there for our third annual fly-fishing adventure, and I had a serious case of what some fishermen call "the bug." Plainly put, "the bug" is an insatiable desire to fish, and I was on fire to catch a fish before the sun went down. So we dumped off our gear, pulled on our waders, grabbed our rods and headed for the river.

I waded upstream, leaving my father behind. It wasn't long before I noticed several trout stirring through the water in a dark pool some thirty yards up from me. I began a frantic search through the pockets of my fly vest, where an extensive collection of dry flies and nymphs waited. Several hours and several flies later I hadn't gotten as much as a nibble.

"God, what's the problem?" I prayed crossly. "I've been looking forward to this trip for months and nothing's happening!"

"Hey, no fair! You've got the best spot on the river!" my father's voice interrupted.

"Yeah, right, Dad," I snapped back sarcastically, glaring into my fly box, "These fish have all got lockjaw...."

"Brock, look up. You've got a perfect view!"

I tore my eyes away from my tackle and shot an aggravated glance at my father. He was pointing over my shoulder past massive green pine trees and up the side of the mountain, where a magnificent sunset was breaking across the sky. I held my breath, caught in this blaze of purple, orange and pink.

In my rush to catch a fish, I had forgotten my real reasons for making the trip: to enjoy nature and share time with my father. Now I stood quietly as Dad and I watched the sun sink below the mountain's crest.

God, how quickly I lose my perspective. Open my eyes. Open my heart. —BROCK KIDD

5

I looked for some to take pity, but there was none; and for comforters, but I found none. —PSALM 69:20

Every morning I read three psalms. I don't look for something that strikes my mood. I let the words speak to me wherever I am. Often the phrases, recalling wars or kings or ancient enemies, seem to have no direct application to my life, but still I find comfort in them. Through the thoughts of the Psalmist, expressed in utter honesty, I feel connected with the Lord.

My friend Peter writes children's books, sometimes as many as a dozen a year. He has had enormous success, but not long ago he was feeling stymied by a project. By the time his wife Tina came home, he had worked himself into a tizzy of frustration and rage. He was angry at his publisher, angry at his editor and furious at himself. "Peter," his wife said, "people have felt frustrated like this as far back as...." She searched for words. "As far back as King David in the Psalms."

"Really?" he said.

As if to prove her point she picked up her Bible, turned to the Psalms and began reading at random. Stretched out on the sofa, Peter closed his eyes and listened. And he kept listening as Tina read psalm after psalm. He allowed the words to wash over him, not only the exultant ones of praise, but the indignant ones crying out in rage. They gave his frustrations a voice, and gradually, that summer evening, as the sun disappeared from the sky outside, he felt at peace.

Hear my cries, Lord, and help me in my need.   —RICK HAMLIN

6

We are the children of God: And if children, then heirs....
—ROMANS 8:16–17

Looking through the window of the studio where I work, I am watching the awesome wonder of a misty-green century plant getting ready to bloom. The *agave americana* is misnamed the "century plant"— in most areas it takes forty to sixty years, rather than a hundred, to bloom. In our warm and friendly California climate, these plants bloom within two or three years of their planting.

From a cluster of tall leaves (each five feet or more and tipped with a needle-sharp spike), the plant shoots a thick green stem twenty to thirty feet up into the air. This branches out into clusters of yellow-green flowers, honey sweet, so bees and hummingbirds hover around them. After blooming the plant dies, but it has already thrown out small baseline suckers, which, in their good time, grow and renew the process.

It seems providential that our plant blooms as we get ready to turn the century. I think of those who planted the original cluster in our garden, long before I was born. Now I'm looking toward a generation who will grapple with the twenty-first century, one of whom may someday sit where I am sitting and watch the miracle of our century plant blooming.

Tucked into my Bible is a quote passed down to me from my father. It was written by Sir Francis Drake, the first Englishman to sail around the world. "Men pass away, but people abide. See that you hold fast the heritage we leave you. Yea, and teach your children its value, that never in the coming centuries their hearts may fail them or their hands grow weak."

Lord, in the continuous blooming of our lives—of those who went before us, and now those who will come after us—I pray for steadfast hearts and strong hands. —FAY ANGUS

7

"Let the children come to me...for to such belongs the kingdom of God." —MARK 10:14 (RSV)

Just the prospect of spending the day at Aunt Alice's filled me with anticipation. There were cousins to play with and all sorts of interesting things we could do. They lived out in the country in a small house without all the conveniences we're used to today. Water was drawn from the well in the front yard, and the cooking was done on a cast-iron, wood-burning stove. There was a porch across the front of the house and a clear, gravel-bottomed creek running through the property. At night the house was lighted with kerosene lamps.

My cousins and I spent the morning playing in the creek and catching crawdads. Our equipment was simple—a piece of bacon rind tied on a string attached to a willow stick. When the crawdad grabbed the bait with its claw, we lifted it gently up and shook it off into a bucket.

When the container was full, we took the crawdads to the house, and I asked Aunt Alice, "If we clean them, would you cook them for us?" She agreed without hesitation and sent us to the front porch to shell out the tiny, shrimplike morsels. She sprinkled them with salt and pepper, gave them a dusting of cornmeal, and fried them crisp in her iron skillet.

At the time, it didn't occur to me that honoring my childish request meant a lot of work for Aunt Alice. She had to gather kindling and wood to build a fire in the stove, and we created a whole stack of dishes that would require washing. But it was such a special experience for me that I remember it fondly sixty-plus years later.

I hope that one day when some child comes to me with a ridiculous request, I'll give it the same serious consideration.

Dear God, give me the capacity more often to look at life with the eyes of a child.   —KENNETH CHAFIN

8

For he will give his angels charge of you to guard you in all your ways.   —PSALM 91:11 (RSV)

My backpack was heavy. Despite the fog and early morning chill, I was hot—and I still had another mile to walk to the Edinburgh train station. Suddenly, out of the fog, looking like he'd just stepped out of a Sir Walter Scott novel, a man approached. I grew apprehensive.

"Good morn'. Can I help ye out, ma'am?" he asked.

"No, thank you."

"I don't mind. Ye look a wee burdened."

"I'm certain, thank you!"

He shrugged. "I'll mosey on then."

The next morning, in a completely different part of town, I was holding a heavy bag and waiting for a city bus. Suddenly, out of the mist, the same stranger.

"'Ello, ma'am. Can I help ye today?"

I shook my head.

He leaned against the wall beside me. My apprehension increased. Not a single bus for half an hour! I prayed, *Now is a good time for a bus to come along, God!*

In answer to my prayer, my fear vanished, and though I'm not a person who hears God talk, I heard: *He's here to help you.*

The man stood by. We talked a little. Mostly it was quiet, an odd time of calm such as I've never experienced before, or since. Finally, "A bus be along the noon, ma'am," and he vanished into the fog.

I was not surprised when, less than a minute later, a bus wheezed out of the mist.

"No buses Sunday mornins, lass," the driver hollered. "I'm special run! But ye hop on! 'Tis not safe here!"

People to whom I tell the story often wonder if I'd met an angel. One thing I know, whoever he was, he was of God, sent to help and protect me.

Dear Lord, help me always to accept Your help and protection in whatever form it comes. —BRENDA WILBEE

9

Be thankful unto him, and bless his name. —PSALM 100:4

Shirley and I took the grandchildren—Jessica, Ashley and David—with us to our lake cottage in Indiana again last summer, and I think they enjoy the times in that rustic setting almost as much as we do. After several weeklong vacations together, we have developed certain rituals that we repeat each year. We swim at the same spot, fish in the creek, play golf, birdwatch, go on nature hikes and at night play games like Rook. There is something else we do: rake up the debris in the yard and use the twigs for a wiener roast. There's nothing quite as tasty as a sooty hot dog cooked over an open fire, or so my grand-kids think.

And after hot dogs come S'mores. I imagine most of you have fixed them. If not, the recipe is easy. All you need is a green stick upon which to impale marshmallows that are then heated (read that *set afire*) over hot coals; a box of graham crackers and some chocolate bars. A hot marshmallow and a piece of chocolate are sandwiched between two crackers and *voilà!* you have a S'more. Of course, they're so good that one treat is never enough. You must have *s'more*.

After my second sandwich, I got to pondering the name. I don't have a clue who christened this calorie-laden snack, and I don't think I've heard it in any other context—unless it's when I'm praying. Too often I think I ask God for *s'more* this and *s'more* that, overlooking the mountain of blessings He has already given me. Perhaps you're guilty of the same mistake. If so, maybe we both need to ask for *s'less* and be thankful *s'more*.

Instead of asking for another plateful,
Teach me, Lord, to be more grateful.
—FRED BAUER

10

The Lord is close to the brokenhearted and saves those who are crushed in spirit. —PSALM 34:18 (NIV)

Dinner was almost over, and the waiter was rustling around the table signaling that it was growing late. Long day. I was tired, tired of chattering, tired of trying to pretend that everything was fine. I felt as if my mind were full of black, nauseating mud.

"You're not well, are you?" said the old friend across the table. I opened my mouth to turn aside the remark with a plea of fatigue or work stress and, suddenly, the tears cascaded down my face without a sound. Few things are more embarrassing than crying in a public place. I bowed my head. Thank goodness the restaurant was romantically dim.

"You should call your doctor," said my friend in a matter-of-fact voice.

"I did," I whispered. "She's on vacation for ten days, and there was some emergency number to call. I just couldn't." The depression had been deepening for several weeks, just as the darkness falls on a summer night. It was too late by now to see my way.

"*I'll* call him, right now," my friend said. I was astounded by her offer, unable to answer. She disappeared to the pay phone at the back of the restaurant.

"Let's go," she said on her return. "He's calling you at home in half an hour." And he did. One quarter, one friend, and I could begin my walk toward the light.

Thank You, Lord, for true and courageous friends, who change our lives. —BRIGITTE WEEKS

11

"Every one who believes in him receives forgiveness of sins through his name." —ACTS 10:43 (RSV)

As I watch the waves dance one after another to the shore, I wonder why I am so drawn to the sea. Is it simply the beauty of the sparkling blue-green water, powerful and unchanging like God Himself? My thoughts are suddenly interrupted by my son Ross, who, after body-surfing for more than an hour, has just ridden a big wave all the way into shore and runs to tell me about it.

"You know what I love about the ocean, Mom?" he says, shaking saltwater off his face. "The waves keep coming. If you miss one, you just have to wait. There's always another one."

His innocent assessment falls into place in my mind like the last piece of a puzzle. *There's always another one.* The ebb and flow of the waves is an echo of God's own voice, calling me back to Him. Only recently I've let go of some destructive feelings, anger at a friend over long-ago hurts that I wouldn't forgive and resentment over her successes. Holding on to those feelings separated me from God, and in my stubbornness I passed up opportunities to be forgiven. Yet like the gentle pull of the tide, I always felt God bidding me to return to Him. And when I was finally ready, so was He—ready to send another cleansing wave of forgiveness to wash away the pain.

Gazing at God's great ocean now, I think I understand its power to comfort me. The steady flow of the sea is a reminder that while in my weakness I may miss many chances God offers me to come to Him, He will see that there's always another wave of His love and grace to carry me into shore.

Lord, wash over me Your love and forgiveness and bring me closer to You. —GINA BRIDGEMAN

12 THURSDAY

He has made everything beautiful in its time....
—ECCLESIASTES 3:11 (NIV)

This morning I dressed in the dark so as not to disturb my wife Julee, who was sleeping in after a late-night singing gig. Imagine my dismay when I arrived at work only to discover a small, ugly stain on my fresh shirt, a stain my neighborhood laundry had vowed to banish. It was virtually unnoticeable, I'm sure, but immediately I imagined that no one who came in contact with me could possibly ignore my blighted appearance. Later at a meeting, I felt utterly self-conscious. At some point I must have told myself, *Look, you're being silly,* but it did no good.

It was a lovely Manhattan day. A bright summer sun bleached the skyscrapers. I was walking from lunch across West 32nd Street with a friend when I detected people staring at me. Yes, I was certain someone pointed. I reminded myself to demand a refund from the laundry. Then I noticed my companion grinning. "You'll never believe this," she said.

"What?" I was growing tense.

"There's a big, beautiful butterfly riding on your shoulder."

Out of the corner of my eye I made out a pulsating smear of color, ocher and orange and blue.

"Careful," she whispered, "you might scare it off."

But it wasn't going anywhere, at least not anywhere I wasn't going. All the way across 32nd Street, west to east, the butterfly perched on my shoulder like a cool flame, and everywhere people stared and pointed and smiled.

"How did you teach him to do that?" one astonished kid asked.

The butterfly stayed with me for a good fifteen minutes, the entire way back to my office building, before fleeing the arctic air conditioning of the lobby. "That was amazing!" my friend said.

Amazing, certainly. But not as amazing as God, Who gives me a nudge when I'm thinking foolishly, and shows me that He made people far more interested in beauty than in ugliness.

Thank You, Lord, for stains and butterflies and sunny days—for everything. —EDWARD GRINNAN

13

FRIDAY

And having done all, to stand. —EPHESIANS 6:13

It was our seven-year-old grandson Ryan's first year in 4-H Club and first county fair. He proudly showed me his reserve champion rabbit and purple-ribbon no-bake cookies, then we went to look at Moonie, his calf. "We'll be in showmanship first," Ryan told me. "I have to lead Moonie around the show ring and make him stand in line with the other calves."

Showmanship! I groaned inwardly. Moonie was definitely not showy! He was a dull black-brown with long Brahma ears, and at one hundred fifty pounds he was the smallest calf in the barn.

When the announcer called, "All junior beef showmen into the ring!" I breathed a quick prayer while our son Patrick gave Ryan final instructions: "No matter what happens, hold tight to Moonie's halter and stand still unless the judge tells you to move."

Ryan dragged a reluctant Moonie into the ring. There were eight other calves plus two steers who weighed over a thousand pounds each. During the second trip around the ring, one of the steers jerked away from his owner. He knocked down two 4-H'ers and spooked three calves before the ringman caught him and tied him to the fence. Through it all, Ryan and Moonie never moved a muscle.

"Weren't you afraid when that big steer got loose?" I asked after the competition was over.

"Not really," Ryan told me. "I was too busy trying to do what Dad said: 'Hold tight to Moonie, and stand still unless the judge says move.' "

Hold tight and stand still. It was good advice for me, too. The mission agency where I work recently experienced some setbacks, and I'd reacted with a frantic burst of activity, pursuing projects and sources of funding that weren't really compatible with our work. Maybe the way to move forward was to do what Ryan did: Hold tight to the task and direction God has already given, and wait for His guidance.

Jesus Lord, forgive me when I think Your work depends on my efforts. Give me the grace to move forward by standing still. Amen.
—PENNEY SCHWAB

14

SATURDAY

Blessed are your eyes, for they see....   —MATTHEW 13:16

My gardening skills are almost nonexistent, but that has never daunted me, and every year I spend many Saturdays enthusiastically planting crops in my tiny garden plot. Every year, just as faithfully, my crops fail. Last year, bugs ate more of my lettuce than I ever did, my strawberries were aptly named (they looked like berries but tasted like straw), my carrots were stunted, and my white, extra-large "globe" onions never got bigger than a thumbnail.

"Another flop," I sighed as I carried my entire harvest into the house in my two hands. Apparently my visiting friend Jean agreed, for I saw her eyeing it with what I assumed was a negative look.

"Those onions—" Jean began. I was about to say, "Aren't they dreadful?" when she continued, "Would it be too greedy if I asked you for a few?" As I stared at her, baffled, she explained, "I just love pearl onions."

Pearl onions! I stared at the tiny vegetables again. I had been looking at my onions as imperfect globes, when, in fact, they were perfect pearls.

"Sure," I said finally. "Let me give you several. And here," I said, thrusting some small orange objects into her outstretched hands, "why don't you take some baby carrots, too?"

Encourage me, God, to see the value in what I have.

—*LINDA NEUKRUG*

15

And he that sat upon the throne said, Behold, I make all things new.... —REVELATION 21:5

The hammering started at 7:00 A.M. It was a muggy summer morning, and I had slept with my dorm room window open, trying to milk any breeze for all it was worth. I looked out the window and groaned when I saw that my beautiful courtyard view had been replaced with scaffolding and workers' scuffling boots. After drawing the curtains shut, I rolled over and buried my head under my pillow, trying to muffle the racket. I had a half-hour more left to sleep before work, and I wanted to savor it.

But the pillow did little to stifle the noise. And it was the same the next morning. And the next. And for a week after that. Though I woke up sour and out of sorts at first, grumbling about the restoration project, I soon became used to the sounds of construction.

Then one morning it was strangely quiet. I awoke with a start. I looked at my clock: 7:00 A.M. I closed my eyes, thinking I would enjoy the blessed silence, but I couldn't get back to sleep. A thin line of sunlight peeked at me from under the curtain. I put on my robe and went to open the window.

The courtyard was amazing. The walls were the color of fresh cream. Pink flowers the size of my hand had blossomed while I wasn't looking. The birds were back, and as I listened, the silence was filled with nature's early morning sounds. I leaned out as far as I could and my fingertips brushed the flowers' velvet petals. It must have been difficult to paint the high walls. Restoring the stone carvings had to be a challenge. And minding the plants and trees must have been a terrible hassle.

It was good to be awake to see this. I smiled and gazed once more at my gorgeous new view before getting ready for work.

Lord, help me see beyond my daily trials to the work of renewal You are doing in my life. —KJERSTIN EASTON

READER'S ROOM

Restful days; love of friends; visits from grandchildren; a birthday of a child who never knew his older brother who had died five years before his birth; he is a blessing to us all—God's gift to hurting parents who longed for a child. My parents' love, lots of sunny days and days of peace. I am a blessed lady.

—GAYMARIE SPARRER, LOCKPORT, NY

MONDAY

16

Be transformed by the renewal of your mind, that you may prove what is the will of God, what is good and acceptable and perfect. —ROMANS 12:2 (RSV)

I wish I liked pickles!

It was a muggy Philadelphia noon in May 1948, and I was watching one of my high school friends bite into a crisp dill pickle that seemed so cool and refreshing, especially when she talked about spearing it from the brine barrel in her delicatessen that morning. But I didn't like pickles. The thought of anything vinegary made my mouth pucker. Yet the idea persisted: *I wish I liked pickles!*

So that summer, I did something about it. Whenever pickles were put on the table, I took a tiny bite. The first ones still made me screw up my face. But a friend had sent us some homemade watermelon pickles; their syrupy sweetness overcame the underlying vinegar. Soon, I wasn't minding the acidity. And by the end of the summer, *I liked pickles!*

Today I opened a jar of my own homemade dill pickles on this hot summer day, and their cool, delicious taste transported me back fifty years, to the summer I learned to like pickles. After lunch I piled my

dishes in the sink, along with the breakfast dishes, last night's supper dishes and the cats' dishes. The sink always seems to be full, now
that I eat all my meals at home. "I hate doing dishes," I said for the
umpteenth time. Then revelation struck. *What would happen if I said,
"I wish I liked washing dishes!"*

Change begins with the wish to change. I'm still in the process,
but I do know that it's getting easier to do the dishes after each meal,
to keep the sink and counter clean and the kitchen generally tidy. And
I do like a clean sink.

Now, if only I liked to balance my checkbook!

*Lord, I give myself to You so that my mind can be renewed and
transformed, not only for doing my dishes but for every part of my
life.* —MARY RUTH HOWES

17

Then the people rejoiced, for that they offered willingly....
—I CHRONICLES 29:9

"Where are you heading?"
"To the Spanish Steps."
"Do you mind if I walk with you?"

If truth be told, I did. I was glad to be free of fellow tourists, and,
in Rome for this day, all I wanted was to refresh some old memories.
I walked from the station and this little old lady, also a passenger on
Rotterdam, tagged along. I quickened the pace. She kept up. When I
came to Via del Quinnale, she, breathless, complained. "Are you sure
you know the way?" (As though my guidebook were wrong!)

Then we arrived at the top of the steps. "Oh!" she exclaimed at
the sudden open expanse, the roofs and roof gardens of Rome, the
frequent bursts of pink azaleas, the one hundred and thirty-seven
steps down to Piazza di Espagna (according to my guidebook). "Oh,
it's so beautiful!" Then, turning to me, she said the thing that softened me. "And so are you."

Vanity, vanity. We began to talk. I shared my plan to head to Piazza
Navona, and then to the "wedding cake" of Vittorio Emanuele, then
the Colosseum. She was game. We lunched outside in a cafe beside
bold Bernini figures. ("No, no, *my* check. You've given enough.")

Eventually, tired from a long afternoon of executing my plan, we sank into a cab.

On the train back to the ship, I mused about the day. What would it have been like if I had gone alone? Possibly good, probably not. "You've given enough," she had said. I had given, grudgingly, what I could. And now, when I think of Rome, I think of her.

Lord, help me to give willingly and to receive joyfully.

—VAN VARNER

18   WEDNESDAY

Lightning and hail, snow and clouds, stormy winds that do his bidding....   *—PSALM 148:8 (NIV)*

I am a muller. I like to mull things over in my head while I do dishes or dust or make beds. Sometimes I think deep thoughts about God and life and pain and praise. But just when I think I am getting to the bottom of some profound conundrum, I remember the example of faith that our son John gave me when he was only five years old.

It had been a lowering Ohio summer afternoon and the radio warned of potential tornadoes. John was headed out to play. "Now, John, if you see a tornado approaching, what should you do?" I asked, expecting him to say, "Run home and go down to the basement."

He paused a moment (John is a muller, like me) and said, his gray-blue eyes round and serious, "I'd tell it to go away in the name of Jesus!"

John headed for the door again. Then he stopped and turned to me, his face perplexed. Suddenly, he broke into a world-shattering grin. "And, Mommy, if it didn't, then I'd know it was one of Jesus' and it'd be okay!" The door banged behind him as he bounded happily down the steps.

John's faith that if a bad thing still comes after prayer and spiritual warfare, it comes because of Jesus' loving plan for us, still humbles and inspires me. And mull as I might, I knew I'll never do better.

Lord, thank You for the faith of our children and for the memories that linger and nurture our own faith when they are grown.

—ROBERTA ROGERS

19

A dull axe requires great strength; be wise and sharpen the blade. —ECCLESIASTES 10:10 (TLB)

A bad dream woke me this morning. In it I was standing up in the classroom to teach, but I couldn't remember what to say. I think it was a warning.

Later, on the way home from the library, I paused to watch a tree trimmer at work. He was taking down a dead oak that was dangerous to pedestrians. He stood in a white, hydraulic bucket that took him up, down and around the old tree. His chain saw was the smallest I've seen—little bigger than a ukulele. Yet he lopped off limbs with no more effort than a housewife snapping off stalks of celery. Then he sliced the trunk in sections, like you would slice a carrot. In fifteen minutes he was done, without bothering traffic or endangering anyone.

"You make it look easy," I said when he came down to earth.

He smiled a proud smile. "It's trickier than it looks." He held up his little saw. "You've got to have good equipment. You can get a chain saw for a hundred bucks, but this little dandy cost me seven hundred." He wiped the shine from his face. "Good equipment and good preparation. I keep this chain as sharp as glass, keep everything oiled and fixed. It's a lot of preparation, but it makes the job fun."

I pondered his words on the way home, sensing a nudge from God in the incident. When I got home, I made a list of all the things I needed to do before school starts: type course plans; buy some newer books; remodel my office. Just making the list relaxed me and gave me confidence that I will be ready.

"Good equipment and good preparation" sounds like a formula that might apply to almost any situation I might be facing.

Remind me, Lord, to sharpen my tools if I want to make my work easier. —DANIEL SCHANTZ

20

For he shall deliver the needy when he crieth....

—PSALM 72:12

Money was tighter than ever that sweltering August. I had given up my job at the local newspaper in order to stay at home with my four small children. I was trying to make a living from freelance work, but attending to the children's needs took up most of my time, and both my productivity and my income had taken a nosedive. Soon they would need clothes for school. *Will the child support arrive this month?* I brooded. *God, are You even listening?* To take my mind off the heat and my dilemma, I put up my feet and reached for *So Big* by Edna Ferber.

My pastor Charles Taylor had introduced me to this story of a plucky Midwestern mother who supports herself and her son by raising vegetables. Perhaps I had told him about the year I spent eleven cents on seeds and sold a hundred and fifty pounds of pumpkin. He had given me a secondhand copy of the classic book as a Christmas present. I wrote a thank-you note and put away the gift on a shelf next to my desk.

Now, I propped myself up on some pillows, stretched out and began to read. Suddenly, a crisp twenty-dollar bill fluttered out of the book and landed on my chest. *Leave it to Father Taylor to be imaginative like that!* I thought. *He must have wondered why I didn't thank him for the money.* Smiling to myself, I opened the book again. Another twenty fell out, then another. Barely breathing, I slowly turned the pages and found two more twenties tucked between them, for a total of a hundred dollars. My smile broadened, then turned into laughter—laughter that my listening Lord could hear all the way to heaven.

Dear Lord, even when You don't hand down twenties from heaven, I know that You will provide for me. —GAIL THORELL SCHILLING

21 *Cast thy burden upon the Lord....* SATURDAY —PSALM 55:22

Last summer I spent a long weekend with my goddaughter Neva at her parents' home in Lake George, New York. It came at a time when the lease on the comfortable apartment where I've lived for more than twenty years was about to expire. I was worried because my dog barked, and I thought it might be a reason to deny me a renewal.

One afternoon while I was sitting on the lakeside dock, I watched as Neva tried to convince her four-year-old son Nikolas to jump from the dock into the knee-high water where she stood. Nikolas was wearing his water wings and a life vest, but still he hesitated. "Come on, Nikolas!" Neva called out. "I'll catch you. Just throw yourself on me."

Throw yourself on me, I thought. *Where do those words come from?* And then I recalled the words of St. Augustine of Hippo, the Christian church father and philosopher, who, when counseling his flock, said, "Do not be afraid to throw yourself on the Lord! He will not draw back and let you fall. Put your worries aside and throw yourself on Him." Just then, Nikolas made the leap and landed in Neva's outstretched arms, where he beamed up at me over his accomplishment.

That night during my prayer time, I recalled the incident and mentally threw myself on the Lord. And when I returned to the city, guess what? The new lease was waiting.

Lord, how easy it is to cast my cares on You. Thank You!

—*ELEANOR SASS*

JOURNEY OF THE SOUL

The prophet Elijah, the First Book of Kings tells us, journeyed to Mt. Horeb, where the Lord spoke to him as a still, small voice. Sometimes if we want to listen to God's voice, we must hush the everyday voices around us and let Him lead us to a place apart. This week, Marilyn Morgan Helleberg invites us to join her as she seeks God's guidance in prayer and solitude. Along the way, she'll show us some ways to create our own places of quiet right here, in the midst of life's distractions. —THE EDITORS

22

FACING THE MOUNTAIN
He went up into a mountain apart to pray....
—*MATTHEW 14:23*

Thomas Merton wrote, "All people need enough solitude in their lives to enable the deep inner voice of the soul to be heard." As I read his words, something within me says, *Yes! I know it's true.* So why do I often neglect the contemplative aspect of my spiritual life? In this busy, achievement-oriented world, it's so very difficult to carve out time for solitude. Yet I see a hopeful shift of focus arising among people of faith as we near the millennium. More and more of us ordinary folks are hungering for a deeper connection with the Divine. And we're actively seeking it, too, not just for our own personal gratification, but in order that we may better serve God and others in our everyday, push-rush-pull world.

It's for this reason that I decided to spend a month alone at our family's mountain cabin. I know that's not an option most of us have, but what became clear to me there is that *it is possible to connect with God in a deep way by carving out small slices of solitude, even in the midst of busyness and stress.* In fact, stress makes it a *necessity.*

When my soul is fed during time alone with God, I'm invariably led right back into the everyday world, with a challenge and a responsibility to live it out in my daily life, and to distribute the loaves and fishes Jesus has multiplied on the mountain.

I've come to see this time apart as deep and valid work that grounds me in God's truth. In fact, it may be the most truthful work I've ever been called to do. If your soul is hungering for a deeper relationship with God, thirsting for a more vivid awareness of Christ walking beside you along the road of your life, I invite you to join me for a week in a little cabin on the side of a Colorado mountain, to see what gifts we may bring back into everyday life.

May we be present with You, Lord Jesus, at Your place apart on the mountain.
                                        —MARILYN MORGAN HELLEBERG

23

JOY IN THE JOURNEY
The Lord thy God is with thee whithersoever thou goest.
                                        —JOSHUA 1:9

I'd come to a time of questioning the value of my life. More than anything, I'd wanted to be a perfect wife and mother. Now that I was divorced and my children grown, my failure to live up to that ideal seemed painfully clear. My relationship with God had always been vital and fulfilling, but lately even that had lost its savor. I desperately needed to reconnect with Him.

How many years have I been making the trip to the little cabin on the side of a mountain? All of my life. That's sixty-six years. Now, on Interstate 80 somewhere between Sterling and Denver, the sky opens up and takes me into itself. Oh, not just the sky but also the shape-shifting clouds, the 360-degree horizon, the long, quiet highway un-rolling itself before me and especially the still-distant mountains ris-ing abruptly out of the silent, spacious plains. As my little blue Mazda purrs along, licking up the remaining miles, even the other cars on the road, with their unknown passengers, have become part of this no-longer-surprising yet always stunning sense of God's presence.

How can I bring this back with me into everyday life? Perhaps I can make it a point, whenever I drive on the highway, or ride a bus or subway, or travel by air, to count that time as a gift. Instead of fret-ting about what's ahead of me or how long it's taking me to get there, perhaps I can allow myself just to relax into the scene; to open the windows of my awareness and let it all in; to say, with my Creator, "It is very good."

Oh, great Creator of all that is, may I see this time en route not as time wasted but as time given. Let it be a time to touch and to be touched by Your presence. —MARILYN MORGAN HELLEBERG

24 TUESDAY

AFFIRMING LIFE
To every thing there is a season, and a time to every pur-pose under the heaven. —ECCLESIASTES 3:1

The traffic is getting thicker and more impatient as I pull into Denver. I glance at the clock—5:15 P.M. Rush hour! You'd think I'd learn to time things better. Oh well, I might as well pull off and have dinner. I settle into the booth, place my order, squeeze lemon into my iced tea and take a long, cool drink. Then I notice a young family with two small, tired and whining children, a fussy baby, a frazzled mother, and an impatient dad. Taking another sip of tea, I breathe a long sigh, remembering how it was to travel with small children.

In the booth across from me, an old man sits mumbling into his coffee cup. As he gets up to complain to the waiter, I notice how stooped over he is. His comments to the waiter are a bit incoherent, and I realize that his command over his body and mind has begun to leave him.

In these two little vignettes being played out before me, I see my past and possible future, and I know I'm closer to the latter than the former. But right now, in this clear, free moment, I am present, alive and aware. For an instant, I imagine myself flying free, up above the scene, embracing it all. And it's all okay.

I'll try to remember this moment when I'm home in the busy rush of my life, hurrying toward a work deadline, shopping in a crowded store or hosting a grandchild's birthday party. I'll let the moment come alive by focusing on the sights, sounds and smells around me. I'll try really *to notice life happening.* And even if these old bones ache, I'll embrace it all, knowing Whose hand sustains me.

Thank You, great Creator, for this priceless, ordinary moment.
—MARILYN MORGAN HELLEBERG

25 A PRESENCE ON THE ROAD
All the paths of the Lord are mercy and truth....
—PSALM 25:10

I was tired when I arrived last night, but the pine-scented air, the star-sprinkled sky undimmed by city lights and the crackling fire I built felt like welcoming arms. This morning as I sit, coffee cup in hand, gazing out the window at the mountain I know so well, I do not feel alone. I sense the lingering presence of my grandparents, parents, brother, aunts, uncles, cousins and my own immediate family, all of those who've lived within these walls. And yet there's something missing, some vital spark within me that refuses to come back to life.

I reach for my pen and spiral notebook and write, "What is this longing that pulls so strongly at my heart?" Almost as soon as I've written the words, I know. It's a longing for God. Though my mind knows that my Companion on the journey has never left me, my heart sometimes forgets!

I close my eyes and envision my life as a road, and I ask, *At what points of the journey have I been most aware of Christ walking with me?* Memories come quickly: of a child swinging under a wisteria arbor feeling surrounded by God's love; of a lonely teenager in Chicago during World War II whose invisible Friend was Jesus; of a young mother walking the floor with a colicky baby, aware of other Arms upholding her; of a mother in a hospital chapel the night of her son's tragic accident, carried through by the words, "Peace, be still!"; of a woman nearing sixty going through a painful divorce, knowing she was not alone. Many, many other moments come to mind, glad ones and sad ones, eight pages of them!

Feeling both emptied and filled, I glance out the window again. A gentle, powdered sugar snow is falling with such grace and beauty I want to kiss the ground where it falls. And I *know* Who shares the moment with me.

Though the journey's end is not yet in sight, Lord, I know You walk the road with me. —MARILYN MORGAN HELLEBERG

26

THURSDAY

LEARNING TO LET GO
Study to be quiet.... —I THESSALONIANS 4:11

It's my fourth day here, and I'm feeling a vague heaviness. What is it? I think I had some unrealistic expectations about this time apart. What I'm finding is that instead of "getting away from it all," I've brought my problems and worries with me! Whenever I get quiet, I find myself turning them over in my mind. *What about the health problems that showed up on my last physical exam? Are my grandchildren getting a good education? Will I ever get caught up on all the mail waiting to be answered?* Then all of those self-inflicted "shoulds" start parading across my mind. Along with the many graces of a quiet retreat, time apart does tend to bring up all the stuff that busyness has pushed out of sight.

I see that it's time to begin my practice of the "letting-go prayer" that has been so meaningful to me for more than twenty years. I change from my jeans to full-cut pants and a loose shirt, do a few stretching exercises to loosen up my body, and get comfortable in the soft chair with the straight, firm back. Next, I take a few long, slow, deep breaths to help me relax, let my eyelids close and then begin to call upon the name of the Lord. Sometimes I just repeat, "Jesus, Lord Jesus," and sometimes I simply use the name "Love" as my way of calling upon our God Who *is* love.

Usually within a very short time, I notice that my mind has wandered away, often to a problem or worry. Then I just make a mental note of what the thought's about, offer that situation to God and *let go of it* by again returning to the name of the Lord. What I notice is that even though the same thought may return many times, as I just keep releasing each concern to my heavenly Father, the load gets lighter. The bonus is that often, later in the day, as I'm washing dishes or doing some other mundane task, a solution to a problem presents itself!

When I'm at home, I practice the letting-go prayer twice a day. It's the best prayer gift I've ever received.

As I still my mind, Lord, Your precious name releases my burdens. I am eternally grateful.   —MARILYN MORGAN HELLEBERG

27 FRIDAY

FAITH-WALKING
I will lift up mine eyes unto the hills, from whence cometh my help.   —PSALM 121:1

It's become a ritual for me, each time I come here, to hike up the mountain to the foot of the falls. About halfway up, there's a large boulder I sit on to rest and to absorb the beauty and wonder of the place. Often, chipmunks and even birds come near enough to eat sunflower seeds from my hand, and I'm aware, once more, of God's stunning presence in all creation. But I've never before been here in winter, and there's snow and some ice on the mountain now. I've recently been diagnosed with osteoporosis. Do I dare make the climb? I offer the question to God, and every bone in my body answers, "Yes!" I know Who has called me here, and I trust that call.

The snow on top of the pine needles makes it slippery and hard to get a footing. About halfway up to the falls, the going becomes treacherous, and I keep slipping. I begin to realize that this is the most difficult climb I've yet made. The path ahead looks worse, so I look back and notice I made a wrong choice some time back. I see that if I'd go back down, across and then up, the trail might be easier. Yet I seem to hear an inner command: *Hold the ground you've gained.* "Okay, God. I'm trusting You to get me through."

I pick my way carefully upward a few more steps, and there by my right foot is a dead branch. I pick it up, break off the top, test its sturdiness and accept God's gift of a hiking stick! Though I've never used one before, the timing is beyond coincidence. When there's nothing to hold on to, I can place it solidly where my next step will be and pull myself up with it. It helps me to reach the rock that has become a sacred place for me.

After brushing the snow from the rock, I sit down and allow myself to be filled with the wonder of it all. Then I notice, for the first time, the sound of the falls. I let it seep into every cell in my body. Thankfulness overflows. A silver-white dove hovers near. I'll take my hiking stick home, to remind me that I can dare hard things because the One Who walks with me will provide for my needs.

Thank You, my trustworthy Friend. Because of You, my spirit soars.

—MARILYN MORGAN HELLEBERG

28 SATURDAY

SHARING THE FRUITS
Come ye yourselves apart...and rest a while....

—MARK 6:31

I have only a few days left in which to savor this time apart with God. I came here questioning the value of my life. Have my questions been answered? My time here hasn't enabled me to relive the past or to see clearly where the road ahead may lead. But it has helped me to reconnect with the eternal Beloved, Who has fed my soul in the deepest possible way. Who could ever ask for more?

There are other gifts I'll take home with me, too. A deeper trust—in God and in the great mystery that life is. And I'll bring home a new appreciation of the ordinary: the big black crow sitting, still as a snapshot, on a snowy branch in an all-white world; the squirrel on the weathered wood fence peering in the window at me; the gently falling snow; the stillness at dusk; the moonlight shining, oblique and silver, on Grandmother Banta's faded print tablecloth. Best of all is the hiking stick, the gift that taught me trust. Little things, ordinary things, rendered priceless by love.

But now I'm noticing a shift. Something inside says, *Okay, enough. I'm ready now to go back out.* Already, my arms are aching to hold my grandchildren. Today, I'll shop for a few small gifts to bring back to those I love. Yet I know in my heart that the intangible gifts I carry home will outlast all the souvenirs.

Two thousand years ago, Jesus said to His disciples, "Come ye yourselves apart...and rest a while." While they were there, He fed not only the twelve but also the multitudes, with two small fish and five loaves, the meager gift of a small boy. Sometimes I have only a few brief minutes to offer Him, but He receives them with grace, and then multiplies them. When I return home, I will find time to "come apart and rest a while" with Him, even on the busiest day.

Lord, I offer You my small gifts of minutes apart with You. Feed my soul and then multiply the gifts.

—MARILYN MORGAN HELLEBERG

29
SUNDAY

"The rain came down, the streams rose, and the winds blew and beat against that house; yet it did not fall, because it had its foundation on the rock."

—MATTHEW 7:25 (NIV)

The house where I was raised was old, even then. Its two-story frame was built on top of a hand-dug basement. One of my jobs was to go down in this basement and get whatever canned goods we needed for mealtime. The creaky stairs ended in a dank cellar where canned peaches and green beans, pickled beets and sauerkraut lined the shelves. Long-legged spiders skittered into corners with my approach.

I never liked the basement much until storms came. Then that dark, spidery enclosure became a welcome refuge. Winds could wail and rain beat down, but I knew we were safe here. I could place my hands on the huge rocks, cemented together half a century ago, and know that our foundation was sure. Nothing could harm us.

My husband builds houses now, and most foundations are poured concrete. No one takes time to lay stones one upon another before erecting a home. But while the material may have changed, the principle hasn't: Every structure needs a strong foundation.

I've found that's true for lives as well as houses. The foundations on which I build—often themselves unseen—determine how well I stand the storms of life. When I build on the solid rock of faith and forgiveness, God provides me with an edifice that will never be shaken. No matter how strong life's winds blow.

Oh, Rock of my salvation, I would build my life on You!

—MARY LOU CARNEY

30

I will give you back your health again and heal your wounds.... —*JEREMIAH 30:17 (TLB)*

School is starting, and we'll all be changing our routines somewhat. *Ah ha,* the perfect time to start a new habit! How about an exercise habit?

Before my youngest child Andrew left for college last fall, I'd get up at 6:15 each school day and jump into my casual clothes and walking shoes. I'd fix Andrew's breakfast and my tea. We'd enjoy thirty minutes together while he ate and got ready for school. Then, as soon as he was out the door at 7:05, I'd take off walking. Fast walking, mind you. Even though Andrew's two thousand miles away now, my walking habit is still with me.

Sometimes I wear a radio headset that is tuned to the oldies station. All those great rock and roll tunes of the fifties, sixties and seventies keep me moving fast. In between the tunes I hear the news. Often, I leave the radio at home and meditate, plan my day, or just commune with nature on the beautiful bike path along the creek just two blocks from my house. It's a great way to start the morning. Half an hour later, I return home, shower, eat breakfast and head for my home office. That's *my* exercise routine.

Now let me tell you about Anne Clark's exercise habit. She's competed in more than five hundred running races worldwide and is the proud owner of more than thirty age-related running records in races that range from short 5Ks to marathons. What's so unusual about that, you say? Nothing, except for the fact that Anne didn't start running until she was sixty-nine years old and in 1996, at age eighty-seven, she was still running races. Anne says that running has cured her age-related aches and pains, including back pain, arthritis and bursitis. To look at her sleek physique and rosy complexion, you'd think she was in her early sixties.

When I read about people like Anne Clark, it reminds me that God meant for our bodies to remain young and healthy well into old age. But we have to do our part. The good news is that it's never too late to begin a fitness habit. Let's start today...for the rest of our lives.

Lord, help me to cherish the body You gave me by keeping it active. Don't let me be a slacker. Keep me walking, running, skating, swimming, whatever...all year long. —*PATRICIA LORENZ*

31

Beloved, if God so loved us, we ought also to love one another. —I JOHN 4:11

One afternoon I saw my friend Kimi in the mall. She looked so frail, as if she might fade away. And her round, usually cheerful face was somber and shadowed beneath a soft dark hat. When I asked what was wrong, I learned she had recently lost Mari, the handicapped daughter to whom she'd given twenty-five years of constant, tender care. It was a terrible blow for her. Her heart was "shock," she said. She went on to tell me how God was comforting her with glimpses of sunflowers wherever she went. In them, she saw Mari's smile.

An idea blossomed in my mind. I arranged a surprise "sunflower lunch" with Kimi's friends. We bought her gifts that included or pictured these bright, shaggy flowers. She was thrilled. Once the waitress paused at our table to ask if it was Kimi's birthday. "No," she said with a smile, "they just love me."

Her words, less than a year later, ring in my ears. Her conviction that she was truly loved is a comfort to me. For now it is my turn to say my heart is "shock." Just a few days ago, Kimi died suddenly. I am still trying to absorb the knowledge.

And today, as I reflect on my good times with Kimi, my daughter walked into the room wearing a T-shirt I haven't seen in a while. It happens to be decorated with sunflowers. And it's true, they really do smile.

Compassionate Savior, may those I love see it clearly, like a sunflower growing tall on a warm summer day. —CAROL KNAPP

MY FAITH JOURNEY

1 *[handwritten] Beautiful sunny day HHH. Paul made bacon, egg + potatoes for breakfast. I took a 2 hr nap. Butch came over.*

1 Missed kids. Beautiful sunny day 95° HHH. Paul & I went for papers coffee, we came home & relaxed.

2 Butch stopped over.

3 Missed kids. Beautiful sunny day 93° No HHH. I did 4 hrs O.T. Paul & I showered & watched soaps.

3 Missed kids. Beautiful sunny day 85°. I did 4 hrs O.T. Came home & Paul & I showered & watched soaps.

5 Missed kids. Beautiful sunny day 88°. I did 4 hrs O.T. Came home & Paul & I showered & watched soaps.

6 Missed kids. Beautiful sunny day 90° very busy at work. I did 4 hrs O.T. Butch stopped over.

7 Missed kids. Beautiful sunny day 90°. very busy at work.

8 Cloudy rainy day & very humid 90°. Papers & Kelsey's birthday party at 1:30. Came shrimp

9 Missed kids. Kelsey's birthday. Called & sang to her. Walked to old house. I sat outside till 8:15. Made salad

10 Missed kids. Beautiful sunny day 80°. But went to dump & Ames. We had toy gather for supper

11 Missed kids. Beautiful sunny day w/ few showers. 90°. HHH. Worked 4 hrs O.T. Paul & I had BLT for supper & watched soaps

Missed kids 4 hrs O.T. — Beautiful sunny day HHH. I waked Aunt Tim at 5:00A. Paul & I showered & watched soaps, an retired at 9:00.

12

Missed kids — Beautiful partly cloudy day 91°. Took VAC day & Paul & I went to Paitre Pio Center & see Boche.

13

Missed kids — Rainy cloudy day 80°. Did 8 hrs O.T. from 5:00 - 1 PM. Came home & napped w/Paul. Bad storms. Watched soaps.

14

Cloudy rainy day. Chantell & Bob & the kids stopped over to take Boches dresses to her. Paul & I went to 8:30 Mass.

15

Missed kids — Beautiful sunny day. Did 4 hrs O.T. Came home & Paul & I made salad & showed & watched soaps. Paul had sharp pain in abdomen.

16

Missed kids — Beautiful sunny day 90°. HHH. Worked 4 hrs O.T. & Paul & I had spagetti for supper. Watched soaps.

17

Missed kids — Beautiful sunny day 85°. Not quite so humid. Worked 4 hrs O.T. Leftover spagetti & watched soaps.

18

Missed kids — Beautiful sunny day 80°. Very breesy at work. Hot sour storm. Paul & I watched. Chinese lunch for supper. Watched soaps.

19

Missed kids — Rain, Rain Blessed Rain. 80°. Worked 4 hrs O.T. Called Chantell on my way home. Butch called PM.

20

Missed kids — Rain AM, Cloudy cool day 70°. Worked 8 hrs O.T. Came home & napped for 2 hrs. Brought Mickey D's for lunch. Paul & I showed & went to IGA after Mass in New Egypt.

21

Missed kids — Beautiful sunny cool day 75°. Paul & I went for papers & relaxed most of day. Washed

22 linen & clothes & dried. Called Dutch.
Missed kids — Beautiful sunny day 85°. very uneasy as work. Did 4 hrs O.T.

23 Paul & I made salad. watched soap.
Missed kids — Beautiful sunny day 85°. uneasy as work. Did 4 hrs O.

24 Came home & watched soap.
Missed kids — Beautiful sunny day 80°. very uneasy as work. Paul called

25 Dr. Goldsteins office - Worked 4 hr O.T.
Missed kids — Beautiful sunny day 90° very uneasy as work. Did 4 hrs o.t.

26 Worked (52) hrs O.T. in 2 weeks.
Missed kids — Beautiful sunny day HHH 90°. Paul & I went for my haircuts. Padre Pio

27 Mass, confession & gloves & to see Boche
Beautiful sunny day 90° H.H.H.
Paul & I went to Bobby & Kelsey

28 football games Carteres & Arthus'.
Beautiful sunny day 90° H.H.H.
Bobby & Kelsey spent the night.

29 We went to 5:00 PM Mass at St. Raphael.
H.B. Paul — Cloudy, cool day 70°. Bobby spent the night. I made pork roast for

30 Chantel & girls came over & we went to show.
Missed kids — Cloudy, dreary day 75° Partly sunny. Did 1 hr O.T. Very tired.

31 Came home at 3:00 & Paul wasn't home. Tired as dumps. Laid in bed & watched G.H. Retired 10:

September

Thou anointest my head with oil....
—PSALM 23:5 (RSV)

S	M	T	W	T	F	S
			1	2	3	4
5	6	7	8	9	10	11
12	13	14	15	16	17	18
19	20	21	22	23	24	25
26	27	28	29	30		

LESSONS IN LISTENING

1

WIDENING THE CIRCLE
For the same Lord over all is rich unto all that call upon him.
—ROMANS 10:12

We spent most of our year in Africa in newly independent Uganda. With changes coming fast, people in various ministries met to seek guidance each Friday in the capital, Kampala. One medical missionary from England faced an especially hard decision. Sybil had a retarded thirty-two-year-old son whose assisted-living facility back in England was about to close. In addition, her elderly parents would soon be unable to stay alone in their home in Kent. Before long we were spending every Friday on Sybil's dilemma. Should she return to England to care for her son and parents? Who would continue her work in Uganda?

Well, we had opinions and advice for her in plenty, but no real answers. Round in circles we went, week after week, storming a silent heaven on Sybil's behalf. At last a wise old Mennonite on leave from Congo spoke up.

"Your receiver's stuck on a single band," he said, a reference to the shortwave radios many of us used. "When nothing comes through, you have to listen at another wavelength. You never know where you'll pick up God's signal."

Sure enough, once we opened those Friday sessions to other concerns, answers came for Sybil. An older missionary, due to retire, prayed to find affordable housing back home in England. "Prices have gone up so since I came to Uganda forty years ago!" God's solution was to stay with Sybil's parents in Kent, allowing the elderly couple to stay put.

The director of a Kampala orphanage needed a cook's assistant. "We can provide food and lodging, but no salary." When my husband and I left Uganda, Sybil's son had been in Kampala three months, "with real purpose in his life for the very first time," she told us, in that orphanage kitchen.

Enlarge my caring, Father. Your perfect plan for me embraces the needs of many people. —ELIZABETH SHERRILL

2

Every man according as he purposeth in his heart, so let him give.... —II CORINTHIANS 9:7

My late husband George and I used to spend a lot of time at our cottage on Lake Erie.

We had some land around the cottage, which had to be mowed and kept in trim. George had a mower to help him with the grass, but it was getting old. His sons Jeff and George Jr. did the best they could when they were there, and he often hired other help. But the trees, grass and weeds were always threatening to get out of control.

Then one day a neighbor arrived at our door in a huge vehicle that put all mowers to shame. It could not only cut the grass and weeds, it could also cut trees, if necessary, and even grind them into chips if you wanted! Most amazing of all, it could clean up afterward.

To our amazement, the man handed a key to George. "Here, take it. It's yours!" he said.

"Oh, no, don't be silly!" George gasped. "I can't accept it!"

"Okay, then let's just say it's *ours.* Use it whenever you want, and let your boys use it whenever they're here. I really want to do this for you, Doc. I'm not rich, and I don't own much, but I sure get a kick out of sharing what I've got."

Lord, help me to be generous with the blessings You've given me.
—MARJORIE HOLMES

3

Have no anxiety about anything...let your requests be made known to God. —PHILIPPIANS 4:6 (RSV)

Our dog Cookie is a worrier. Her favorite perch is the windowsill in our son Ross' room where she keeps an eye on everything in the neighborhood that needs watching: early morning joggers; kids getting on the school bus; and especially other dogs. But her biggest worry is our swimming pool. Every time we jump in, especially if Ross does one of his wild, splashy dives, Cookie barks and runs around the perimeter of the pool, getting more agitated and exhausted with each lap. She relaxes only when I take her into the house and settle her into her bed.

"I wish we could make Cookie understand that running around in circles worrying doesn't do any good," I said to the kids one day after taking her inside.

Only after I heard myself say it did I realize that Cookie's worrying wasn't any different from my own. She runs in circles and makes a lot of noise, but her efforts do no good; they just wear her out. My worries have the same effect on me, especially when I wake up in the night with a head full of them. *Will Ross be safe at his Scout campout? How will Maria handle her first day at her new school? Should I have agreed to teach a new class this fall? How will I get the work done?*

My mind goes in circles with the noise of all these thoughts, and the worrying alone changes nothing. Too often it's only at the point of exhaustion that I'll turn to God. But I suspect that's the wrong approach. Bishop Fulton Sheen said, "All worry is atheism because it is a want of trust in God." Just as Cookie seems to lack faith that we know what we're doing when we jump into the pool, so my own worry reveals a gap in my trust in God. Instead of running in circles, I need to run straight to Him.

Lord, forgive my worry and bring me peace. —GINA BRIDGEMAN

4

A time to weep, and a time to laugh; a time to mourn, and a time to dance. —ECCLESIASTES 3:4

Our friend Phyllis called us early on an August morning. She had recently lost a son, and I held my breath as I waited to hear what she had to say.

"Can I borrow your church directory?" she asked.

"Of course," I answered.

"I'll be there as soon as I can." For Phyllis, that meant a twenty-mile drive.

When Phyllis arrived, she told us what she was planning. Her sister Jean and her brother-in-law Henry, who were members of our church, were about to celebrate their twenty-fifth wedding anniversary. "I want to give them a party, and I want to give it at their summer home in Maine, and I'd like it to be a surprise!"

Ruby and I gasped. Although it was a wonderful idea, it didn't seem very practical. And what's more, Phyllis planned to hold the party on the Saturday before Labor Day, when friends are apt to be as scattered as fallen leaves.

"You know their friends at church," Phyllis said. "I want to invite as many as I can, and I want you to call them. And don't forget—it's a secret!"

The day of the party arrived, and Ruby and I drove ninety miles to Maine, to the town next to the one where Henry and Jean lived. Phyllis was there waiting for us. Henry and Jean had houseguests who were in on the secret, and who had taken them on a sightseeing outing that morning. We hurried to the house, where we were met by Jean's father and her four brothers, who erected a tent and set up tables and chairs while the ladies prepared a feast. When Henry, Jean and their visitors arrived, everything was ready. Later Jean said, "When I came around the corner and saw all those people and the tent, I was mad! I thought someone was holding a yard sale on our property!"

The afternoon was filled with joy, as Jean and Henry accepted the congratulations of the more than one hundred guests—a family of caring friends brought together by Phyllis, whose love had swept away her sorrow.

Dear Savior, help me to find joy in bringing joy to others.

—OSCAR GREENE

5

A time to love....   —ECCLESIASTES 3:8

How we deal with people different from ourselves says much about our Christian growth and maturity. Need was the determining factor in Jesus' ministry, not race or sex or social standing or religion.

This point was underscored for me again when Mother Teresa died and obituaries reviewed her life of Christian service. One story in particular caught my attention. When she first arrived in Calcutta and tried to establish a hospice for the homeless who had theretofore died on the streets, the saintly nun and her fellow sisters faced neighborhood hostility. They didn't want the church's "Home for the Dying" in their backyard. And because the Catholic mission was located next to a Hindu temple, neither did its holy men.

But then one of the Hindu priests came down with terminal tuberculosis, and because the city hospital admitted only people who could be cured, he was denied a bed. There seemed no place for him to go. That's when Mother Teresa stepped in. He could come to her hospice and she would tend to him. When the priest died, she delivered his body to the temple for Hindu rites. News of her ecumenical compassion spread throughout the city, and the rest, as they say, is history.

Mother Teresa's secret and the secret of all the giants of faith were the same. They didn't outlive their detractors, they out-loved them.

Forgive me, God, for being deaf when the needy cried,
And I passed by on the other side.

—FRED BAUER

6

Better is the end of a thing than the beginning thereof....
—ECCLESIASTES 7:8

A tool factory is an unlikely place for romance, but the Mac Tool Company where I worked summers in high school was an adventure.

I loved to watch the creative process. A muscular hand would grab a bar of ebony-blue steel, slap it into a powerful press and *bam!* Out came a crude wrench. With a *twaaang* it bounced away to a grinder, who manicured the burrs away in a shower of fireworks. At last the wrench was plated with bright chrome. Hundreds of identical wrenches in the final bin gleamed like a treasure chest of jewelry.

It was not all so artful, however. My job was merely to assemble screwdrivers. I stamped the company name on the handle, then drove a blade into it. After making several billion of these, I began to feel like an android. To keep myself alert, I tapped my foot in time with the presses and sang Elvis Presley tunes.

What kept me going, when other high schoolers were at the beach, was the feeling that I was producing a valuable product. "Mechanics depend on good tools," my father said, and I knew he was right. I was already a backyard mechanic myself, so with my first paycheck I bought a set of Mac tools for myself.

I don't suppose anyone escapes boredom altogether. Sure, the maintenance crew gets bored vacuuming the boss's carpets, and the secretaries tire of form letters, but the boss himself must sit through interminable meetings. Even basketball players tire of routine exercises, and movie stars weary of retakes.

As a college teacher I spend countless hours grading dull papers. But when one of my former students calls to say, "I was just named teacher of the year," then I remember what it's all about: Keep looking forward to that final bin of gleaming treasures, whether it's clean floors, bigger contracts, winning games...or making a positive difference in someone's life.

Lord, on this Labor Day, help me to keep my eye on the big picture and not get lost in details. —DANIEL SCHANTZ

7

TUESDAY

Good sense makes a man slow to anger, and it is his glory to overlook an offense....Listen to advice and accept instruction.... —PROVERBS 19:11, 20 (RSV)

My Norfolk pine looks pitiful. Last Christmas it was lush, sparkling with lights and tiny ornaments. Now most of the branches are brown. Today, my husband Alex looked at the dying plant and said, "Just toss it." But I can't.

The pine has been failing for a while. But after being away for two weeks this summer visiting my family, we returned to find it covered with dead branches. Setting the plant on the kitchen table, I ponder my painful memories of our time at my mom's. The children irritated her, she criticized my parenting, and we exploded at each other. We apologized, but the tension was thick for the rest of the visit. Our relationship is like my Norfolk pine—once lush and full, now dry and scraggly.

I'm tempted to avoid Mom. But just as I can't accept Alex's suggestion to toss the pine, I can't just withdraw. As I begin cutting away the dead brown branches, God whispers, *Cut away your resentment and hurt.* I plead, "Please help me forgive and let go."

The tree needs more light. I clear a spot near a window. *Look at this problem in My light.* Can I find some truth in what Mom said? She asked, "Why do you give in all the time?" I do let the children manipulate me. I do need to set firm limits, to be stricter.

I add soil and fertilizer. *Think of ways to nourish your relationship.* Yes, I decide. I'll talk with Mom, tell her my troubles in parenting and seek her advice. I'll call and write more often; we can spend some special time together.

I rinse my dishes in the sink and dry them on a towel. With a last look at the pine, I turn and walk to the phone.

Thank You, Lord, for my relationship with Mom and for my beautiful Norfolk pine—that are both flourishing again!

—MARY BROWN

8

WEDNESDAY

And I saw another angel flying in midheaven, having an eternal gospel to preach to those who live on the earth....

—REVELATION 14:6 (NAS)

In the mid-seventies a dream came true, and I was selected to attend the Guideposts Writers Workshop in New York. Although I'd never flown before, I was feeling more excitement than fear as my husband Jerry drove me to the airport. But when my plane was announced, terror hit the pit of my stomach, and I whispered, "I don't think I want to go." Jerry managed to get me on the plane with the help of a smiling flight attendant. They pushed me down into my aisle seat and fastened my seat belt.

"First flight," Jerry told the serene woman sitting next to me. I glanced at her briefly. She was elderly, chipper, with fluffy white hair piled on her head, kindly eyes smiling from behind round glasses. In her lap was a well-worn Bible. She winked at Jerry, and he left me on the plane. I glued my eyes to the burgundy carpet, determined to stare at it all the way to New York—if we made it.

Trying desperately to help me, my seatmate asked lots of questions. When she found out that I wanted to learn to write, she asked, "What do you write about, dear?"

I swallowed hard, studying the swirling pattern on the carpet, and said, without looking up, "My faith."

When we were no longer on the ground, I started to hyperventilate. "Look, dear, please look," she said, taking my hand. "We are up in God's heavens. You don't want to miss this." I squinted until my eyes were almost shut and turned my head ever so slightly toward the window, fiercely holding on to my seat. Right outside our window, breathtaking clouds invited me to marvel. They were astonishing, miraculous. I opened my eyes and my mouth formed a perfect O as I leaned across the lap of my newfound friend. God's majesty once again proved greater than my old enemy—fear.

Father, surely You have other new experiences for me. Give me the courage to embrace them. Amen. —MARION BOND WEST

	THURSDAY

9 *Keep fervent in your love for one another, because love covers a multitude of sins.* —I PETER 4:8 (NAS)

Leo and I had been dating for several months, but although I had agreed to marry him, I secretly had second thoughts. We just didn't see eye to eye in regard to finances. I wanted to spend for the present; he wanted to invest for the future. Before we were even engaged, he had bought some land and was busy building a house on speculation.

I confided my misgivings to Gudrun, an elderly friend. "He thinks he's the persevering type, but I think he's just plain stubborn."

"Ah, but a person needs a mind of his own," she replied.

"But he thinks real estate is a good investment. I think it's just a big risk," I complained.

"Ah, but a person should think of the future," she said.

"But he's so busy building the house he doesn't have any time for *me*," I whined.

"Ah, but don't you see? He's doing it *all* for you. He's a hard worker, a good man. Just marry him, and *love him hard.*"

I took her advice.

I still think Leo is stubborn, and we still have some heated spats, but you know something? He must have talked with Gudrun, too, because we've been "loving each other hard" for forty years.

God, it is only Your love that has cemented together the relationship we have built. Thank You. —ALMA BARKMAN

10

Grace be to you, and peace, from God our Father, and from the Lord Jesus Christ. —EPHESIANS 1:2

Ephesus. What was it that troubled me? We'd driven the twelve miles from Kusadasi, where *Rotterdam* docked, to this place that Luke had cited in Acts. Paul spent more than two years here, working at his trade as tentmaker, preaching, creating a Christian church, which was, in time, to flourish.

I couldn't complain about the sights I'd seen. The excavations, only five percent uncovered, just went to show what a fabulous city it had been. The Romans had taken the Ionian Greek town and turned it into one of the great cities of the Empire. The temples, houses, fountains, baths, library—everything was outlined. So, too, were the grand colonnades, the Marble Way, on which you could see the tracks of chariots, and the Arcadian Way, which once led down to the sea with shops and covered archways. That was before the silting of the harbor. Now it was three miles to the ocean, the principal reason that Ephesus was abandoned.

"The bus will leave in half an hour," a fellow passenger let me know.

"Thanks," I said wearily. We were in the theater, so well-preserved it could still hold twenty-four thousand people. I sat and looked out toward the marsh where the harbor had been. Then it struck me: Ruins. Uninhabited ruins. That was why I was troubled. Paul, and others, had worked and succeeded in establishing a vigorous church—but where was that church now? Gone. Vanished....

And yet, Paul in his letter to the Ephesians was writing about God and the universe, not about *a* church, but about *the* church. A light went on in my dim head. It didn't matter *where* it was, but *that* it was. A congregation can disappear, but the Lord's Word in it, never.

I climbed back onto the bus and took another look at Ephesus.

Lord, I remember now: Your kingdom is not of this earth.

—VAN VARNER

SATURDAY

11

Set an example for the believers in speech, in life, in love, in faith and in purity. —*I TIMOTHY 4:12 (NIV)*

When I was entering my teen years, my brother Robert left our small West Virginia town to attend college in Chicago. He was five years older than I was, and while I held him in awe, I really didn't know him all that well.

To be perfectly honest, I was looking forward to exchanging the cramped quarters I shared with my two younger sisters for the bliss of having a room of my own. Robert was leaving behind beautiful mahogany bedroom furniture, complete with a huge desk and bookcase and a wonderful set of encyclopedias—not to mention his hi-fi and his impressive collection of 45s.

The first week that Robert was gone, I played his Everly Brothers records so many times that I managed to break his turntable. I cured that problem by setting a can of deodorant on the tonearm. Then I carelessly put a bottle of cola on his bureau, leaving an ugly white ring on the wood finish.

But during that confusing time, from ages twelve to fourteen, I made a discovery that would remain a part of my life long after the Everly Brothers tunes had faded from memory. On Robert's bulging bookshelves were many books that addressed the role of God in the life of a teenager. Those volumes became my silent mentors as I read by flashlight far into the night.

Robert was hundreds of miles away, and even if he had been at home, I don't know that I would have taken my questions to him. But in the pages of his books, I was able to find some important answers. Because of them, I resolved to use my teenage years to honor God. And I can't help but wonder who I might be today had God not spoken to me through my brother's books.

Thank You, dear Lord, for the men and women of faith who have left us their legacy in books. And thank You for all of those who have brought that legacy into my life. —*ROBERTA MESSNER*

12

"God does speak...though man may not perceive it."

—JOB 33:14 (NIV)

Our oldest son Jeff was off on his freshman year at Duke University in Durham, North Carolina, three hundred miles from home. I found myself standing at the silverware drawer at dinnertime counting out five forks, then realizing my mistake and letting one clatter back down into the drawer. I thought bleakly, *I really don't want to fix dinner.* That one negative thought invited others, and by the time I sat down at the kitchen table across from Jeff's empty chair, I felt as if God had moved out of the house, too.

Then in early September I became worried sick when Hurricane Fran hit Durham, with seventy-nine-mile-per-hour winds and heavy rains. *Was Jeff all right?* I called him on Friday night. No answer. I called Saturday, again and again. No answer. By Sunday morning, I was quite worried.

Finally, at four on Sunday afternoon, Jeff telephoned. "I'm fine," he assured me when I told him how worried I'd been.

"Were you evacuated?" I asked.

"No," he answered.

"Well, was the telephone system knocked out by the storm?"

"No," he admitted.

"Well, why on earth didn't you answer the phone for three days?"

There was a pause on the other end of the line. "Um," Jeff said, "somehow the ringer got turned off on the phone and we didn't notice it."

After I hung up, I thought about the three days' worth of worry that had been caused by a simple switched-off ringer. My difficulty in adjusting to Jeff's absence had been sounding in my mind so loud and clear that I hadn't been hearing much else. The next night when I again counted out one too many forks, instead of seeing it as an unwelcome reminder of the changes we had been through I thought, *Maybe God's trying to tell me to say a quick prayer for Jeff.* "Lord, help him enjoy this wonderful opportunity," I prayed. As the fork fell back into the drawer, my ears perked to the sound of a clear—and meaningful—ring.

I beg Your pardon, God. How long has it taken me to get Your message?

—KAREN BARBER

13

An old man's grandchildren are his crowning glory....
—PROVERBS 17:6 (TLB)

My fiftieth year was a blockbuster. I went to Europe for the first time in my life, chaperoning twenty-six teenagers! And that summer I even water-skied behind my brother's speedboat on the Ohio River. But the most important thing that happened to me that year after I turned fifty was becoming a grandmother for the second time.

Hannah was born a month early with a head full of thick, shocking red hair. The first time I saw her she was still in the neonatal intensive care unit at the hospital, attached to all sorts of wires and monitors and sleeping in a heated bassinet. Her back seemed only a few inches wide as she snuggled into my hand. Her skinny little arms were punctuated with perfectly formed fingers that squeezed my little finger.

Holding and rocking my dainty, darling redheaded granddaughter in that hospital brought on such feelings of joy that during my two-day visit I practically begged my son, Hannah's dad, to let me go in instead of him during the few minutes each hour that one of us was allowed in the intensive care unit. Most of the time Michael gave in and stood outside looking through the thick windows of the nursery while I rocked and cuddled my precious grandchild.

As Hannah and I snuggled, I knew without a doubt that no matter what adventures I have, where I go or what I accomplish in my next fifty years, absolutely *nothing* can come close to the intense feelings and joy of being a mother—and a grandmother.

Heavenly Father, today, on Grandparents Day, I thank You for the beautiful grandchildren who renew my life with joy.
—PATRICIA LORENZ

14

Encourage the timid, help the weak, be patient with everyone.
—I THESSALONIANS 5:14 (NIV)

I had a retarded brother who was four years older and idolized me. One afternoon, shortly after I started attending school for full days, Bobby, who only went in the mornings, thought he would do me a favor and change the water in the little bowl where I kept my pet green turtles Sarge and George. They'd come from the local five-and-ten.

I arrived home that afternoon and went directly to feed my turtles. But Sarge and George weren't hungry. They would never be hungry again. Bobby had unknowingly filled the bowl with boiling hot tap water. My turtles could not even escape to the little island with the plastic palm tree, for he had submerged it. I was angry at what he'd done, and also frightened that he could have made such a dreadful mistake.

Just then Bobby and Mom walked into my room. "You stupid—" I started to shout and caught myself. Too late. Bobby's pale blue eyes, which according to my mother had not changed color since the day he was born, bloomed with hurt. Mom sent him out back to play. I felt horrible. I think she was as close to striking me as she would ever come. She grabbed my shoulders instead, and said in a voice so full of seriousness and conviction it startled me, "Just remember, God put us here to help him."

Today Mom, who struggles with Alzheimer's, is in many ways more helpless than her retarded little boy was, and I'm ashamed to admit that I sometimes become impatient with her, too. The other day, for instance, she refused to put on socks, all the while complaining noisily about how cold the floor felt on her bare feet. "Mom..." I sighed, exasperated. Part of it, I'm sure, is my sheer human irritability; and part of it, on a deeper level, is my fear that my mother is no longer someone I can reach to for help, as I had for so many years. But holding the pair of socks in my hand, I recalled something she taught me one day when I was little. I remember Bobby, who will be a little boy forever. And I remind myself, *We are here to help.*

Lord, I have received so much help in my life. Help me to help others.
—EDWARD GRINNAN

15

WEDNESDAY

Tell of all his wonderful works! —PSALM 105:2 (RSV)

Yesterday seemed an ordinary sort of day. I didn't have to go to work, so after my husband Lynn left, I pulled some weeds in the early morning coolness, talked to my brother on the telephone and tackled the piles on my desk. Mid-afternoon, as I headed to the kitchen for a snack, I glanced out the window toward the mountains and gasped in awe. There, about a mile away, below a bank of dark ominous clouds, was a perfect funnel cloud. A tornado! I'd read about tornadoes out on the plains, on television, I'd seen the devastation they caused, but I'd never seen one near our home in Boulder, Colorado.

Eerie-sounding sirens wailed in the distance, but I stood stone-still and mesmerized as the funnel cloud moved across the valley and then seemed to stop in the middle of a lake, pulling the green water up into a huge funnel spout. Then it lifted off the ground and disappeared back up into the clouds.

"Wow!" I said out loud to myself, wanting to tell everyone about what I'd just seen. I flipped on the television and, sure enough, a news bulletin confirmed a tornado in our area, but they didn't know if it had touched down. So I rushed to the phone, called the station and reported what I'd seen. Then I called Lynn at his office. Then a friend who lives close to the lake. Later, I eagerly shared my description with neighbors I hadn't talked to for weeks.

Today, the community is reflecting on the unusual tornado. The front page of the newspaper has big headlines and several stories. Amazingly, only one home was damaged and no one was hurt. But I am reflecting on my own response. Why did it take a tornado to get me excited enough to tell others what I'd seen? Why did it take a tornado to get me talking to my neighbors? Did I recognize the hand of the same Creator in the beauty of the early morning sky, the wonder of the root system of a weed or the reconciled relationship in my brother's life? Did I think to share the greatness of *those* miracles with anyone else?

Father, help me to notice and name Your greatness in big and little things every day.
—CAROL KUYKENDALL

READER'S ROOM

"Everyday Wonders"...here are a few of mine: a class of kindergartners, so full of wonder at everything (I am a substitute teacher); six pairs of my husband's freshly washed jeans hanging on the clothesline; a baby shower for a friend's first grandchild.
—LINDA HAMILTON, LAS VEGAS, NV

16

And one of them, when he saw that he was healed, turned back, and with a loud voice glorified God, And fell down on his face...giving [Jesus] thanks.... —LUKE 17:15–16

"Say thank you to the girls who helped you, honey."

"I *won't!*" Elizabeth didn't want to leave the playground, and she was acting her age: two. Embarrassed by her rudeness, I floundered.

"But if you don't say thank you, how will they know you liked what they did? Maybe they'll think you didn't want their help, or that you didn't care. Then perhaps the next time they won't want to help you."

The words rang hollow in both Elizabeth's ears and mine. I said a silent prayer for patience, then began to sing a song so I wouldn't attempt further arguments. The reasons I'd given for saying thank you were the wrong ones. But what were the right ones? I'd never really thought about it. Now as we walked home I began to wonder.

"This little light of mine, I'm gonna let it shine...." The song I'd unconsciously chosen to sing was one of Elizabeth's favorites. Not wanting me to see she was enjoying it, Elizabeth surreptitiously wiggled her index finger, pretending it was a candle. I stopped the stroller and squatted down to be at eye level with her.

"Sweetie, I think I told you the wrong reason for why we say thank you to people. We don't do it because we want them to be nice to us again." Interest lit up in Elizabeth's eyes. I had her full attention. "When people are kind to us, we see a little bit of Jesus shining in their souls. They're letting their little lights shine, and that helps us know God a bit better. We say thank you to them because in a way we are saying thank you to God."

Elizabeth pondered that for a moment, then offered, "One man came back and said thank you after Jesus made him better."

I smiled and nodded. Then *I* said a silent thank you for prayers answered, and answers given.

Come, Holy Spirit; erase from my heart the feeble explanations the world offers, and fill my heart and mind with truth.

—JULIA ATTAWAY

17

And be ye kind to one another, tenderhearted, forgiving one another, even as God for Christ's sake hath forgiven you.
—*EPHESIANS 4:32*

I hadn't seen my uncle and aunt in a dozen years or more, so I was excited to attend a family reunion in California in honor of my Uncle Lokki's eightieth birthday. One evening we were invited to dinner in a neighboring community and stopped along the way for the ice cream my aunt had promised to provide. Since my uncle was not entirely certain of the "back door" route to the house from the store, he just started zigzagging every which way, heading toward the general vicinity of a water-tower landmark.

Meanwhile, my eighty-one-year-old Aunt Pat, who had reached our hostess on the cellular phone, found it impossible to direct her determined husband, who was switching streets fast enough to make our heads spin. My mother and I, grinning helplessly in the backseat, further aggravated matters. My aunt got so frustrated that she jabbed Uncle Lokki in the shoulder and sputtered, "I'm not speaking to you the rest of the night!"

We finally arrived at the house, called a truce during the meal and eventually headed home. The sunroof was open to the starry night sky, letting in the mellow summer evening. From out of the stillness my uncle's contrite voice asked, "Have you forgiven me for the way I acted today?"

My aunt responded, "You haven't asked me to."

He paused, took the plunge and respectfully said, "Honey, will you forgive me?" She reached over and squeezed his hand, and it was done.

After fifty-five years of marriage, a loving relationship still comes down to forgiving and being forgiven.

Lord of mercy, we're never too young nor too old to know forgiveness—for like You, it is timeless.
—*CAROL KNAPP*

18

O house of Jacob, come ye, and let us walk in the light of the Lord.
—*ISAIAH 2:5*

The whining motor on the treadmill seemed to throb in time with my steps. Walk, walk, walk, walk. How I hated to exercise! To me, all that huffing and puffing just led to aching muscles and a sweaty body. But the doctor had insisted I put in four miles each day.

While wondering how I could break the monotony of it all, I spotted the box of gospel tapes that my husband and I usually keep in our truck. Pretty soon the familiar strains of an old hymn were filling the little room where the treadmill hummed softly beneath my feet.

Precious Lord, take my hand, lead me on, let me stand.... The words stirred my leaden spirit, and my sluggish steps picked up a bit. *When we walk with the Lord, in the light of His word, what a glory He sheds on our way....* I closed my eyes, letting the words sink into my heart.

Walk, walk, walk, walk. Over a mile already, and it had hardly hurt a bit. That's when it occurred to me that this wasn't the first time my steps had been made light by the knowledge that God was walking with me. He had shone His glory on my path every day for a full year while my husband Larry was in Okinawa with the Navy. He had illumined my way through two major surgeries, a long stint with depression, and the ups and downs of raising two children. Why should He stop now?

Maybe your path seems a little dark at this moment. Won't you join me in singing that old hymn, which has gladdened many a heart? *And He walks with me and He talks with me, and He tells me I am His own. And the joy we share as we tarry there, none other has ever known.*

Father, like a faithful old lighthouse, Your radiant presence in my life dispels all darkness.
                                                          —LIBBIE ADAMS

19 *Love bears all things, believes all things, hopes all things, endures all things.* —I CORINTHIANS 13:7 (RSV)

My friends Noreen and Will were devoted to their grandson Bobby, who suffered from multiple sclerosis from the time he was an infant. MS attacks the muscles, and Bobby spent most of his time in a wheelchair. He needed a lot of care, and Noreen and Will helped Bobby's parents look after him so that the boy could remain at home.

When Bobby died at the age of twelve, his family was devastated. Like all their other friends, I worried about them, wishing I could do something to help. But whenever any of us reached out to them, they turned away. All we could do was pray that God would heal the pain of their loss. Unfortunately, Noreen and Will seemed to be turning away from God, too, and they stopped coming to church. They used to be active in so many of our events that it was hard to go on without them, but we kept praying for them.

About a year passed, and one Sunday Noreen and Will showed up again. After the service they stood in the vestibule as we all gathered around them, tearful and smiling. Then Will held up his hand; he had something to say. He and Noreen were remodeling their house so they could open a day-care center for disabled and handicapped children. "It's something we know how to do," he said, "and it's something that needs to be done."

When I left the church and walked out into the bright sunlight, I closed my eyes and thanked God for answering our prayers for Noreen and Will. But God had done more than heal their pain. He had inspired them to offer their love for Bobby to as many other children as they could fit into their home. He had turned a terrible loss into a beautiful gift.

Thank You, Lord, for the many times You have brought something good out of our suffering. —PHYLLIS HOBE

20

MONDAY

The desert shall rejoice, and blossom as the rose.
—ISAIAH 35:1

In a show of support, friends had sent a miniature rosebush to my office the first day of my new job at Guideposts. It was covered with red blooms the shade of my favorite lipstick. I had placed it near a sunny window and said a quick prayer. My success rate with plants is low.

Every day of that first week I greeted and watered my rosebush. When I had left for the weekend, everything was fine. Now on Monday morning it looked dead. The flowers were deep-fried and the leaves were crumbly to the touch. It was toast.

And I could relate. I had worked in publishing before, and after a year I was completely burned out. The high stress and long hours were too much for me. My next job had been in another line of work, but now I was back in the field I had left behind. I had moved to New York to become an editor, and I was ready for a second chance. I hoped my rose would have one, too.

Co-workers dropped by to offer advice. "Soak it overnight," said Mary Ann. "Trim the dead leaves," suggested Alan. "Just call the florist and have it replaced," said Celeste. *She's right—there's not much hope,* I thought.

Then Dago visited. "What a shame. But don't worry. It's not dead." He pointed to branches that were still green. "I'll find the problem." He checked beneath the decorative moss at the base of the plant. "Ah, you see," he said, "there's no soil under here. Roses need to dig their roots deep." That afternoon I replanted the bush.

A month later it was as lush and green as the day it arrived. There were even three buds on the highest branch. I had begun to take root as well, learning the ropes and settling into a new routine. I loved my job reading mail from readers and writing features. Most of all I enjoyed my colleagues and appreciated the expertise they shared. I figured in time, I might bloom, too.

God, plant me firmly in Your will.   —ALLISON SAMPLE

21

"They are no longer two but one flesh...."
—MATTHEW 19:6 (RSV)

I had been needing them for some time, but my pride kept me from admitting it. Last night, I finally gave in. I didn't tell a soul. I just went to the pharmacy, quietly bought my first pair of reading glasses and crept out into the night.

When I got home, my wife Beth was already in bed, propped up on a mountain of pillows, lost in the twisting plot of another novel. I changed into my pajamas, picked up the glasses and went into the bathroom. After brushing my teeth, I put on the glasses and gazed into the mirror. I was shocked at how much I looked like my father. Silently raging against time and age, I slipped under the covers, glasses sitting on my nose.

I didn't say a word; I wanted to see how long it would take Beth to notice. A minute went by in silence, then two. Finally, I turned to face my unsuspecting wife. As she lifted her head from her book, my eyes grew wide and my mouth flew open. There was Beth, a pair of reading glasses perched on the end of her own nose.

We're both reading better now that we've got our glasses; a little wounded vanity is a small price to pay for life without squinting. And as the years pass and more changes than just our eyes, Beth and I, God willing, will see it through—together.

Father, thank You for the people with whom we travel through the years.
—SCOTT WALKER

WEDNESDAY

22

I have rejoiced in the way of thy testimonies....

—*PSALM 119:14*

Like most people, I have a set of files that help keep my life in order. There's a file for unpaid bills and another for paid bills. There's a file for unanswered mail and one where I stow information about Keri's college expenses. Pretty normal, I'd guess, except for one: The last folder in my drawer is labeled "Things I Want to Read Again." When life gets tedious, that's my folder of choice.

One day I was just plain blue. Keri was away at school; David's meetings would stretch on into the evening. I went to my file for a lift and pulled out a piece of notebook paper half covered with stickers of butterflies and little bears and flowers: "Happy Hop Hop Day! Here's a name poem for Momma:

P-recious and dear to her family though her
A-ccent is so Southern! She was just made
M-om of the year!"

Other times, I reach for my "folder runneth over" when I need purpose, inspiration or just a good chuckle. There's a "Prayer for Children" by Ina Hughs that reminds me to pray for children "whose pictures aren't on anybody's dresser." There's a newspaper article quoting our son Brock as an investment expert and a funny note from David thanking me for cooking chili for a long-ago meal at church.

As you read this, I hope ideas for your own folder are forming in your head. But even if you never get around to organizing your favorite writings into a neat little packet, there's another source of "Things I Want to Read Again" that you might want to pull out when your own life gets tedious. The Holy Bible is chock full of adventure and intrigue, pithy quotes, sound advice and plenty of reassurance from the One Who loves you most. Open it now. You'll be glad you did.

Father, thank You for this marvelous collection of "good reads" we call the Bible: a testimony of Your comfort and care and even Your good humor!

—*PAM KIDD*

23

Forgetting those things which are behind....

—PHILIPPIANS 3:13

I'm at that time in my life when I need to give a lot of my books away, and I'm discovering that it isn't easy. I had no books as a child, and the one-room school I attended didn't have textbooks for all the classes. During the Depression, we moved to a city where the elementary school had a librarian. She guided me carefully into the world of books and changed my life.

I escaped from plainness to palaces where kings entertained knights at round tables. I dived for pearls in the Pacific and panned for gold in Alaska. I read everything I could get my hands on, and eventually I was able to begin buying books. In the process of going to school and then pastoring and teaching for five decades, I accumulated a sizable library.

When I retired, I gave sets of commentaries to the church library, moved books I'd need in writing or teaching to my office, and stored the rest in an empty room at the church. But I didn't realize how attached I was to them until I took a young pastor by to give him some books on preaching.

As we started through the boxes and I began to hand him books, I realized they were all wrapped in wonderful memories, and I felt like I was giving away old friends. Then it suddenly dawned on me that I was being selfish, that I needed to give as so many others had given to me. And as I helped him load the books into his car, I felt that God was somehow making me a part of this friend's future, and it felt good.

So I'm now in the process of placing the tapes of my pulpit ministry in a library that shares them with people everywhere, and I'm actively hunting for places where all those boxes of books will meet people's needs.

Dear God, help me to find joy in passing on to others the blessings I have received. —KENNETH CHAFIN

24

Because thy lovingkindness is better than life, my lips shall praise thee. —PSALM 63:3

My father was a wholesale grocery salesman, calling on stores in the small Georgia towns surrounding Macon, where we lived. Often in the fall at cotton harvesting time, my sister Leila and I accompanied him on his rounds as an all-day outing.

Once at the only general store in one of those hamlets, we watched Sam, a middle-aged man in overalls, unroll a wad of paper money to pay the big bill he owed Mr. Charlie, the storekeeper. Sam had sold his cotton crop and had come to "settle up" for the provisions he and his family had charged all year against crop time. Then, placing the remainder of the roll in his pocket, he left the store grinning at being out of debt.

Mr. Charlie joined us as we opened the lunch basket Mother had packed for all of us. We were having a leisurely meal until Mr. Charlie suddenly sprang to his feet. Sam was walking across the dirt road, his arms loaded with two large sacks of groceries. Mr. Charlie dropped his sandwich and strode toward the man, meeting him at the railroad track that ran down the center of the road.

"Sam!" Mr. Charlie growled, snatching at the top of one bag. "You've been up at that new A&P store and loaded up with groceries! I carried you all year long on my books, and as soon as you get some money, you rush to spend it up there!"

Sam's mouth popped open in amazement, and both bags fell, bursting as they hit the tracks.

"Oh, gee, Mr. Charlie," he cried innocently, "I didn't know you sold for cash!"

Mr. Charlie started laughing. He forgave Sam his ignorance, helped him resack the groceries in bags from his own store and sent him on his way.

Every time I recall that incident, I am reminded—and ashamed— of how often I forget that Jesus carried my debt of sin and that He marked it "Paid" on Calvary. Surely all my gratitude and praise is due to my beloved Savior.

Thank You again, dear Lord, for Your redeeming love.

—*DRUE DUKE*

25

There was no peace to him that went out....
—*II CHRONICLES 15:5*

My friend Edith took me on the tour of the *Queen Mary,* now in dry dock in Long Beach, California, for my birthday. After it was over, the guide announced that we were free to wander on our own, and we should not forget to visit the shops on the promenade deck. Edith and I climbed to the very top deck where we could see all of the harbor and most of Long Beach. We were leaning on the rail, side by side, talking about nothing much, when the ship's whistle blew.

The whistle on the *Queen Mary* can be heard for ten miles. We were standing right under it. The physical assault of the noise blew us halfway across the little deck, and we ended up clutching each other and screaming to release the pressure buildup in our bodies. It was disorienting and terrifying. When the whistle stopped, we fell to the deck, still holding on to each other, laughing hysterically, our legs like cotton floss.

Eventually we recovered enough to decide maybe we should go visit the shops on the promenade deck. We browsed happily for half an hour when the PA system went on and a voice said, "Warning. The ship's whistle will blow in one minute. Warning." The message was repeated three times.

Edith and I stared at each other, open-mouthed. They warned everybody on the ship except the poor fools standing right under the whistle!

The lesson of the *Queen Mary*? I only get warnings when I'm still far enough away from the danger to do something about it. If I get in too deep, I won't hear the warnings anymore. I'll only get blasted by the whistle.

Dear God, keep me within hearing distance of You.

—*RHODA BLECKER*

26

SUNDAY

They shall mount up with wings as eagles....

—*ISAIAH 40:31*

In our town we have a young minister who likes to challenge people with provocative questions. The other day he asked some of us to describe the role we'd like to have God play in our lives. "In just one word," he said, "tell me what you'd like Him to be."

Well, an interesting collection of words came forth: Protector, Redeemer, Guide, Comforter, Friend and so on. But there was one unexpected reply. "I'd like Him," this man said, "to be my chauffeur."

All of us were taken aback until he explained his choice. "When hot-air ballooning was invented some two hundred years ago in

France," he said, "the man in charge of the fire underneath the balloon that produced the hot air was known as the chauffeur, from the French word *chauffer,* meaning to heat. Without the work of the chauffeur, the balloon couldn't soar. It couldn't even rise. Now do you see the connection? I like the thought of God breathing His lifegiving spirit into me every single day, so that I can rise above trials and difficulties and preoccupation with material things. Without the lift that God supplies I can do nothing."

God as the eternal chauffeur of the human spirit. It's a comforting thought, isn't it? And an elevating one, too!

Father, help us to seek and find the power that comes to those who "wait upon the Lord."　　　　　　　　　　—ARTHUR GORDON

27　　　　　　　　　　　　　　　　　　　　MONDAY

God does not judge by external appearance....
—GALATIANS 2:6 (NIV)

Hurrying to the school nearby, a stocky teenage boy crossed my path. "Ma'am, excuse me. Do you know what time it is, please?" As my eyes swept down to my watch, I gasped, thinking, *Oh, my gosh! He's losing his pants! His underwear is showing!* Then his friend approached, and I saw that his baggy jeans were falling in exactly the same way. I came to my senses. *Oh—both of them are dressed alike. It must be a style!*

Shaken, but much relieved that I hadn't blurted my thoughts, I gave them the time, then walked on, musing, *Why on earth would they think that looks attractive? They look so sloppy. Who could possibly find that appealing?* I stopped mid-thought, remembering when a man asked my friend Ally and me, "Are you sisters?" We'd been astonished and protested, "No!" wondering how he'd mistaken a petite hazel-eyed blonde and taller brunette with brown eyes for siblings. Last year, seeing a snapshot, I'd laughed out loud. Amy and I had been dressed nearly identically: the same wide bell-bottomed pants; the same "poor boy" ribbed sweaters; the same strappy sandals.

Now I told myself firmly, "*You* don't have to like their style. Teens are developing a sense of who they are, trying to blend in and at the same time figuring out who they are as individuals." And they were polite. They called me ma'am and said "please" and "thank you." As the boys caught up with two teenage girls dressed identically (to my eyes) in flannel shirts with torn jeans, I smiled. Style is style, politeness is eternal. They were the ones with the schoolbooks, but I'd learned a lesson!

God, may I not judge others by their appearance today.

—*LINDA NEUKRUG*

28 Let each esteem other better than themselves.

—*PHILIPPIANS 2:3*

The task seemed most tedious. My boss had asked me to write down the names of all the people at work who had helped me with my job. For a year I had been in charge of fillers and shorts at the magazine, all those one-line quotes and brief anecdotes that fit at the bottom of the page. And now it was taking me a good part of two days to look back through the files for twelve issues, recording who had found each item. *What an incalculable waste of time,* I thought. *I could be doing a lot more productive things.*

But as the list of names grew, I came to be astonished at how many people had helped me in the past year. *That quote came from Sidney....Dana discovered this anecdote....Celeste passed on that manuscript, which was sent to her by a longtime reader.* As I typed the information into my computer, the task that had seemed so odious filled me with appreciation. I had never realized how much help with my job I had received from my colleagues. In fact, I was deeply indebted to them. I couldn't have done it without them.

"Here," I said to my boss, giving him the typed list.

"Great," he replied. "Now I want you to pass it around the office with some explanation."

It was the easiest memo I ever wrote. And the consequences were great—more contributions flooding my in-box.

As my boss said, "You can never go wrong with appreciation."

Good God, let me express my thankfulness to You and the people who fill my days.

—*RICK HAMLIN*

29

Be thou faithful...and I will give thee a crown of life.
—*REVELATION 2:10*

Do you know how many daffodil bulbs are in a twenty-five-pound sack? Neither did we, but we couldn't resist the nursery's end-of-season clearance price.

My husband Harry, always fascinated by numbers, counted them carefully as he transferred them into buckets. "About two hundred seventy six," he announced, "not counting the five or six dried-up ones I threw out."

It took us most of the day, but we finally got them all into the ground. Harry dug the holes, I sprinkled a little bonemeal and dropped in each bulb. They were deceptively dead-looking, but heavy with the promise of life in the spring.

As I tucked each crinkly-skinned bulb into its dark resting place, I hoped the experts were right in saying that deer don't eat daffodil bulbs. I imagined hundreds of bright yellow heads on tall green stems waving in the spring breezes, popping up amongst the piñon and juniper trees. "This is faith," I said to myself. And it seemed a perfect time to pray.

I knelt in the soft pine mulch or alongside the nose-tingling sage, and with each cluster of bulbs I talked to my Father about something. Praise for this beautiful autumn day, the mountains against the cloudless blue sky, the dusky smell of fresh-turned earth. I brought Him each of our six kids and their particular needs and concerns, and our church's building program. I prayed for our neighbors and their baby Emma, scheduled for heart surgery next week, and for particular areas in my own life where I'd like to see growth.

I know, from many years of experience, that spring follows winter. The oak brush will sprout new leaves, wildflowers will bloom again, the buried bulbs will push their green noses up through the earth. And from long experience I also know that God hears my prayers, and His faithfulness surrounds me.

Heavenly Father, I rejoice in You as Creator and Sustainer of all life—including mine. Thank You. —*MARY JANE CLARK*

30

"New wine must be put into fresh wineskins."

—*LUKE 5:38 (RSV)*

Since late summer I've had an all-new kitchen. My sink has moved from its old place kitty-corner across the room as far from the stove as it could be to a convenient right angle beside the stove. I have all-new cabinets, and more of them. And some of the old cabinets have been put above the washer and dryer, which are now behind folding doors. Walls and cabinets are bright white, and the open area in the room has increased.

In spite of all this, I am experiencing regret! Funny, I miss my queer, old, ugly kitchen with its exposed pipes; where I had to zigzag around the furnace partition to get to the sink from the stove; but where with much ingenuity I created storage or hanging space for everything, from pots and pans to tissue boxes and canned goods, much of it in plain sight. Now, even with all the new cupboard space, I still don't know where all my stuff should go, and I feel dislocated and frustrated.

Then today I read Jesus' words in Luke 5:33-39 about the new and the old. When I got to His last comment about preferring the old, I felt as though Jesus reached out to put His arm around my shoulder and say, "Don't worry. I understand how it is."

Part of the problem is that with work still going on in the living room, the workman's tools in front of cupboard and folding doors, and plaster and tile dust sifting into everything, I haven't gotten the kitchen really straightened out. And I haven't stopped to study how to be as ingenious with my things as in the old kitchen.

Yes, I had made the old kitchen good and useful. But I have a new kitchen. It's time to rejoice in it—to leave the old and live with the new. And unlike new vs. old wine, my new kitchen really *is* better than the old!

Thank You, Jesus, that You understand my difficulty parting with the past. I do believe that the new is better, including the new wine of Your Spirit.　　　　　　　　　　　　　　—*MARY RUTH HOWES*

Missed Kids — Beautiful sunny day 90°. Very busy at work. Did 3 hrs O.T. Called Chantel. She's leaving Bob tomorrow. Wants job in AFIS.

1 Beautiful sunny day. 90°. Did 1 hr O.T. Chantel came home w/ kids & left Bob.

2 Used Kids — Beautiful sunny day 90°. Bob came after Chantel & kids & they went home at 10:30. Worked 1 hr O.T.

3 Beautiful sunny day 90°. Chantel called. Butch was here. 5:00 Mass & Red Star Pizza.

4 Missed Kids — Cloudy, rainy day. Paul & I went to Bobby's game & Kelsey's cheers at 9:00 for 9:00.

5 Cloudy partly & HHH. Paul & I were lazy bums today. I washed & made spaghetti sauce. Butch & Jan came over.

6 Missed Kids — Rainy day 90° HHH. Worked 1 hr O.T. Paul & I here & watched soaps.

7 Used Kids — Partly sunny day 90° HHH. Did 3 hrs O.T. Walked to Butches house.

8 Missed Kids — Cloudy, rainy day 90°. HHH. Worked 4 hrs O.T. Watched soaps.

9 Used Kids — Partly cloudy day Rain AM 85°. Paul & I went to Ron Skelles for supper.

10 Beautiful sunny day 85°. Paul & I & Seth went to Bobby & Kelsey football game.

11 Missed Kids — Beautiful sunny day 85°. Paul & I went to Bradleys. They were there & T & A & Chesterfield BBQ chicken.

12 Used Kids — Beautiful sunny day 85°. Very busy at work. Did 4 hrs O.T. Butch was here & called Bob.

13 Missed Kids — Beautiful sunny day 85°. Worked 1 hr. Called Dr. K at 2:00. Starkman Paul in hosp.

14 Missed Kids — Cloudy, rainy day. I got sick day. Took Paul to Dr. K. & Dr. K. to hosp. Emergency appendectomy surgery 6:00 PM. Live 12:00. Stayed with them w/ kids til 1:30 A.M. Chantel spent the night.

15

SEPTEMBER 1999

Missed kids — Rain, Rain. Rain, Hurricane Floyd Paul is doing much better still in pain but looking much better.

16 _____

Missed Bowling League — Beautiful sunny day 75°. Paul g

17 Moved to room 343 my old room

Missed kids — Beautiful sunny day 75°. Paul looks

18 better every day. Moved to Room 442 9:00

Missed kids — Beautiful sunny day 75°. Paul look

19 better every day. Communion at last

Beautiful sunny day 75°. Paul looks

20 better every day. Came home. Paul came home today.

Missed kids — Beautiful sunny day 75°. Paul is more

21 comfortable as home.

Missed kids — Beautiful sunny day 75° Paul look

22 better every day. Very tired Dr. Brown

Missed kids — Beautiful sunny day 75°. Paul looks

23 better every day. Very tired Brown

Missed kids — Beautiful sunny day 75°. we got letter

24 from lawyer about the hosp. bill.

Missed — Butch came over after work &

25 Mowed lawn. Went to 5:00 Mass alone

Chantelle Bob & kids came over

after football game I made

26 Spaghetti for supper.

27 _____

Missed kids —
28

Paul went to Dr. Brown's & had

29 staples out today.

30 _____

October

My cup overflows.

—PSALM 23:5 (RSV)

S	M	T	W	T	F	S
					1	2
3	4	5	6	7	8	9
10	11	12	13	14	15	16
17	18	19	20	21	22	23
24	25	26	27	28	29	30
31						

LESSONS IN LISTENING

1

HEARING THE WORD
And he said to them, "Follow me...."

—*MATTHEW 4:19 (RSV)*

Almost thirty years ago I faced a decision. Should I quit my salaried job at a magazine to help my husband launch a new business? On one side, a regular income in the family, work I enjoyed. On the other, challenge, risk, the excitement of pioneering together.

"When I have a choice to make," our minister advised me, "I simply go to the Bible."

Simple for him, maybe—he knew the Bible inside out. But where would I even begin looking? I remembered a friend telling about getting a Bible verse over the phone when he had to make a choice. "The caller couldn't possibly have known my situation, yet the verse he gave me was my answer!"

No such phone call came for me.

"I pray for guidance," another friend said, "then just let the Bible fall open." I tried this. I closed my eyes, put my finger on a page and read, "Ozias begat Joatham; and Joatham begat Achaz; and Achaz..." (Matthew 1:9).

When I laughed about this with a neighbor, Co Holby, she nodded. "That time my husband was so ill, I did just what you did, opened the Bible at random looking for guidance." Instead, Co found herself staring at the blank page between the Old Testament and the New. "The only words there were 'The Gospel.'"

We started to laugh again—then realized what she'd said. *The Gospel!* That's where Co and I and every Christian would find direction. Asking God for a specific verse for a particular situation, after all, is asking for a miniature miracle—wonderful when it happens, but not something I can summon on demand. My husband and I began a daily reading of the Gospels in terms of my decision, finding our fears, our egos, our hidden motives exposed to the light of Jesus' life and teaching. In the end I quit my job, but what came out of that time was something more important: a pattern for bringing every decision before Him Who followed His Father's will without fail.

Show me Your Son today, Father, as I read Your Word.

—*ELIZABETH SHERRILL*

2

Praise be to...the God of all comfort, who comforts us in all our troubles, so that we can comfort those in any trouble with the comfort we ourselves have received from God. —*II CORINTHIANS 1:3–4 (NIV)*

"You don't know me, and I hope you don't mind my calling," a woman told me when I answered the phone one Saturday morning, "but someone gave me your name." Her voice broke. "My teenage daughter has the same problem your daughter had."

Immediately, a strong bond of shared experience connected me to this stranger, and my heart hurt for her as she began to describe her daughter's autoimmune disease, alopecia aerata. It's a baffling condition in which the body's immune system attacks the hair follicles, causing partial or total loss of hair. Sometimes the hair grows back; sometimes it does not. Even if it grows back, sometimes you lose it again. You have the disease for life, and for self-conscious teenage girls, it is particularly life-altering.

"I don't know what to do. I don't know how to help her," this mother told me. For nearly an hour, I listened and tried to encourage her. As we talked, I reached into a file drawer and pulled out some papers with names and phone numbers and pieces of information I had gathered two years earlier. I tried not to offer too much advice; I remembered that when I started down this same path with Kendall, I couldn't take in too much advice at once. But before we hung up, I encouraged her to call me anytime.

"Thank you," she said.

"Thank you, too," I said, though she probably didn't understand what I meant. When this disease struck eighteen-year-old Kendall and she lost all her hair, I couldn't imagine any good coming out of the struggle. But now Kendall is off at college, and she has hair on her head. Though we live with the ongoing reality of the disease, we have passed through the place where this other mother and daughter now find themselves, and I now understand one of God's truths more clearly: Our pain is not wasted when we can reach around and comfort another coming along behind us on the same path.

Father, thank You for the comfort that comes in comforting another. —CAROL KUYKENDALL

3 ———————————————————— SUNDAY

And we, who with unveiled faces all reflect the Lord's glory, are being transformed into his likeness....
—II CORINTHIANS 3:18 (NIV)

Glory is one of the ideas I like to mull over while I'm dusting. It's an idea far bigger than my mind can comprehend, but it's fun to try. And one Sunday, recently, I saw for a brief moment a picture of what glory looks like.

In our church, we offer Communion every Sunday. I love it because it gives me a starting-all-over-new moment for the week ahead. Usually, I have my eyes closed as the plates of broken matzo and the grape juice in small plastic cups are passed around, but on this Sunday I looked up and was astounded. The faces of the servers working their way up the aisle were all aglow. Since we meet in a windowless high school auditorium, I was puzzled about where this white-gold light was coming from.

Then I saw. The rim of the silver Communion plate, holding the bread that symbolized the Lord Jesus, caught the rays from bright lights high up in the auditorium ceiling and reflected that light into the faces of my friends.

Glory!

Lord, imagine the glow on my face when I move on and see You face to face! May my life and service here give others a brief glimpse of that glory, a taste of what is to come. —ROBERTA ROGERS

4 ———————————————————— MONDAY

He does great things beyond our understanding.
—JOB 37:5 (NIV)

My husband Whitney and I were waiting in line to board a crowded flight from Portland, Oregon, to Dallas, Texas. Outside it was gray and raining. Inside, on the chilled ramp leading to the plane, the line had stopped. We waited, human islands of dull silence. Ahead of me was a tall young man with a ponytail, wearing a denim jacket. Through the crook of his elbows, I saw a glass box cupped in his big hands like a treasure.

"Butterflies!" I gasped.

He turned around grinning. Inside the cage, five brilliant, orange and black monarchs fluttered like exquisite jewels. Excited murmurs surged through the line. A packed circle gathered round, *oohing* and *aahing.* "They're from my cousin's biology class," the man said. "They hatched from their cocoons too late to migrate safely to Mexico, so I promised the class I'd give them a lift to Dallas. From there, they'll make it."

"I'd forgotten they fly that far," said a man in a suit, carrying a briefcase. "Isn't it amazing?"

A child traced a finger on the glass. "Pretty," she said.

Someone else said, "You know, their brains are the size of a pinhead. Yet they know the way to Mexico. Can you believe it?"

"And those colors, the design so perfect on each wing," a woman added. Then the line began to move. We stepped back into formation, now bonded together by reverence, wonder, joy.

Oh, Master Artist, Your handiwork on even the smallest of canvases brings praise to our lips. —SHARI SMYTH

5

TUESDAY

I can do all things through Christ which strengtheneth me. —PHILIPPIANS 4:13

Camera slung around my neck, I savored one last look at bottle-green Saddlebag Lake, 11,200 feet up in the Wind River Mountains. I had been covering a story on acid-rain testing by the U.S. Forest Service. Suddenly, a gust of icy wind knocked me off balance. I slammed into a boulder the size of a compact car, breaking my fall with elbows, knees and telephoto lens. *No more photo ops this trip,* I thought as I examined my dented equipment.

But my throbbing kneecap! How was I going to hike out eight miles with rangers who walked these hills for a living? Until now, my treks were sprints to the clothesline or rambles with my dog Spot. I tried one tentative step. Limped another. Then another.

With pack goats carrying our gear, we picked our way down the steep, crumbly rock faces. Once we were below the timberline, a colleague hewed a walking stick for me from a fallen lodgepole pine. Now I could shift the weight off my aching knee and stop myself when I skidded on slopes carpeted with pine needles.

After bushwhacking for three miles through the timber, we emerged at swampy Atlantic Meadows and straddled from hummock to hummock, splashing into calf-deep water when we missed. By the time we reached Roaring Fork Trail, our five-mile "home stretch," the team hydrologist and I chatted, yodeled and hobbled on as the pack animals and other rangers disappeared down the trail.

When we finally limped to the trailhead a full hour after the others, I felt exhilarated by my endurance and pain threshold. Perhaps I expected a heroine's welcome, but there was no fuss, no fanfare. "You might want to take an aspirin when you get home," one of the rangers suggested. The outdoorsmen had known all along I could do it. The surprised one was me!

Dear God, with Your help I can bushwhack life's toughest trails one step at a time. —GAIL THORELL SCHILLING

6 WEDNESDAY

For the Lord taketh pleasure in his people: he will beautify the meek with salvation. —PSALM 149:4

I find children perfectly charming, and it's because of their imperfections. Take malaprops, for example, those little slips of tongue that children commit because they don't know the right word.

Our daughter Natalie never could say "watermelon." It always came out "willermeller." At a football game, my nephew Jeremy kept asking to go to the "confession stand." His sister Karissa listened to her dad tell about two bicycle builders from Dayton who invented the airplane. She interrupted to say, "Oh, I know: the Righteous Brothers."

Boldly children make their mistakes, then laugh with us when we laugh at them. They are endearing because they know they don't know everything.

Somewhere on the way to adulthood I got the idea that I was no longer allowed to make mistakes or I would be rejected. To have egg on my face would be an unpardonable sin. I would "just die" if I gave the wrong statistics when I was teaching, and I would be "absolutely humiliated" if I mispronounced an important name or forgot someone's birthday.

It's funny, but the people I love most are those childlike, vulnerable types who are able to laugh at their frequent flubs. So I've been praying:

Lord, help me to relax and to enjoy the beauty that comes with meekness. Don't let me take myself so seriously that I lose the charm of imperfection. —DANIEL SCHANTZ

7 THURSDAY

David and the whole house of Israel were celebrating with all their might before the Lord....
—II SAMUEL 6:5 (NIV)

As a family, we believe that too much of a good thing is never enough. We celebrate everything and anything. Most of all we celebrate birthdays, especially the big zeros: 10, 20, 30, 40, 50.... For these we try to plan something hilariously outrageous, wickedly generous and passionately memorable.

When our neighbor turned forty, her husband hid forty small gifts in tuck-away places around the house and yard: her favorite perfume; a glitzy pen; a new pair of gardening gloves; a book on her "want to read" list; and on and on. Each was tied to an alarm clock or timer, preset to buzz one after the other every fifteen minutes. She had a frantic, fun-filled day, especially as the gifts were so well hidden that before she found one another was buzzing.

We loved this idea, so on my husband's fiftieth birthday we scoured the stores for fifty different candy bars, especially those he fondly remembered from his Canadian childhood. We hid these around the house, not with buzzers, but with a paper trail of clues, one leading to the other. The final clue took him to a card with reservations for dinner at his favorite restaurant.

Life is the gift of God's superlative imagination! Fill it with love and have fun living it.

Thank You, Father, for all Your good gifts. —FAY ANGUS

8

Whatsoever things are of good report...think on these things. —PHILIPPIANS 4:8

Life these days comes with plenty of stress. I guess that's why our family loves to escape to our cabin in Alabama. There, on a little island surrounded by a tranquil lake edged by a mountain chain, it's easy to recenter ourselves.

Since I was a young girl, one of the delights of the island has been a huge forest of pine and hardwood trees. Designated common property by the original owner, the trees had been owned by no one except the owls who hooted there at night and the mourning doves who called out from the tall pines at daybreak.

Common property, that is, until last year. First I noticed that certain trees had been ringed with red paint. "What's going on?" I asked neighbors, but no one knew. Oh well, I reasoned, nothing could ever happen to this wonderful stretch of thick woods.

And then the call came. Our daughter Keri had driven to the cabin from college. Cresting the hill from the causeway, she discovered our forest in ruins. Most of the trees had been cut and hauled off for timber. Then bulldozers had ripped through the ground and pushed all the leftover limbs and smaller trees into huge piles.

"Our woods are gone," she wept to Brock, who had happened to answer the phone. "Everything's ruined...ruined," she cried.

Catching the gist of the conversation, my heart sank to my heels. And then I heard Brock calm his sister's distress with a few gentle words. "Keri," he said firmly, "I want you to hang up this phone and I want you to start walking down toward the lake. About halfway down, I want you to stop. Look at the lake. Look at the mountains. Remember how it feels to sit on the pier and watch the sunset. As long as we live, the lake and the mountains and the sunsets will always be there for us. Don't think about the lost woods across the road. Think about the things no one can take away from us."

Father, I can't keep everything just the way I want it to be. You are the One Constant no one can take away from me. —PAM KIDD

9

For this reason I bow my knees before the Father, from whom every family in heaven and on earth is named.
—EPHESIANS 3:14–15 (RSV)

Recently, when I was visiting my sister in Michigan, I noticed her clipping hockey articles from the Detroit sports pages to send to my nephew Justin, who had just started art school in Chicago.

"Ah," I said with a chuckle, "upholding a fine old family practice, are you?"

Mary Lou looked at me quizzically. I was surprised she didn't get my reference.

"When I went away to college," I explained, "Mom used to send me every single article from the local papers about the Tigers. It became kind of a dormitory joke, in fact, because there was always a huge stack of baseball clippings in my room. But I would have been even more homesick without them."

My sister laughed. "I never knew that! I guess I'm more like her than I realize."

Funny how these things develop, even subconsciously. My wife Julee says I laugh just like my mom. At night I always get out of bed to double-check that the front door is locked, a ritual of my father's that always annoyed me. So did his jiggling his change in his pocket, yet I catch myself doing the same thing. My brother and I both insist on sitting on the aisle in church or at the movies, a habit we cultivated separately.

I watched Mary Lou write out Justin's address on a roomy manila envelope, her hasty scrawl (nearly identical to Mom's handwriting) that says, "I have so much to get done." I was satisfied to think how much my family has given me to take through life, even the little things. Especially the little things—a gesture, a mannerism, a figure of speech. Something that says who I am and where I came from. Next time I catch myself laughing and jiggling the change in my pocket, I'll keep in mind where I learned.

Father, where would I be without the family You've given me?
—EDWARD GRINNAN

10

In the world ye shall have tribulation.... —JOHN 16:33

While my father was stationed in Chicago during World War II, I was transplanted from a small-town junior high in Nebraska to a large, sophisticated city school, where I felt very lonely. We didn't talk much about feelings in our family. In fact, a rosy, look-on-the-bright-side attitude was the way we denied our pain. Every night in bed, I'd comfort myself by reading the service for evening prayer from *The Book of Common Prayer.* It's a habit I've kept up through all the years since. There is one prayer that soothes me more than any other. These are its words:

> Keep watch, dear Lord, with those who work, or watch, or weep this night, and give your angels charge over those who sleep. Tend the sick, Lord Christ; give rest to the weary, bless the dying, soothe the suffering, pity the afflicted, shield the joyous, and all for your love's sake. Amen.

I think it comforts me because it *acknowledges suffering.* What a great relief it is to stop pretending life is all joy and peace and light, to admit that people do get old and sick and die, that hearts break, that this very night there are people crying themselves to sleep. Why is that a relief? Because it lets me admit the truth that, mixed in with the love, the unexpected blessings and the great joys of my life, there is also deep pain...and that I am not alone in this.

Many times the prayer has come back to console me, when I've been one of the sick or weary or weeping. As I pray those words, I know that I am somehow joined with all others who suffer. It's also a great comfort at those times to know that somewhere in the world, at that very moment, someone else is praying that prayer. Tonight perhaps you'll add your voice.

Keep watch, dear Lord, with those who work or watch or weep this night.
—*MARILYN MORGAN HELLEBERG*

11

You have come to thousands upon thousands of angels in joyful assembly. —HEBREWS 12:22 (NIV)

As I headed up the driveway for my morning walk, I was struck by how beautiful the world was. The air was crisp, leaves were turning, a few clouds sat quietly on the horizon. All was wondrous, but what took my breath away were thousands of jewels sparkling in the early morning sunlight.

I bent down and looked. Spiders had been at work spinning webs over tiny patches of lawn and each web had caught scores of dew-drops, which now acted as prisms breaking the sunlight into bursts of color. I couldn't wait to come back from my walk to show my wife Tib. But when I returned an hour later, the dewdrops had vanished.

Or had they? I knelt to look more closely and saw that the tiny droplets still clung to the webs, but the sun's rays no longer hit them at the right angle to create these flashes of color. The gems were there, but conditions were not right for me to see them.

The Bible speaks of angels surrounding us in their thousands. Yet only rarely have I met someone who has actually seen an angel. After that early morning experience with the jewels sparkling on our lawn, I understand a little better how this can be. Angelic hosts are indeed surrounding us always, even though the spiritual conditions are not right for us to see them.

Father, as I go about my routines today, help me to appreciate the heavenly hosts who are always with us. —JOHN SHERRILL

12 TUESDAY

The sun rises and sets and hurries around to rise again.
—ECCLESIASTES 1:5 (TLB)

Today, October 12, is the official day for Columbus Day. It's also my birthday. And it was the day in 1987 when my youngest son Andrew, who was seven at the time, and I arose in the wee hours, drove the two miles from our home to Lake Michigan and waited to see some-thing Andrew had never seen before—the sunrise.

At 6:30 A.M., we arrived at the deserted lakefront with our jug of hot cocoa and spread a blanket in the sand. Andrew and I snuggled close in the forty-degree weather as the cold lake wind slapped our faces.

We waited, shivered, snuggled closer, talked, sipped our cocoa and watched the clouds change color over the massive expanse of icy blue water. In the dusky haze of almost-light, I felt a sense of melancholy at being another year older. More light escaped over the thick clouds lying flat against the horizon. We talked about how flat the world looked from here. No wonder the early explorers were confused.

Suddenly, at 7:01 A.M., we both saw it. An incredibly bright concentrated speck of orange light. In seconds the speck became an arc the size of a crescent moon and hopped up on the horizon like the top of a neon pumpkin. Andrew jumped up and started dancing in the sand. "Mom! We did it! We did it! We saw the sunrise!" Throwing up his arms in victory as if he himself caused this incredible event, he flashed a grin as wide as a jack-o-lantern's and asked me to take his picture.

Suddenly, I felt a sense of timelessness. My birthday dreariness disappeared. Instead, I felt a kinship with Christopher Columbus who, five hundred years before, must have felt the same elation as he watched land appear on the horizon just ahead. That one sunrise moment promised the chance for a better life, an opportunity to start over.

Lord, when everything seems to be just "more of the same," surprise me with the amazing grace Your sunrise offers every day.

—PATRICIA LORENZ

13

My eyes are ever on the Lord, for only he will release my feet from the snare. —PSALM 25:15 (NIV)

Riding a rented bicycle with marginal brakes into a four-way intersection on an unsurfaced road is no game for the fainthearted—and I *am* fainthearted. But while on a trip to Vietnam last year, that is exactly the situation in which I was horrified to find myself. There are few motorcars in Hanoi and almost no public transportation, but there are hundreds of thousands of bicycles and small motorcycles racing around the city, guided by no apparent rules.

The first couple of times I lived through this trial by terror, I vowed to return the bicycle and take to my feet, but that meant missing so much of the city. *What a waste of so long a journey,* I told myself, deciding to give it one more try. On the second day, I approached the city's largest intersection. Taking a deep breath, I plunged into what appeared to be a dense and fast-moving morass of vehicles, all going in different directions, many with multiple passengers and alarming amounts of merchandise.

Everywhere vehicles were coming at me at impossible speeds. "Please, God," I gasped, "get me out of this alive." Then I noticed something. Each of the other riders kept his or her eyes glued to the four- or five-foot swath of road right in front of them. There was much swerving and weaving, but clearly you only had to take evasive action if another rider intruded into that space in front of you.

I'm a quick study in a tight situation. *Eyes front,* I told myself, and with one or two close calls I got across intersections without bodily harm for the next two weeks and, more important, without a trace of the ghastly sense of panic I had experienced that first day. God didn't help me escape; He helped me to see order in the midst of chaos.

In moments of fear and chaos, God, help me to listen for Your directions, sent in so many quiet and subtle ways. —BRIGITTE WEEKS

14

"This is my name for ever, and thus I am to be remembered throughout all generations." —EXODUS 3:15 (RSV)

I was reminded of the above verse the other day when we were discussing what to name our new dog, who now answers to Teddy, because he looks like a teddy bear. Names are taken very seriously at our house, and everyone gets involved in the process. We seem to name everything—rooms, cars, trees, flowers, houseplants (one of the kids had a spider plant named "Kamikaze" because it kept jumping out of its pot) and, of course, pets and people. People we like a lot are given nicknames.

I'm interested in both given and surnames, and I often inquire of new acquaintances how they got their names or what they mean. My parents named me after my Bavarian-born grandfather Friedrich, for example; Bauer means farmer in German. My wife Shirley was born when a moptop named Shirley Temple was the rage of films, which explains why she and thousands of others were so christened. Shirley's maiden name was Snyder, which in German means "to cut," as in tailor.

But there are other names we give people, unspoken ones that, perhaps, are the most important of all. Unthinkingly, we sometimes silently label people *failures, awkward, ignorant, homely* and worse. In subtle ways the tone of our voice or our manner can convey disapproval or condescension. This can be particularly harmful to our children, who need our encouragement and reassurance—just as we need to know that we are treasured by our heavenly Father.

What I hear Him calling you and me today is "Special, Precious,

Forgiven, Welcome, Wanted, Wonderful, Worthwhile, Beautiful, Accepted, Esteemed, Unconditionally Loved." Those are names we all like to be called.

Make us sensitive, God, to names we bestow,
Choosing kind ones that help people grow.

—FRED BAUER

15 FRIDAY

Whatever is true....do; and the God of peace will be with you. —PHILIPPIANS 4:8–9 (RSV)

This fall I've been doing one of my "once in a blue moon cleanings." But to throw out my treasures—though I no longer need them—feels like a betrayal of the people responsible for enriching my life. Then an idea comes to mind: I can either pass my treasures on with prayers of thanksgiving for the blessings they represent, or resurrect them with new meaning!

Here are my many angels, each one given me by someone I love. I put some in the Goodwill bag, wrapped in prayer for the niece, sister or friend who thought of me. I pray, too, for God's blessings on the person who might someday receive them.

Here are the flannel graph figures and backdrops I used twenty years ago when I taught Sunday school. I can give them to a neighbor who holds Good News Clubs in her home. They're better off being used.

And what of my children's schoolwork? Their priceless art? Their stories about what they wanted to do when they grew up? Ideas play in my mind as to how I can reuse them. Blake's autumn poem, written when he was eight, I've already framed and hung by the front door. Phil's drawing of a neighbor boy crying (sketched when Phil was twelve and Robbie was three), I've matted and will take to Robbie's mother. And Heather's sixth-grade journal letters, written each Friday as a school project? Perhaps I can make her a scrapbook, with pictures to illustrate.

My angst has turned into delight, for I have ways to give new life to the good things that have been mine.

Count your blessings.
Name them one by one.
Count your many blessings.
See what God has done. —BRENDA WILBEE

READER'S ROOM

I find early mornings especially nice to spend time with the Lord and let Him fill me with His words of comfort. One particular morning the song in my ear was "God is worthy of praise," and I lifted my head toward heaven and experienced the most beautiful full moon I've ever seen. It spoke to me of God's light that shines brighter than all my darkness. God's light fills my world, and I'm thankful that I remember the wonder of that moon that morning. —*CARRIE HAMILTON, LIVINGSTON, TX*

16

SATURDAY

Trust in the Lord, and do good.... —PSALM 37:3

When a few families from Hillsboro Presbyterian in Nashville, Tennessee, put up the money to buy an old, rundown house, reactions were mixed. The idea was to fix up the house for an older woman, who was on the verge of being homeless.

"There's no way the people of this church can do the work required to make that house fit to live in," one man said. "Our own church building needs a fair share of work, we should take care of our own responsibilities first," a woman said. "It will take years to make that old place livable," someone else predicted.

Others held fast in their resolve to answer the prayers of a woman in need. "It's time to move forward in trust and do the work the Lord has put before us," my father, who is Hillsboro's senior minister, said from the pulpit one morning.

And so a few Saturdays later, I found myself perched on top of a steeply pitched roof, tearing off about a hundred years' worth of shingles and tossing them down into the yard below. "Maybe those guys were right about overextending ourselves," I muttered to myself as I wondered if my favorite football team had scored in today's game.

When we broke for lunch, the lady next door came. "The whole neighborhood is behind you," she said. "This house had been attracting some mighty shady people before you folks bought it. They were doin' drugs and all sorts of bad things. It was bringin' down our spirit."

After lunch, I walked across the street for a better view of the old

house. Before, I had seen a hopelessly dilapidated place with a sagging porch and rotted-out eaves. From this perspective, I saw a proud old house calling out for another chance. I saw people from all walks of life sitting around in the yard, munching on sandwiches and getting to know each other. I saw renewal on neighbors' faces and pure joy on the face of the house's future occupant, who had come by to help.

"Move forward and trust," my dad had said.

"Then stand back and see just how far I will spread your good works," God seemed to be answering.

God, choosing good and trusting You, that's the way I want to live.

—BROCK KIDD

17 SUNDAY

He put a new song in my mouth.... —PSALM 40:3 (NAS)

I grew up in the church. My husband Jerry and I took our children to church three times a week. I was very religious, but in my mid-thirties, I could no longer ignore a restlessness deep within me.

While vacuuming one day, I became desperate enough to cry out to God audibly, "If I don't really know You personally, I want to. I'll do anything...." My plea was the beginning of a life-changing revival that happened right there, in my toy-strewn den. The sudden joy that touched me was almost unbearable, and I suddenly longed to praise God. I sang hymns, singing one in particular over and over. The song—"Out of My Bondage"—was new to me, and I didn't know all the words.

Almost immediately, I began to discern a patient, loving Voice speaking to my heart. The next Sunday in church, the Voice urged, *Go forward publicly to commit yourself to Me.* I refused for two weeks. What would people think?

On the third Sunday, when church began, so did the kind Voice. Silently, I explained to Him, *I'll go if they sing my new favorite song at the end of church.* The song had become mine, as surely as the children sitting with me were mine. As I reached for the bulletin to check the invitation hymn, the Voice urged, *Trust Me. Don't even look at the bulletin.* I obeyed, and at the end of the service I recognized the first three sweetly familiar notes and stepped into the aisle. Obedience felt marvelous, but I had no idea what I'd say to my minister, who waited up front. Just as the minister took my hand, the Voice prompted me to say, "This isn't just a rededication—it's all of me."

In the years since that Sunday, I've had many other experiences with the Voice, inviting me to new ways of living out my Christian commitment. But my theme song remains the same:

Out of my bondage, sorrow and night, Jesus, I come....
Out of unrest and arrogant pride, Jesus I come to Thee.

—MARION BOND WEST

A FORK IN THE ROAD

Changes in our lives can challenge us to deepen our faith in God's plan. Last year, Eric Fellman faced a series of changes in the things he'd taken for granted—his job, his home and his family. This week, he'll take us with him through those stressful times and help us to discover a renewed trust in God's loving care. —THE EDITORS

18

MONDAY

DAY 1

So that your trust may be in the Lord, I teach you today....

—PROVERBS 22:19 (NIV)

When an unexpected career change hit me this year, I found myself frozen with doubt as the challenge of finding another job loomed before me. There was the financial burden of having two kids in college and another headed that way. Then there was the daunting prospect of diving into the cold waters of the job market. Would anyone hire me? Would the new job be as satisfying and rewarding as the last one? Would we have to move? If so, where? Would our new neighbors like us, and would we like them?

After an early morning men's meeting one Wednesday, I stood in our church parking lot, pouring out all of my doubts to my friend Len. Shivering a bit in the chill morning air, I noticed that Len seemed to be looking past me, and I was annoyed that he wasn't paying full attention to my tale of woe. Suddenly, he blurted out, "Well, will you look at that?"

I turned around, but I couldn't see anything special. The sky was clear and the sun was peeking above the trees on the ridge behind us. "Look at what?" I asked.

"Why, it's amazing," he replied with a grin. "Eric Fellman has lost his job, and the sun is still coming up!"

My astonishment was just turning into anger when Len continued. "Eric, how long have you and Joy been married?"

"Almost twenty-one years," I replied. "Why?"

"How many days have you gone hungry in twenty-one years?"

"None."

"How many days homeless?"

"None."

"So, if God has taken care of you for twenty-one years, why do you think He is going to stop suddenly now? Has He stopped bringing up the sun or sending the rain or anything else you can notice?"

"No."

"So quit whining and get on with it."

With that Len climbed into his vehicle and drove away. I climbed into my car, looked at the rising sun and got on with it.

Lord, let me know the power of Your promises today, and help me to trust the wisdom of Your leading. —ERIC FELLMAN

19

DAY 2

"If you know these things, blessed are you if you do them." —JOHN 13:17 (RSV)

I thought selling my fishing boat would be one of the toughest things about moving. But the boys were all away at school and there was no room to store the boat at our new place. So I promised Joy I'd try to sell it to avoid storage fees. But my sales method was not designed for success. I parked the boat along the edge of our lawn that ran along a dead-end street. The "For Sale" sign was large, but only six or eight neighbors could see it. One week before the move, I was rolling the boat back to our house when a family pulled up in a van and asked, "Is your boat still for sale?"

"I guess so," I reluctantly replied.

Out jumped a boy about ten and a girl about twelve years old. Their eyes sparkled as they ran around, climbed in, and sorted through the boat and equipment. But their father's look told me he thought it was worth more than he could pay. Calling the kids to him he said wistfully, "It's probably worth about twenty-five hundred dollars, right?"

I didn't really hear him, because my heart was captured by those two eager faces at his side. So ignoring his question I said, "What are you offering?"

"Well, I can only afford fifteen hundred," he said.

"That's funny," I replied, "I was just thinking I'd have to sell it for fourteen hundred because it has no child-sized life jackets."

His kids squealed, "Let's take it, Dad!" and ran over to scramble aboard once more.

He looked at me and said, "It's worth much more than that. Are you sure?"

"Look, friend," I replied, "you'll pay me cash, but they"—I pointed to his kids—"are paying me joy. I figure I'm ahead."

Lord, thank You for once again showing me the healing power there is in passing along happiness. —ERIC FELLMAN

20

DAY 3

We have...a house not made with hands, eternal in the heavens. —II CORINTHIANS 5:1 (NAS)

When you've lived in a house for thirteen years and raised your family there, it has a special place in your heart. I was trying to ignore this reality as we sold our home in Pawling, New York, and prepared to move to a new place in Virginia. I wasn't being very successful. In the last week, I had found myself wandering the yard, looking at favorite trees, listening to the gurgle of the swimming pool filter and wondering in how many more weeks the lawn would need cutting.

While the papers were being signed at our closing, I realized I had left a bicycle leaning against the big maple outside the garage, intending to pack it last on our pickup truck. The buyer said it would be no problem for me to come and get it the next morning.

Joy and I spent the night several miles away at the home of friends, and I got up early to drive over and retrieve the bike. When I pulled into the driveway, I saw the buyer's two young sons playing soccer in the side yard, just as my sons had done years ago. I got out of the truck, and as I lifted the bike into the pickup, the boys came running up to me. "Watcha doin', mister?" one of them asked. I told them I was getting a bike I had left behind. "Oh, you're the owner!" the boy said.

With just a little hesitation, I leaned down between them, put a hand on each one's shoulder and replied, "No, boys, now you guys are the owners." As I watched them run off, laughing and kicking their ball, the ache in my heart told me I had let myself get too attached to an earthly treasure. The house had never been mine; God had just loaned it to our family for a while, and although it would now be another family's home, the love and happiness we had shared there would be with us wherever life's journey might lead.

Lord, help me to remember that our real treasures are the gifts of the spirit that come from You. —ERIC FELLMAN

21 THURSDAY

DAY 4

The eyes of the Lord are in every place....

—PROVERBS 15:3

Our move from Pawling, New York, to Falls Church, Virginia, was a big change in lifestyle. Pawling was definitely rural: only five thousand people in a region of farms and horses. Falls Church is definitely urban, inside the Washington Beltway, just seven miles from the White House. For Joy, the change has been wonderful; she grew up in a large city and the remoteness of Pawling was always a struggle for her. For me, it's another matter.

We moved from a house on two acres to a townhouse with a twenty-foot backyard. Our front window looks out on the street, and the back window overlooks a church parking lot. At night the streetlights are so bright you can hardly see any stars, and the local wildlife is the kind that draws police sirens, not birdwatchers. The worst thing for me, after four weeks, was a loss of the sense of the presence of God. I have always seen Him clearest in the shade of a giant maple tree or heard Him in the gurgle of a brook or felt Him in the pull of a bass at the end of my line. It seemed to me He was gone in the noise and traffic of metropolitan life.

One morning, after a fitful night of sirens and flashing lights, I got up early to have a cup of coffee on our second-floor deck. I was about to pour my heart out in bitter prayer and ask God where He had gone when a loud "chirrrrrrrr" sound rose up from overhead. Perched on our rain gutter was a fat gray squirrel who promptly ran down the drain spout, sat on the deck railing and cocked its head to chirp at me once more. Then it scampered down the post to the ground and ran across the street to collect acorns beneath an oak tree. All I could do was laugh and say, "Okay, Lord, I get the message."

Thanks, Lord for Your presence with me wherever I am—even if I have to look a little closer to find You.　　—ERIC FELLMAN

22
FRIDAY

DAY 5

Not that I have already obtained it, or have already become perfect, but I press on....　　—PHILIPPIANS 3:12 (NAS)

Joy and I have lived in several houses, but we have never purchased one under construction. So we thought our new townhouse, where we were able to choose everything from the placement of rooms to the color of the carpet, would be perfect. Wrong. The light in the dining room was off center, and there were sections of the bedroom trim that the painter missed. One bathtub had no hot water, and on the first cold night the furnace wouldn't light.

In the middle of all this, I was trying to start a new job and felt that everything I did was wrong because I didn't know the background of the situation or the people involved. It seemed I was constantly trying to learn simple policies or procedures without knowing where the forms were or where to send them when I found them.

One night I arrived home very discouraged to find Joy in another painful discussion with the builder. Coming up the walk, I heard him say, "Please be patient, Mrs. Fellman. It takes time to finish a house. We'll get everything right in the end."

"Please be patient." It seemed as if I'd heard that before. Going to my desk, I rummaged through a box of stuff I had meant to throw out in the move, and there it was: a button with the bold letters PBPGINFWMY printed on a blue background. Someone had given it to me years ago. The letters stood for "Please Be Patient, God Is Not Finished With Me Yet." Looking out my window at the new section of townhouses rising from their foundations, the meaning of the button became even clearer. We are *all* under construction, and it takes time to get it right. But God doesn't quit; He sticks with it until we *are* perfect.

So I'm wearing my button again. If you need one, just let me know.

Lord, hurry up and make some more progress on me.

—ERIC FELLMAN

EDITOR'S NOTE: A month from today, on Monday, November 22, we will observe our sixth annual Guideposts Family Day of Prayer. We want you to be part of our praying family. Please send your prayer requests to Guideposts Prayer Fellowship, PO Box 8001, Pawling, NY 12564. Enclose a picture if you can.

23

SATURDAY

DAY 6
Behold, children are a gift of the Lord....

—PSALM 127:3 (NAS)

One of the results of our move this year was an instant empty nest. Our second son, Nathan, was off to college and our youngest, Jonathan, decided to become a boarder at his school in Connecticut. Previously, the boys had attended boarding school as day students, but now Jon wanted to stay behind and finish his high school studies there. So Joy and I arrived in Falls Church, Virginia, with just two cats and all our stuff. The first few days were filled with all the activity of a move. But there came a night when we sat down amidst the boxes and clutter and looked at one another and said, "It's pretty quiet. We miss the boys." The next morning the phones were finally installed and immediately began to ring.

"Mom, where have you guys been?" asked Jonathan. "I've been calling the number for two days and no one answers. Are you guys driving up for Parents' Weekend?"

"Mom, get Dad on the phone," said Jason, our oldest. "The brakes on my car are making an awful noise, and I need to know what to do."

"Dad, this is Nathan. Can you pick me up at the train tomorrow?

I have to get out of this dorm and get a paper done!"

By noon, Joy and I looked at each other and started laughing. They might not be here right now, but they certainly were not gone—not yet, anyway. But those first few days were a good lesson. We're trying to learn that our relationship with our children, like all human relationships, is a gift from God, a gift to be treasured and nurtured through all of life's changes.

Lord, help me never to take Your gift of my loved ones for granted and always to do what is necessary to keep our relationships strong in the midst of change. —ERIC FELLMAN

24

DAY 7

"How much more shall your Father who is in heaven give what is good to those who ask Him!"
—MATTHEW 7:11 (NAS)

If you are like me, during tumultuous and disconcerting events like our career change and move, there are days when you cry out and think God is not listening. During one of those moments, a minister friend told me about a phone call he had recently received. One night, at one or two in the morning, he was awakened by a caller who was clearly upset, sobbing and rambling on in a way that made no sense. Trying to wake up, calm the caller and make sense of the problem all at once, my friend became exasperated and said sternly, "Now settle down, get a grip on yourself and tell me your name."

In a moment came the startled reply, "But, Dad, it's me, Joel!"

Instantly my friend was wide awake, totally sympathetic, filled with love and compassion, listening to a tale of woe only a college student pressured by grades, girls and loneliness can experience. Why the sudden change? It was his child. No one on earth mattered more to him.

As he told me the story, he didn't have to make the point. When I am pressured and frazzled and call out to God, He responds with total understanding, compassion and love. For I am His child. And so are you.

Lord, thank You for being my Father. When my problems get to be too much for me, help me to remember that You are always waiting on the other end of the line. —ERIC FELLMAN

25

And let us not be weary in well doing: for in due season we shall reap, if we faint not. —GALATIANS 6:9

Carving faces on pumpkins is one thing, I thought as I watched several experts give a demonstration. *Carving faces on a mountain is another.*

The comparison resulted from a recent talk with Orville Worman, who'd helped carve Washington, Jefferson, Lincoln and Theodore Roosevelt out of South Dakota's Mount Rushmore sixty years ago.

"Working on that monument must have been exciting work," I said to Orville.

"At first I thought the job was kind of a crazy one. But I had a wife and child to support, and it paid fifty cents an hour."

"It must be satisfying to look up there now and know you helped chisel four presidents' heads out of solid rock."

"Well, I don't see just four presidents...I see Don and Glen and Howdy and Red and a lot of other buddies I worked with. I was a mere driller. Others had more important jobs than I did. I guess that's taught me a valuable lesson: We don't always have important positions in life. Sometimes those tedious day-to-day tasks that seem unimportant right then add up to something you can look back on and be proud of."

He's right, I concluded, remembering the seemingly unimportant tasks I often felt saddled with, especially during the days when my sons were growing up: changing diapers; washing dishes; cleaning windows; cooking meals; running errands. Now I seldom remember those tedious day-by-day tasks. I look at the fine men my sons have become. They're my monument.

Keep molding me daily, Father, into the person You want me to be.
—ISABEL WOLSELEY

26

How forcible are right words!... —JOB 6:25

I love e-mail. I love the way you can send a message whenever it's convenient (11:30 at night for me), and you don't have to worry about interrupting your recipients because they'll access it and read it when they're free. I love it that you can say little, silly things or long, serious things and that you can have a discussion back and forth through cyberspace for days, punching the reply box each time until you've created a document that would fill pages. I love the way you can communicate with people in the office next door or thousands of miles away, all for the cost of a short phone call.

But once I became very frustrated with the limitations of e-mail. A friend, whom I hadn't seen for months, and I were having a heated argument by e-mail. In an apologetic, writerly way, he wrote some very frank words. I was grateful for his honest criticism and said so in my reply. Our friendship would survive this agreement to disagree, but in the space of our last two messages I noticed an excess of politeness entering our dialogue, as though we were each scared of hurting the other. *Lord,* I prayed, *I wish I could see Arthur.*

Two days later I was walking down Fifth Avenue at lunchtime when I spotted my e-mail friend crossing the street toward me. We practically fell into each other's arms. "I'm so sorry I upset you," he said to me. "Don't be ridiculous," I responded. "I was grateful for your honesty." We spoke for five minutes before rushing in opposite directions, but the moment of face-to-face communication served its purpose. The static that had entered a friendship was wiped away. That night as I penned a new e-mail message to Arthur, I thanked God for His direct ways.

God in heaven, You know the yearnings of my heart. Let me express myself with clarity in what I write and what I say. —RICK HAMLIN

27

"Only take heed...lest you forget the things which your eyes have seen...." —DEUTERONOMY 4:9 (RSV)

Back in the sixties and early seventies, I was aboard her three times when she was the *France,* the most elegant way to cross the Atlantic you can imagine. The longest ship in the world and beautiful, she was the pride of France. Then, in 1973, it ended; the economy and air travel caught up with her, and she lay unused and neglected in the port of Le Havre. One day a Norwegian came to see what her chances of becoming a single-class cruise ship were, and they took her away from France. She was given the name *Norway,* and by 1979 she was out into service in the Caribbean.

Seventeen years passed. Word came that she was going to make a crossing—the first time up from Miami to New York, and the first time back to France. I signed on with a bittersweet feeling. I was prepared for the changes—the new double row of cabins, the smoking room now walled in, the promenade deck became Broadway on the starboard side and the Champs Elysées on the port. But I was startled by one thing: the great number of French passengers aboard. They had flown over for the return voyage. Then there were the invited French chefs who created meals *a là France,* and the lectures about the defunct French Line. Nothing, however, could have surprised me more than sailing into Le Havre.

I stood on the promenade foredeck to be a part of an event that made the whole trip worthwhile. A flotilla of boats on every side greeted us beyond the harbor and brought us in. The fireboats sprayed us, the ship's whistle boomed, and people, thousands of them, lined the shore for miles—a reception larger than for any maiden voyage greeted our prodigal ship. Bands played, officials spoke, and all day the people came. Until nine that night when the ship departed for Southampton, it went on, when at last we were bade farewell with fireworks on land and sea.

She is *Norway,* but she is French at heart, *sans doute.*

I thank You, God, that You let us remember greatness and beauty.
—VAN VARNER

28
THURSDAY

He appointed twelve...that they might be with him and that he might send them out to preach....
—MARK 3:14 (NIV)

Our move to Atlanta felt more like a thousand giant steps backward than a move forward. Our oldest son Jeff was off at college for the first time and his new, empty room seemed so strange and still. Our fifteen-year-old Chris was moping around friendless in his new high school. My husband Gordon seemed to be gone all the time, exhausting himself in his new job and the long commute through heavy traffic.

About the only one who seemed to be taking to our new home was our six-year-old John, who scampered all over the neighborhood riding bikes with the other children. *That's fine for him,* I thought, *but I don't fit in with all of these young mothers. What on earth am I doing here?*

On Sunday I forced myself out of bed to attend church, but as I settled down in the pew, the familiar resistance burned in my throat. *This isn't my church. I don't know anybody here.* Then my eyes fell on a notice in the bulletin for a Stephen Ministry class, training to help people in crisis, that I had been too busy to take in my old church. After several weeks of procrastination, I telephoned the church just before the training date. The two Stephen leaders arranged a meeting with me, and I found myself signing up. As I left the meeting, I stopped outside the closed office door to get out my car keys. The resistance resurfaced. *What have you gotten yourself into? You're going to feel awkward working with strangers.*

Just then I was startled by a sound from behind the closed door. It was an unmistakable outburst of laughter. The two women who had just spoken with me were carrying on with enough "all rights!" and "amens!" to be heard right through the door. *What on earth are they so happy about?* I wondered.

At the first Stephen meeting I found out. Half a year earlier, when the pair had begun developing the ministry, they had prayed for twelve volunteers to train. Although they had run announcements in the bulletin for six months in a church with more than a thousand members, until I moved to the area, there had only been eleven volunteers.

I opened my training manual, wondering how many other times I had gone kicking and screaming, only to land right where God not only needed me, but had already counted me in. Only this time I'd been allowed to hear with my own ears the rejoicing on the other side of the door.

Father, help me to count on Your grace until I discover where You've already counted me in. —KAREN BARBER

29 FRIDAY

But the desires of the diligent are fully satisfied.
—PROVERBS 13:4 (NIV)

I glared at the sheet music in front of me: third-chair trombone. I had played second and lead the year before. And I was in the running for section leader. The results of the jazz band auditions had just been posted, and I was sure there had been a mistake. Maybe the new director had it in for me. I should have been first chair, I was certain, maybe second if Erik had practiced a lot. I ran my tongue over my lip where the day-old cut was healing. I had explained that I couldn't play my trombone very well with my cut, that I was afraid it might open up again.

But the truth was, the cut wasn't all that deep. I was so nervous, I probably couldn't have played even without the handicap. The truth was, I should have practiced more, and though it hurt to admit it, I believed my friend deserved the honor.

Sometimes it takes a wake-up call to make me realize the obvious: Hard work helps to earn a good reputation, but I can't just stop there. In the end, effort and the will to improve will take me much further.

It took a few minutes for me to swallow my anger and my ego. I prayed for composure and went to congratulate Bryant on making second chair. That earned me a firm handshake and a surprised grin from him before I went to congratulate Erik on playing—no, earning—the lead.

Dear Lord, when it's time to be humble, help me to congratulate others on a job well done. —KJERSTIN EASTON

30

SATURDAY

"This is what the Lord Almighty says: '...show mercy and compassion to one another." —ZECHARIAH 7:9 (NIV)

I'd had a strange week. Monday, a crying little girl rang my doorbell. She had taken the wrong school bus and needed my help. When I drove her home, her mother said to me, "Robin's guardian angel must have sent her to your house." Tuesday, I found a gold watch on the floor of a theater where I had just seen a new play. When I turned it in, the usher said, "Somebody will be awfully glad you were here tonight." Wednesday, a woman called looking for my help concerning a court case on which I'd served as a juror several years before. "I looked through the phone book praying I'd find you," she said. And on Friday, a friend called me, frantic that she'd lost her purse. "Pray that I find it, Gina," she said, and I did. She found it the next day.

In each case the need was so obvious that I didn't have to think hard to know how to help. In a lighthearted way I pictured each of those people praying for help, and each day God looking down to see me once again in the perfect spot to be of some assistance. But it made me think: Are there times when God asks me to help someone and I don't hear the question?

I thought of a young boy I'd met at church the week before whose negative attitude and rude language elicited a quick reprimand from me. I wonder if he really was asking for the attention that he's not getting anywhere else. Next time I'll try to respond more positively. What about my older friend who painfully recounted the difficulty of caring for her ill husband? Maybe I can offer her more than an understanding ear, even though she didn't ask for it.

Once I started listening for these "unasked questions," I began hearing them all around me. By taking the time to hear the cry in a child's voice, or really see the look on the face of a friend or stranger, I might discover a hidden need that God wants me to respond to, knowing that in that face-to-face moment, I'm the only one who can.

Lord, help me daily to be someone You can count on to hear even the silent cry for help that comes my way. —GINA BRIDGEMAN

31

SUNDAY

Then let us no more pass judgment on one another, but rather.... Let us then pursue what makes for peace and for mutual upbuilding. —ROMANS 14:13, 19 (RSV)

Perhaps it was the gray, drizzly weather or my own uneasy restlessness after church, but last Sunday afternoon while my husband Alex and the children were napping, I impulsively drove to rural Laingsburg to look at houses for sale. Alex and I had been thinking about living in the country, perhaps by a lake, but decided not to move for at least three years. But today I felt strangely compelled to go see this new development.

After driving around the lake, inspecting the subdivision, I knew it wasn't for us. I headed into the town, looking for another lake nearby. I didn't find it, but in front of a small, white-frame church I spotted the reason I'd been prompted to drive out here. On a simple sign were the words: "The sin of criticism is far worse than the sin you criticize."

For me this was much more than a clever phrase. It was a light to guide my response to the turmoil in our church. I'd been deeply upset by the removal of our pastor and the resulting division and strife. And, yes, I had been criticizing—both those who were leaving ("Why can't they stay and work things out?") and the new pastor ("Can't he do more to help people stay? Why is he making such big changes so quickly?").

But the sign by the little country church spoke to me. I am not to judge. My fault-finding can be more harmful than the wrongs I think I see.

Oh, Lord, please help me not to criticize, but to understand and accept and encourage.
                                                                —MARY BROWN

MY FAITH JOURNEY

Missed kids

1. Paul & I watched T.V. Paul needs to do more things for himself

Missed kids

2. Paul took a nap & went to Mass w/ me. I was so thankful. Noodles & cottage cheese for supper.

Made Turkey dinner & all the kids & grandkids came over.

3. Put up Halloween decorations

Missed kids

4. Rain, Rain, Rain. Pauls improving every day. We had turkey dinner for lunch

Missed kids

5. Went to dump as 7:00 & IGA. Paul was up more today. He looks Much better.

Missed kids

6. Went to Dr. K. He had Theresa in his office both do les ahus bills. She was very nice. Went to Hallicks girl

Missed Boys & Albers

7. Chantelle Baby & I went to Columbus outside & then to luncheon at Methodist Church in Pemberton. I saw Jeanne & Alan, Aunt & Judy Cole. Ice Cream for dinner

issed kids Paul finally went for a week to Builders louse w/me. We also sat outside a while. I went for papers & tomatoe pie from Red Star in

8 Crosswick. Delicious!!
Paul & I showed & watched kids at Chantells from 11:00 – 3:00 Came home

9 Paul napped & my went to Church at 5:00
issed kids Rain. Rain. Rain. I went for papers.

10 Paul & I relaxed all day. Watched football & made stuffed cabbage.
Beautiful sunny day 70°. Made pork roast, mashed potatoes & corn. Chantell

11 came over & Paul & Bobby got haircuts
Beautiful sunny day 70° went back to work. Chantell & Bob & kids came over & had supper & brought lima beans

12 Beautiful sunny day 70°. very busy at
issed kids work. Came home & husk corn & shell

13 lima beans. Paul & I showed & watched soaps
issed kids Beautiful sunny day 65° very busy at work. Called Paul at lunch time.

14 Paul & I watched soaps. Butch was here
used kids Beautiful sunny day. Paul & I walked to take pictures of Butchies house.

15 Talked w/Tony & Ricky. watched soaps
used kids Beautiful sunny day. Relaxed all day. Butch stopped over & Brian

16 called & talked over 1 hr. 5:00 Mass
Beautiful sunny day AM & Rain P.M.
Paul & I went to Bobby last

17 football game, turkey dinner Maria Allentown
issed kids Beautiful sunny day. Took VAC Day. Paul & I went to see Marion

18 dedication Church in Brick, dinner
issed kids Beautiful sunny day. very busy at work. Paul & I went to clean after work. Butch

19 stopped to see Paul. Chantell called from Atlanta, Georgia. They went down w/kids to see Mets game.

Missed kids

Rain, Rain, Rain. Very busy at work. Came home & Showed & Paul + I went to find papers + kids

20 pictures from Mets game (Baby)

Missed kids

Beautiful sunny day. Took a VAC day from work. Paul & I ate lunch &

21 napped to go see Maria & St. Peters.

Missed kids

Beautiful sunny day. I took an A/L day to relax w/ Paul. to get

22 see Maria Esperanza at visitation.

Missed kids

Beautiful sunny day 55°. Butch came over for lunch. Paul & I napped

23 + went to Wedding Oyster Dinner & church.

Missed kids

Beautiful sunny day 50°. Paul & I went for papers & relaxed all day

24 w/ papers & football. Made spaghetti

Missed kids

Beautiful sunny day. 60°. Started to go back to work. Cried. Butch

25 stopped by at supper time.

Missed kids

Beautiful sunny day 60°. Paul has blood in his urine again. We have

26 appt. w/ urologist tomorrow.

Missed kids

Beautiful sunny day 60° went to Dr Urosh & Paul had cistoscope

27 They let me come in. Rush to hosp.

Missed kids

Beautiful sunny day 60° x-rays + cardiograms + blood work. Put

28 Paul on cancer floor. Private room.

Missed kids

Beautiful sunny day. 60° brought in bed to lab. Paul to surgeon

29 Dr said NO. Problem with his heart

Missed kids

Beautiful sunny day 60°. Paul had surgery yesterday & is doing

30 wonderful.

Missed kids

Beautiful sunny day. 70°. Paul came home from hospital today

31 We got home about 4:00. I walked down to the house w/ Butch + gem

November

Surely goodness and mercy shall follow me
all the days of my life....
—PSALM 23:6 (RSV)

S	M	T	W	T	F	S
	1	2	3	4	5	6
7	8	9	10	11	12	13
14	15	16	17	18	19	20
21	22	23	24	25	26	27
28	29	30				

1

Ye that love the Lord, hate evil: he preserveth the souls of his saints; he delivereth them out of the hand of the wicked.
—PSALM 97:10

On a recent Sunday morning, our pastor began his sermon by asking, "How many of you are saints?" A scattering of hands ventured up.

"How many are sinners?" he inquired. Throughout the church, many hands shot up.

I wish I had raised my hand for both questions. In the Bible, the word *saint* describes all those who know the Lord and seek to serve Him. St. Paul tells the Christians at Rome that they are all "called to be saints" (Romans 1:7). But like many in the congregation, I thought that my affirmative answer to the second question disqualified me from saying yes to the first.

So often I fall short when it comes to the things Jesus has told us to do: feeding the poor; visiting the sick; praying for the lonely; loving the unlovable—all saintly endeavors. But when that happens, I try and remember something else Paul tells the same Christians: "All have sinned, and come short of the glory of God." *All*—not just Drue, but Peter and Paul and Luke and John. And feeling a bit more courageous, I ask God to send me more opportunities to share His love with others and grow into my saintly calling.

Lord, today let me hear You calling me to be one of your saints.
—DRUE DUKE

2

He that ruleth over men must be just.... —II SAMUEL 23:3

Mother and Father had voted each November as long as I could recall. They were interested in good government, and they felt voting was not a duty but a privilege. So why was I entering the voting booth for the first time in November 1948? Why had I waited until I was thirty years old to cast my vote? Was it apathy or disgust with the world of politics?

From 1941, when I turned twenty-three, until 1948, I was continually relocating, never remaining in one place long enough to vote there. When I moved to Medford in 1946, I commuted to my job, returning home only on weekends. But by 1948 I was settled, registered and available to vote.

I left the polling place that Tuesday morning filled with joy. I was now an active citizen, a member of the community. I had a voice—even if it was just a tiny one—in our national, state and city government. I felt a real sense of accomplishment.

Twelve years later, in 1960, we received a letter from our cousin Richard, a Harvard-trained Ph.D. and a university professor. He told us he had been denied the right to vote because he had "failed" a literacy test administered by a grammar school dropout. Amazingly, Richard had managed to keep his good humor and seemed more amused than outraged by the situation.

From then on, each time I voted, I thought of Richard. But on August 6, 1965, President Johnson signed the first Voting Rights Act into law. The act was designed to stop discrimination at the polls, and it suspended literacy tests and other devices aimed at disqualifying minority voters. "I'm free to vote," Richard wrote us. "I imagine my adversary will have to find other employment!"

All I could say was "Amen!"

Father, as I vote today, let me remember not to take this freedom for granted. —OSCAR GREENE

LESSONS IN LISTENING

3

WEDNESDAY

FRESH PERSPECTIVES
In an abundance of counselors there is safety.
—PROVERBS 11:14 (RSV)

Years ago I believed I heard God tell me to write a biography. I spent three years working on it before learning that the core of the story was untrue. How can we confirm the guidance we think we're hearing?

My friend Charles Blair offered me one answer he found at a cost that makes my three misspent years seem cheap. With faith and determination Charles had built the largest church in Denver. Seven thousand people drove to hear him preach each Sunday. He had a daily radio program and went into a million and a half homes on TV each week.

Then in the early 1970s he believed God was telling him to build a badly needed housing and medical complex for the elderly. "Trusting God" for the money, he borrowed huge sums, then borrowed more to pay interest on the first loan, and so on. At last, hopelessly in debt, Charles realized that he'd mistaken his own can-do spirit for God's directive. My husband and I flew out to be with him.

"Of course I knew," Charles told us, "that before any major decision, guidance must be submitted to a group of wise counselors. I'd done that." What he hadn't done was select advisers with *different* outlooks from his own. "I listened only to people who, like me, believed that with enough faith you could do anything."

For the past twenty-five years Charles has labored to pay off that staggering debt. Today his last dollar has been repaid; Charles' ministry is back on track. And his counselors include the cautious along with the bold, the practical as well as the visionary.

His wisdom came too late for my book project. Like him, I'd checked my guidance only with people as excited about the subject as I was. Nowadays, since suffering with Charles through his ordeal, I seek out personalities very different from my own to confirm or deny what I hear. "The body of Christ" has new meaning for me—different organs, different functions, as necessary to each other in our differences as the eye is to the hand.

What fuller understanding of You, Father, will someone give to me today?
                                                —ELIZABETH SHERRILL

4

Even though I walk through the valley of the shadow of death, I will fear no evil, for you are with me....
                                                —PSALM 23:4 (NIV)

Whitney has a brain tumor. She is a beautiful girl, not yet married and thirty years old. She is the daughter of friends about our ages, so I still think of her as a girl instead of as a woman. Tonight, we who are family friends are responding to a request from her parents: *Come, please, to a prayer gathering in our driveway at dusk and surround our home with your prayers.*

And so we have gathered outside Whitney's window with her parents, grandmother, friends and neighbors. We are the people who watched her grow up, who prayed for her five years ago at the onset of this disease. We rejoiced with her a year later when the tumor seemed gone. We cried at the news of the tumor's reappearance two months ago.

Now Whitney lies in a coma upstairs in her bedroom, and we've gathered outside her window, hoping she can hear our songs and feel our prayers as we light candles and lift her up on the wings of our faith. We don't understand these painful circumstances, but as we entwine our arms and form a tight circle around this house, we remember that we don't have to understand. We have to trust...that God knows and cares and goes before Whitney and each member of this family and that He will provide and be sufficient and hold up His light so that Whitney and each of us can take just one small step at a time. Always. No matter how difficult the path may be.

Father, thank You for the privilege of standing in a circle of Your love. Hold Whitney in Your everlasting arms, and give Your continued comfort to her family. —CAROL KUYKENDALL

---

5 FRIDAY

Thine heart was lifted up because of thy beauty....
—EZEKIEL 28:17

I felt rather blue as I sat at my desk. Unanswered letters were stacked to my right. On my left, a file of new work assignments waited. But I couldn't find the inspiration to attack either pile. Some weeks earlier, a dear friend had died and just a few months before that, we had lost David's mother. And now, an e-mail from our daughter Keri, who was studying in China, confirmed that she wouldn't be home until January.

In this first week of November, the thought of the holidays ahead struck a hollow chord in my heart. Thanksgiving and then Christmas without three of my favorite people loomed empty and cold.

As I gazed out the window, a single yellow leaf drifted slowly by.

It seemed almost like a finger beckoning me outside. I went to the hall closet, pulled out my husband David's blue fleece jacket and wrapped myself in its safe softness.

Outside, the day was brisk. Rain was on the way. I walked back toward the creek where a row of maples and sycamores had shed a lovely, yellow-brown carpet all along the bank. A red leaf swirled in the stream below.

Funny, I thought to myself, *I used to dread fall, and now I find myself drawn to this season of change.* Once autumn seemed an ending, but today I sensed a sort of rebirth: a pattern. A perfect plan. Beautiful leaves, falling, mulching together in the ground, dying so they might live again. The leaf that floated past my window suddenly seemed an invitation straight from God. *Come, step back into life,* it beckoned, *where the seasons come and go, and God makes everything beautiful in His time.*

I found myself impatient to get back in the house and attack the work that waited on my desk. Thanksgiving and then Christmas lay ahead. I had a lot to do.

Father, let me rest awhile in Your perfect plan and then step joyfully into the new day that waits. —PAM KIDD

6 *I will bless the Lord at all times: his praise shall continually be in my mouth.* —PSALM 34:1

One Saturday a few weeks ago, my husband and I drove out into the country to a little restaurant we like. We were looking forward to the hickory-smoked barbecue and homemade coconut cake for which Billy's is famous. So when we arrived and found they had closed early, we were keenly disappointed.

"Well, where do we go from here?" Larry grumbled, as we pulled back onto the road. We were miles from any of our usual eating places, but as we rounded a curve, we spotted a rundown café.

"Do you want to try this place?" I asked. "It doesn't look like much, but then we don't have much choice." We hesitated a moment, then decided to take the plunge.

Once inside we were glad we had. On the menu we discovered old-fashioned hamburgers made with a mixture of flour and onions. The friendly waitress brought them to us piping hot, and they tasted like those we had enjoyed when we were children. The atmosphere was warm and inviting, with local folks stopping by our table to greet us as if we were friends. We left feeling pampered and content, and thankful, too, that circumstances had brought us to this unique little place.

Sometimes it's hard for me to let go of my disappointments long enough to see that something better may be in store for me. But I found that the detours in my life often lead to special experiences that I could never have planned on my own.

Father, I'm thankful that my detours are already known to You. Help me to see in them Your good gifts. —LIBBIE ADAMS

7

SUNDAY

Today, if you would hear His voice, Do not harden your hearts.... —PSALM 95:7-8 (NAS)

Recently, I was invited to speak at a conference on children and adoption in Toronto, Canada. I arrived on Friday afternoon, but I wasn't due to speak until the closing session on Sunday. The conference's theme was "Building Bridges for Children and Families," and I had carefully planned a message that would encourage the participants to go out and be bridge-builders themselves.

I spent Friday afternoon and Saturday attending a variety of lectures and workshops. The material being presented was helpful and fascinating, but one thing troubled me: None of the speakers was giving any acknowledgment of God's role in building families.

During my prayer time on Sunday morning, I felt the need to go over my talk again. The Lord led me to see that something was missing. In all my talk about bridge-building, I'd left out the most important bridge of all: the Cross of Christ. The Cross is the bridge that joins a holy God to a sinful humanity, and without it, the message I was getting ready to share was really incomplete. But how could I talk about the Cross to this secular, sophisticated audience? Would they be offended by my message? Would they laugh at it? Then the Lord brought Psalm 95 to my mind: "Today, if you would hear His voice, Do not harden your hearts."

When the time came for me to speak, I shared my convictions about our need for God and the Cross as the way we can have access to Him. My message was courteously and warmly received. No one was offended. In fact, the meeting organizers were pleased with what I had to say.

Every day, I am learning more and more to listen to the voice of God and not to my own fears and misgivings. All I have to do is follow where He leads me, and leave the results to Him.

Lord, give me an open heart to hear Your voice. —DOLPHUS WEARY

8 MONDAY
Be ye therefore followers of God, as dear children.
—EPHESIANS 5:1

One of my most joyous responsibilities is editing *Guideposts for Kids,* a bimonthly magazine for children ages seven to twelve. Last year we were pleased to be visited by Hubert Chicou, an editor from Paris. He brought with him several magazines his company publishes for children. Carefully he translated the titles for me.

One cover had a picture of Moses carrying the Ten Commandments. I pointed to its rather long subtitle. "What does this say?" I asked.

"It reads: 'For children who are curious about God.'"

Curious about God. I liked that! It's too easy for me to get stuck reading the same devotional materials. Praying in the same position. Looking for God in the expected places. So I'm trying to be more curious these days. To read a different translation of the Bible. To try a fresh approach to prayer. To look for God in the faces of stooped widows or unruly children. And I'm finding that God is broader than I imagined, which makes me even more curious....

Oh, Lord, keep me from predictable parameters of worship. I want to seek You with the eager curiosity of a child. —MARY LOU CARNEY

9 TUESDAY
Accept one another.... —ROMANS 15:7 (NAS)

Lovey, our golden retriever/Labrador, wags her tail at everything that moves—squirrels, butterflies, strangers, even cars whizzing by. Most of the time, they don't respond. But that doesn't faze Lovey. She keeps wagging her tail as if the whole world loved her.

Maybe dogs don't worry about being rejected, but I do. I'm afraid to make friends because I'm afraid I'll lose them. Whether it's a gradual cooling of friendly feelings, a change in circumstances that forces someone to move away or the forces of life over which we have no control, like sickness and death, something will happen to take my friend away from me.

As we walk, Lovey pulls hard on the leash and begins to wag her tail furiously. A neighbor we hardly know is approaching her mailbox. She bends down to give Lovey a pat. Lovey looks back at me, panting with wild delight, as if to say, "See, she accepts me. I am loved!" Then I remember that this neighbor is going through a family crisis. Reluctant to get involved, I say a polite "Hi," planning to move on quickly. But Lovey drags me to within inches of the woman. I can see the agony in her face. I'm startled, shocked. "Are you okay?" I ask her.

She starts to cry right there by the mailbox. Not neat little tears, from the corners of her eyes—the kind you can dab away—but deep, racking sobs. Even as she cries, her gentle eyes hold mine.

"Listen, let me put the dog in the house and I'll be right back, okay?"

She nods and stands there and waits for me at the mailbox. I hurry.

Father, help me overcome my fear of rejection and get on with the things You have for me to do. —MARION BOND WEST

10

WEDNESDAY

As he thinketh in his heart, so is he. —PROVERBS 23:7

There is a nice neighborhood grocery store between our home and my office. When I discovered that they made sandwiches, I began stopping each morning to pick up lunch. Their employees were helpful, their shelves crowded with interesting foods, and the aroma of freshly ground coffee was often in the air.

It was an enjoyable stop, except on those mornings when one particular counterman waited on me. He was good at his job, but seemed preoccupied and often angry. I felt that while he was making my sandwich, his mind was somewhere else.

One morning when I was in the store, he wasn't there, so I asked about him. The man who waited on me said, "He's at the hospital with his wife." Then I learned that a year before, the angry counterman's wife had undergone a heart transplant that her body was still trying to reject. During the past ten months he had been in and out of the hospital with her many times. From that day on, no matter who took care of my order when I was there, I took a minute to speak to him and inquire how he was, what kind of a week he was having, and about his wife.

This morning it was early when I went in, and he was the only sandwich-maker there. I was glad, because it gave us time for a leisurely visit, and I headed to my office feeling good. He hasn't changed. His personality still shows the effects of the terrible load he must continue to bear. It isn't going to get any better for him.

It's my attitude that has changed.

Dear God, help me to be aware of those around me whose loads are too heavy to carry alone. —KENNETH CHAFIN

11

Peter went over the side of the boat and walked on the water toward Jesus. But when he looked around at the high waves, he was terrified and began to sink. "Save me, Lord!" he shouted. Instantly Jesus reached out his hand and rescued him.... —MATTHEW 14:29–31 (TLB)

One of the most frightening times of my life happened on the way home to Wisconsin from Kentucky. I was driving my beautiful, eighteen-year-old niece Kirstie and my fourteen-year-old son Andrew home after visiting my brother and his family in Louisville for a week. Andrew was asleep in the backseat when, near Chicago, I had to change highways. Unfortunately, I got off the interstate at the wrong exit and ended up on a deserted, dead-end, dirt-and-gravel road. I turned around, got back on the main highway and tried to get off again, only to end up at the same spot.

This time as I got off, I noticed a car following me down the deserted road. Quickly, I made a U-turn just as the other car sped up and pulled alongside me. Five or six jeering men started to get out of the car. Terrified, I locked my car door and gunned the engine, spewing dust and rocks behind me. I raced back toward the interstate, praying like gangbusters, drenched in fear. Five minutes later the right exit appeared and we headed home, out of danger.

For the next hour of the trip I said prayers of thanksgiving and took lots of deep breaths. I recalled stories my dad told about his experiences as a World War II fighter pilot in the South Pacific.

"Weren't you scared?" I'd ask. He'd say he just remembers flying one mile after another, trying not to think about what could happen, knowing that God was his copilot.

Whether we're facing an enemy in war, an ambush on a deserted road or struggling to make it through the next paycheck...if we just have faith that God is there guiding us mile after mile, then we'll make it to safety.

Lord, on this Veteran's Day, help my faith to grow so that I can reach out to You and find comfort, no matter how dangerous the waters are. —PATRICIA LORENZ

12

Such as I have give I thee....

FRIDAY

—ACTS 3:6

When I was seventeen, I had open-heart surgery. For a time, I felt self-conscious about my scar, but after a time, the feeling faded. Unfortunately, so did the feelings of gratitude that my operation had at first kindled in me, gratitude toward the doctors and nurses and to my family and friends, who'd visited me faithfully.

Then one day I was reading a magazine article on the "blessings of the twentieth century." To my surprise, there was open-heart surgery, along with microwave ovens and television. I got the chills when I realized that if I'd been born just a half-century earlier, the operation that healed me (I'd been born with a hole in my heart) wouldn't even have existed.

I wish there were something I could do to express my gratitude, I thought. But to whom? And what? I couldn't afford to donate a wing to a hospital! The very next page of the magazine held my answer: "Only two percent of those eligible donate blood. You can help—give blood."

Who, me? Suddenly, giving back didn't seem to be so urgent. *Wouldn't it hurt? Or take hours? Besides, they wouldn't take my blood, would they?* Well, they would and they did—and it was *easy!* It took about fifteen minutes, it didn't hurt me at all—and I got to guzzle all the oatmeal cookies and apple juice that I could. The nurse slapped a heart-shaped sticker on my sweater: "Be nice to me," it said. "I gave blood today."

"Thank you," she told me.

"Thank *you*!" I said, and I meant it. It felt good to give back.

God, is there something I'm grateful for in my life—my family, job, friends? Today, let me find a way to give back. —LINDA NEUKRUG

13

Thou shalt not be afraid for the terror by night; nor for the arrow that flieth by day. —PSALM 91:5

My wife Julee and I were up in our mountain cabin last weekend when an incredible thunderstorm struck. Branches were torn from trees, rudely dispersing the last of the autumn leaves, and rain pummeled the roof. We were glad to be safe and dry inside by the snapping fire. Marty, our oversized yellow Lab, curled up in a tight ball under the coffee table until the racket was over—the typical reaction for a dog. Ferocious as he can appear, he's really quite fainthearted when it comes to storms. But Sally, our diminutive cocker spaniel, is another story altogether.

Unlike the timid Marty, Sally defiantly plants herself at the window, awaiting the boom of thunder, then barks furiously in response. It's as if she is saying, "Stay away from my house! Stay away from my family!" I try to take her on my lap and comfort her, but she'll have none of it. With the next clap of thunder she springs toward the window to stand her ground, hair raised, ears up, neck stretched—a small brown monument to pure instinctual animal courage. She will not back down.

Last weekend I found myself marveling at Sally's bravery and asking myself, *Do I stand up to my fears the way she does? Firm and straight on?* I am not endowed with the unambiguous bravery of pure instinct, like Sally. There are times in life when I am confused, frightened, when storms break and I don't know where to turn, when I want to run. Those are the moments when I must remember the Source of *my* courage.

You are there, God, to give me the courage to weather life's storms.
—EDWARD GRINNAN

14 | SUNDAY
Now set your heart and your soul to seek the Lord your God.... —I CHRONICLES 22:19

To spiritually mark the closing of the twentieth century, I decided to make a pilgrimage of the soul, a walk through a winding labyrinth of meditation, reflection, gratitude and prayer.

Over eight hundred years ago, Benedictine monks laid a labyrinth into the floor of Chartres Cathedral in France. This was set as a spiritual tool for those who walk it to draw closer to the heart of God. All Saints Episcopal Church in our neighboring city of Pasadena, California, has a replica. It is a huge canvas circle (symbolic of the world), thirty-seven feet in diameter, with a winding pathway painted in sepia tones that leads to the center, where one may linger for worship and prayer. Unlike a maze, the labyrinth has no wrong turns or dead ends. There is only one path.

As I entered, I consecrated my meditation to remembrance. The most poignant belonged to those I love who did not see the century through. My missionary grandparents who brought the Gospel to China; my mother and father; my little brother (do children stay as children, or do they grow up in heaven?). As I walked their memory, I praised God that love remembered is never lost, and those now with the Lord are more alive than ever before.

I twisted around a turn and remembered Pearl Harbor and the war; I stopped to consecrate the trauma of my imprisonment as a POW while others stepped around me. The pathway of the soul was filled with pilgrims.

Reaching the center, I looked to the labyrinth notes given to each walker for spiritual direction: "PURGATION—release the details of your life and seek only the presence of the Lord." *Forgive the hurts I have received, Lord, and those hurts I have given. I release my sorrows, griefs and tears.* "ILLUMINATION—let the glory of God's power flood your soul." *Energize me, blessed Holy Spirit; in all my weakness, be my strength.* "UNION—feel God's all-embracing love." *Jesus, Lover of my soul, wrap me in the shelter of Your arms.*

My heart was exalted. I had sought the Lord and found a new dimension of His love.

Father, Son and Holy Spirit, the Source and Center of all that is, and was, and yet will be, I worship and adore You. —FAY ANGUS

15

"Be merciful, just as your Father is merciful."

—*LUKE 6:36 (NIV)*

"Hey, Mrs. Bonnette!" one of my teenage students called out as he approached my desk one morning before school started.

I looked up from my lesson plan. *Great,* I thought, *another morning interrupted.*

"Hi, Coleman," I replied, looking back down quickly. I had so much work to do before the bell rang. "I don't have time to talk right now."

"Oh," he said, "okay. See ya later." He picked up his book bag, slung it over his shoulder and walked out.

Gee, I've probably embarrassed him. Well, I have things to do. Anyway, I'm not his baby-sitter.

As I turned back to my lesson plan, I remembered something that happened to me when I was in first grade. My parents had dropped me off early at school one morning, and I had to wait in the principal's office until the other kids arrived. I sat on a large wooden bench, staring down at my patent leather shoes. My teacher walked in, surprised to see me sitting there. The principal looked up from his papers, nodded toward me and said, "Seems I'm the baby-sitter this morning." My face turned red as my sweater.

My teacher walked over and reached for my hand. She squeezed it tightly and smiled. "Why, I was hoping I could get some help this morning. Would you like to wash my blackboard?"

I jumped up from the bench. "Yes, ma'am!"

Returning from my thoughts, I got up from my desk and walked down the hall to the commons area where the students wait for the bell to ring. It was empty except for one boy, leaning against the wall. I walked over to him.

"Hey, Coleman," I asked. "Want to wash the blackboard in my room?"

He smiled broadly. "Cool."

Lord, help me to remember that what I do for others I do for You.

—*MELODY BONNETTE*

16
TUESDAY

He leadeth me beside the still waters. —PSALM 23:2

Sometimes people with Alzheimer's become agitated without any apparent reason. When it happens to my father, the staff at the nursing home usually can calm him down with reassuring words. But one day the head nurse called me and asked if I could come over to see him right away. "He's very upset," she said, "and maybe you can help."

When I arrived at Dad's room, he was wheeling his chair back and forth, and he kept looking behind him as if he thought someone or something threatening was there. I had never seen his eyes so haunted. "We don't dare leave him alone," the nurse said. "He keeps trying to get up, and we're afraid he'll fall."

I put my arms around him and said, "Hi, Dad, it's me." I could see he didn't know me—sometimes that happened.

Lord, I prayed, *I don't know what to do. Help me!* If the professionals couldn't do anything for him, how could I?

Then I remembered that whenever I'm upset—really upset—I read the Twenty-third Psalm. It's like medicine for my soul. There was a Bible in Dad's night table, and I opened it to the Psalms. I held it in one hand and put my other arm around Dad's shoulder. "The Lord is my shepherd," I began, holding the Bible in front of him so he could see the words.

By the time I got to "I will fear no evil," I felt Dad's shoulders relax and he breathed more slowly. The nurse nodded and smiled.

When I finished, Dad looked at me and knew me. "Again," he said. We went through the psalm two more times, and he was calm. So was I. The Twenty-third Psalm had restored our souls.

Thank You, Lord, for the comfort of Your words. —PHYLLIS HOBE

17
WEDNESDAY

He who answers before listening—that is his folly and his shame. —PROVERBS 18:13 (NIV)

I looked out the window and saw that the little blue car was back. It had circled the block and was now parked in front of the house. A few minutes later I noticed the driver was still sitting in the car, so I decided to go out and see if she needed help.

There was sadness in her voice. "I just wanted to see this house again. We almost bought this property last year, but the owner had just accepted your offer an hour before."

It was a wonderful old house, built in the early 1900s with high ceilings, wood floors, a fireplace, a vintage tub and a basement—almost unheard of in Texas. Plenty of space for our active young family and the several college students who boarded with us.

I invited her in, and as we walked around she told me the ideas and plans she had had for the various rooms. "This is a great old house," I remarked. "We're so grateful to live here. God is so good. It seems like He just saved this house for us."

She turned sharply and looked me right in the eye. "Well, that's great for you, but what does that say for how God feels about me?" Then she told me why she had wanted this house so desperately. Her toddler son had drowned in their backyard swimming pool, and she couldn't bear to continue living in their house. Her husband was reluctant to move, but finally she had persuaded him. This house had been on the market for many months, so they were shocked when they submitted their offer and found that they were just an hour too late. With tears in her eyes she said good-bye.

I have replayed that exchange many times in my mind since then. I thought I was expressing my gratitude for God's expression of love to us in giving us this house, but I realized later that what it conveyed to her was arrogance, a presumption that God was exclusively on *my* side. In my all too typical way, I hadn't thought through the implications of my words.

I don't know what effect that exchange had on her—perhaps God used it for good in her life in spite of me. But I know it's made me more aware of the need to listen. I won't stop speaking of God's goodness to me, but I want it to be a thoughtful, sensitive dialogue—not a glib pronouncement.

Lord Jesus, help me to share with others the importance of my relationship with You, without being arrogant or presumptuous.

—MARY JANE CLARK

READER'S ROOM

Back in November '96 the phone rang, and when I answered it our grandson Alex said, "Grandma, I was baptized today." Well, I was so surprised and thankful because I had been praying for this for so long. —CAROLYN BALTHASER, FORKED RIVER, NJ

18

THURSDAY

There is a friend who sticks closer than a brother.
—PROVERBS 18:24 (NIV)

In my job as patient-education coordinator at a large hospital, I work with many people who want to stop smoking. Breaking the cigarette habit is the single most important thing a smoker can do for his or her present and future health. But it's also one of the most difficult. That's because cigarette smoking represents a double addiction: physical and psychological. Nicotine-replacement therapy in the form of a patch or gum helps with the physical addiction, but the psychological bondage is quite another story.

"Giving up cigarettes is like saying good-bye to my best friend," my patient Gary once explained. "The friend who was there for me when my daughter got cancer, the one who calmed my nerves when they were downsizing at the plant. I'd be hard pressed to name a person who's done all that for me."

I wondered if Gary would stick with our smoking-cessation program. But on the day of his two-week follow-up appointment, he sauntered into the clinic smiling. "I'm a nonsmoker!" he announced to no one in particular in the waiting room. "I haven't smoked a lick in fifteen days. Prayer and the patch—that's how I did it. A double-barreled approach."

Prayer and the patch. What a winning combination, I thought, thanking God for Gary's practical insight and his victory. Through medical advances, God has given us many of the tools we need to be healthier. But what power is ours when those tools are coupled with prayer! Not to mention all the yet-to-be-discovered blessings of Gary's new Best Friend.

Dear Lord, please give an extra measure of Your strength to those who say yes to "No Smoking" today. —ROBERTA MESSNER

19

This is the day which the Lord hath made....

—PSALM 118:24

There are people who complain about rainy days, and I must confess that at times I have been one of them. Too damp, too gloomy, too dreary, too depressing.... I have said all these things.

But a letter came the other day that may have changed me somewhat. In her note Virginia Skillman tells me that she *likes* rainy days, and always has. Why? Because as a child just beginning to read she came across an idea in a book for children that made an indelible impression on her young mind. It was the thought that "as raindrops land on the pavement they are instantly transformed into tiny, dancing fairies, flitting to and fro like a myriad of fireflies on a summer's evening."

Her letter goes on: "Although the years have robbed me of many of childhood's delightful imaginings, this dream of fairies dancing in the streets on rainy days has never left me...and never will."

So thank you, Virginia Skillman, for sharing your dream and changing my attitude after all these years. Next time it rains, I won't complain so much. I'll be too busy looking at the fairies!

Lord, remind us that whether You send days of sunshine or of rain, it's how we perceive them that counts. —ARTHUR GORDON

20

Love never fails.... —I CORINTHIANS 13:8 (NIV)

Love letters are a treasured and tangible part of family life. I met a woman recently named Linda Bremner. When her son Andy became ill with cancer, Linda discovered how much cards and letters from friends and well-wishers meant to him. But over time, the mail for Andy dwindled. That's when Linda began to write letters to Andy herself, signing them, "Love, Your Secret Pal."

One day she came upon Andy drawing a picture. He hid the picture, claiming it was for his secret pal. When he fell asleep, Linda peeked at the drawing. At the bottom, Andy had written, "I love you, Mommy."

Later, after the cancer had taken ten-year-old Andy away from her, Linda found a box with her typewritten letters to Andy at the back of his closet. Every one had been saved. They had meant the world to her son.

And that gave Linda the idea for Love Letters, the organization through which she and many volunteers keep letters and cards and gifts coming to terminally ill children.

Lord, what can I do to make someone's life better today? Please give me Your guidance. —RUTH STAFFORD PEALE

EDITOR'S NOTE: If you would like to help out Love Letters, contact them at 436 A Eisenhower Lane, Lombard, IL 60148-5404.

21

SUNDAY

All scripture is given by inspiration of God, and is profitable for doctrine, for reproof, for correction, for instruction in righteousness. —II TIMOTHY 3:16

I don't remember exactly how I found it or how long ago it came into my life. I think it was left on a subway seat and I picked it up, thumbing through the pages of the green, pocket-sized edition of the New Testament and Psalms. Someone's green ballpoint pen had marked parts in childish scribble, and a few page ends were dog-eared. The cover had a lighted lamp embossed in gold, symbol of Gideon International. Perhaps a Gideon volunteer left it on that subway seat, or maybe someone had picked it up in a hotel room on a business trip. At any rate, I stuffed it in my briefcase and kept it.

I have fancier versions of the Bible on my shelves, newer translations, study versions with extensive notes and concordances. When I look up a lesson for Sunday school, I usually use a heavy parallel Bible that has the text in four translations, a book so mighty it could prop open a screen door or press wildflowers. But the pocket version goes everywhere I go, in the zippered pocket of my briefcase.

In the mornings, when I'm looking for inspiration on my subway ride to work, I take it out and read the stately King James language. I can see by my markings over the years how a particular passage has captured me, marking my progress in my pilgrimage to God. Sometimes I can recall how a verse struck me two years back or more. Someday, perhaps, I'll know the Bible so well that I'll be able to turn automatically to the chapters and verses I'm looking for or I'll have them in my memory. But in the meanwhile, this is the book that I have depended on. It has grown on me, and I have grown with it. It's a reminder, a companion, a sacred friend. I rarely leave home without it.

This morning, Lord, I turn to Your Word for guidance.

—RICK HAMLIN

22

MONDAY

These all continued with one accord in prayer and supplication, with the women....   —ACTS 1:14

On the night of October 13, 1994, I sat in my neighbor Neva Patterson's living room with eleven other members of Copeland United Methodist Women, listening to a lesson on prayer. Near the end, Neva turned out the lights, leaving only the glow of a tall, white Christ Candle on a makeshift altar. It was surrounded by a dozen small, unlit candles—one for each of us. Margaret Unruh, the lesson leader, gave instructions: "One at a time, light your candle from the Christ Candle. As the flame catches, give God the deepest desire of your heart, spoken if you wish, silent if you don't. As each candle is lit, we will all pray for that need."

I intended to make my prayer a silent one. But when I lit the candle my words tumbled out: "Lord Jesus, I ask You to give my daughter a child." Rebecca and her husband Frank longed for a baby, but a team of infertility specialists had confirmed her own physician's diagnosis: Rebecca wasn't likely to conceive, and none of the "miracle" treatments was an option.

I don't know how many of the prayers we offered that night have been answered. I do know that exactly fourteen months later, on December 13, 1995, Caleb Anthony Clancy entered the world via emergency C-section. Last December Olivia Dawn completed their family.

Most of my prayers don't receive dramatic answers, and faithful people remain childless despite years of fervent prayer. At the same time, I'm becoming more and more aware of the power of shared "heart prayers"—giving up our deepest desires to God and allowing others to pray in our behalf. My journal records the results: Our little church is assigned a "just right" pastor; an eighty-five-year-old friend, Clara, finds a wonderful, affordable retirement home; a woman with cancer is upheld by faithful friends and loving caregivers. And each time three-year-old Caleb grabs my hand and says, "Come play, Grandma!" I offer another prayer:

Thank You, Lord, that where two or three are gathered together in Your name, You are in our midst. And thank You for my own faithful group of pray-ers. —PENNEY SCHWAB

EDITOR'S NOTE: Today is Guideposts Family Day of Prayer. Please join us as we bring the needs of our whole *Daily Guideposts* family before the Lord.

23

TUESDAY

Everlasting joy shall be upon their heads; they shall obtain joy and gladness.... —ISAIAH 35:10 (RSV)

One day when my daughter Maria and I were playing on the bed, she suddenly pointed to the fine lines beside my eyes.

"What are these?" she asked.

"Wrinkles," I said, thinking, *Oh, great, now my two-year-old has to remind me I'm not getting any younger.*

"Twinkles," she said, pleased with herself.

"No, wrin—" I stopped in mid-correction. "You know, that makes them sound like something good, Maria. Twinkles they are."

That night as I looked in the mirror, I realized that my twinkles do come from smiling and laughing, forming a kind of road map of the great joy with which God has blessed my life. From parents who filled our house with laughter and taught us not to take ourselves too seriously and brothers who are still two of the funniest people I know, I learned the value of a laugh a day. If there's one gift God has given me in abundance, it's joy, and I have the twinkles to prove it.

I'm turning forty in December, and while I haven't been particularly excited about it, or about those subtle lines or my one pesky gray hair that returns each time I snip it off, I'm ready to look at it all in a new way. Mark Twain wrote, "Wrinkles should merely indicate where smiles have been." So, rejoice in the twinkles! They're a sign to the world that God has given me a lot to smile and laugh about.

Joyful Creator, in Your grace continue to fill my life with laughter, joy and an abundance of twinkles. —GINA BRIDGEMAN

24

By love serve one another. —GALATIANS 5:13

Recently, on my way to do some shopping, I ran out of gas. As I coasted to the shoulder of the expressway, I noticed that all the service stations were on the other side. Rather than cross six lanes, I decided to go under the highway bridge over a railway cut. Sliding down the steep embankment, I worried about the bushes and brambles. But I discovered a well-worn path and soon came out close to a station.

A young man named Jim helped me. As I struggled with the gasoline, he offered to drive me back to my car. I accepted gratefully.

"So you came through there," Jim said, pointing toward the hole in the fence.

"Yes," I replied. "I was surprised to find a path under the bridge. Who would be walking around under there?"

"Homeless people," he said quietly. "They have no place else to go. Sometimes they sleep under the bridge."

I looked at him in amazement. "Do you mean there are homeless people here in our community?"

"Oh, don't worry," he said, misunderstanding my look. "They wouldn't harm anyone. Sometimes I give them food or money. They're just down on their luck."

We arrived at my car, and Jim poured the gas in the tank for me. "I'll wait to see you get started," he said.

Through the rearview mirror, I watched Jim waving as I drove away. I could see God's love shining from his face, and in turn I wanted to help someone as I had been helped. That afternoon I found the local shelter and made a donation. Soon after, I joined the board of the Putnam Salvation Army and made it my business to find out what I could do to help others in my community.

If there are other needs in my own backyard I haven't noticed, I hope I won't have to run out of gas to find them.

Lord, show me how to thank You by helping my neighbor.

—*SUSAN SCHEFFLEIN*

25

In every thing, give thanks....   —*I THESSALONIANS 5:18*

It was Thanksgiving Day. Our family had gathered for a delicious holiday meal, and now we were lounging around the fireplace in the den. The boys were glued to a football game on television, and I was fighting the sure signs of an approaching nap. Like a sleepy old bear, I wandered upstairs to my study and plopped down in my easy chair. I began to ponder the Thanksgiving message I was supposed to preach that evening at our church.

With a yawn, I gathered up a stack of notes I had made and sifted through it. My eyes fell on a poem by the seventeenth-century English clergyman and poet George Herbert. As a young man he had taken his pen in hand and jotted a note to God:

> Thou who hast given so much to me,
> Give one thing more—a grateful heart.

Herbert's words riveted me and helped me to see a great truth: The most important ingredient for happiness is not fortunate circumstances or great possessions, but a heart that knows how to be grateful. Gratefulness is the root of contentment and peace.

Dear God, on this Thanksgiving Day and every day, give me a grateful heart.   —*SCOTT WALKER*

26

Putting to sea from there.... We sailed slowly for a number of days, and arrived with difficulty....

—*ACTS 27:4, 7 (RSV)*

This past summer my niece Elizabeth, who was visiting from England, and I went for a sail on the hundred-foot sloop *Clearwater,* which plies the Hudson helping to educate and campaign for a cleaned-up river. Unfortunately, the one day Elizabeth's visit and the sloop's schedule coincided, it rained, but enough hardy travelers turned out in all kinds of rain gear that the crew decided they and we would brave the elements.

So in the rain, with the engines running, we took off from Haverstraw, New York. In the middle of the river, all of us—children, women and men—strained to raise the mainsail and the jib to a heave and a ho of a traditional sea chantey. We made the sails fast, and as the wind caught them, we headed downriver.

It's hard work hoisting a sail on a hundred-foot ship. And it's harder in the rain trying to hold on to the huge wet lines with water streaming down your face and arms and the wind and the rain penetrating your supposedly rainproof gear. Elizabeth and I got down below for a few minutes to see how the *Clearwater*'s crew lived and ate—in very cramped quarters with very little privacy. But most of the time we stood on deck, getting steadily wetter. After only three hours we were very glad to get off the ship.

From that short trip I had gained a new appreciation for the men and women, some of them my own ancestors, who left home in the seventeenth and eighteenth centuries and crossed the Atlantic Ocean on sailing ships. They spent three to four months on their ships! What courage and strength that took!

I honor them. And I am grateful not only that they braved the seas, but that they passed on their faith in God and belief in freedom to me.

Help me, God, to be as willing to endure hardship for You as my ancestors were. —MARY RUTH HOWES

27 SATURDAY
Every man shall give as he is able, according to the blessing of the Lord thy God which he hath given thee.
—DEUTERONOMY 16:17

Today, my local newspaper reported something surprising to me, namely that there are seventy-five American graduate schools offering advanced degrees in philanthropy, and that thousands of students are pursuing diplomas in the art of giving. What does one study in order to earn a master's degree in philanthropy (from the Greek *philos*, "loving," and *anthropos*, "man")? According to the article, students are not taught how to give, but rather how to encourage others to support worthy causes. They're taught fund-raising and how to administer nonprofit organizations that engage in outreach programs. All of which is necessary, the article explains, because government is now doing less and the private sector is hard-pressed to make up the difference.

I suppose I should be pleased that so much emphasis is being put on helping others; when natural disasters strike and organizations such as the Salvation Army and Red Cross, two of my favorites, respond, I am always heartened. Yet, there is something that gives me pause about all this professionalism. I long for simpler times when neighbor looked after neighbor, but I must concede that sometimes the problem is bigger than a local one.

My point? The heart *of* giving is a heart *for* giving. My Grandma Strayer, who knew all about widow's-mite sacrifices, didn't learn her generosity from a book, and neither will we, unless it is the Good Book that tells us it is more blessed to give than to receive. Maybe some of us have got that turned around and need to be reschooled; the rest of us only need practice what we already know.

Remind us, God...

We don't need bigger barns to store our treasure,
But bigger hearts to share Your measure.

—*FRED BAUER*

THE PATHS TO CHRISTMAS

Christmas is a time of expectations, of hopes both holy and mundane. Yet though our hopes may stay the same, our journey to Bethlehem is always different. This year Julia Attaway takes us with her along some of the unexpected paths that have led her to a richer understanding of Christmas. —THE EDITORS

28

SUNDAY

THE PATH OF HUMILITY
Prepare ye the way of the Lord, make his paths straight.
—*MATTHEW 3:3*

It had been a long haul. For months, three-year-old Elizabeth had been having a difficult time in church. Week after week, we'd spent Sundays alternately hushing her and taking her out to calm down. Now, as Advent approached, it appeared she was finally settling down. I was thrilled. Aside from looking forward to simply sitting through a church service once again, I was eager to really *prepare* for Christmas.

We decided to start Advent by doing something special: We went to a church where they have a lovely music program. The choir entered, voices soaring in plainsong. The processional hymn was "O Come, O Come, Emmanuel"—one of my favorites. Months of tension began to melt away as I listened to the music.

Then, just before the Gospel reading, Elizabeth began to wail. Something in me snapped. Furious, I snatched my daughter from the pew, clamping my lips together to prevent the uncharitable thoughts in my head from escaping, and headed for the door.

It took many attempts before both Elizabeth and I calmed down enough to go back into church. We arrived just as the last hymn started. I sat down and put my head in my hands to pray, but ended up sobbing with frustration instead.

On the way home, I said sadly to my husband, "I feel like I can't even prepare for Christmas."

Andrew was thoughtful. "I don't suppose they had much time to prepare for the first Christmas."

Now it was my turn to ponder. "You're probably right. I remember when I was nine months pregnant. I sure wouldn't have wanted to ride seventy miles on a donkey!"

The thought made me smile, just a bit. I looked over at Elizabeth, who was now singing happily to herself. Maybe the room I'd been hoping to prepare in my heart for Christ wasn't the kind of room He wanted to be born in. After all, a stable isn't beautiful, or warm, or quiet. It's humble.

Lord Jesus, help me prepare a humble heart in which to receive You this Christmas.
                                                          —JULIA ATTAWAY

29
MONDAY

Casting all your anxiety upon Him.... —I PETER 5:7 (NAS)

The branches of the fir tree scrape against the window pane, needling me to get out of bed. It's a sure sign that a blizzard has blown in very early on this November morning. I look out the window, where the only sign of life is a tardy flicker that missed fall migration. I feel helpless watching that beautiful bird scavenge in vain for berries among the vines. *What do flickers eat, anyway?*

I put on my parka and boots, drop some suet into a mesh bag and scoop up some birdseed. As I push open the storm door, it scrapes away an arc of snow from the drift on the back step. Sinking deeper and deeper into the drifts, I plunge along to the bird feeder and then retrace my steps.

Stamping the snow off my boots in the back entrance, I worry whether the flicker will be able to withstand the storm. Surely such weather will prompt it to fly south. If not, I hope it will eat the food I've put out for it.

As I turn on the radio, the morning disc jockey is cautioning his listeners to take the storm in stride. "Remember, folks, not everything in life is fixable, so don't sweat it."

He's right, Lord. There's nothing more I can do.

While waiting for the blizzard to blow itself out, I make a big pot of coffee. And then during my quiet time I mentally release that stormbound bird into the hands of God.

Lord, I waste so much time worrying over something I can't help. May I spend that energy carrying it to You in prayer.

—*ALMA BARKMAN*

30

TUESDAY

Thou hast taken account of my wanderings; Put my tears in Thy bottle; Are they not in Thy book?—PSALM 56:8 (NAS)

For two years I lived in historic Hannibal, Missouri, a pretty town set on a hundred hills. It features dozens of captivating views of the Mississippi River and countless reminders of its classic citizen Mark Twain.

On my days off I would hike along the rugged limestone river bluffs, pretending to be Tom Sawyer or Huckleberry Finn. I crawled into caves and collected arrowheads. Often I found myself wondering, *Do you suppose Mark Twain stood in this very spot and admired this graceful river bend?*

No one will ever write a book about *my* life on the Mississippi, but my life is just as real and historic as Twain's, and God is recording my every move. Whether I'm whitewashing my own picket fence or teasing a Becky Thatcher at the library, He sees it. He notices how I treat that Puddn'head Wilson at the office, and how often I visit my Aunt Polly. He notes when I take garden tomatoes to my neighbor Big Jim, but He also notices how I avoid that eccentric old guy on the corner who wears white suits, smokes cigars, and claims to be a writer and river pilot.

When I stand up in the classroom, I am Mr. Dobbins, the schoolmaster. When I am harsh with my daughters, I am Huckleberry's dad. When I go abroad, I can be innocent or I can be guilty of ugliness. By my attitude, I am a prince or a pauper.

I don't see God as a spy, but rather as a loving Father who is keeping a journal on His beloved children. He cheers me when I do well, and weeps with me when I fumble the ball. I wonder what God will write in the chapter titled, "Daniel Schantz, 1999"? I guess it's up to me.

Lord, help make my life worth writing about to Your glory.

—DANIEL SCHANTZ

MY FAITH JOURNEY

[Handwritten journal entries]

1 — Missed kids. Beautiful sunny day. I started work at 5:00 & left at 12:00. I did the report. Paul's doing fine.

2 — Missed kids. Cloudy rainy day 50°. Day off for election day. Paul & I [?] move out of the house. Talked [?]

3 — Missed kids. Cloudy, wintry looking day. Very [few?] at work. Got a thank you from [?]. Bob welch for report I did for him.

4 — Missed kids. Beautiful sunny day 68° very busy at work. Took care of Solomon's. Butch stopped over.

5 — Missed kids. Beautiful sunny day 60°. Very busy at work. Came home & laid down w/Paul.

6 — Missed kids. Beautiful sunny day 60°. Paul & I went to dump, GA & shop rite. We took a nap. Butch stopped for lunch & we went to winterlow oyster dinner. Delicious. Came very [?] home.

7 Beautiful sunny day but chilly 50°. Paul + I showed + went to 7:00 A.M. Mass. We got papers + I made pork roast + we watched kids while Chantel + Bob went to Egypt opening New.

Missed kids

8 Beautiful sunny day 50°. Very busy at work. Brought bean soup home for supper w/Borca Buger. Watched soaps.

Missed kids

9 Beautiful sunny day 70°. very busy at work. Brought roast beef dinner + Beef Burley soup home. Went to dump.

Missed kids

10 Beautiful sunny day 73°. very busy at work. Started at 5:00 A.M. Left at 9:00 to take Paul to Dr. Josephson as Dr. K. off.

Missed

11 Beautiful sunny day 50°. Worked on dining room + living room. Took a nap + Chantel + kids came over.

Missed kids

12 Beautiful, partly sunny day 50° Worked on dining room. Paul + I watched soaps + went to Ames for phone card.

Missed kids

13 Beautiful sunny day 50 worked on dining room. Paul + I took a nap, showed + went to Harriets after dinner. (terrible)

Missed kids

14 Beautiful partly sunny day 65°. Paul + I went for papers early + got an egg sandwich + hash brown. We relaxed all day.

Missed kids

15 Beautiful partly sunny day 50° very busy at work. Came home + relaxed w/GH + showed + relaxed w/Y + R.

Missed kids

16 Beautiful sunny day 50° Retirement seminar at work. Bob home at 5:00. Brought soup home for supper.

Missed kids

17 Beautiful sunny day 50°. very busy at work. Stopped at Shop Rite. Paul made linguini w/ peas + onion.

Missed kids

18 Beautiful sunny day 59°. Retirement seminar at work. Pas brother Bill taken to hospital with a possible heart attack. Got home at 4:15. Showed + watched soaps. Butch called. I called Chantel home

Missed Kids

19 Beautiful sunny day 65°. Very bu__ as work. Called Chantell on my phone & left a message. Paul & I took a walk & took pictures.

Missed Kids

20 Beautiful sunny day 65°. Toured apt. all day. Called u____ Christmas ____ for kids. _____

Missed Kids

21 Beautiful sunny day 70°. Paul & I went for papers & ____ for free turkey. Watched football

Missed Kids

22 Foggy, cloudy, dreary day 65°. very busy as work. Chantell called. Paul & I watched soaps.

Missed Kids

23 Foggy, cloudy dreary day 70°. Very busy as work ____ at 5:00 left at 12:00 to take Paul to Dr. Reeves

Missed Kids

24 Cloudy dreary day & foggy AM & beautiful sunny day PM. Very busy at work. Called Chantell.

Missed Kids

25 Cloudy, rainy day. 50°. I wrapped some Christmas present. We went to Chantell's for dinner at 1:30.

Missed Kids

26 Cloudy rainy day 65°. Worked on bedroom & clothes for vacation. Called Chantell & Butch ____

Missed Kids

27 Cloudy AM & sunny P.M. 55° Worked on utility room. Paul helped. Went to 5:00 Mass.

Missed Kids

28 Beautiful sunny day 50°. Kids called to thank me for Advent calendars. Talked w/ Butch & Chantell

Missed Kids

29 Beautiful sunny day 45° very busy at work. Hair cut after work & I found red pants. Watched soaps.

30 Beautiful sunny day 45° very busy at work. Picked up Chantell & kids & went for baileys for Paul & Bobby. Went to Red Star for supper

December

And I shall dwell in the house of
the Lord for ever.

—*PSALM 23:6 (RSV)*

S	M	T	W	T	F	S
			1	2	3	4
5	6	7	8	9	10	11
12	13	14	15	16	17	18
19	20	21	22	23	24	25
26	27	28	29	30	31	

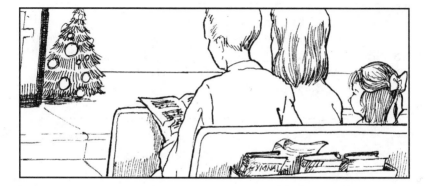

LESSONS IN LISTENING

1

WAITING

But when the fulness of the time was come, God sent forth his Son.... —GALATIANS 4:4

December is the month when we celebrate this "fulness of time"— God's time to be born into human history. How different God's clock is from our own! How long did it take to prepare a human family for the birth of His Son? How many centuries till there were Roman roads to speed the good news, a *lingua franca* to proclaim it? How many generations had waited for this perfect time?

Perhaps the hardest of all lessons in listening is that I must ask not only *what* God wills, but *when.* I remember a Christmas when I "heard" that I was to wrap a gift for "Ruth" who would spend Christmas with us. Not only that, the gift was to be a book of poems. I knew no one named Ruth who would be likely to visit during the holidays. No Ruth who was especially interested in poetry.

But so clear did the message seem, and such confidence had I gained in the reality of guidance, that I actually went out and bought the book, a lovely, little red leather edition of Emily Dickinson. I wrapped it in red foil paper and attached a card to it, "For Ruth." But the holidays came and went—no Ruth.

Time passed. The little book in its foil wrapping sat untouched on a shelf, a silent reproach to the notion of God's guidance in the minutiae of my life. But every time I thought of taking it down, removing the card, giving it to someone else, I seemed to hear, "Not yet."

It was six years before a secretary at Guideposts, who had no family to go to, spent her Christmas vacation with us. A wonderful guest, she grabbed a dish towel without being asked and spent hours playing Monopoly with the kids on the living-room floor. We had so much fun, in fact, that I never thought of the little package until, late Christmas night, I found Ruth Dallier glancing through our books: "I'm looking for something by Emily Dickinson."

Give me a listening ear, Father, to hear Your voice amid the sounds of the new century—and grace to await the working out of Your purpose in Your perfect time. —ELIZABETH SHERRILL

2 THURSDAY

Put on the whole armour of God.... —EPHESIANS 6:11

I couldn't have been more than twelve, but I still remember the fear that filled my heart when my father told me that he had to go to the hospital to have surgery. "Brock, you will have to be responsible for things while I'm gone. I'll need you to feed the horses every night."

I swallowed hard. "Uh, sure, Dad. No problem."

We lived in a rural area of Tennessee, in a wonderful place called Leipers Fork. We had just enough land to support the two horses that had been given to us by a family friend. I didn't mind feeding those horses one bit. It was the "night" part of the request that made me worry. Our barn, where the horses stayed at night, was several hundred yards from the house, surrounded by dark woods way up on a hill. The barn had a tin roof, so any noise was significantly heightened.

The first night my father was away, I looked out the window at the barn. It looked awfully dark up there. "Dear God," I whispered, "help me not to be afraid."

I made my way toward my father's shop at the back of the house and went straight to his flashlight. I gave it a thorough examination to make sure that the batteries wouldn't give out on me. As I opened the back door, I noticed Dad's coat hanging there on a hook. It was comforting to see it there. I shed my own coat and pulled his off the door.

The coat was entirely too big for me; the sleeves went down past my knees. But as I zipped it up, it gave me the feeling that my father was there with me. I walked out of the lit shop into the cold darkness. As I got closer to the barn, I was no longer afraid. My father's coat gave me all of the security I needed.

Today, whenever a decision looms like a dark barn set back in the woods, I like to remind myself of a simple truth: Like a warm coat, God's love is always by the door that leads out into the darkness. All I have to do is put it on.

God, Your love protects me from life's insecurities. Thank You.

—BROCK KIDD

FRIDAY

3

How great is the love the Father has lavished on us, that we should be called the children of God!...

—I JOHN 3:1 (NIV)

"You know, Mom," my then-seven-year-old daughter Elizabeth declared one afternoon while we were kneading bread together, "sometimes I feel like God is giving me a big hug!"

"You do? Why, that's wonderful!"

Later I found myself wondering, *When have I felt like God was giving me a big hug?* Often I'm so preoccupied talking *to* God, I forget that sometimes I can simply be *with* Him.

Since hearing Elizabeth's comment, I've been trying to put aside all my "grown-up" preoccupations when I pray and picture God enfolding me in His loving presence.

It's hard, though. I squirm out of quiet contemplation just as my two-year-old son Mark wriggles out of my lap when I try to cuddle him these days. He has become so active and independent. I love watching him run, kick balls and play with trucks, yet I also yearn to hold him and have him nestle close again.

But there is one time Mark will still cuddle on my lap: when we read books before bedtime. How I treasure those moments! Last night after we read his favorite animal and farm and truck books, Mark snuggled a long time and we talked and sang.

Mark has given me an idea. Perhaps reading God's Word is a way I can calm my restlessness and settle down for quiet, receptive prayer. Sinking into my favorite armchair, I read my Bible for a while, then close my eyes and picture myself nestling in for a loving hug....

Abba, Father.

—MARY BROWN

4

No sooner are they planted, no sooner are they sown, no sooner do they take root in the ground, than he blows on them and they wither, and a whirlwind sweeps them away like chaff. —ISAIAH 40:24 (NIV)

I am married to a "messie." True, Bill keeps his messes in neat piles—neat piles strewn all over the house in every room. Since I am a "neatnik," this has meant major adjustments in our thirty-two years of marriage. I have had to learn to live around his piles, and he has had to put up with my occasional up-to-my-ears-in-piles outbursts.

"God isn't disorderly!" I yelled one day recently. "Why can't you be more like God?"

Bill only grinned and tossed a pile of freshly cut branches into the woods where they landed on past years' accumulations of cut brush. I slammed the car door and headed off to the grocery.

As I slowed for a stop sign, my eyes glanced into the thick woods along the road, then riveted on what I was really seeing: A bad storm sometime in the past few years had broken and bent many of the trees. They leaned and lay in a jumble of bare branches all over each other. Some tops touched the ground. Others crushed low bushes struggling to grow around them. Those woods were just plain messy. And God had done it.

I still loathe the piles, but I love Bill. And when I think of his messes, I remember God and the storm-ravaged woodlot.

Lord, You are a God of order, but You are also a God of messes. Open my heart to all ways of being. —ROBERTA ROGERS

THE PATHS TO CHRISTMAS

5

THE PATH OF DARKNESS
The light shines in the darkness, and the darkness has not overcome it. —JOHN 1:5 (RSV)

My feet seemed to have more faith than my heart. They dragged me to church each Sunday, plodded to the Sunday school pageant and brought me to the midnight service on Christmas Eve. Yet none of it seemed to matter.

I felt alone, terribly alone. No beautiful carols, no glittering tree, no seasonal cheer was able to penetrate the emptiness in my heart. It took enormous effort to go to Christmas dinner at a friend's house; the mere thought of having to carry on a pleasant conversation was excruciating. Numbly, automatically, I did the best I could. "Christ is born!" I told others. To myself I added, *Even if it doesn't feel like it.* I was stumbling through the holiday in darkness, unable to see His light. All I could do was trust that it was there.

At dinner, embarrassment was added to depression. A man with whom I worked on several church committees gave me a gift— *Dialogues of the Carmelites,* an opera on CD. I had no idea why he did it; I had no gift to give him in exchange. I said a polite thank-you and left as soon as it was possible to do so gracefully. Back at home, I crawled into bed, where I could be sad and alone in peace.

Years later, I can look back on that Christmas and make out a pin-prick of light in the darkness. I could not see it at the time, nor even in the months that followed. Yet Christ was born and at work in my heart that December. In the midst of my deep loneliness, He kindled a spark that eventually sputtered into flame, for that unexpected musical gift came from the man who, a year and a half later, would become my husband.

Light of the World, You were born in darkness. Help me walk to Bethlehem guided only by faith in Your unending love.

—JULIA ATTAWAY

6 MONDAY

How sweet are thy words unto my taste!...

—PSALM 119:103

Confined to bed for a couple of days with a minor back injury, I occupied myself with books while my husband Gene made me feel pampered. As he left for the store to pick up a few groceries, he asked, "Anything you want?"

Immediately, I envisioned the candy counter at the nearby grocery store, and I could almost taste the chocolate-covered peanuts. "Yes! Bring me a bag of—" Then I remembered my plan to lose five pounds. With much less enthusiasm, I completed my request, "—hard candies." I knew their fat content was much less than what I really wanted.

"You sure?" Gene hesitated.

"Yes," I sighed with resignation.

He was back in a short while, and by the time I read the last chapter of my book, I had finished the bag of candy. But no—wait, there was one more on the very bottom of the bag. I reached in and pulled out a cluster of chocolate-covered peanuts! I popped it into my mouth and savored the sweetness of the chocolate and the taste of the peanuts. My sweet tooth had been satisfied—and so had my soul.

I'm up and about now, and back to my regular routine. But whenever my spirits start to sag or I feel stuck in a rut, I think back to that sweet surprise. I pause and savor the taste of the chocolate and then get back to work. Who knows what God has waiting for me on the bottom of the bag?

Lord, You find the most marvelous ways to remind me of Your love. Amen. —MARION BOND WEST

7

Have always a conscience void of offence toward God, and toward men. —ACTS 24:16

"Mom, I need to talk to you about my puppy," my son Derek told me in a recent phone conversation. He sounded tired and discouraged, a tone that triggers an instinctive maternal response in my heart. Derek is in the third year of his first post-college job, and he got the eight-week-old yellow Lab a few months earlier to fill in a hole of loneliness because he lives alone. But he didn't know how much time a puppy requires.

"I realize now that I'm not home enough to train him and take good care of him. I feel like I'm ruining him." A long pause. "Mom, would you and Dad consider keeping him for a while until I'm in a better place?" The next long pause was mine.

We're "dog people," which means our house is dog-friendly, and I liked the puppy, who had already spent time at our house when Derek visited. The puppy had a few accidents on the carpet and rolled around a bit vigorously on the kitchen floor with our four-year-old golden retriever. But he romped happily in our fenced backyard and slept in a crate at night. Still, I wasn't a bit sure I wanted the hassle and responsibility of caring for a puppy.

"Let me think about it, Derek, and talk to Dad."

For the next couple of days, we wrestled with this decision. Derek's predicament was no surprise. In fact, we'd warned him of all these possibilities before he got the puppy. And other "empty nest" parents reminded us of the commonly accepted rules of parenting adult children: Don't rescue them. Set boundaries. Define the difference between "your problems" and "their problems." But something else kept nudging our hearts: the desire to help our son and his puppy through a hard place.

So we now have a "grand-dog" living at our house. Yes, we've had some accidents, and he wakes up earlier than we do, but as I said, we're "dog people." More importantly, I hope we're also "Jesus people."

Father, help me to know when heart nudges are more important than rule-keeping.
— CAROL KUYKENDALL

---

8 | WEDNESDAY

It is the gift of God—not by works, so that no one can boast.
—EPHESIANS 2:8-9 (NIV)

I always feel underappreciated at Christmas. This year, true to tradition, by the second week in December I was well on my way to feeling taken for granted. Our two teenage boys had yet to make up a Christmas list; my husband Gordon hadn't thanked me for the three days I had spent searching for the right present for his mother; and our six-year-old John? Well, I was interrogating toy store clerks all over town about the latest must-have toys, and I wasn't going to get any credit for that.

As I emptied the boxes of decorations from the attic, I picked up a tin can and heard something rattling around inside. It was a small set of plastic nativity figures from the dollar store. I was about to throw them back into the box when John begged to have them. Later that evening, worn out from decorating and still stewing about how little thanks it had gotten me from my family, I went into John's room to get the dirty laundry. John had set up a nativity scene on his desk. Instead of the usual display with Mary and Joseph lined up on each side of the baby, the shepherds on one side and the wise men on the other, John had made a circular scene. The manger was in the center and every figure had their backs turned to the observer and their faces hidden.

I found myself peering over the shoulders of the anonymous, backward figures to see what everyone was staring at. In that small quiet moment as my eyes fell upon the Christ Child in the manger, I found myself moving out of the center of attention and back into my rightful place as part of the wider circle. Every purchase I had made, every gift was made possible by the greater gifts of life, time, health, intellect, creativity and love that had all come directly from God. If I kept my gaze steadily on the Christ Child, half of the time outside observers wouldn't even glimpse my face. I left John's room with the dirty laundry, deciding it was time to start a new holiday tradition: to keep my eyes off myself and on the One Who gave His name to Christmas.

As You use me today, Lord, to find, prepare or give a gift, open my eyes anew to the gracious heaven behind it. —KAREN BARBER

9

A merry heart maketh a cheerful countenance....
—PROVERBS 15:13

When my mother-in-law Joy Briggs was a young woman she played the piano for silent movies. She used to entertain us with stories about the days when she sat in a darkened theater in Ipswich, South Dakota, accompanying the adventures of Rudolf Valentino and Lillian Gish and Buster Keaton. She had no musical scores to guide her; she'd simply improvise, her fingers flying up and down the scales for a chase scene, thundering in the bass as the locomotive bore down on the helpless heroine, shifting to a minor key when true love seemed doomed.

It was during those nightly stints before the flickering screen that she made a remarkable discovery. She could alter the way people reacted to the plot simply by changing the mood of the music. If, for example, Charlie Chaplin was being jilted by a proud society beauty, Joy could move the audience to tears with a mournful melody. The next night, by playing a farcical tune, she could set people giggling at the very same scene.

She'd stumbled onto a truth I've never forgotten. Just as important as what happens to me is how I interpret what's happened. Identical experiences will be received differently, depending on the background music of our lives. I know people who hear tragic strains behind every event. Others go through life to the beat of a march or the lilt of a waltz. And some, the fortunate ones, to the harmony of a hymn.

Father, help me to hear the celestial music that places the joys and sorrows of my small life in Your eternal symphony.

—JOHN SHERRILL

10 FRIDAY

Let this mind be in you, which was also in Christ Jesus: Who, being in the form of God, thought it not robbery to be equal with God: But made himself of no reputation, and took upon him the form of a servant....

—PHILIPPIANS 2:5–7

The first glimpses of Christmas in New York bring me great angst. Lights and wreaths and ribbons start sneaking out well before Thanksgiving and the heralded arrival of Santa, courtesy of Macy's. *I can't believe the year is ending already!* I fret. *Think of all the things I didn't get done!* Then there are the gifts I must find, the people I must see, the plane reservations and time off work and money to pay for it all. The mental list overflows with obligations and worries. I find myself turning away from that initial splash of red and green and wishing it was still the red, white and blue of July Fourth when the year still held such promise!

But I have an antidote. It's a memory from a December day the year after I graduated from college. In the grip of wanderlust, I had gone south, through the Caribbean to Central and South America. I was picking my way through a bustling little marketplace high in the Ecuadorian Andes, at the far edge of the northern hemisphere. Natives had traveled many rugged miles to display their wares on blankets and in makeshift stalls, as they had been doing for centuries. Beneath a tree at the edge of the market I saw what looked to be an old baby doll resting in a pile of straw and cloth, almost as if a child had abandoned her toy. When I looked closer, I noticed a crude wooden cross stuck in the dirt and a plain box, which my companion explained was for donations for the needy.

No blinking lights, no jolly St. Nicks, no midnight madness sales. Not even the figures of Mary and Joseph or the wise men. Just the Christ Child and the simple message that He was among us.

I didn't know at the time how persistent a memory it would become, that simplest of Nativity scenes in the Andean marketplace. But today, when the frenzy of this season gets to me here in New York, I think back to it and consider what it said to me.

Lord, You came among us in humbleness so that we would be humbled. In the celebration of Your birth, I will not forget that.

—EDWARD GRINNAN

11 Keep thy heart with all diligence.... —PROVERBS 4:23

SATURDAY

As a lad I loved football. In 1933, Columbia University was my favorite team, and Cliff Montgomery, Columbia's diminutive quarterback and team captain, was my hero. Every Saturday during the season, I huddled near our radio listening to their games.

I was anguished when Columbia lost, 20–0, to a surprisingly strong Princeton team on October 20. But I cheered when they went undefeated the rest of the way.

Then came a surprise. Two powerful Eastern teams, Army and Duke, were upset late in the season and eliminated as contenders for the Rose Bowl. Michigan and Princeton declined invitations, and Columbia was unexpectedly invited. I was elated! But many football fans belittled the choice. They pointed out that Virginia State, which Columbia beat 15–6, had lost to Ohio State 75–0 the week before. We were reminded that Columbia had just managed to slip by Cornell, 9–6, a team that Michigan had trounced 40–0. Columbia's record was not impressive.

As the team traveled west by train, the newspapers sang the praises of Stanford, their Rose Bowl opponent. A young team composed mostly of sophomores, Stanford had outstanding strength and deception. By comparison, Columbia seemed puny. It was predicted that Stanford would win 85–0!

On January 1, 1934, I sat glued to our radio, my heart pounding as Stanford raced up and down the field. Stanford racked up almost twice the passing yards of Columbia, and outrushed them three to one. But in the end, the score was Columbia 7, Stanford 0. The lone touchdown came on a hidden-ball play from Cliff Montgomery to halfback Al Barabas.

Despite their physical disadvantage and the popular wisdom, my team had worked hard and never stopped believing they could win.

Where brawn failed them, they had used their brains. That night, I vowed to study, practice and work hard at whatever tasks I was given. Maybe someday I, too, would beat the odds!

Lord, You have promised that victory doesn't always go to the swift or the strong, but to the true of heart. —OSCAR GREENE

THE PATHS TO CHRISTMAS

12

THE PATH OF STILLNESS
Be still, and know that I am God.... —PSALM 46:10

As Christmas Eve approached, my husband Andrew and I wondered if we should attempt going to the evening service. John Joseph was five months old; Elizabeth was almost two and a half. We were exhausted from our move, from my recent bout with asthma, from adapting to life with more than one child. And the logistics of going to church were a nightmare. We could walk through a fairly unsafe neighborhood to one church, or else take a twenty-five-minute bus ride—right at the kids' bedtime—to get to a different one.

December 24 arrived, bitterly cold. Knowing we were courting disaster, we decided to take the bus. We dressed the kids in two layers of pajamas, put on their jackets and wrapped them in blankets.

A nonstop stream of what-ifs ran through my head: *Would the kids fall asleep on the way? If so, would they wake up when we stepped out into the frigid air? What were the chances they would sleep through most of the service? Were we going a long way for nothing?*

Thankfully, we arrived with two sleeping children. We stepped inside—only to find an empty, dark church. Mystified, we tiptoed in and laid the children on a pew. I knelt to say a quick prayer, with the efficiency of a mother who expects to have to deal with some small crisis every thirty seconds. As I got up, my eyes met Andrew's. Were we early? Late? What should we do?

The most incredible thought crossed our sleep-deprived, parent-weary minds at the same time: *We could use this time to pray!*

I knelt again and prayed for several minutes. No interruptions, no noise—what a luxury! I checked on the kids, who were still sleeping soundly. Then, almost giddy with freedom, I knelt and prayed some more.

Half an hour later, a few lights flickered on. Twenty minutes after that, our fellow churchgoers began wandering in. By the time the choir entered and the service began, Andrew and I had savored nearly an hour of exquisite quiet time, kneeling together before God. It was a totally unexpected gift. A silent night.

Lord Jesus, still the noise in my preoccupied heart, that I may hear Your voice within me this Christmas. —JULIA ATTAWAY

13 MONDAY

He which soweth bountifully shall reap also bountifully.
—II CORINTHIANS 9:6

At this writing we have two homes, one in New Jersey and one in Florida, with the second one getting more and more use. Cold weather and old bones are the main reason. I come in contact with more retirees these days, and I'm amazed at the way people age. Some seventy-five-year-olds look and act like fifty-five, and some fifty-five-year-olds could easily be mistaken for people in their seventies.

Recently in a grocery store I was talking to a man (age seventy-three) who had come out of retirement to work four hours a day, five days a week. "It keeps me from getting bored," he said with a toss of his white hair.

"You're lucky to be in such good health," I commented.

"Not quite," he replied. "I've got a pacemaker and arthritis that makes it difficult to get out of bed some days."

But he does get out of bed, and he works to feel alive. Retirement may be a time for slowing down, but not for full-time chair-rocking. Seniors I admire are still involved in church and volunteer work, reading new books, seeing plays and films, going to concerts, engaged in hobbies, sharing their skills, talents and knowledge.

Some people think they must have perfect health to be involved, forgetting the old adage that says, "Half the world's work is done by people who don't feel well." They sit around and complain. Others, just as physically challenged, thank God for the strength and energy they've got and stay busy, proving that health, like many others, is a case of mind over matter. You know the rest: "If you don't mind, it doesn't matter."

Lord, keep me in the camp of those who shout:
Let me die of wear, not rusting out!
—FRED BAUER

14

Before they call, I will answer.... —ISAIAH 65:24

Several years ago, I developed a hand tremor. It has since been diagnosed as a mild case of Parkinson's disease. Most of the time, medication keeps it under control. But when I am tense or worried, the tremor can get out of control.

The other day, I went to the post office for stamps. The lines for postal-worker service were enormous, so I decided to use one of the stamp machines. Since I was holding envelopes in my left hand, with no place to set them down, it was difficult to keep the bills flat as I tried to feed them into the machine with my right hand. The machine kept rejecting them with the notation "Be sure your bills are flat." After several tries, I became aware that a line was forming behind me.

Then I heard a pleasant female voice say, "Would you like for me to do that for you?"

I cringed. *Someone is watching me,* I thought. *Now I'll never get these bills into the machine!*

In my retirement years I find that I'm deeply sensitive to offers for help with things that I could do all by myself just ten years ago. As I turned to answer the woman, a still, small voice seemed to say, *Let her help you.* So instead of muttering something like "Thank you, but no thanks," I said, "Yes, please." She stepped forward and within ten seconds I had my stamps.

As we left the post office, I thanked the young woman and briefly explained my problem. "That's okay," she answered, "I understand."

Ever since, I never hesitate to accept help when I need it. It's what God wants me to do.

Lord, I thank You for assistance that is so very available.

—ELEANOR SASS

15

"I tell you the truth, whatever you did not do for one of the least of these, you did not do for me."

—MATTHEW 25:45 (NIV)

The knock at our door came at about nine at night. We were having two volunteer groups over for dessert and a time of sharing in our home. I went to the door, and there stood a thin man in his late twenties. He said, "Reverend Weary, I'm hungry. Could you loan me twenty dollars to get some food?"

As I stood in the doorway, many negative thoughts ran through my mind. Here was a young black male wanting a handout. *Was he really hungry, or was he only looking for money to buy alcohol or drugs? Or was he hungry because he spent all of his money on alcohol or drugs and then expected me to feed him?*

Usually, if someone came to my door asking for a handout, I would take him to the store and buy some food for him. But with the house full of visitors, I didn't have the time. I had to make a quick judgment. So I prayed, *Lord, use this gift to bless this man.* I gave him a little money and encouraged him to accept it as a token of God's love.

"Reverend Weary," he said, "I'm going to pay you back."

"No," I said, "this is a gift from God. Use it to glorify Christ."

He walked away, and I returned to my guests. I was feeling a little uneasy. *Had I contributed to his bad habits? Had I encouraged him to think that he could make his way through life begging from others? Had he taken advantage of me, and was he now laughing to himself about what a soft touch I'd been?*

But no, none of that mattered. In the person of that beggar, Jesus wasn't asking me to be a social worker, a psychologist or a judge. He was asking me to give, as best I could, and to leave the results to Him.

Lord, when I see You in the least of my brothers and sisters, let me respond in love. —DOLPHUS WEARY

READER'S ROOM

My everyday miracle is that God loves me each and every day. He has loved me from the second I was conceived over forty-six years ago. He has loved me through all of my failings and fallings. He loved me even though I was really, really angry with Him after my mother died. He has loved me through my doubts. He has loved me through my fears. He has loved me through some not-so-wise decisions. No matter what I do, or where I go, or what I say, God loves me. And there is no better feeling, and there is no greater miracle.

—CYNTHIA DOUGHTY, PHOENIX, AZ

16

Believe in the light, that ye may be the children of light....
—JOHN 12:36

Most nurses like to "fix" things, and I guess I'm no exception. So when my dad's cancer spread to his bones, I wanted to make everything better in one fell swoop. But every day, it seemed he was confronted with a new enemy—pain, fatigue, more and more difficulty walking. There was so little I could do except be with him, listen, and make sure he had everything he needed for pain management and supportive care.

What good were all those years of studying to be a nurse if I can't even help my own dad? I lamented one chilly December afternoon. As I gazed out the snow-speckled window, I thought of days like this during my childhood, when Dad had taken us sleigh riding in Ritter Park.

Just then a delivery truck pulled up in the driveway, dropping off a shipment of punched-tin night-lights I'd ordered for Christmas presents. I tore into the box and plugged the lights into every available wall socket in our sunroom. The bulbs were a dim four watts, and their light was scarcely noticeable in the blinding afternoon sun.

But while I was out shopping, night came. I returned home to find angels, stars, Christmas trees, reindeer and stockings softly lighting my path through the darkness of the sunroom. The lights were dim, but each one played a part in lighting my way.

Maybe with enough little acts of love, I could help Dad see his way more clearly through the frightening darkness of incurable illness. I filled a tin with some freshly baked chocolate-chip cookies and drove into town for a visit with him. I'd ask Dad to tell me a story about Katydid, his pet goat when he was a boy. He always lit up when someone asked him for a story. I thought again of all those night-lights, each one tiny, each one different, like little works of love, making the darkness light.

Lord, let my light always shine for Your glory. —ROBERTA MESSNER

17

Your promise renews my life.   —PSALM 119:50 (NIV)

My husband's mental illness coupled with the stresses of a growing family have plunged me into one crisis after another. Throughout the past eleven years, many friends and acquaintances have offered me welcome comfort. Practical help, like shoveling the driveway after a blizzard or repairing a wall. Social comfort, like a dinner invitation or an outing to the theater. Warm, fuzzy comfort, like a sincere word of praise or affirmation.

But no comfort has the enduring value of a Scripture verse shared either on the telephone or in person. Whenever someone shares a verse with me, I mark it in my Bible and in the margin I write the name of the friend who offered it. So when loneliness and anxiety engulf me, I grab my Bible and flip through its pages in search of the highlighted verses, marked with special names.

"So do not fear, for I am with you; do not be dismayed for I am your God" (Isaiah 41:10, NIV). Lucille.

"The Lord...will satisfy your needs in a sun-scorched land" (Isaiah 58:11, NIV). Agnes.

"The Lord...will make...her wastelands like the garden of the Lord" (Isaiah 51:3, NIV). Olga.

Now as I reread each Scripture promise, I remember my friends Lucille, Agnes, Olga and many others. Out of their own comfort from Scripture, they have offered me solace. Often they couple their words of blessing or promise with an "I'll pray for you."

Suddenly, I feel surrounded by friends. (Are some of them praying for me right now?) Fellow pilgrims they are who have experienced God's presence on the journey. *I do not travel this road alone. God is with me and so are a host of people of goodwill.*

Father, I thank You for the solid comfort of Your Word and those who share it with me. —HELEN GRACE LESCHEID

18

SATURDAY

The gift of God is eternal life through Jesus Christ our Lord. —ROMANS 6:23

When I opened the box that had just come in the mail, a shock of surprise zinged through my body. In my hands lay a baby pillow made from a quilt block that had my name embroidered on it in my late mother's handwriting. The accompanying letter explained that the sender and my mother had belonged to the same women's club back in the 1930s. The members had made quilt blocks for their children, intending to piece them in a communal quilt.

"The quilt never got finished," the sender added, "but I've kept your mother's block all these years. Now I hear that you have a new granddaughter, so I've used the block to make this pillow for her."

My heart warmed with gratitude for such a kind, thoughtful gift. As I caressed my mother's embroidery, the years melted away and I sensed once more my mother's love, spanning two-thirds of a century. In memory I saw her sitting near a window in a home where we'd once lived, her brown hair and unlined face bathed in morning sunlight. Now she had moved on to live in God's home.

Precious gifts that tie the years together: a parent's love; a new grandchild; a pillow from a generous friend. And eternal life from God, our greatest Friend of all.

Thank You, Father, for letting us share in Your timeless love. Amen.
—*MADGE HARRAH*

THE PATHS TO CHRISTMAS

SUNDAY

19

THE PATH OF LOVE
And the Word was made flesh, and dwelt among us....
—*JOHN 1:14*

I'm finding it hard to prepare for Christmas this year. A month ago, a lump the size of a golf ball appeared on my sixteen-month-old son's neck. It is something called a thyroglossal duct cyst, and it has to be taken out. Surgery is scheduled for this week.

Frankly, our personal situation threatens to supersede Christmas. How can I possibly think about the birth of another baby when someone is going to cut open my own? I dutifully await the Christ Child, and end up clasping my boy close to my chest instead—when he pauses from his giddy round of toddler mayhem long enough to let me.

Did Jesus squeal and race across the room the way my John does? Did He play hide-and-seek with His mother, draping wet clothes over His head while she did the wash? Was He obsessed with all vehicles equipped with wheels? Did He fling His head back and spread His arms wide with joy, shouting *"Trees!"* on a beautiful fall day?

Was the Baby born in Bethlehem *that* real?

Knowing that even straightforward surgery can go wrong, this Advent I am oh-so-intensely aware of how deeply I love my son. What a tremendous gift God has given me! And then, in the briefest moment of understanding, I'm struck with wonder: How could He stand giving me His *own* son, too?

Heavenly Father, may the infant Christ, in all His humanity, teach me the glory of Your unending love. —JULIA ATTAWAY

20

MONDAY

So God created...every winged bird according to its kind. And God saw that it was good. —GENESIS 1:21 (RSV)

In Canada where I grew up, "Christmas crackers" sit alongside each plate at the table, part of the festivities. Made of paper tubes wrapped in festive paper and tied at the ends, they resemble oversized Tootsie Rolls. Inside is a little prize, a tissue-paper "crown" you unfold and wear and a printed joke. Running through the cracker is a special, explosive paper stick, which you seize and pull. *Pop!* Out tumbles your prize, crown and joke!

One year, my sister found a joke shop that sold the explosive strips and decided that she and her daughters would make crackers for our family celebration. To our surprise and joy, when we finished the fun of popping our Christmas crackers, we discovered that Erica, seven, and Celena, five, had discarded the jokes for philosophy. Each thought, straight from their hearts, was poignant and refreshing. The one I remember and treasure is my own. *If you want to hear the birds sing, open the window.*

So often I sit pining after something without ever taking the steps to make it my own. If I want an orderly garage, I have to clean it. If I want a better relationship with someone, I have to make an effort.

"Thank you, Erica! Thank you, Celena!" I told my nieces.

"You're welcome, Auntie! Merry Christmas!"

Thank You, dear Lord, for the simple wisdom of a child. And help me to remember to keep opening my windows! —BRENDA WILBEE

21

Each of you should look not only to your own interests, but also to the interests of others.

—*PHILIPPIANS 2:4 (NIV)*

The traffic signal was a green dot in the distance, but the vehicles ahead of mine seemed rooted to the road. "What's the matter with you?" I muttered at their drivers. "You've got the light. *Go!*"

Finally, the sluggish line did move, but half a block before I reached the intersection, the signal turned red. Lines of cars—four lanes deep and curb to curb—stretched to infinity in all directions. *This is like being in a herd of turtles. In fact,* I fumed, *at this rate, turtles could zip past me in a cloud of dust.*

Just then I noticed a harried young woman trying to exit a parking lot on my right. Four obviously tired youngsters chafed in car seats. The smallest of the quartet wailed while his siblings offered a Christmas cacophony of "Rudolph," "Jingle Bells" and "O Little Town of Bethlehem." *That mother has a worse problem than I do.*

When the light finally turned green, I caught her eye, then held my car in place and waved her in ahead of me. She flashed a radiant—and relieved—smile and popped into the opening I provided. Just before disappearing into the sea of cars, she blew me a kiss.

I actually enjoyed the rest of my trip home! Since then, I've blown a few kisses to courteous drivers myself. It's such a simple way to "pass it on."

Father, help me to remember that a simple courteous gesture is one way to apply the golden rule. —*ISABEL WOLSELEY*

22

Don't forget to do good and to share what you have with those in need.... —*HEBREWS 13:16 (TLB)*

Christmas week it rained. "A little damp won't hurt us," I said as I zipped up the children's jackets and bundled them into the car. We had a long list of things to buy: fruit; nuts; cookies; more tinsel for the tree. The afternoon was great fun as we sloshed through puddles and scurried from store to store, and on the way home I had a sense of satisfaction that now at last I could relax, everything was done.

"Daddy's home! Look, the front door's open," Ian squealed as we pulled into the driveway.

Strange, I thought, *his car's not here.* Suddenly, queasy with apprehension, I held the children back. "Let me go in first."

As we crept into the living room we saw that the tree so lovingly trimmed had been pushed over, its brilliant star crushed. Every carefully wrapped package was torn open, gift boxes yawning emptiness. Throughout the house, drawers were turned upside down, their contents spilled onto the floor in heart-stopping disarray.

"The Grinch done stole'd our Christmas," Ian whimpered, his five-year-old eyes welling up with tears.

The police arrived, neighbors came over, and by the time my husband pulled into the driveway, it was a circus of chaos. We spent the evening restoring order and listing the missing valuables.

"The gifts, the children..." I whispered to John. "What will we do?"

He held me close, "We'll figure something out, honey."

It was after eleven that night when we heard the singing—Christmas carols, out front. Our driveway was a sea of umbrellas, people we knew and people we didn't, some with children droopy-eyed in sleepers. Piled on our porch were gifts they had taken from under their family Christmas trees to fill the emptiness under ours.

We sat on the porch steps and cried tears of joy. "Where there's love to be shared," we told the children, "not even a Grinch can steal the spirit of Christmas!"

Loving and caring, giving and sharing...help us, Lord, spread these blessings in all that we do, not only at Christmas, but all the year through. —FAY ANGUS

23

THURSDAY

Now when this was noised abroad, the multitude came together, and were confounded, because that every man heard them speak in his own language. —ACTS 2:6

I was twenty-two years old, I had just graduated from college, and I was spending the year in Italy teaching English as a foreign language. For Christmas I visited a French family who had been friends with my family in California for years. I was so thrilled with the sights of Paris and so proud of my independence that I don't remember being particularly homesick. It was only on Christmas Eve that I wished that I could be flown home for just a few minutes, to sing carols at our half-timbered church, to embrace my old high school friends beneath the palm trees outside, to worship in a familiar way.

My French family were Huguenots, part of the Protestant church that dates back to John Calvin in the 1500s, and on Christmas Eve we went to their small church in a Parisian suburb. There were a hundred people there at most, with no choir, and an organ that wheezed and squawked through the hymns. Worst of all, I struggled to comprehend the French of the service, always finding myself stuck on a phrase, translating in my head as the rest of the congregation moved forward.

For Communion we stood in a circle and passed the elements one to another. The papa of the family (as I called him) was on my right, and when he turned to me with the wine, saying, *"Le sang de Dieu, eh?"* I suddenly understood. Yes, this was the mystery of faith, as hard to translate as a page of Proust, and yet completely comprehensible when it was shared between two who believed in Him. "The blood of Christ" was a concept as clear as day in Papa's foreign tongue.

God, give me understanding. —RICK HAMLIN

THE PATHS TO CHRISTMAS

24 THE UNSEEN PATH
Walk as children of light. —EPHESIANS 5:8

The year Elizabeth was born, I awaited Christmas with the giddiness of a first-time mother. I baked cookies, anticipating the years when my daughter would bake them with me. Andrew and I had serious, parentlike talks about how many gifts to give, so as not to spoil her. We debated the essentials, like white versus colored Christmas lights, and even reached a truce on the critical issue of tinsel on the tree.

Christmas Eve arrived cold and clear, a perfect night for feeling warm and snug in church. The first hymn was "Joy to the World." As the organ began to play, Elizabeth awoke with a start. Her four-month-old lungs let out a loud and not-so-joyful sound, so I quickly took her out to the parish hall to calm her down.

But she would not calm down. I rocked her. I sang to her. I tried to nurse her. I changed her diaper. Nothing worked. Elizabeth shrieked and wailed until she was purple. Other mothers came and went with their fussy babies—and came back a second time.

In desperation, I wrapped Elizabeth in a blanket and took her outside. Maybe the cold air would shock her out of her fit. Not a chance. Now tears began to roll down my face, too. Overhead the stained-glass windows glowed with color; carols wafted through air. We were alone. It was cold. My baby was crying, and I was losing control. I shut my eyes and began to pray out loud, walking to the rhythm of the words: "Lord Jesus Christ, Son of God, have mercy on me, a sinner."

I walked and prayed; Elizabeth cried. The beat of the prayer slowly worked its way into my soul. "Lord Jesus Christ..." Mary and Joseph were alone that night, too. Everyone else was at the inn. "Son of God..." Was it cold in that stable? Did God really choose to be as little—and loud—as my baby? "Have mercy on me, a sinner."

"O Come All Ye Faithful" drifted into the night air, and I looked up. There, illuminated from within, blazed a stained-glass picture of a lamb, the Lamb of God. From inside the church I could not have seen it against the dark night. Instinctively, I dropped to my knees. Elizabeth hiccuped and stopped crying. Christ was here. It was Christmas.

Come, Lord Jesus. Cleanse my heart of false expectations, so that I may celebrate Your birth in truth and love. —JULIA ATTAWAY

THE PATHS TO CHRISTMAS

25
SATURDAY

THE PATH OF THE HEART
For this is the message that ye heard from the beginning, that we should love one another. —I JOHN 3:11

The Christmas after Elizabeth turned one, two little eyelids fluttered open on cue as the first hymn of the midnight service began. But this year she was a toddler, not an infant. I picked her up and whispered, "It's Christmas. Baby Jesus is born!"

She didn't let out a sound. Her eyes blinked and grew huge as she took in the flickering candles, the red and gold decorations, the sound of hundreds of people raised in song, the cascade of poinsettias over the altar. I watched her watch, and through her I saw that the church truly looked fit for a king.

But where was He? Children are literalists, and I could see the question in Elizabeth's eighteen-month-old eyes. The church was glorious, but where was Baby Jesus?

"Watch," I said. "Do you see that little girl?" The procession to the crèche had started. "Do you see her carrying something, close to her heart? She is bringing the figure of Baby Jesus to the manger."

Elizabeth craned her neck, and with various gestures and words made it clear that watching from the sidelines was not adequate. She wanted to *be* there. *Sure,* I thought, *that's the point of a crèche—to bring us closer to Christ's birth.* I slipped out of the pew and across the church.

Elizabeth's eyes glowed as the Baby was placed in the Christmas crib. After prayers, the procession headed to the front of the church and I turned to go back to our pew. But Elizabeth wanted to see more. She stretched out her little arms, reaching for the figure of the Christ Child. "No, no," I whispered, as I held her hands gently, "we don't need to pick up the figurine. Jesus is born in our hearts, if we ask Him to live there. He's right here, inside of you." I touched her chest.

Elizabeth looked at the figurine, then at her chest. *Will she get it?* I wondered. My explanation of the incarnate God—God Who chose to be seen, touched and heard—seemed so abstract. But Elizabeth heard the eternal message. She wrapped her arms around her chest, and gave her heart a hug.

Lord Jesus, You made Yourself so small that to hold You in our arms we must drop everything else. Open my heart to receive You.

—JULIA ATTAWAY

26

Renew a right spirit within me.

SUNDAY

—PSALM 51:10

Christmas day had dawned near perfect. The night before, we had celebrated with my mother and my stepfather Herb. A lovely candlelight communion at our church, a warm supper of vegetable soup, turkey sandwiches and boiled custard (all prepared in advance by me), then presents and family fun.

The next morning I was up early pulling big pans of cheese grits and sausage casserole and sweetbreads out of the refrigerator. By the time an assortment of guests arrived for our traditional Christmas-morning breakfast, the grits were bubbling and the smell of spicy wassail was wafting through the house. Later, as the breakfast wound down, I sat in the living room amid carols and laughter and thought: *Perfect. Now all I have to do is round up the family for a visit to Frances, then come home, set the table, pop dinner in the oven, put the music on, re-warm the wassail…and the day will have been a masterpiece of organization.*

"Mama, can I talk to you?" my daughter Keri beckoned from the hallway. "Charlie"—one of our breakfast guests, recently divorced—"is going over to the Salvation Army to help with the dinner for the homeless. I wish I could go."

"Now, Keri, our day is planned. First Frances, then Herb's family for dinner. I need you here."

A few minutes later I saw Keri standing at the window. A single tear rolled down her cheek. She was watching Charlie walk alone to his car. It didn't take me half a second to toss aside my plans. What difference would a couple of hours make to Frances, our dinner guests or to me, the perfect planner? "Wait, Charlie!" I called as I ran out the front door. "Wait for Keri!"

Later, when we finally got around to dinner, Keri confided, "You should have seen how happy we made those homeless people, Mama. It was my best Christmas ever."

I had a lot I wanted to tell Keri, but just then there was a lump in my throat about as big as a partridge in a pear tree.

Father, in this season, and all year through, keep me open to Your invitations.　　　　　　　　　　　　　　　—PAM KIDD

27
"I am with you always, to the close of the age."
—MATTHEW 28:20 (RSV)

"Everyone longs for a simpler time," read the headline on a magazine article about ways to simplify life. But I had to chuckle at a couple of the suggestions. "Use e-mail" and "Let your voice mail take your calls" sound helpful, but they don't exactly make me nostalgic for a bygone era.

I admit that life in the late twentieth century has moved faster than I can keep up. As my techno-minded brother likes to tease, I'm afraid I'm still waiting at a rest stop along the information superhighway. I move slowly with change, one of the last people around to start using the bank's automatic teller machines and one who's still waiting to go on-line.

In spite of the rapid changes I'm expecting in the new century, a recent trip to my hometown reminded me of something that hasn't changed. As I stood inside the quiet sanctuary of the church where I grew up, I saw its simple, wooden pews, stained-glass panels and carved stations of the cross just as I remembered them from twenty years before. But beyond these tangible things, I realized the most important constant: the loving presence of God. I recalled the mystery of the confessional, the wonder of my first Holy Communion and the excitement of my confirmation as I grew in my faith. I felt the comforting strength of God guiding me through those times, just as He has guided me through all transitions in my life.

Some of the tools of worship have changed for me now. I sit in a different building, sing from a different book and say slightly different words. But God's tools, His love, forgiveness and grace, have remained unchanged. That is His great gift linking me to the past and the future, to the faith of my great-grandparents and of my children's grandchildren.

I may be a little intimidated about entering a new millennium, but I know one thing with certainty: God won't send me into the twenty-first century on my own, but will be right beside me, steadfast and unchanged.

The future is unknown, but, Lord, You are not. Let me know You better. —GINA BRIDGEMAN

28

TUESDAY

Our heart is not turned back, neither have our steps declined from thy way. —PSALM 44:18

I've seen him every Christmas since he was born, and many times in between. My great-nephew Eric lived in the Midwest and I lived in New York, and I realize now that I never saw him alone; he was just another family member. We had some amusing times that went on year after year—when I was King Kong frightening him with my shaggy bear overcoat—but gradually he grew. He would entertain me; it was always the piano or a horn of some sort. I'm not musical, but I was impressed that he was good enough to be in the band. His high school band went to the Rose Bowl, and later, at the University of Michigan, he went there again. Not bad, I thought, for a lark.

It was the bassoon that waked me. He had a series of them, and casually I asked how much the latest cost. "About twenty-four thousand, Uncle Van."

"Twenty-four thousand *dollars?*" I was assured that a genuine Heckel cost that sum when, if possible, you could get one. That's when I began to look at him with new eyes. Was he really serious about playing that bassoon as a *career?* I showed up for a solo performance he gave for credit at Michigan (it was an eye-opener), and then he was off to Germany for an audition, which he passed.

In the summer I asked him what he had planned. "Another year of study in Germany," he said. "Then I'll be ready to apply for a job over there, and after five or six years, I'll be ready for the U.S." So matter-of-fact, so sure, so resolute. He had been that way all the time; I just hadn't seen it.

More and more, as I add to my seventy-four years, the younger generation amazes and thrills me. It starts with Eric, now twenty-three, a strong, God-fearing man...first Eric, my great-nephew, now Eric the bassoonist.

Bless the young, Lord, who seek to use the talents You have given them. —VAN VARNER

29
WEDNESDAY

I will give thanks to the Lord with my whole heart; I will tell of all thy wonderful deeds. —PSALM 9:1 (RSV)

It had rained every day since Christmas. And as much as I loved the mild, sultry Louisiana weather, the warm and humid holidays were getting the best of me. Worse yet, I was already missing my daughter Kristen, who had just left to return to Texas A & M. Her one-week visit had been so short. My mood was as gray as the clouds.

The house seemed damp that morning. I reached for a sweater to wrap around me as I had my morning cup of tea. Disappointed over yet another day of overcast skies, I began my housework. I turned on all of the lights in the living room, trying to perk up my canary Luke. Even he was not singing today.

I pulled out the vacuum cleaner and began vacuuming. My husband Roy, walking down the stairs, stopped short. "Look!" he exclaimed, as he pointed to the backyard. "Sun!"

A little patch of sun had bravely fought its way out among the clouds and was shining down on a small section of our deck. I looked at it briefly, then continued vacuuming. *Too bad it's just a sliver of sun,* I thought.

Roy walked out of the back door and stood right in the middle of the sunbeam with his arms outstretched, as if giving thanks for this tiny, precious gift. I stopped and watched my husband bask in this small bit of sunshine. And I whispered a prayer of gratitude that Kristen had been able to share Christmas with us. It *had* been brief, but it was also rich with sharing laughter and cups of hot tea.

In a few moments, the gray clouds covered up the sun once again—a loving reminder to take the time to give thanks for all God's gifts, however fleeting, however small.

Lord, help me to see Your glory in all things. —MELODY BONNETTE

30
THURSDAY

If anything is excellent or praiseworthy—think about such things. —PHILIPPIANS 4:8 (NIV)

Every New Year's Eve, my husband Gary and I get all dressed up and go to Long John Silver's. That's right, the fast-food place. We do it to commemorate a dinner we had there several years ago.

We were on our way to a friend's house for an evening of games and goodies, so we stopped off for a quick fish dinner. The place was almost empty. A lovely, young girl with wide, sad eyes was sweeping the floor. She smiled at us as she passed the broom in front of our booth. "Happy New Year," she said.

"Happy New Year to you," I replied. We left the restaurant and stopped by our house to pick up a game to take with us. The phone was ringing. I watched Gary's face whiten as he said, "Yes, this is he." He reached for his back pocket. His wallet was gone. Seems it had fallen out when we got up to leave the restaurant.

We hurried back to the place. Gary had received a large amount of cash that day and had been unable to get to the bank before closing. It was all there—bill after bill after bill. "Who found it?" he asked. The sad-eyed girl stepped forward. Gary pulled out a hundred-dollar bill and gave it to her. "Thank you so much."

Overcome, the girl began to cry. "Oh, you don't know what this means—I have two babies at home!"

There's no denying that the world is full of evil and meanness. But Gary and I like to remind ourselves that it's also full of honesty and hard work. What better way to welcome in a new year?

Through Your grace, Father, I am born into optimism. It's going to be a very good year! —MARY LOU CARNEY

31 *The Lord is my shepherd....*

FRIDAY

—PSALM 23:1

Lord, I am so confused. My life seems like a series of accidents. I'm getting nowhere.

I am the shepherd. You are a lamb. It's not your job to know the way, but to follow Me. Through all the twists and turns, I am leading you in paths of righteousness. You'll see when you arrive.

But, Lord, I'm falling behind financially. Who's going to pay all these bills?

You shall not want. Your daily cup is running over. Remember when I fed you in the presence of your enemies? And the time I anointed your head with healing oil, when you were very ill? Trust Me, one day at a time.

But I get so weary, Lord. So very tired.

I know, and I want you to lie down in green pastures. I can restore your soul, if you will give Me a chance. But you continue to worry and work as if I were not here, and as if everything depended on you alone.

Doesn't it?

Not at all. I am leading you for My name's sake, not because you are so wonderful. My name is "The Good Shepherd" and I intend to keep My good name by caring for you. It's what I do.

But I'm getting older, God. Sometimes I wake in the night, thinking about dying.

Even when you walk through that dark valley, I will be there with you. I've already been through death, and I know the way. When you come out on the other side, it will be to dwell with Me in My house forever.

But I have so many regrets. Things I said and did that fill me with shame. Just settle down. My goodness and mercy have been following you everywhere. I am healing those old wounds and cleaning up the messes you made. Leave the past—and the future—to Me. Pay attention to this day—it's the only one you have for sure.

Lord, as I come to the beginning of a new year—and a new millennium—help me to go forward in faith, knowing that You, the Lord of all the times, are leading me on. —DANIEL SCHANTZ

MY FAITH JOURNEY

1 Beautiful sunny day 40° very busy at work. Stopped as Shop Rite. God van serviced. Helen picked me up.

2 Beautiful sunny day 40°. Bored at work. Stopped at Shop Rite. Called about trip. Destiny ready

3 Cloudy partly sunny day 45°. We left for Lake Placid at 1:00. arrived at 2:30. Beautiful

4 Partly sunny day 40°. Went to Hungry Trout for delicious breakfast then to Santas workshop. dinner + Santa

5 Beautiful sunny day 40°. Went for breakfast by 9:00 & Paul & I went to church. Packed up to go home

6 Rain, Rain, Rain 45°. Very busy at work. Got repairs done. Came home & laid down. Exhausted!

7 Beautiful sunny day 50°. Very busy at work. Came home & laid down. Almost real bad. Paul & I please + went to Mass for Holy Day. Retired to bedroom at 10:00.

Missed Kids — Beautiful sunny day 50°. Bored at work today BB went home sick. Came home & watched GH & went to take tape back to

8 Dr. Reeves, watched Y&R I read papers. Sunday

Missed Kids — Beautiful sunny day 50°. Christmas Party at work. Frank was

9 Santa Claus. Food was cold.

Missed Dad — Rain, rain, rain 50°. Bored at work. Stopped at drug store & got my blood

10 pressure pills. Relaxed w/soaps.

Missed Kids — Beautiful sunny day & windy, cold 35°. Worked on dining room again. Paul &

11 I showered & went to 5:00 Mass.

Missed family church — Beautiful sunny day 45°. Paul & I went to OLS for Kissup DOLS party

12 for grandparents from 12:00 – 1:00.

Missed Kids — Rain, rain, rain 45°. Bored as usual after I did the reports. Stopped at Shoprite

13 for paper products. Paul made potato soup.

Missed Kids — Rain, Rain, Rain 45°. Bored at work. Came home & watched GH & then

14 Y&R, Cut coupons.

Missed Kids — Cloudy dreary day 45°. Bored at work today. Came home & laid

15 down. Flesh was feeling real bad.

Missed Kids — Beautiful sunny day 40°. Paul & I went to Polish Store in

16 Bellmawr. Spent $80.00.

Missed Kids — Beautiful sunny day 35°. Paul & I went to Wal. Mass & Sams. Jim feeling a little better.

17

Beautiful sunny day. Met Chantell & Bob & kids at SD Police to see

18 Santa. Went to Georges for birthday

Beautiful sunny day 40°. Paul & I slept till 9:30. We had breakfast

19 & went for papers. Aunt Ruth & Ernie came over & then we went to hear Bobby sing in choir at OLS.

DECEMBER 1999

Missed kids — Rain, Rain. Rain 50°. Very busy at work. Catching up reports, Billed PM, Hair cut after work. Paul & I took a nap
20 8:00. Watched Raymond & soaps.

Missed kids — Cloudy, partly sunny day 35° Went to Cherry Hill & Neocesterom mall. Red Stain for sup
21 went to Fletcher's building supplies

Missed kids — Beautiful snow AM & sun PM. Went to S, R & Acme. Got Butch
22 filet & Paul crab legs & salmon

Missed kids — Beautiful sunny day 30°. Paul & I showered & had breakfast. I wrapp
23 presents. We went to SR & Acme & Dr. K.

Beautiful sunny day. We cooked shrimp & crabs. We had salmon for lunch. We shower & went to 5:00 Mas
24

Beautiful sunny day 30°, I finish wrapping. Paul & I had shrimp & crabs for lunch. We went to Chantell's
25

Beautiful sunny day 30° Paul & I went to 8:30 AM Mass at St Mary's. Made dinner for our family, turkey
26

Missed kids — Cloudy snow flurry day 30°. Very busy at work. Running a temp, not feeling well.
27

Missed kids — Partly sunny day 30°. Paul & I are so sick we couldn't get our blood work. Dr. S called in antibiotic.
28

Missed kids — Beautiful sunny day 30° Paul & I are still quite sick. Kelsey called us. Butch was here.
29

Missed kids — Beautiful sunny day, 50°. I washed bed things. Butch totaled Auburn fam on Chess Rd. God was with him.
30

Beautiful sunny day 40° Chantell brought groceries & the kids to see us. Butch was here, Connie Rutland came over, I called Aunt Ritt Carol Mann, kids. Jojee painted Brian called me.
31

FELLOWSHIP CORNER

Welcome to the Fellowship Corner, where our fifty-two Daily Guideposts *writers are waiting to tell you where God's been leading them during the past year. If you've been with us before, you know there are old friends here waiting to say hello and some new folks who'd like to introduce themselves. If you're new to our family, this is a good place to get acquainted. Come right in and join our family circle!*

 LIBBIE ADAMS and her husband Larry live in Richlands, North Carolina, where her roots stretch back for generations. "We've been married 27 years and have two sons. Greg is engaged to be married to Kim, an emergency room nurse from New Hampshire. Jeff is our youngest. We own a custom woodworking business, and it keeps us traveling down the beautiful back roads of North Carolina, delivering doghouses and sheds to our many customers. It's a job and lifestyle we love, but we also enjoy touring other states. Last year we traded in our 12-year-old trailer for a brand-new one, and this year we hope to christen it properly when we travel to Indiana for a family visit, then to New Hampshire for Greg and Kim's wedding."

 FAY ANGUS of Sierra Madre, California, writes, "My cousin Yvonne lives in a 17th-century cottage in the English countryside. I slept under open beams salvaged from sailing ships out of Southampton harbor. I blinked awake to hundreds of rabbits blurring the hillside, as white Hascombe deer foraged the hedgerow. Here I met clusters of cousins, some several times removed. We pored over family photos that led us all over the world: Australia, China, Canada, USA. 'We're much traveled,' I said. 'Now more than ever,' they replied as we hugged one another. Through the years God has led our family across seas and continents; this is the year He brought us together. We are strangers no more, and it is good."

"Life moves by so quickly when you're trying to keep up with a preschooler and a toddler," says tired-but-happy *Daily Guideposts* editor ANDREW ATTAWAY of New York City. "When I have a moment for reflection between reading to Elizabeth about dinosaurs and volcanoes (her two new favorites) and playing trucks with John, I'm struck with wonder at how marvelously God has led me. He brought Julia and me together, and through us He brought Elizabeth and John into the world. And as if that weren't enough, He's given me a second family at Guideposts—colleagues and writers and readers sharing our joys and sorrows in a community of prayer and caring. Even the bumps in the road (I'll let Julia tell you about them) help us keep our eyes on the Cross. I don't know what the year 2000 may have in store, but it will be what God knows is best for us. Praise Him!"

"This year was like a tossed salad of the mundane and the truly difficult," writes JULIA ATTAWAY of New York City. Mixed in among the everyday joys of raising small children and watching them grow was son John's neck surgery, a pacemaker for Julia's mother, and a newborn niece whose first weeks were spent in intensive care. "Sometimes the hardest thing in the world is to say, 'Thy will be done,' " says Julia. "I say it every day, for it is part of how Jesus taught us to pray. Yet I often don't comprehend the immensity of that little phrase until I am forced to decide whether or not I am willing to let God lead me in all things—even on paths I don't want to travel."

In her October 28 devotional, KAREN BARBER of Alpharetta, Georgia, tells how she was led to take a Stephen Ministry training course. She completed it and received her first assignment: supporting a woman coping with a serious illness. "In the training we are taught that our number-one ministry is to listen. We're not supposed to offer cure-alls or give advice. When my care-receiver struggles for direction, I close my mouth and open my ears. I found that not only does God lead me but that He leads others best when I step aside and let Him. The astonishing part is that when my friend finally makes her own best decision, she tells me how wonderfully smart I am!" Karen has also put her listening skills to good use with her sons Jeff, a second-year engineering student at Duke University, Chris, a junior in high school, John, a second-grader, and her husband Gordon.

"This year we suffered a poignant loss when my 95-year-old mother passed away," says ALMA BARKMAN of Winnipeg, Canada, "taking with her almost a century of life experiences. On the other hand, we celebrated a delightful gain when we welcomed into the family her namesake, Rose Ellis, who is grandchild number seven for us. As I rocked that new pink bundle to sleep, I pondered what changes she would encounter if she should live to be as old as her great-grandmother. At the rate the world is changing, such contemplation can be almost frightening, except when I look back upon my own life. Then I can sing with conviction, 'He leadeth me, O blessed thought, O words with heavenly comfort fraught.' It is a very old hymn—and an effective lullaby, too, I might add."

"Finally, my wife Shirley and I spent a whole winter in Florida," FRED BAUER of Princeton, New Jersey, reports. "And it was splendid—except for a few El Niño-influenced storms and some hospitalization." Fred had to undergo some additional treatment for lymphoma last year. "But the warm, sandy beach out in front of our new place in Englewood on the Gulf of Mexico was a perfect spot to recuperate"—which he did. "One thing illness teaches, if we didn't already know it, is that our lives are finite and totally in God's hands. He is indeed the author and the finisher of our days. Those who trust their future to Him need not fear. Our concern in life, to quote Peter Marshall, should be less about its duration and more about its donation."

"Keith and I celebrated our 20th anniversary," says RHODA BLECKER of Los Angeles, California. "And everyone said it wouldn't last! We lost our wonderful foundling dog Spunky, who hung on through discernible discomfort and probable pain until I finally assured her we were safe, so she could stop guarding us and go on to her reward. That leaves us with just Perky, Jessif and Hobo (the dogs), and a very feisty orange and white cat, Tau, who rules them all. And our home did not wash away in El Niño, so we are infinitely grateful. Our roof is sound and our lawn green. You can't ask for more than that."

"My love for God and country often merge," writes first-time *Daily Guideposts* contributor MELODY BONNETTE of Mandeville, Louisiana. "I prayed about wanting a big American flag for my American history classroom and God led me to one. My husband Roy and I were strolling through the French Quarter when we happened upon an old, rumpled American flag for sale. Much to my astonishment, it measured a whopping eight by ten feet and had only forty-five stars. Needless to say, I bought it. Now my students and I get to pledge our allegiance every morning to this 103-year-old flag!" It comes home every summer so Melody's family can enjoy it. That includes daughter Misty, who, along with husband Indelethio, is acting and dancing professionally in New York City; daughter Kristen, who is finishing up a psychology degree at Texas A&M; and sons Christopher, 18, and Kevin, 15.

GINA BRIDGEMAN of Scottsdale, Arizona, her husband Paul, and their children Ross, 9, and Maria, 4, spent much of last summer doing what many Arizona families did: watching the new major league baseball Arizona Diamondbacks play their inaugural season. "We became fans the moment the team first took the field," Gina says. Following the Diamondbacks is especially exciting because Gina's oldest brother Joe is the team's general manager and her dad, Hall of Fame announcer Joe Garagiola, broadcasts some of the games on TV. "With our kids so active and growing up so quickly, our life is going in many different directions. This next decade will bring two teenagers into our house, but I trust God will continue to keep us centered through Him and His church, and lead us on together."

For MARY BROWN, usually from East Lansing, Michigan, the past year has been a whirlwind of travel with professor husband Alex as his sabbatical has taken their family to Europe, the Middle East and South Africa. Ten-year-old Elizabeth and 5-year-old Mark have learned German and found that a friend can be any nationality. Mary says, "In each new country God has guided us to apartments, schools, churches and new friends. In the throes of a decision, I cling to His promise: 'I will lead them...by ways they have not known, along unfamiliar paths I will guide them' (Isaiah 42:16, NIV)." On this year's theme, Elizabeth remarked, "The most important thing I have to remember is sometimes the Lord works slowly, and be patient. Sometimes I wait and wait and wait, then finally something works out and I know what to do."

"I've been so aware this year of the seasons changing," says MARY LOU CARNEY of Chesterton, Indiana. "Maybe that's because so many things in my life have been changing, too." Mary Lou continues to edit *Guideposts for Kids,* a bimonthly magazine read by hundreds of thousands of children, but this year she added to her staff. Becoming more of a manager is a new challenge for Mary Lou. So was creating a special issue of *Guideposts for Teens,* a magazine featuring real-life stories for 13- to 18-year-olds. Daughter Amy Jo came through a painful divorce, moving back in with Mary Lou and her husband Gary for a few months. Brett continues to work in the excavation business with his father. Last year, Brett became a landlord, moving into one of the apartments in a three-unit he built. "How amazing to know that in the midst of changes God remains the same: loving me, forgiving me and leading me—day by day by day."

"It's been a good year," KENNETH CHAFIN says. "Barbara and I decided, at least for now, to stay in Louisville, Kentucky. But we'll spend the spring months in Texas at Windy Hill enjoying all the wildflowers. Hospital time in March, while doctors dealt with a blocked artery, put me in touch with my mortality but also made me grateful for new medical knowledge. I spent a great week in Illinois helping my mother celebrate her 89th birthday. With a push from my children, I went on-line this year, but I still need a map and a guide to find the information highway. I've always been interested in art, so I decided to enroll in a watercoloring class. On the first day I felt like crying and telling my mother I wasn't going back, but it's gotten to be fun. In all the ups and downs of the year, I've always had a keen sense of God's love and guidance."

MARY JANE CLARK's highlight of the year: Finally all six kids got together in the same place at the same time—a first in her and Harry's almost ten years of married life. Kennedy, the oldest, married Deb on Thanksgiving weekend in Durango, Colorado—the occasion for the clan gathering. Todd and wife Angie plan to travel around the United States this summer before settling back in North Carolina. Wynne announced her engagement to Matt; they plan a September wedding. Jeff and wife Jessica returned from Africa to pursue his Ph.D. at Colorado State University. Jessica finished a nine-month refugee studies program at Oxford, England. Ethan, a University of Colorado student at Boulder, fractured his foot on his skateboard just one day after purchasing a season pass for snowboarding. "I look back and see how lovingly God has led us, especially in these fifteen years since my first husband's death, and I marvel at the ways God has brought us and the things He has taught us."

"At the time of this writing," reports DRUE DUKE of Sheffield, Alabama, "I am propped up in a hospital bed—I fell and broke my right hip. I am doing well—I know I am, the nurses tell me so! My husband Bob and I have had a quiet, loving year with our family. Daughter Emily embarked on a new job, which is more diversified and offers greater potential. Granddaughter Christy completed the first year of graduate work on her master's degree in Business and Human Resources; grandson Bob went on an all-expense paid trip to Europe in the summer. As a high school history teacher, he served as counselor for a group of youngsters. All of the experiences we are gaining—even my learning to walk again through rehabilitation—are outfitting us to step with excitement and great expectations into 2000!"

KJERSTIN EASTON, an undergraduate at Caltech in Pasadena, California, keeps busy with her electrical engineering courses and shares her dorm room with a special roommate: her kitten Antimony. Kjerstin says, "Call me Grace, but I was fixing my ceiling fan when I fell and injured my hip. Antimony wandered over and perched on my chest like a sentinel until one of my friends came by to help me up. I ruined a lot of connective tissue in my right hip, but Antimony has been the perfect companion, keeping my spirits up and chasing the tip of my cane as I totter around." The year brings a few big changes, with Kjerstin's brother marrying one of her best friends and her mother teaching at a new school. God has certainly been a leading force—even though Kjerstin is sometimes following on crutches.

ERIC FELLMAN writes, "This year's theme is a great one for my family and me. As I made a career change, my family went through the process of moving from Pawling, New York, to Falls Church, Virginia. We all needed to feel God's leading as we went through the various details that made up our personal life changes. The phrase 'He leadeth me' is concluded in Psalm 23 with 'beside the still waters.' I think I felt this most as our son Jason struggled with thoughts of transferring colleges, Nathan went off as a freshman, Jon stayed behind as a boarding student at his high school, and my wife Joy left a job she enjoyed. All along the way we could have been torn apart by the turmoil, but instead we were led beside still waters, which calmed, reassured and refreshed us."

ARTHUR GORDON of Savannah, Georgia, writes, "As anyone who reaches the age of 80 knows, reminders of death become more frequent as loved ones complete their journey through this life and move on into eternity. It's a solemn transition, certainly, one that awaits us all. Some of us seem to regard it with apprehension, others with tranquillity. My father belonged in this second category. 'For me, it's very simple,' he said, 'because it's right there in the Twenty-third Psalm. The first line tells us that the Lord is our Shepherd. Then the second verse says that He is leading us. That's the key word. So if the Good Shepherd is leading us, we don't have to worry about anything. All we have to do is follow.' Let the Good Shepherd lead. Perhaps that's all the advice any of us needs. In life or in death."

This was a year of the unexpected for OSCAR GREENE of West Medford, Massachusetts. After 23 years, he resigned from his beloved Trash and Treasure at the church fair. Oscar visited and spoke at a treatment center for youngsters, ages 15 to 17, and learned the meaning of "another direction, another chance." He served as worship leader at a University of Life

Lenten service, an opportunity usually reserved for the clergy. Oscar was asked by the families to provide ushering service at several funerals, including one for the sister of aviatrix Amelia Earhart. Oscar witnessed the power of "He leadeth me" when a dreadful, midnight fire engulfed the home where he was vacationing. Seven people escaped, including one person with advanced Parkinson's disease. The deputy fire chief called this "a miracle!"

"I spent a lot of time traveling this year, usually trying to catch up with my wife," EDWARD GRINNAN of New York City informs us. Julee toured extensively as part of Bobby McFerrin's improvisational jazz vocal group Circlesong. "Before a tour, I always envy her exotic itinerary. Then I see how difficult life on the road is. It makes me appreciate how hard Julee works." This year Julee hopes to spend more time recording than touring, keeping her—and Edward—closer to home. But not too close. "Travel is the greatest education there is," Edward maintains. "What better way to spread faith—and find it."

"Carol and I don't seem to get any older, but our kids do," says RICK HAMLIN of New York City. "In recent months we had the pleasure of attending 11-year-old William's class play, in which he played a college student, and 8-year-old Timothy's class concert. Hearing Timo's boy soprano brings back memories of my performances as a kid, and I wonder how my mom and dad stood the anxiety! Sunday mornings, at our church, I help teach the 5th grade class. Last week we played a board game showing the travels of Paul. Anything to keep them interested—and to keep us teachers on our toes. The light of Christ seems most visible in the people I've known who follow Him. The visionaries, the risk takers, but most of all the people who know how to love."

"Looking backward, looking forward, I think that's what everyone is doing as we approach the new millennium," writes MADGE HARRAH of Albuquerque, New Mexico. "In my own lifetime I've seen amazing medical advances and the development of space flight. I've married, brought up children, developed a career, gained a deep faith, enjoyed grandchildren, buried my parents—years filled with much joy, some sorrow. Now I feel excited as we head into the next century, despite some predictions of global disaster. Although I can't fix the international problems, I can try, with God's help, to fix the smaller problems that come my way, keeping in mind Paul's words to Timothy: 'I have fought a good fight, I have finished my course, I have kept the faith' (II Timothy 4:7). Not a bad goal for the years to come."

Several "marker events" have occurred this year for MARILYN MORGAN HELLEBERG of Kearney, Nebraska. The birth of Haley Sierra Helleberg to Paul and Cheryl brought the "grandchildren grand total" (so far!) to eight. Fun! Also, Karen and John both graduated *summa cum laude* from the University of Nebraska at Kearney. Marilyn enjoyed a canoe trip in the Ozarks, visits to relatives in Topeka, Kansas, and San Francisco, some time at her Colorado cabin, and retreats in Seattle, Denver and Manhattan, Kansas. As John heads off to graduate school at the University of Illinois at Urbana-Champaign, Marilyn is planning a move to Colorado Springs. "I look forward to the upcoming changes," she says. "I have no doubt that the One Who has guided me all of my life will continue to lead me on this new segment of my soul's journey."

PHYLLIS HOBE of East Greenville, Pennsylvania, writes, "When my father, who has Alzheimer's, had to go into a nursing home, I felt frustrated because I wanted to help him in some way, yet didn't know what I could do. Then I learned that some family members were forming a volunteer group to work with the staff. 'You see things we don't,' said the head of the nursing home, 'and we want your suggestions.' What a difference that group has made in my life! We're small in number, but we move mountains! Our first suggestion was doorstops for the heavy front doors so that residents in wheelchairs could be moved outside more easily. Now we're raising money for a screened pavilion where our loved ones can enjoy the summer weather. We, too, have been blessed by our efforts. We're discovering that, with God's help, we can still be useful to our family members and learn new ways to care for them."

"This year I have sad news," writes MARJORIE HOLMES of Manassas, Virginia, "the loss of my youngest daughter Melanie after even the doctors believed her cancer had healed. Our 'baby angel,' we called her, born when I was 40. She was a beautiful dancer, appearing with the finest companies. She also taught tap and ballet. Some of her students performed at her service. 'Now she's dancing in God's garden,' the minister said, 'where we'll meet her again someday.' She was taken from her family just after Christmas: a husband and two sons, 13 and 15, both musicians like their father. One of Melanie's last requests was that they keep very close to me. So I see them often. The boys bring their friends here to fish and swim, and her husband calls or comes every Sunday."

MARY RUTH HOWES of Jersey City, New Jersey, writes, "It has been said that we live life forward, but we understand it backward. That is true for me as I look for God's leading in my life. I don't necessarily understand the present, but I can see God's hand in the past. My father from Canada and my mother from Arizona met in China and married there, where I was born. My father's grandfather was a homeopathic doctor in upstate New York, and my grandmother brought that knowledge with her to Canada. My father took homeopathic medicine to China with him—and as a result I recovered from typhoid fever. My parents were readers and letter-writers. As a result, I've been a book person and reader all my life—and a family letter-writer. In my present life, I find the Lord directs me most often through His Word, often as I prepare a study to share with others in church."

"The past year has brought a lot of good things my way," says BROCK KIDD, "including buying my own home in Nashville, Tennessee, and being named a vice president in my company's investment division. It was certainly the thrills and chills of the stocks and bonds market that attracted me to my present work, but after four-plus years as a financial consultant, I have found deeper meaning in my career. I've come to see my work as a special ministry, serving others as I help clients plan for a child's education, a dream home or a worry-free retirement. So, in the early morning, before opening up *The Wall Street Journal*, I try to consult with the ultimate Adviser: 'Whom can I help for You today, Lord?' "

It's full steam ahead for PAM KIDD's family as the new millennium approaches: Keri has chosen a graduate school and will be studying for a career as a psychotherapist. Brock, a vice president of an investment bank, recently bought his own home. David just celebrated his 25th anniversary as minister of Hillsboro Presbyterian Church in Nashville, and Pam continues to relish her number-one job as wife and mother. "David and I are delighted to discover that the dreaded empty nest syndrome has been greatly exaggerated. Our fledglings are out soaring somewhere, and sooner or later they come home bringing great affection, exciting stories and the hint of new adventures. We look forward to every minute we spend with Brock and Keri and their friends, but our time alone together is just as satisfying! So together, we move forward in faith, believing that God is always leading us and that His angels hover near. Moving ahead, life is very, very good."

"After a gap of twenty years," writes CAROL KNAPP of Big Lake, Alaska, "Terry and I are once again experiencing the joy of new life with the birth of Zachary Peter to our daughter Tamara and husband Rich. Our speed-loving son Phil is driving oil exploration equipment, which moves about five miles per hour, on Alaska's North Slope. Kelly, a King College senior, flew to Barcelona to attend Spanish Language Institute. Brenda, a junior nursing major at the University of Alaska, spent a summer on the catching end of a fishing line, stocking our freezer with king salmon. I rediscovered a small red leather New Testament that once belonged to my father and eagerly began reading it. The closer walk with Jesus that resulted led me to be rebaptized by immersion on a rainy August Sunday in Fish Creek, near where I live. I felt as if it were the River Jordan and Jesus Himself Whom I had come to meet. Time fell away, and I fell in love with my Savior Who is the same 'yesterday, and today, and forever' (Hebrews 13:8)."

CAROL KUYKENDALL of Boulder, Colorado, writes, "My husband Lynn and I spent three weeks in Australia and New Zealand where I started new groups and trained leaders for the worldwide ministry MOPS (Mothers of Preschoolers). What a joy to discover that God has poured the same maternal instincts into the hearts of *mums* the world around! At Christmastime, we celebrated Lindsay's move to a new job in San Diego, Kendall's decision to participate in an urban internship in San Francisco, and the engagement of Derek to Alexandra Hogan from Seattle. According to tradition, the mother of the groom is supposed to 'wear beige and keep her mouth closed.' That demure role sounds like a near impossibility for me, but whenever I move through uncharted waters, I think of Jesus' call to Peter when the disciples were in the boat on stormy waters. 'Come!' Jesus commanded. As long as Peter kept his eyes on Jesus, he was able to move forward, in spite of the seeming impossibility."

HELEN GRACE LESCHEID writes, "Leaving our home of almost twenty-seven years in southern British Columbia was extremely hard. Every nook and cranny held a precious memory. Yet now our five grown children had left home, my husband was in a group home, and it was time for me to move on. I made a wish list for where I'd like to live: a rancher with a gas fireplace; a view; a little plot where I could plant a rosebush. Two months after I drafted my wish list, I settled into a new town house in Sumas, Washington. I've been able to check off every item on my wish list, plus I added the extras God had given. At a recent family gathering in my new home, I listened to the happy chatter around our family's oak table—new memories added to old ones. How rich I felt. 'Thank You, Lord. It's great to follow You.' "

After thirty years of full-time (mostly single) parenting, PATRICIA LORENZ's youngest child Andrew is a freshman at Arizona State University, nearly two thousand miles from their Oak Creek, Wisconsin, home. Daughter Jeanne received her master's degree in art at Yale last year and is working in New York. Julia, a wellness specialist, is married to a wonderful teacher named Chris. Michael is a high school band director, married to Amy, a nurse. Pat finished her third and fourth books: *Great American Outhouse Stories by Sixty Great Americans* and *Life's Too Short to Fold Your Underwear.* "The Lord is leading me to all sorts of wonderful places, so I don't think the empty nest is going to be so bad after all. I just hope someday one of those places is in a warmer climate with a good man at my side!"

This year has been an especially challenging one for ROBERTA MESSNER of Sweet Run, West Virginia, as she has faced new challenges in her own personal health as well as both parents battling diagnoses of cancer. "It's been overwhelming at times," she admits, "but God's leading has amazed me with its unfailing precision." So often God's guidance has taken the form of people He has placed in her path at just the right moment. "One of my dearest blessings has been the support of my *Daily Guideposts* family. So many have written, with some saying they pray for me *every day.* I'm convinced we won't know until heaven the enormous impact of the love and prayers of our *Daily Guideposts* readers."

LINDA NEUKRUG of Walnut Creek, California, writes, "This year God leadeth me into busyness. I am still volunteer-tutoring my Russian emigrant Mrs. Menina, and have been to New York and England to visit my family and my husband Paul's family. One of the most fun things I've done is begin teaching a one-night class called 'Clutter Be Gone' at the adult education school. I began the class by lugging in five huge trash bags filled with outdated calendars, used books I haven't read in years, clothes that 'might come back in style' and things that 'might come in handy some day.' This was so the students would realize I'm no expert, although I did have many tips to share, like 'Don't put it down—put it away.' This is also a good tip, I've found, for old grudges and hurts. I'm also trying to simplify my prayer life—by setting aside a regular time in the morning to pray."

RUTH STAFFORD PEALE of Pawling, New York, fills her days with answering letters, counseling people over the telephone, attending meetings, traveling to speaking engagements and having wonderful fellowship with the staff at Peale Center for Christian Living, a division of Guideposts where the magazines *Plus* and *Positive Living* are published. "Our prayer mail totals between 11,000-18,000 requests every month. We consider it a privilege to be prayer partners, and we pray by name and problem for each request we receive. We have organized and trained volunteers who come to our chapel daily and are an important part of our ministry. I am also blessed with a very closely knit family, and even though I am living alone, I have a faithful farm manager and his wife on the property. My mind is full of gratitude, for there are more than one million persons reading *Daily Guideposts* every day. God wants us to make a difference as we live out each day."

"The waters by which the Lord led our family this past year were not quiet," says ROBERTA ROGERS of White Plains, Maryland. "For each of us, dreams died. Yet already green shoots of new ones are rising, and none of the inundations drowned our faith or our love for each other. So we take a fresh breath and look forward. My mother Kathryn Stoddard, 89, continues to be an encouragement to those in the retirement community where she lives. My husband Bill's mother Marian, 92, broke a hip, but she is now at home on her own again, walking unaided. Our son David is about to be a college senior! This year I found that the still waters by which the Lord leads us can be those deep within, where His peace resides in the midst of pain and turmoil. What a wonderful Shepherd He is!"

"No one was more surprised than I was when God led me to the least used area of my tiny Brooklyn, New York, apartment—the kitchen," says first-time *Daily Guideposts* contributor ALLISON SAMPLE. "When I was growing up in Alabama, oatmeal cookies were practically breakfast food. But I had no idea I had a knack for baking cookies until I decided to give them as Christmas gifts." As a result, Allison launched her own cookie business last summer. "Spending more time in front of the oven, I've learned to be more patient with myself. Each step—mixing, rolling, baking, cooling and savoring—is important and has its own rewards." Allison, an assistant editor for *Guideposts* magazine, occasionally shows up for work with a little flour in her hair.

ELEANOR SASS of New York City says, "Everyone who knows me knows what a notorious jaywalker I used to be. My friends called me 'Cut-through Ellie' because I'd never walk to the corner and wait for the green light if I thought I could save some time by jaywalking in the middle of the block. All that has changed now. One of the joys of being retired comes to me each Wednesday when I pick up my goddaughter's daughter Hannah and take her to Central Park in her stroller. To get there we must cross a few busy streets, and it is then that I know God is leading me. In fact, I can almost hear His voice: 'No cut-through tactics, now.' It's a nice warm feeling to know that I'm obeying the city's rules and God's orders. This slowing down on my part benefits my dog Wally, too. He's 6 now, and loves to stroll along sniffing the trash bags and greeting other canine friends."

DANIEL SCHANTZ has passed the 30-year marker as a teacher at Central Christian College in Moberly, Missouri. He and his wife Sharon became grandparents for the third time in February 1998, when Rossetti Sharon was born to younger daughter Natalie Cleeton and husband Matt, who already had one child, Hannah Mae. Older daughter Teresa and husband Dan have their hands full, caring for son Silas Tennyson Williams, who is in his "Tricky Twos." Dan's college is going through growing pains, and sometimes he wonders how it will all turn out, but he comforts himself with the thought of God's leading. A favorite hymn of his is "He Leadeth Me," which speaks of how God leads: "Sometimes mid scenes of deepest gloom, Sometimes where Eden's bowers bloom... still 'tis God's hand that leadeth me."

"God has been guiding us toward a world of love ever since the birth of His Son two thousand years ago," writes SUSAN SCHEFFLEIN of Putnam Valley, New York. "Each day He gives us the power and the choice to add our love to the mix. I try to show my love by volunteering for groups that work to improve life for others. Count the number of people you know who perform acts of kindness (including yourself). That makes for a lot of love in the world. 'Love one another' (John 13:34). That's what Jesus wanted us to do then, and that's what He wants us to do today, and tomorrow, and always."

Daily Guideposts newcomer GAIL THORELL SCHILLING lives with her children Greg, 15, Tom, 14, and Trina, 12, in Lander, Wyoming, in the foothills of the Wind River Mountains. Her daughter Tess, 18, attends school in Spokane, Washington. After two and a half years of study, Gail finally completed her career change from journalism to education and earned an elementary teaching certificate from Regis University in Denver, Colorado. Even a tumble that broke her foot didn't stop her. "I began student-teaching while sporting crutches and a cast. These thoroughly intrigued my third-graders during Show and Tell! Since I couldn't drive for three months, my kind friends ferried me to school, to church, to the grocery store—everywhere. Friends and family also helped when funds ran low. As God leads me toward my new profession, He consistently provides helpers to ease the journey."

" 'He Leadeth Me' was one of the first hymns I learned to pick out on my grandma's piano when I was four," says PENNEY SCHWAB of Copeland, Kansas. "Today, the personal journal I've kept for many years provides a clear and consistent record of God's guiding presence." Penney and her husband Don celebrated the birth of their first granddaughter, Olivia, in December 1997. Olivia joins brother Caleb and cousins Ryan, David and Mark. It's been a year of growth and change for United Methodist Mexican-American Ministries, where Penney works, but God has continued to open the way for new areas of service.

 ELIZABETH (Tib) SHERRILL of Chappaqua, New York, celebrated her Valentine birthday last year in Hollywood, California, where she was born 70 years ago. Tib and her husband John went by ship, from New York to Los Angeles through the Panama Canal. "After six days sailing south," she recalls, "the ship abruptly changed direction. It passed through that narrow channel and headed north instead. Like John's and my life journey: setting out as nonbelievers; passing through the 'straight gate' of conversion; heading a different way." Looking back, Tib can detect God's guidance even when she was unaware of it. "Especially then! Long before I knew Him, He was bringing people and events into my life in a design only love could have devised."

 JOHN SHERRILL and his wife Tib were not married in a religious ceremony, only in a civil service. "We weren't Christians at the time," John explains. Last winter, they celebrated their 50th wedding anniversary aboard the QE2. "A sentimental journey. We met on the first Queen Elizabeth." During the trip, the ship's chaplain invited couples to renew their marriage vows. John reports that when they were—belatedly—standing before a minister exchanging the promises of a Christian marriage, both he and Tib were fighting tears. "They were tears of realization," John says. "We had been *led* to each other before we knew the One Who did the leading."

 SHARI SMYTH says, "Here in Nashville, Tennessee, I've found a friend, Mary Richards, who loves history as much as I. Together we've been touring historical mansions with names like Belle Meade, Belmont and Hermitage. The sweeping entrances and grand staircases are lined with gilt-framed portraits, sober faces staring down at us. I shiver, remembering that a mere one hundred years ago our footsteps were theirs. Now, the millennium is beating the door. Meanwhile, Whitney's and my house in the country plunges into the woods, and at night from the back deck, I observe dark shapes and nocturnal stirrings, while our three dogs and two cats prowl the jagged perimeters. We are high

on a hill. Stars hang in the trees. The wind is restless. I am content and happy. God is present."

"Some people have the idea that I spend most of my time cruising the world," says VAN VARNER of New York City. "That's a nice thought, but hardly true. A few weeks out of the year, maybe. With different sights and sounds, of course, I am given the chance for new thoughts for *Daily Guideposts,* though they're only new because they are different. Alas, I'm a man bent upon the past, riding in the grand old ships while they last, and fearful that I'll have to adjust to humongous ships that are everywhere now. Somehow I guess I know I'll adapt, for I love the sea, and the Power behind it won't let me down. And so, after a brief voyage, I'll come home to the people I love, and the work that I love, and settle down in my apartment with my dog Shep, whose eyes will be asking, 'Why were you away so long?' "

"The past year was a great time for me, my wife Beth, and our children, Drew, 15, Luke, 12, and Jodi, 9," writes SCOTT WALKER of Waco, Texas. "We enjoyed some brisk vacation time hiking in the Colorado Rockies, as well as discovering the beauty and wonder of New Mexico and Arizona. Last spring, I published *Glimpses of God* with Augsburg Press, and they published a new and expanded version of *Life-Rails* in the fall. I am also completing a book on the American Civil War. I am finishing my twenty-third year as a pastor and realize more than ever what a privilege this has been. And the Guideposts family—what a joy it is to know that wherever I go there is someone with whom I share a personal friendship through *Daily Guideposts.*"

DOLPHUS WEARY still lives in Mendenhall, Mississippi, but after 26 years with Mendenhall Ministries, he is now the executive director of Mission Mississippi, which works to encourage unity in the body of Christ across racial, social, economic and denominational lines throughout the state. Dolphus finished his doctoral dissertation and is now officially

"Dr. Dolphus Weary." This year, he and Rosie will celebrate 29 years of marriage. Danita is in her third year of medical school; Reggie will graduate in May from Tougaloo College, majoring in business/economics; 11-year-old Ryan is a sixth-grader at Genesis One Christian School. "God has a wonderful sense of humor to take a guy who wanted to run away from Mississippi and now use him and his family to help make a difference in the whole state."

BRIGITTE WEEKS writes that this year has been a quiet and thoughtful period. When children grow up and make their own way in life, parents often watch them with wonder. They try to see where life is taking those who so recently were on their way to school or, reluctantly, to bed. The path that the Lord maps out is never quite what one expects, she says: "The five of us spent a wonderful couple of weeks in Tanzania, marveling at the wildlife and at how much we enjoyed each other's company as grown-ups! Not a single squabble about who sat where in the Jeep or who slept in which tent. Back in busy Manhattan, my husband Edward and I watch over our family from a comfortable distance. He teaches high school while I try to make the best books that I can for Guideposts readers. So looking back and looking forward, my year's thoughts are both grateful and tranquil."

"This has been a sentimental year for me," says MARION BOND WEST of Watkinsville, Georgia, "as I've enjoyed recalling over and over the details of how I became Mrs. Gene Acuff after my first husband died. It's hard to believe that nearly twelve years have passed since I answered an interesting letter from a Guideposts reader, a professor/minister. Six months later we were married. Gene smiles and reminds me that living in the past is a sure sign of growing old. I don't agree at all. Loving Gene keeps me young." This past Father's Day, Marion's son Jeremy, who'd taken his own good time warming up to Gene, sent him a card that announced in bold, blue letters, "Happy Father's Day to a Wonderful Dad!" "Sometimes I know I miss God's leading, but He surely led me each step of the way as I waited for Him to answer my prayer to become a wife again."

BRENDA WILBEE of Bellingham, Washington, a freelance writer and novelist, is enjoying her youngest child's last year at home. The last play, the last awards dinner, the last band concert, the last college application…. "Where 'He Leadeth' after Blake graduates remains to be seen! In the meantime, I brace myself for 'empty nest syndrome' and continue to putter around in my garden, design and illustrate greeting cards, and sew guardian angels and dolls for local arts and craft shows. In between, I look forward to, and enjoy, the many letters sent me from our *Daily Guideposts* family. This year, my prayer is that in seeking God's lead, we dare to follow. So many new things ahead!"

ISABEL WOLSELEY of Syracuse, New York, writes, "This year I tired of a kitchen whose cupboards screamed, 'Made back in the 1940s!' I convinced my husband Roland—who prefers to keep things as they are—to remove the dinosaur cupboards and replace them with new ones. I'm 75, but it's time to move ahead, and it'd be nice to enjoy a new kitchen. We enlarged it onto the adjoining porch and combined it with a family room. My status, too, is moving on. A phone call from the oldest of my six grandchildren let me know I'll soon change from Grandma to Great-Grandma. I'm looking forward to a new baby to squeeze. My son John Champ, Jr. and his family serve with Wycliffe Bible Translators, and my other son Kelly Champ and his family are preparing for him to enter seminary training."

AUTHORS, TITLES AND SUBJECTS INDEX

A NOTE FROM THE EDITORS

This original Guideposts book was created by the book division of the company that publishes *Guideposts,* a monthly magazine filled with true stories of people's adventures in faith.

If you have found enjoyment in *Daily Guideposts, 1999,* and would like to order additional copies for yourself or as gifts, the cost is $13.95 for either the regular print or the large print edition. Orders should be sent to Guideposts, 39 Seminary Hill Road, Carmel, New York 10512.

We also think you'll find monthly enjoyment—and inspiration—in the exciting and faith-filled stories that appear in our magazine. *Guideposts* is not sold on the newsstand. It's available by subscription only. And subscribing is easy. All you have to do is write to Guideposts, 39 Seminary Hill Road, Carmel, New York 10512. When you subscribe, each month you can count on receiving exciting new evidence of God's presence, His guidance and His limitless love for all of us.

Guideposts is also available on the Internet by accessing our homepage on the World Wide Web at http://www.guideposts.org. Send prayer requests to our Monday morning Prayer Fellowship. Read stories from recent issues of our magazines, *Guideposts, Angels on Earth, Positive Living,* and *Guideposts for Kids,* and follow our popular book of devotionals, *Daily Guideposts.* Excerpts from some of our best-selling books are also available.